Heidegger and Criticism

Heidegger and Criticism
Retrieving the Cultural Politics of Destruction

William V. Spanos

Foreword by Donald E. Pease

University of Minnesota Press
Minneapolis • London

Chapters 2, 3, 4, and 6 originally appeared in *boundary 2*, vol. 5 (Winter 1977); *boundary 2*, vol. 4 (Winter 1976); *Society for Critical Exchange Reports*, 8 (Fall 1980); and *boundary 2*, vol. 17 (Summer 1990), respectively.

Published by the University of Minnesota Press
2037 University Avenue Southeast, Minneapolis, MN 55455-3092
Printed in the United States of America on acid-free paper

Library of Congress Cataloging-in-Publication Data
Spanos, William V.
    Heidegger and criticism : retrieving the cultural politics of destruction / William V. Spanos : foreword by Donald E. Pease.
        p.   cm.
    Includes bibliographical references and index.
        ISBN 0-8166-2096-2 (HC : acid-free paper).—ISBN 0-8166-2097-0 (pbk. : acid-free paper)
        1. Heidegger, Martin, 1889–1976.   2. Criticism (Philosophy)
    3. Philosophy and civilization.   I. Title.
    B3279.H49S59   1993
    193—dc20   92-32422
                                                                              CIP

For my son, Adam

Child of November
golden-mouth troper
beast-namer with a
disconcerting twist

When tradition thus becomes master, it does so in such a way that what it "trans-mits" is made so inaccessible, proximally and for the most part, that it rather becomes concealed. Tradition takes what has come down to us and delivers it over to self-evidence; it blocks our access to those primordial "sources" from which the categories and concepts handed down to us have been quite genuinely drawn.

Martin Heidegger, *Being and Time*

The historical sense can evade metaphysics and become a privileged instrument of genealogy if it refuses the certainty of absolutes. Given this, it corresponds to the acuity of a glance that distinguishes, separates, and disperses, that is capable of liberating divergence and marginal elements—the kind of dissociating view that is capable of decomposing itself, capable of shattering the unity of man's being through which it was thought that he could extend his sovereignty to the events of his past.

Michel Foucault, "Nietzsche, Genealogy, History"

Contents

Foreword
Donald E. Pease

I consider it my responsibility in this foreword to William Spanos's *Heidegger and Criticism: Retrieving the Cultural Politics of Destruction* to sketch out the significance of its occasion—the possible erasure of Heidegger's influence from American criticism—as well as the figures marking it. Those figures include such proper names as "Heidegger," "Dresden," "Auschwitz," "Vietnam," and they share as a common property only the absence of any speculative instrument capable of conceptualizing their interrelationship. As grounds for his erasure, Heidegger's critics propose that the Heidegger who persevered in undermining the "forgetting of Being" should have understood himself to be under no obligation to remember Auschwitz (which instantiated what Lévinas has called the "otherwise than being")[1] indicated an unpardonable lapse in his thinking; and that the key words from the Nazi propaganda machine (e.g., *Volk, Arbeit, Führungprinzip*) that appeared as well in Heidegger's works entailed nothing less than the engendering, sedimentation, and support of Nazi ideology from *within* Heidegger's philosophy. Heidegger's refusal to speak about Auschwitz bears significant witness to the obstacles Heidegger's involvement with Nazism poses for responsible thinking about the "Heidegger controversy."

While the Heidegger controversy does not become an explicit topic until Spanos's final chapter, it nevertheless informs the book's overall rationale: the "destruction" (in the Heideggerian sense of disassembling the structure in which the forgetting of being is enabled) of liberal humanism as a discourse appropriate to adjudicate the controversy. Arnold Davidson's introduction to "Symposium on Heidegger and Nazism" in a special issue of *Critical Inquiry*[2] provoked Spanos to discriminate the American from the European "appropriation" of the Heidegger question in an essay that he first published in a special issue of *boundary 2*,[3] entitled "Heidegger, Nazism and the Repressive Hypothesis: The American Appropriation of the Question."[4] The terms in Spanos's title call renewed attention to the difficulty of addressing the topic. In taking the "American appropriation" of the Heidegger question as his central concern, Spanos first displaces the European debate over the political and philosophical implications of Heidegger's adherence to Nazism, then he replaces the Nazis' extermination of the Jews with the United States' genocidal policies against Vietnam as the pertinent historical context. The overall result of Spanos's rhetorical strategy is the substitution of the 1960s antiwar controversy for the 1990s Heidegger controversy. In focusing on the "repressive hypothesis" as the Americanist instrument of appropriation in the Heidegger controversy, Spanos is not conducting a defense of Heidegger but expressing concern over the potential loss of the question (Man's being in the world) to which Heidegger's thinking gave access. Spanos identifies Davidson's "liberal humanist" critique (free-standing, disinterested inquiry certain of its power conceptually to grasp the truth of the matter) as itself the object of Heidegger's persistent critique, and a vestigial trace of Nazi humanism. Davidson's liberal humanism, Spanos argues, depends on presuppositions from the ontotheological tradition for its power and it displays that tradition's capacity to reconstitute its central premises at the very site of the Heidegger controversy.

The occasion for Spanos's retrieval of the cultural politics of destruction derives from his concern that if it were situated within the Heidegger controversy the question of Being would be forgotten. In focusing on Davidson's active forgetting of Heidegger's question (of the be-ing of Being), however, Spanos has himself almost forgotten about the question of Heidegger and Nazism, and thereby disclosed the problematic of forgetting as an unthematized site for his inquiry. While I cannot do justice to this problematic in the brief span of this foreword, I do hope to let the questions it poses return repeatedly to this site.

The *Critical Inquiry* symposium included position papers by such post-Heideggerian European philosophers as Jacques Derrida, Emmanuel Lévinas, Philippe Lacoue-Labarthe, Hans-Georg Gadamer, and Jean-François Lyotard, as well as the anti-Heideggerian Jürgen Habermas, each of whom (with the possible exception of Habermas, who understood Nazism as the *sole* sociopolitical referent for Heidegger's thought), with varying degrees of success, struggled to analyze nonreductively Heidegger's involvement with Nazism. Instead of constructing causal paradigms able to assimilate Nazism to his thinking or derive the one category from the other, these philosophers attempted to read Heidegger under a double obligation: to acknowledge the seriousness of his political involvement with Nazism as well as the complexity of his thought. Spanos does not excuse Heidegger against these criticisms, but emphasizes what Davidson left unmentioned about the European critique, namely, its indebtedness to Heidegger's philosophical practice for its efficacy. In calling attention to the Europeans' ambivalent response, their continued dependence upon Heidegger's philosophical thought for the dismantling of his politics, Spanos isolated, as what might be termed the political unconscious of the American appropriation, Davidson's will to make Nazism the absolute scapegoat for occidental humanism and thereby to forget the mass destruction of civilian populations in Vietnam, Dresden, and Hiroshima.

At issue in Spanos's countercharge is Arnold Davidson's representative humanist reaction to Heidegger's notorious 1949 pronouncement: "Agriculture is now a mechanized food industry. As for its essence, it is the same thing as the manufacture of corpses in the gas chambers, the same thing as the blockade and reduction of countries to famine, the same thing as the manufacture of hydrogen bombs."[5] After citing this passage, Davidson writes: "When one encounters Heidegger's 1949 pronouncement, one cannot but be staggered by his inability—call it metaphysical inability—to acknowledge the everyday fate of bodies and souls, as if the bureaucratized burning of selected human beings were not all that different from the threat to humanity posed in the organization of the food industry by the forces of technology."[6] In his own response to this passage, Spanos, unlike Davidson and the Europeans he cites in *Critical Inquiry*, does not confine himself to remarks about Heidegger's insensitivity but provides the passage with a gloss: "For Heidegger the essence of the West, i.e., that which *increasingly* determines its self-representation and historical practices (including the Nazis' manufacture of corpses in gas chambers and death camps), is the logic of technology."[7] According to Spanos, the forces of technology (rather than Heidegger) do indeed regard the bureaucratized burning of human bodies and the organization of the food industry to be *essentially* the same and he cites the complicity between U.S. agricultural and military technologies in Vietnam as evidence confirming this claim. Then he meets Davidson's charge that Heidegger cannot pronounce the name of the Jews with a countercharge of his own: that Davidson is unable to pronounce the name Vietnam.

By this counteraccusation Spanos does not, I think, intend a strict homology between the extermination of Jews at Auschwitz and the military horrors of Vietnam. He intends, instead, to return Davidson to the site of a previous Americanist appropriation of Heidegger, when Spanos himself deployed Heidegger's "destructive hermeneutics" against the U.S. war powers. During the Vietnam War, the bureaucratized burning of bodies did in fact become the task of a product of American agribusiness called Agent Orange.

Spanos's recollection of the Vietnam controversy thus enabled him to contrast Davidson's appropriation of the Heidegger question in the 1990s with the very different usage to which Spanos had put Heidegger in the 1960s; that is, as "counter-memory" directed against the United States' official cultural memory. At that time, Spanos understood Heidegger's thinking to be recollective of the historical character of what Heidegger named *Dasein*, as the one in whom the question of being takes the form of an originary temporality, an endless deferral of structuration. Spanos directed this way of thinking against the ontotheological tradition, which masked the fact that "Man" exists according to the dimension of history, rather than from within the spatial enclosures affiliated with the ideology of domination and the war powers.

Throughout the Vietnam era Spanos appropriated the Heideggerian inquiry into the question of Being to undermine the privileged status of such masterful academic practices as the New Criticism, structuralism, phenomenological analysis, and literary modernism. All of these efforts, Spanos argued, were grounded in the same unexamined assumptions, namely, that identity is ontologically prior to difference, that the end of time is antecedent to temporal process. These assumptions in turn justified, in the name of disinterested inquiry and American exceptionalism, masterful interpretive as well as dominative militaristic practices, with the result that the temporality of the text was reduced to a spatial form and Vietnam to a U.S. military colony. In his interpretive strategy, Spanos never tired of breaking these metaphysical enclosures, retrieving the temporality of being against the tradition's forgetting, and reassigning the interpreter to historical *Dasein*—that is, to temporal being in the world.

The difference between Spanos's "destructions" of the late 1960s and those of the 1990s entailed his belated recognition (in the wake of the Heidegger controversy) that this retrieval was not enough; that it required for its historical efficacy a correlation of Heidegger's ontological critique with Foucault's genealogical method. Without "completion" by the other's method, both Heidegger and Foucault failed to realize their critique. Heidegger emphasized the site of ontology but minimized the historically specific sociopolitical site. On the other hand, Foucault emphasized sociopolitical concerns but minimized the ontological question, with the potentially disastrous result that his counter-memory to the disciplinary society became particularly vulnerable to amnesia in the 1990s. In combining Heidegger's destructive hermeneutics with Foucault's genealogical method, Spanos undermined any possible reconciliation of be-ing with Being. As a result of this conjuncture, Spanos now understood the temporality of being in the world as not confined to one site but as an always changing, unevenly developed lateral field of already constituted forces, encompassing all the regions between ontology and sociopolitics.

These observations require a redescription of Davidson's efforts as a reappropriation of the Heidegger question. In the 1960s Spanos deployed Heidegger as a means of recovering an originary Greek thinking against the grain of a U.S. foreign policy intent on "Romanizing" the globe. He further understood himself as a figure whose experience during the Dresden firebombing had resulted in an existential experience of Dread before the annihilation of being *at this site*.

Spanos recounts this experience at the moment in his critical exchange when Davidson argues that the description "face to face with horror" can be properly assigned *solely* to "the production of corpses and death camps":

> However illiberal, indecorous, and improper it may seem to liberal humanist academics committed to the "autonomy of philosophy," I will contaminate my discourse by reference to a personal experience: I was a prisoner of war in Dresden at the time of the massive Allied firebombing, and I experienced the horror not only of that dreadful night and day, but also of the following days when those of us who were still alive in the *Arbeiten Kommandos* were assigned the task of searching the charred rubble for bodies of the incinerated dead, piling them into horse-drawn wagons, and hauling them away for mass burial. That, I can assure Professor Davidson, was not potential. It was immediate and actual—a "face to face experience of horror."[8]

Spanos's task of gathering charred bodies stands behind his description of the relay of sites, the indissoluble and interpenetrating force field of lived discursive practices constitutive of the history of the occident. As the critic who had already been positioned at the site where the unspeakable could become forgotten, the Spanos of the 1990s recalls the Being of *Being and Time* against the prospect of Davidson's liberal humanism forgetting this question yet again. The existential Dread he experienced at Dresden renders Spanos immune to Davidson's efforts at humanist accommodation. Whereas Davidson struggles to assimilate the "discursive explosion" released in the Heidegger controversy to the "disinterested" truth claims of liberal humanism, Spanos identifies Davidson's efforts as synecdochal of the process of reconstitutions underwriting the sociopolitical dimension of the ontotheological tradition. Refusing to accommodate himself to this discourse, Spanos resituates his destructive inquiry at the interpretive site wherein his experience of Dread before the nothingness of historical temporality could be persistently retrieved as well.

With Dresden understood as the backdrop against which he conducts his destructive reading of Davidson's reappropriation Spanos can also be understood to provide the missing referents for "Eastern Germans" mentioned by Heidegger in a letter to Herbert Marcuse on January 20, 1948:

> To the charges of dubious validity that you express "about a regime that murdered millions of Jews, that made terror into an everyday phenomenon, and that turned everything that pertains to the ideas of spirit, freedom and truth into its bloody opposite," I can merely add that if instead of "Jews" you had written "East Germans" [i.e., Germans of the eastern territories], then the same holds true for one of the allies, with the difference that everything that has occurred since 1945 has become public knowledge, while the bloody terror of the Nazis in point of fact had been kept a secret from the German people.[9]

In this passage, Heidegger constructs a lateral continuum that links Auschwitz together with Dresden (and the public knowledge of the resettlement of East Germans), and Spanos confirms this linkage by way of an autobiographical anecdote. Then Spanos pronounces the name Dresden as well as those of Auschwitz and Vietnam and finds in all of these "events" essentially the same technological paradigm at work.

But if these events cannot be appropriated by the cultural memory of official history, and they thereby disclose its repressive powers, how can they occupy the sites in the lateral continuum forever reconstitutive of that history? Is not Spanos's ability to pronounce the names Dresden, Vietnam, and Auschwitz a "liberal humanist" forgetfulness of the alternative eventfulness they disclose? Is not his banishing of Davidson from the site of his prior appropriation of the Heidegger question by way of the pronunciation of these names a return of the totalizing gesture these names symptomatize? Consequently, do these names not return us to the site of the Heidegger controversy?

The incontrovertible historical facts are that Heidegger's sympathy for National Socialism influenced his appointment to the rectorate at Freiburg, that his official plans for university reform corroborated Hitler's vision of German renewal, that he publicly supported several of Hitler's political initiatives, that he urged future leaders to work for the state, and that he remained a dues-paying member of the Party until the collapse of the Reich.[10]

In addressing these historical facts Heidegger's European commentators constructed a complex philosophical trope, intertwining Heidegger's earlier "destruction" of the metaphysical tradition with that tradition's return (in what is called the *Kehre*) in Heidegger's affirmation of National Socialism (as Germany's historical destiny). For Lacoue-Labarthe and Derrida in particular, Heidegger's identification of the temporality of being with the destiny of the German *Volk* released a series of related mimetological lures at work in Heidegger's writing—the "clearing," "Spirit," the "unnameable"—and activated the problematic "forgetting of being" as a process of infinite self-reappropriation at work in Heidegger's writing. Lacoue-Labarthe and Derrida then demonstrated the relationship between the self-forgetting of being and Heidegger's inability to speak about Auschwitz.

Both speech acts depend upon a thinking of the forgotten in terms of Being, but Auschwitz, insofar as it describes an "event" that is "otherwise than Being," forecloses Heidegger's capacity to think. Its "forgetting of what is otherwise than Being" instantiates a difference from the forgotten Being that Heidegger alone recalls. Instead of thereby rationalizing Heidegger's failure to speak of the holocaust, these commentators find this silence an essential feature of his philosophy and the basis for its linkage with his politics. By recollecting the way of Being in place of Auschwitz, Heidegger rendered unforgettable what Jean-François Lyotard has called the *abjection* that Lyotard also finds essential to Heidegger's politics.

Spanos's contribution to the *European* appropriation of the Heidegger affair includes his recharacterization of the European debate as a repression of the commentators' own residual Heideggerianism. In constructing Heidegger's problematic of temporality as a scapegoat for the "return of metaphysics" to his thinking, they authorized its replacement with their deconstructionist problematic of writing, which liberated them from any further obligation to Heidegger's project. Unlike the Europeans, Spanos does not distinguish the later from the earlier Heidegger, but finds in such later writings as "The Age of the World Picture," *On the Way to Language*, and *The End of Philosophy* ways of foregrounding the sociocultural consequences of the spatialization of time. The references to Being and the other ontological traces that Lacoue-Labarthe and Derrida cite from the later works should not, Spanos claims, be understood as Heidegger's recuperation of a metaphysics of presence, but read as already "erased" by the destructive hermeneutics of *Being and Time*. Following this "destruction" of their readings of the *Kehre* writings,

Spanos faults the European philosophers for their collective effort to exploit the Heidegger question to corroborate their own turn—away from ontological and toward specifically linguistic concerns—as itself an attempt to evade existential problems: the occasionality of history and the unrepresentable temporality of the infinitely deferred difference that is human finitude. According to Spanos, Jacques Derrida in particular has overlooked the worldly dimensions of Heidegger's critical ontology by persistently transcribing ontological difference into writerly *differance*, and has thereby trapped temporality within the endlessly deferring relays of textuality.

Spanos's intervention disclosed the political consequences of th Europeans' appropriation to be twofold: they authorized their belated American followers to understand Heidegger's texts as "superfluous" and to institutionalize a representation of temporal difference as Derridean "textuality." In essence, Spanos rediscovers in these post-Heideggerians the fault that originated with Heidegger; that is, the failure to theorize the political implication of a historically polyvalent logocenter, which restricts their critical discourse to the generalized site of ontology at the expense of sociopolitical critique. Having thereby "retrieved" a *second* Heideggerianism as the European post-Heideggerians' failure to theorize the lateral continuum of Being, Spanos exports this new post-Heideggerian tradition to the site of the American appropriation, where it counters Davidson's recuperative "retrieval" of liberal humanism.

That Spanos finds the entire lateral continuum itself in danger of disappearing at the site of the American appropriation of the Heidegger question discloses the stakes of Spanos's project. In "retrieving" Heidegger's destructive hermeneutics in a site *missing* from Heidegger's own project, Spanos quite literally produces, as an *after-the-fact extenuating circumstance*, the sociopolitical critique that, had it been available at the time of Heidegger's wartime writings, would have rendered him immune to Nazism.

Insofar as it depends on "upping the anti" of Heidegger's antihumanism (with Spanos's anti-Davidson's anti-antihumanism), however, Spanos's counterseduction of Heidegger's attraction to Nazism depends upon a dedifferentiation (of liberal humanism and Nazism) he earlier identified as the telltale effect of the ontotheological tradition. Moreover, the "destruction" of Davidson's project that he enacts on this site cannot in fact be distinguished from Davidson's humanist critique of Heidegger. Consequently "Spanos/Davidson" cannot in truth be said to have effected a "retrieval" of the temporality of be-ing, but as the institutionalization of an American Heideggerian tradition the Spanos/Davidson debate is essentially intertwined (as its internal distance) with liberal humanism.

Having dis-covered the liberal humanism at work in Spanos's own retrieval of Heidegger, it is difficult not to affiliate this factor with the Nazi residue sedimented in Heidegger's philosophy. Philippe Lacoue-Labarthe gave this interanimation of Nazism and humanism the following description:

> Nazism is a humanism in that it rests on a determination of *humanitas*, which is in its eyes more powerful, i.e., more effective, than any other. The subject of absolute self-creation, even if it transcends all the determinations of the modern subject in an immediately natural position (the particularity of race), brings together and concretizes these same determinations (as does Stalinism with the subject of absolute self-production) and sets itself up as *the* subject, absolutely speaking. The fact that this subject lacks the universality that seems to define the *humanitas* of humanism in the usual sense does not, however, make Nazism an anti-humanism. Quite simply it fits Nazism into the logic, of which there are many other examples, of the realization and concretization of "abstractions."[11]

But if Heidegger's adherence to Nazism cannot, in the last instance, be understood as separable from the liberal humanism of his detractors, can Spanos's "destruction" of liberal humanism be understood as a tacit reconstruction of (Heidegger's) residual adherence to Nazi humanism? Spanos explains why it definitely *cannot* in the following succinct account of Heidegger's involvement with Nazism:

> It will have to suffice for this context to suggest all too summarily that Heidegger's failure to perceive and fulfill the practical (i.e., sociopolitical) emancipatory imperatives of his destructive ontological project in the context of his own historically specific occasion—to make thinking overtly a "critical theory," as it were— was in some fundamental sense, perhaps, the result of a combination of his vestigial nostalgic loyalty to the separation of *theoria* and *praxis* inscribed by the post-Socratics into the philosophical tradition and an unexamined nationalism that reinscribed, against his destructive discourse, the principle of ethnic (not racial) identity. Whatever the source of this failure. . . . It is possible . . . that his apparent complicity with Nazism was the result of the tension on the one hand between the political circumstances in which he was teaching and writing, circumstances, that is, which demanded an indirect rather than overt confrontation of the brutal excesses of the Nazi regime, and on the other, his overdetermined commitment to the critique of Western technological imperialism. To focus his discourse after the brief period of the rectorship (April 1933 to February 1934) on the enormities of the Nazis' atrocities would . . .

especially after the war, be to read it as a tacit acknowledgement and confirmation of the Western metaphysical principle that, according to his essential thought, had come to its end in the globalization of *technik*. It would, in short, tacitly reprieve the West's essential complicity in the making of the Nazi machine and the horrors it perpetrated.

Because *Heidegger and Criticism: Retrieving the Cultural Politics of Destruction* depends for its historical effectiveness on the genealogy of William Spanos's literary career, I consider it the final responsibility of this foreword to indicate the importance of that career for American criticism. Over the last twenty-five years, William Spanos has dedicated himself in his several personae as critic, founding editor of *boundary 2*, theorist, teacher, and scholar to the retrieval for American literary criticism of a standpoint of thinking about literature and culture answerable to the description destructive/projective hermeneutics. While Spanos refers to Heidegger's *Sein und Zeit* as the source for his *praxis*, Spanos's "appropriation" of Heidegger resulted from a complex matrix of reception composed of a revisionist reading of the Christian existentialist orientation of his first book, *The Christian Tradition in Modern British Drama* (1966), the student antiwar movement of the 1960s, Spanos's experience of the Dresden firebombing, his witness to the American government's complicity with a military dictatorship while serving as a Fulbright professor of American literature at the University of Athens, and his founding of the journal *boundary 2* in 1972. The overall result of this reception was Spanos's identification of the "retrieval of an originary temporality" (the difference that temporality always already disseminates from the structuration of Being) as the site for his critical project. Because competing methodologies in the humanities as well as the natural sciences were dedicated to the covering over of this site, Spanos's "retrieval" often entailed his painstaking destruction of both ways of thinking (instrumental or calculative reason) as well as their ideological precipitate (liberal humanism). These methods, Spanos argued, depended upon a logic that was underwritten by a supervisory form of thinking that inevitably reified being's temporality into spatial forms requiring Spanos's destructive hermeneutics.

Understood from this standpoint, the key term in the title *Heidegger and Criticism: Retrieving the Cultural Politics of Destruction* is "retrieving," the recovery of the site of ontological critique at the moment of its possible cover-up through a "destruction" of the responsible instrumentalities. As the chapter titles indicate, the various essays gathered here describe Spanos's deployment of Heidegger's hermeneutics to read, against the grain, respectively, the new critical formalism, Christian existentialism, Derridean poststructuralism and Foucaultian posthumanism. The text as a whole is consequently answerable to two different characterizations: it is a genealogy of the post-Heideggerian, antihumanist reorientation of Spanos's cultural politics, and it is a highly polemical reading of Heidegger's critics. The polemical thrust of the final chapter anchors the others. Because Spanos finds the critique directed against Heidegger's collaborationism to be complicit with a more generalized reaction-formation (recuperative of a pre-Vietnam version of liberal humanism as the hegemonic agency for the post-Cold War world order), he found it necessary to bring the reading of Heidegger he developed during the antiwar movement of the 1970s into contestatory relationship with the liberal humanist prosecution of Heidegger.

After Spanos returns to the Heidegger project he constructed during the 1970s, he finds Heidegger's critics involved in a collaborationism of their own—not with Nazism but with Bloom's and Bellow's and Bennett's liberal humanism. In place of defending Heidegger the historical person against the charge of collaborationism (which he concedes to be for the most part factually accurate), Spanos finds the liberal humanist critique to be a defensive reaction against the antihumanism informing the Heideggerian project. According to Spanos, the liberal humanists' counterrevolution against Heidegger's antihumanist "destruction" (of which the Nazi charge is symptomatic) has been gathering force throughout the academic and the state institutions with which it was laterally affiliated throughout the post-Vietnam era. But the liberal humanists' reading of the end of the Cold War as the triumph of democratic over communist values was epochal, Spanos claims, in that it allowed for a large-scale redescription of the Vietnam event as a temporary relapse from the liberal humanist's "truth" that the New World Order retrieved. Because Heidegger's project enabled a devastating critique of liberal humanism, Spanos concludes, the revival of liberal humanism necessitated the discrediting of his entire project.

In place of this calumny, Spanos reactivates against Heidegger's detractors the critique he had previously directed against the war powers. As the only Greek Heideggerian on the American literary scene, Spanos never read Heidegger as corroborative of either German or American nationalism, but as a means of recovering originary *Greek* thinking against the accretions of Empire. Moreover, because his reading of Heidegger always reactivated in Spanos the dread he experienced at Dresden, his interpretive project cannot forget the "otherwise than Being" recorded at this site.

The ultimate occasion for Spanos's book might be understood then as protection against the loss of this site. Because this site, which Spanos names the "postmodern occasion," alone holds out access to the question of being, Spanos's retrieval of this occasion becomes all the more urgent on the verge of a New World Order and the renewed forgetfulness it inaugurates:

> In this historical context it seems to me quite justifiable to use the word "postmodern" to describe a contemporary literature that is neither a fulfillment nor a belated echo. . . . Rather, "postmodern" describes a literature that radically interrogates the authorizing logocentric forms and rhetorics of the entire literary tradition culminating in modernism in order to retrieve and explore the temporality—and the differences that temporality disseminates— that these "spatial forms" have repressed by exclusion or assimilation and forgotten.[12]

Acknowledgments

"We understand backward but live forward." I encountered this resonant sentence from Søren Kierkegaard's journals when I was an undergraduate at Wesleyan University. It led me to Heidegger's *Being and Time* and to virtually an academic lifetime devoted to thinking its self-evident and baffling content, not least its revolutionary cultural and sociopolitical implications. The essays published in this book constitute a synecdoche of this interminable itinerary.

This is not to say that my intellectual journey has been "self"-produced. Though my personal occasion instigated the process of rethinking the relation between conceptualization and living, essence and existence, inscribed by my schooling, it has been continually renewed by my encounters with a multitude of resistant voices engaged by the question. Indeed, these agonistic encounters—Heidegger would call them *Auseinandersetzungen*—account for the unpredictable swerves—the dis-courses—in my discourse, and whatever is "original" in it. It is impossible to acknowledge the debts I have incurred on the way because Memory forgets. It will have to suffice to express my general gratitude to all those now anonymous but still active voices that have in one way or another contributed to my project. But it would be remiss on my part if I did not single out a number of colleagues and/or students whose variously expressed resistances to my efforts to conceptualize—and arrive at—a destination of my engagement with Heidegger's text have been and continue to be decisive, especially in instigating the turns in

my "Heideggerian" thinking: Jonathan Arac, Paul Bové, Joseph But-
tigieg, Daniel O'Hara, Michael Hays, Margaret Ferguson, Nancy Fraser,
Donald Pease, and Cornel West (all members of the *boundary 2* editorial
collective), Jim Merod, Christopher Fynsk, David Randall, R. Rad-
hakrishnan, Patrick McHugh, Sandra Jamieson, and Jeanette McVicker.
More than agreements, I hope these friends will recognize those occasions in my texts that bear the immiscible imprint of their individual
critical responses to my "Heideggerianism." For it is not so much their
positive contributions to my understanding of Heidegger I prize, however substantial they have been, as it is their negative ones: their insti-
gation of the need to rethink my thinking. It is, finally, their insistent
"reciprocal rejoinders" to my various "Heideggers" that helped me to
arrive at the inconclusive conclusion I have drawn from my engagement
with Heidegger's antihumanist discourse: to think the relation between
understanding and being-in-the-world is not simply to remain in but
always already to instigate the rift between world and earth.

This book owes its publication to Biodun Iginla's continuing support
of my work. Unlike the editor and director of a university press that
originally solicited the manuscript and, despite its strong recommendation by the readers, rejected it on ideological grounds but in the name of
disinterested inquiry, Biodun found my appropriation of Heidegger's
"antihumanism" in behalf of an emancipatory practice worthy of a hearing. I also want to thank Ann Klefstad for her meticulously intelligent
copyediting, a difficult task given the idiosyncrasies of a style intended
to evoke multiple and often contradictory meanings.

Finally, I dedicate this book to my nine-year-old son, Adam, who has
taught me, simply by *being there*, how to *see* differently.

Four of the six chapters of this book constitute revised versions of the
following previously published essays: "Heidegger, Kierkegaard, and the
Hermeneutic Circle: Toward a Postmodern Theory of Interpretation as
Dis-closure," *boundary 2* 4 (Winter 1976), pp. 455–88; "Breaking the
Circle: Hermeneutics as Dis-closure," *boundary 2* 5 (Winter 1977), pp.
421–60; "Retrieving Heidegger's Destruction: A Response to Barbara
Johnson," *Society for Critical Exchange Reports* 8 (Fall 1980) (an extended
version of this piece was published in *Annals of Scholarship*); and "Heidegger, Nazism, and the Repressive Hypothesis: The American Appropriation of the Question," *boundary 2* 17 (Summer 1990), pp. 199–280. I
wish to thank the editors of these journals for permission to reprint.

Chapter 1
On Heidegger's Destruction and the Metaphorics of Following:
An Introduction

The real "movement" of the sciences takes place when their basic concepts undergo a more or less radical revision transparent to itself. The level a science has reached is determined by how far it is capable of a crisis in its basic concepts. *In such immanent crises the very relationship between positively investigative inquiry and those things themselves under interrogation comes to the point where it begins to totter. Among the various disciplines everywhere today there are freshly awakened tendencies to put research on new foundations. . . . In those* humane sciences which are historiological in character [*In den historischen Geisteswissenschaften*], *the urge towards historical actuality* [Geschichte] *itself has been strengthened in the course of time by tradition and by the way tradition has been presented and handed down: the history of literature is to become the history of problems.*

Martin Heidegger, Being and Time

My problem was not at all to say, "Voila, long live discontinuity, we are in the discontinuous and a good thing too," but to pose the question "How is it that at certain moments and in certain orders of knowledge, there are these sudden take-offs, these hastenings of evolution, these transformations which fail to correspond to the calm, continuist image that is normally accredited?" But the important thing here is . . . that this extent and rapidity are only the sign of something else: a modification in the rules of formation of statements which are accepted as scientifically true. . . . In short, there is a problem of the regime, the politics of the scientific statement. At this level it's not so much a matter of knowing what external power imposes itself on science, as of what effects of power circulate among scientific statements, what constitutes, as it were, their internal regime of power, and how and why at certain moments that regime undergoes a global modification.

Michel Foucault, "Truth and Power"

The publication of Victor Farías's *Heidegger and Nazism* in France in 1987 reopened the question concerning the relationship between Heidegger's thought and Nazi politics with the force of scandal. Farías's book contributes little that was not already known about Heidegger's personal affiliation with Nazism.[1] And his analytical effort to implicate Heidegger's thought at large with Nazism is characterized by a superficiality so obvious that, as Philippe Lacoue-Labarthe has observed, it betrays a certain intellectual dishonesty,[2] a dishonesty, I would add, endemic to the future anterior perspective of anthropological inquiry. It suggests that Farías's identification of Heidegger's philosophical writing at large with an anti-Semitic fascism is the tendentious result, not so much of reading Heidegger's texts, as of an inexorably fixed moralistic point of view grounded in the self-evidently damning "facts" of Heidegger's personal adherence to the Nazi Party. Even those who have welcomed Farías's book have more or less conceded that his reading of Heidegger's texts leaves much to be desired. Nevertheless, it has precipitated a massive reaction against not only the historical Heidegger but also, and more significantly, against Heidegger's philosophical discourse from *Being and Time* through the notorious Rectorate Address (*Die Selbstbehauptung der Deutschen Universität*) to his postwar writings on technology, first in France, then in Germany, and most recently in North America. This reaction, not incidentally, has put prominent Heideggerians, especially in France, on the defensive. I am referring to orthodox commentators such as François Fedier, who have followed the uncritical reading of Heidegger's texts (and his engagement with Nazism) proffered by the eminent French Heideggerian, Jean Beaufret; but I am also referring to those dissident Heideggerians such as Jacques Derrida, Philippe Lacoue-Labarthe, Jean-François Lyotard, Maurice Blanchot, and Emmanuel Lévinas, among others, who have always read Heidegger's discourse against itself.

Taking its point of departure from Heidegger's personal affiliation with German National Socialism, this reaction has involved a reexamination of his philosophical discourse at large intended to demonstrate that his insistent interrogation of the ontotheological tradition—especially its modern phase (humanism)—betrays minimally a suppression or atrophy of the human, and maximally its complicity with the appalling antihuman fascist political practices of the Nazis:

> The suppression of the other, the human, in Heidegger's thought accounts, I believe, for the absence, in his writing after the war, of the experience of horror. Horror is always directed toward the human; every object of horror bears the imprint of the *human* will. So Levinas can see in Heidegger's silence about the gas chambers and death camps "a kind of consent to the horror." And Cavell can characterize Nazis as "those who have lost the capacity for being horrified by what they do." Where was Heidegger's horror? How could he have failed to know what he had consented to?[3]

There is, of course, every justification to put Heidegger's philosophical writing to the question of its politics. Given the interrogation by contemporary "theory" of the privileged discourse of disinterested inquiry—especially its assumption of the transparency of language—there is also every justification to put the discourse that has accused Heidegger's philosophical writing of constituting a tacit "consent to the horror" to the same question.

Such an interrogation would "estrange" the familiar moralist structure imposed on the "case" of the politics of Heidegger's discourse by those now prosecuting it. Indeed, it would call this very problematic—the discursive frame of reference they have brought to the debate—into radical question by disclosing it to be the structure of an ideological tribunal.

What has been obscured in the dramatization of this "scandal," especially by those liberal humanists in the United States who have imported the European debate into the North American intellectual milieu, is the ideology informing the attack on Heidegger's discourse enabled by Farías's publication of the "facts" of Heidegger's personal adherence to and practice in behalf of German National Socialism. Whatever its intention, this negative renarrativization of the itinerary of Heidegger's thought in terms of historical anecdote has as its ideological subtext the discrediting of Heidegger's powerful interrogation of the discourse of humanism as such. More important, it also is at some level intended to delegitimate those later, more radical, demystifications of the privileged concept of Man that Heidegger's interrogation catalyzed. I mean the "postmodern" or "poststructuralist" or, as I prefer, "posthumanist" discourses that in the last decade or so have theorized the self-destruction in the 1960s of the "benign" discursive practices of humanism in behalf of specifically emancipatory purposes, especially the self-disclosure of the contradictory will to power informing its profession of "disinterested" and "free" inquiry. Jacques Derrida's recent remarks about the ideological initiative enabled by the publication of Farías's book in France apply as well to its publication in North America:

> Whatever the difference between the two books [Farías's *Heidegger et le nazisme* and Derrida's *De l'esprit*, both published in France in 1987] the question of Nazism was central to them. In certain newspapers and through a kind of rumor one received at that time the violence of a condemnation. This condemnation claimed to reach well beyond Nazism and Heidegger, the very reading of Heidegger, the readers of Heidegger, those who had been able to refer to (even were it to pose on its subject deconstructive questions), still more those who promised to take an interest in (even were it to judge and to think, as rigorously as possible), Nazism and Heidegger's relationship to Nazism. . . . It was not only, but it also was, rather evidently, a question of banning the reading of Heidegger and of exploiting what was believed to be a strategic advantage, in France, in France above all, against all thought that took Heidegger seriously, even if in a critical or deconstructive mode.[4]

The current attack on Heidegger's antihumanist discourse in North America constitutes an initiative at the site of philosophical inquiry that is finally complicitous with the more overt ideological policing initiatives represented by William Bennett, Allan Bloom, Roger Kimball, Dinesh D'Souza, and others in the affiliated spheres of education and cultural production. I mean by this the increasingly vocal campaign that would recuperate the humanist discourse of hegemony in the face of the current crisis of legitimation besetting dominant cultural institutions by invoking the specter of political correctness against posthumanist theory and the multicultural practices it has in part enabled.

What is only implicit in the moralist attacks on Heidegger's thought by American humanists who have recently intervened in the debate is explicit in the similar "anti-antihumanist" attacks mounted against "Heideggerianism" by French humanists in the wake of Farías's book. For it is specifically "the universe of democratic humanism" and "the rights of man" that these humanists would rehabilitate in their effort to delegitimate the "gauchiste" thought of the post-1968 period, which includes the entire spectrum from deconstruction and Lacanian psychoanalysis through neo-Marxism to Foucauldian genealogy:

> The most profound meaning of the debate of which Farías's book and the discussion about Heidegger have been the occasion concerns the philosophical, cultural, and most definitely political question—

even in Derrida—of the eruption of subjectivity in the values of humanism. The controversy surrounding Heidegger is the first phase of another controversy that engages nothing other than the meaning assigned to the logic of modernity: If we are engaged as much as we are today in all this, is it not precisely because it is Heidegger's deconstruction of modernity that has given—in large measure—the French intelligentsia the foundations and the style of its critique of the modern world?[5]

This massive ideological effort to renarrativize the history of the post-humanist moment—to delegitimize the disruptive discourse of a new left by discrediting Heidegger's thought, in order to recuperate the shattered hegemony of humanist rules of discursive formation—has prompted me to gather the following representative essays, written "after Heidegger" over the last decade or so, into one volume.

Collectively the essays constitute a body of "Heideggerian" writing that thematizes the repressive imperatives latent within the "liberal" discursive practices of humanism and explores the projective possibilities these practices close off. As such, the essays stand in recalcitrantly stark contradiction to the representation of Heidegger's thought unleashed by Farías's book: that it is *essentially* a politically reactionary or fascist discourse.

This is *not* to say that this book is intended (like the prevaricating responses of orthodox Heideggerians provoked by *Heidegger et le nazisme*) to exonerate Heidegger's political practice during the period of the rectorship (April 1933–February 1934) and his notorious silence in the post-World War II period about the Nazis' Final Solution for the Jews. It must be acknowledged (as my last essay here clearly does) that Heidegger's historically specific acts, including his failure "to pronounce the name of the Jews," are culpable. I want to suggest that (1) Heidegger's philosophical texts as such, from *Being and Time* to the late essays interrogating the hegemony of *Technik* (including the notorious "Rectorate Address"), resist any simple identification with historical Nazism and Nazi practices; that they exceed the essentially reactionary political purposes attributed to them by his "liberal" humanist detractors; (2) this simplistic identification constitutes an ideological strategy, the ultimate purpose of which is to circumvent the responsibility of thinking that excess: precisely that epochal "antihumanist" thrust in Heidegger's discourse which has exposed the will to power informing the "disinterested" problematic of the humanist subject; and (3) this negative or "destructive" gesture, whatever its limits, has gone far to enable the contemporary emancipatory discursive practices of what traditional humanists, conservative and liberal alike, have pejoratively called "theory." What is at stake in my intervention in the debate is not Heidegger the historically specific man, nor finally is it Heidegger's thought as such. It is rather the discourses and practices, variously called "poststructuralist," "postmodern," or "posthumanist," enabled or catalyzed by Heidegger's interrogation of the anthropologos. I mean by this the discourses and practices that, in demystifying the "sovereign subject" and the "truth" of "disinterested" inquiry, in demonstrating the complicity between truth (and beauty) and power, have precipitated in our time the e-mergence of a multiplicity of resistant "others" hitherto spoken for—which is to say "colonized"—by the privileged concept of "Man."

II

The five essays I have selected for inclusion in this volume do not constitute a book in any traditional sense of the word. They do not collectively represent a completely formulated interpretation of Heidegger's work. In keeping with Heidegger's refusal of the lure of the *telos*, they constitute a selection from a large number of pieces written on the way. They are "essays," which represent the erratic itinerary of my engagement with Heidegger's thought over the last decade or so. But their errancies have one essential and timely impulse in common: they insistently explore the possibilities (which his current detractors now deny) inhering in the excess of Heidegger's excessive texts for a theory of interpretation that, whatever the locus, is simultaneously an emancipatory practice. I mean his de-struction of the concept of Being sedimented in and by the philosophical discourse of the Occidental tradition—the release, or *decolonization*, of the differences that temporality disseminates from the imperial bondage of logocentric structure.

It may be that in the earlier essays, like Jean-Paul Sartre (and probably under his influence), I attribute too much of my own left-oriented (existentialist) philosophical bias to Heidegger's texts, and thus fail to indicate overtly the degree to which his existential analytic is contaminated by a philosophically conservative rhetoric. It is certainly the case that in the later, more politically engaged essays, I have drawn cultural and sociopolitical left implications from Heidegger's texts that go far beyond his intentions vis-à-vis praxis. What needs to be emphasized in the context of the contemporary debate over the politics of Heidegger's philosophical discourse is that these "misreadings" are warranted by Heidegger's texts. They are not impositions from a transcendental End. As the essays themselves will show, the readings constitute discoveries: the consequence of rejecting the "basic concepts" of traditional inquiry in favor of "put[ting] research on new foundations." They are the differential end of reading Heidegger's texts in strict adherence to the interpretive imperatives of his destructive hermeneutics, of the resolute "leap into the [hermeneutic] 'circle,' primordially and wholly,"[6] which, far from confirming the Same, always already precipitates "repetition" (*Wiederholung*): the disclosure of the ifference that the vicious circularity of metaphysical inquiry reduces to identity. In the dialogic term Heidegger uses to characterize this movement in *Being and Time*, these essays are "reciprocal rejoinders" (*Erwiderungen*) enabled by resolute engagement with what Heidegger's texts "hand down" as guide to the "today":

> The resoluteness which comes back to itself and hands itself down, then becomes the *repetition* of a possibility of existence that has come down to us. *Repeating is handing down explicitly*—that is to say, going back into the possibilities of the Dasein that has-been-there. The authentic repetition of a possibility of existence that has been—the possibility that Dasein may choose its hero—is grounded existentially in anticipatory resoluteness; for it is in resoluteness that one first chooses the choice which makes one free for the struggle of loyally following in the footsteps of that which is repeated. But when one has, by repetition, handed down to oneself a possibility that has been, the Dasein that has-been-there is not disclosed in order to beactualized over again. The repeating of that which is possible does not bring again [*Wiederbringen*] something that is "past," nor does it bind the "Present" back to that which has already been "outstripped." . . . Rather, the repetition makes a *reciprocative rejoinder* [*erwidert*] to the possibility of that existence which has-been-there. But when such a rejoinder [*Erwiderung*] is made to this possibility in a resolution, it is *made in a moment of vision* [*Augenblick*]; *and as such* it is at the same time a *disavowal* [*Widerruf*] of that which in the "today" is working itself out as the "past." Repetition does not abandon itself to that which is past, nor does it aim at progress. In the moment of vision authentic existence is indifferent to both these alternatives. (BT, pp. 437–38; Heidegger's emphasis)[7]

I am aware of the characteristically complex ambiguities in this synecdochical passage from *Being and Time*. Given Heidegger's identification of "a possibility of existence that has been" with "the possibility that Dasein may choose its hero," it is seductively easy to interpret its content retrospectively—from the vantage point of Heidegger's practice during the rectorship period or the terrible accomplished history of the Third Reich—as evidence of his early and abiding commitment to the *Führerprinzip* and thus to a National Socialist ideology that would transform human beings into "loyal" (mindless) followers. Indeed, it is essentially passages like this one that have provided the evidence for the recent retrospective reading of Heidegger's discursive itinerary by liberal humanists that indicts his discourse at large as a philosophical justification of the principle of authority and as an appeal to follow unquestioningly its transcendental imperatives:

> The concept of resoluteness and the theme of following and being led become linked [during the period of the rectorship] unforgettably to the *Führer*, and the National Socialist state is apparently identified with the return to the question of Being.

> From the "Rectorship Address" to Heidegger's last writings, the human is always being led, and what leads humanity seems to so envelop or overwhelm it that its disappearance is constantly threatened. Heidegger will never again [after the war] appeal to a *Führer* to lead. The appeal now comes from Being and requires a response that "is a giving way before the appeal." But just as the individual human being disappeared before the arbitrariness of the *Führer*, so the problem of arbitrariness reemerges in the claim of Being: "But precisely here the response may hear wrongly. In this thinking, the choice of going astray is greatest." *Precisely*.[8]

But—and this is what the above criticism, especially the italicized last single-word sentence, occludes—there is nothing either in this early passage (and in the larger context from which it is drawn) or in his later texts that prevents reading it as I have done here and in the essays that follow. There is, in short, nothing that forecloses one's invoking it as an instance of a "circular" mode of inquiry that has as its purpose the *liberation* of human being from the repressive structures enabled by circular inquiry: by the metaphysical philosophical tradition, which, ostensibly presuppositionless, in fact perceives the temporality of being *meta-ta-physika*, from after or beyond or above its disseminations.

Indeed, in exposing the will to power informing metaphysics, Heidegger's text puts the very idea of *following* a leader who embodies the transcendental Word (Logos) under erasure, precisely in order to disable it and all those more insidiously determining discourses of the anthropological tradition which conceal their determinations—and their imperative to follow—behind the rhetoric of "truth" or, in Matthew Arnold's sedimented humanist formulation, the disinterested "discourse of deliverance." The repetition enabled by leaping into the hermeneutic circle primordially and wholly precipitates a "disavowal" of—a refusal of loyalty to—the imperative to follow in the "today" a monolithic past constituted and authorized by a logocentric conception of history. To be "loyal" in this reading means to be engaged in dialogic relationship (that of a "reciprocal rejoinder") grounded in the difference disclosed by repetition, the difference that is the condition for the possibility of identity, and not the other way around.[9] Whatever his personal politics, Heidegger's philosophical discourse, which neither "abandons itself to the past" nor aims at "progress," cannot be represented, as it is by his humanist critics, in the ideologically coded terms of the essentially metaphysical binary, conservative/liberal. To do so in the name of objectivity is to betray a recuperative metaphysical agenda, and also a political one.

Could it not be said of Heidegger's humanist critics that their monolithic indictment of his "authoritarian" ontological and sociopolitical call to follow the leader blindly constitutes an ideological strategy finally intended to obscure *precisely* what the sustained posthumanist interrogation of the sovereign subject has disclosed: that their invocation of "the autonomous individual," "free choice," "disinterestedness," "the rights of Man," and "Western democracy" is itself an ontological and sociopolitical ("politically correct") appeal to follow the authoritarian imperative of "a center elsewhere,"[10] a hidden essentialist imaginary? "By humanism," Michel Foucault says, echoing Heidegger,

> I mean the totality of discourse through which Western man is told: "Even though you don't exercise power, you can still be a ruler. Better yet, the more you deny yourself the exercise of power, the more you submit to those in power, then the more this increases your sovereignty." Humanism invented a whole series of subjected sovereignties: the soul (ruling the body, but subjected to God), consciousness (sovereign in a context of judgment, but subjected to the necessities of truth), the individual (titular control of personal rights subjected to the laws of nature and society), basic freedom (sovereign within, but accepting the demands of an outside world and "aligned with destiny"). In short, humanism is everything in Western civilization that restricts *the desire for power*: it prohibits the desire for power and excludes the possibility of power being seized. The theory of the subject (in the double sense of the word) is at the heart of humanism and this is why our culture has tenaciously rejected anything that could weaken its hold upon us.[11]

Indeed, it could be argued that the recently renewed effort to delegitimize Heidegger's (as well as Paul de Man's) "antihumanist" discourse is implicated in the present massive multisituated effort to recuperate the authority humanism lost in the Vietnam decade, when, in the face of the overt complicity of the institutions of knowledge production (especially the university) in the conduct of the state's colonial war against the Vietnamese people, the students and a large segment of the American public refused their spontaneous consent to its discursive principles. It could be said, further, that this effort to discredit Heidegger's antihumanist discourse and that of the posthumanists it enabled allies itself with that interpretation of the events of 1989 in Central and Eastern Europe that represents them in the global terms of the Cold War narrative: the "fall of communism" or, alternatively, the "triumph of democracy." Is it not possible to read this mounting campaign to delegitimize Heidegger's interrogation of humanism as the closure at the site of ontology of the dominant culture's effort to annul the only critical discourse that, at this historical conjuncture, is capable of resisting the planetary hegemony of the United States? I mean the (neo-)imperialism that now masks itself in the language of the *Pax Americana*: the "end of history" and the "coming of the new world order."[12]

III

What distinguishes the essays collected in this volume from one another, then, is not their ideological content, which can be characterized as an abiding commitment to the temporality, or rather, the differences that temporality disseminates, disclosed by the "interested" mode of inquiry I have called, after Heidegger, de-struction. The difference has primarily to do with the elaboration of the *worldly* scope of this commitment. These essays constitute a chronologically uneven thematization of the critical/projective cultural and sociopolitical imperatives of an engaged interpretive strategy that in Heidegger's discourse is–despite his disastrous foray into politics in the period of the rectorship–more or less limited to ontology. Very broadly, they chronicle the errant itinerary of my engagement with Heidegger's thought: a periplum that opens out from a preoccupation with the ontological question activated by Heidegger's existential analytic—his understanding of *Dasein* not as an essence but as thrown being-in-the-world—to include the indissoluble relay of questions concerning cultural production and consumption and sociopolitical formations activated by the (self-)destruction of the metaphysical discourse of Being.

In this itinerary three general phases or moments can be identified. It begins in the context of the institutional hegemony of Anglo-American Modernism in general and the New Criticism in particular, with an effort to draw out the implications of Heidegger's destructive hermeneutics (his interrogation of the metaphysics of the ontotheological tradition, especially in *Being and Time*) for the act of reading literary texts (and the text of literary history). This is the purpose of chapters 2 and 3, "Breaking the Circle" and "Heidegger, Kierkegaard, and the Hermeneutic Circle." These integrally related texts appropriate Heidegger's version of the hermeneutic circle (derived from Kierkegaard's existentialist destruction of Hegelian recollection [*Er-innerung*]) not only to expose the will to power (over difference) informing the spatializing and dehistoricizing imperatives of the retrospective interpretive practices of the New Criticism and structuralism but also to articulate a temporal and open-ended literary hermeneutics that, in acknowledging the ontological difference, renders both interpreter and text "worldly."

The second phase was precipitated by the concurrence of my encounter with the texts of Michel Foucault (especially *Discipline and Punish* and *The Will to Knowledge*) and of other "worldly" critics such as Antonio Gramsci, Theodor Adorno, Louis Althusser, Fredric Jameson, and Edward Said—and, by way of the too-easy institutionalization in North America of its textual emphasis, my disillusionment with deconstruction as a viable point of departure for the elaboration of an effective oppositional critical discourse. In Foucault's critical genealogy, above all, I found, despite its deliberate distancing from Heidegger's phenomenology, a remarkable parallel with Heidegger's destruction, one that extends Heidegger's (and Derrida's) critique of the centered circle (the logocentrism that accommodates difference to the metaphysical principle of identity) to include its repressive manifestations in the public sphere (the polyvalent diagram of the Panopticon, which accommodates social deviance to the disciplinary principle of normalization). At the same time the difference dramatized the disabling social-political limits of Heidegger's focus on the site of ontology (to which I will return). It thus precipitated an expansion of the horizon of my more or less ontological understanding of being: the recognition, only latent in Heidegger's existential analytic of *Dasein*, that being, however uneven its specific manifestations in any particular historical occasion, constitutes an indissoluble relay of forces extending from ontological and epistemological determinations through linguistic and cultural production to gender relations and sociopolitical formations.

This phase is here represented by the fourth and fifth essays: "The Indifference of *Differance*: Retrieving Heidegger's Destruction" and "Heidegger and Foucault: The Politics of the Commanding Gaze." These pieces appropriate Heidegger's critique of the reifying or spatializing momentum of modern technology—what he calls "the age of the world picture" (*Die Zeit des Weltbildes*)—mediated by Foucault's genealogy of post-Enlightenment power relations: the "panopticism" of the bourgeois/capitalist disciplinary society. They do so in behalf of an oppositional interpretive practice that, without resorting to the essentialist base/superstructure model of classical Marxism, would (1) overcome the dehistoricizing tendencies of deconstruction and (2) expose the complicity of traditional modes of interpretation and the cultural institutions they have legitimated—mainly the "disinterestedness" of humanist inquiry and the institutions of knowledge production it reproduces—with the economic and sociopolitical apparatuses of the state.

The third phase of this Heideggerian itinerary brings the expanding horizon of my destructive hermeneutics to its temporary conclusion.

This last phase, represented here by chapter 6, "Heidegger, Nazism, and the 'Repressive Hypothesis,' " was instigated by the belated American appropriation (and displacement) of the European debate over Heidegger's politics; more specifically, by the traditional humanist campaign to discredit his influential inaugural philosophical thought by culling a dehumanized and dehumanizing fascist essence from its peregrinations. In opposition to this representation of Heidegger's discourse, my essay locates the historical origins of the different but affiliated emancipatory discourses of the present posthumanist occasion not in Heidegger's practice, but in his texts. It would remind the participants in the debate, both those who condemn and those who defend Heidegger's thought, that, more than any other interrogation of post-Enlightenment modernity, it was the transitive (originary) *thinking* Heidegger opposes to the intransitive (secondary or derivative) *philosophy* privileged by the ontotheological tradition that precipitated the crisis of the discourse of humanism. In demystifying the "truth" of humanism, in showing that the philosophical tradition it brings to fulfillment ends, as he puts it in his "Letter on Humanism," in "the dictatorship of the public realm which decides in advance what is intelligible and what must be rejected as unintelligible,"[13] Heidegger's inaugural *Denken* "put research on new foundations" that accommodated "the urge towards historical actuality." However indirectly in some cases, it also provided the philosophical context for the emergence, in the aftermath of the Vietnam War, of the discourses of deconstruction, genealogy, a certain feminism deriving from Lacanian psychoanalysis, and the neo-Marxisms that have shifted their emphasis away from the critique of the economic base to the critique of the now "semiautonomous" superstructural sites of late bourgeois capitalism. These affiliated contemporary theoretical discourses have collectively disclosed the complicity between (the humanistic) discourse of truth and sociopolitical power or, to put it in a way that conflates Gramsci and Althusser, between the discourse of "hegemony" and "the (repressive) state apparatuses."[14]

The essays collected in this book are intended neither as an apology for Heidegger's National Socialist practice during the period of the rectorate nor as a defense of his thought as such. In their retrieval of Heidegger's insistent destruction of the humanist subject and its disinterested inquiry—the exposure of the anthropology determining the discourse of truth (*veritas* or *adequaetio intellectus et rei*)—these essays are intended to foreground what the humanist prosecutors of the case against Heidegger simply refuse to entertain. I mean not simply the interestedness of their "disinterested" discourse in general but also, and above all, the historically specific ideological subtext of their anti-antihumanist trial of his antihumanism: the recuperation (in the face of its self-destruction in the

Vietnam period) of a discursive practice that, as Walter Benjamin reminds us in his "Theses on the Philosophy of History," occludes the history of the inhumanity of humanism and its cultural institutions:

> The answer [to the question "with whom the adherents of historicism actually empathize"] is inevitable: with the victor. And all rulers are the heirs of those who conquered before them. Hence, empathy with the victor invariably benefits rulers. Historical materialists know what that means. Whoever has emerged victorious participates to this day in the triumphal procession in which the present rulers step over those who are lying prostrate. According to traditional practice, the spoils are carried along in the procession. They are called cultural treasures, and a historical materialist views them with cautious detachment. For without exception the cultural treasures he surveys have an origin which he cannot contemplate without horror. They owe their existence not only to the efforts of the great minds and talents who have created them, but also to the anonymous toil of their contemporaries. There is no document of civilization which is not at the same time a document of barbarism. And just as such a document is not free of barbarism, barbarism taints also the manner in which it was transmitted from one owner to another. A historical materialist therefore dissociates himself from it as far as possible. He regards it as his task to brush history against the grain.[15]

This book asks the critical question it does because the real target of those *nouveaux philosophes* and pluralist humanists who have welcomed Farías's "disclosures" about Heidegger's Nazi politics is not Heidegger the man, nor finally Heidegger's discourse as such. Their target is the contemporary posthumanist discourses influenced or catalyzed by Heidegger's destruction of the ontotheological tradition: those emancipatory discourses that, in brushing the narrative of history constructed by the humanist tradition against the grain, have contributed significantly in precipitating the present crisis of humanism and its institutions.

To put the project of this book positively, these essays are intended to demonstrate the continuing use value of a certain Heideggerian initiative of thinking—especially the project of overcoming philosophy—for oppositional intellectuals. Despite the politically conservative bent of his antihumanist discourse, Heidegger's destructive hermeneutics remains viable—indeed, has been rendered crucial by the historical demise of classical Marxism—to the polyvalent task of emancipation in the face of the massive "reform" movement that would relegitimate not simply the discourse of humanism and its cultural institutions, but also the discreetly repressive sociopolitical order it has always served. I mean a movement that is epistemic in scope: not limited to the site of theory, but, as Raymond Williams has observed, extends, however unevenly, into the "specific and indissoluble real processes of living"[16] (of being-in-the-world), from the subject through cultural production and gender and race relations to the domestic and international sociopolitical order.

I will readily concede to his critics that Heidegger's version of the antihumanist project, especially in the period of the rectorate, contributed to the odious political purposes of historical Nazism. But his antihumanism clearly is far more complex than it is now being represented, and should not be used to justify an obfuscation of his epochal positive contribution to a differential discourse of emancipation radically at odds with that privileged in and by the humanist tradition since the Enlightenment. The discourse he inaugurated, in its exposure of the contradictions inhering in the latter, is more adequate than existing oppositional discourses to the analysis and critique of the operations of contemporary power. For in disclosing the will to power informing the privileged understanding of Truth (the determinations of "objective" or "disinterested" inquiry), Heidegger's discourse set the stage for a more radical disclosure: that the humanist representation of Truth as the privileged agency of liberation conceals the complicity of this (ontological) Truth with (ontic) power. Whatever the personal/historical form he gave to his solicitation of the (anthropo)logos, the fact remains that Heidegger's unrelenting commitment to think being exposed the *constituted* (derivative) and increasingly sedimented character of the Occidental discourse of "truth," which, in repressing the difference that temporality disseminates in the name of identity or presence, ends in the totalized representation of being. Which is to say, brings the onto-theo-logical tradition to its fulfillment and end in the detemporalized and indifferent—reified—"age of the world picture." In so doing, it went far to enable not simply the reversal of the metaphysical (essentialist) principle par excellence—that identity is the condition for the possibility of difference—but, more recently, the widespread, however partial, emancipatory "political" discursive projects of posthumanist theory. I mean the projects dedicated to the decolonization (liberation) and empowerment of the historically specific subject and a multiplicity of hitherto subjected cultural and sociopolitical constituencies of the human community: women, blacks, gays, ethnic minorities, and Third World and other subject positions marginalized, repressed, or accommodated in and by the discursive practices of humanist hegemony.

My orientation toward Heidegger's discourse refuses the ruse of anecdotal history so eagerly and all too easily, and often glibly, appropriated by his humanist critics in the wake of the publication of Farías's book. I choose to address the contradictions in his texts. Farías's biography of Heidegger's affiliation with Nazism obscures its reliance on the anecdotal to circumvent or justify a tendential reading of Heidegger's texts. It also conceals the essential, but unacknowledged, determinant informing the discourse of humanism at large—the determinant which it is the purpose of Heidegger's version of the hermeneutic circle (the de-struction) to make explicit: both the anthropo-logocentrism that "overlooks" and forgets or, as in the case of Heidegger's humanist critics, demonizes the difference that would disrupt its authority in the name of identity, and the *ressentiment* that, as Nietzsche has argued, lies behind this repressive strategy. To put it positively, to "leap primordially and wholly" into the circle of the Heideggerian text is not only to encounter its contradictions but also to discover an emancipatory impulse in its solicitation of the humanist representation of being (as Being) and the affiliated relay of binary metaphors this hegemonic representation has constituted, codified, and naturalized: sovereign subject/collective subject, choosing freely/following blindly, knowledge/power, and so forth.

This destructive orientation toward Heidegger's philosophical discourse has informed my writing from its beginnings to the present. It is also this orientation in general that informs the enormously influential writing of those global critics of modernity who have either appropriated Heidegger's discourse or the Heideggerian moment in behalf of a postmetaphysical or, more radically, posthumanist emancipatory philosophy of practice: Jean-Paul Sartre, Jacques Lacan, Jacques Derrida, Jean-François Lyotard, Julia Kristeva, Louis Althusser, Michel Foucault, and, more recently, Gayatri Spivak, Ernesto Laclau, and Chantal Mouffe, to name only some of the most prominent. However assimilated to the specific subject position of particular projects of cultural critique, it is also this destructive orientation that finally informs the discourse and practice of the growing number of North American intellectuals—men and women, teachers and students, whites and blacks—in the humanities, the social sciences, and legal studies, who have refused their spontaneous consent to the hegemonic discourse of humanism and collectively rendered the institutions this discourse is intended to legitimate and reproduce vulnerable to radical critique and transformation.

Could it be said of Heidegger what Foucault says about Marx and Freud, that he was an "initiator of discursive practices": one of those rare epochal authors who "produced not only their work, but the possibility and the rules of formation of other texts"?[17] Whatever one's answer to this question, it is certain—and this should not be forgotten or occluded by the prosecutors' appeal to the damning anecdote—that Heidegger's philosophical discourse, especially *Being and Time*, has generated an intellectual climate in the Occidental world (and elsewhere) characterized by the estrangement of the consensual self-representation of the West. In so doing, it has also instigated the production of a diverse and influential body of transgressive writing that cuts across disciplinary boundaries, or, as in the instances of neo-Marxism and neo-Freudianism, constitutes a radical revision of the founding texts of other discourses. The recent moralist attacks on Heidegger's thought systematically forget, or repress, the influence of Heidegger's texts on contemporary oppositional criticism in the convenient but dubious name of biographical anecdote, that is, "circumstantial evidence." This is precisely why it seems to me now necessary, not to defend Heidegger, but to retrieve his destruction of the onto-theo-logical tradition, especially his disclosure of the complicity of modern humanist inquiry (anthropo-logy, the third phase of this discursive history) with sociopolitical domination: not only the critique, but also the projective impulse that, however occulted, informs his destructive hermeneutics.

IV

All this is not to imply that the essays in this book assume Heidegger's philosophical discourse, whether that of the period of the rectorate or that preceding and following it, to be immune to political critique. If the first two essays withhold reference to the conservative philosophical and sociopolitical gestures in the Heideggerian texts they invoke, it is because they were written during the critical period of the Vietnam War and the civil rights movement: the historically specific moment that spontaneously disclosed the relevant irrelevance of the dominant North American mode of interpretive practice (the New Criticism) in the face of the brutal American intervention in a Third World country in the name of the "free world," and therefore the need to theorize the relationship of its "autotelic" poetics to sociopolitical practice. They were written at a time in the history of American literary studies when one could bracket the well-known question of Heidegger's personal involvement with German National Socialism in favor of invoking his existential analytic in behalf of a *negative critique* of the privileged principle of the autonomous poem and the "objective" reading it authorized. I am referring specifically to its usefulness in disclosing that the New Criticism's "objectivity" was informed by an interest that affiliated it with the ideologically motivated "disinterestedness" of humanist historicism as well as with the "objectivity" of the positivist sciences and technology this criticism was ostensibly opposing. What mattered to me as a member of the profession of literary studies in the United States at that historical conjuncture was the negative phase of Heidegger's destructive hermeneutics. I believe it was also this aspect that appealed to those oppositional intellectuals in and out of the academy who got their Heidegger filtered through the humanist

Existentialist lens of Jean-Paul Sartre, Simone de Beauvoir, Maurice Merleau-Ponty, and Albert Camus or through the Christian Existentialist lens of Paul Tillich, Rudolph Bultmann, and Dietrich Boenhoffer (I am referring to the activist theology of Union Theological Seminary). Heidegger's existential analytic, that is, enabled the critique of a relay of dominant cultural discourses whose metaphysical foundations were concealed in an alleged "objectivity" or a free-floating formalism. In short, it made possible the disclosure of the will to power informing their recollective mode of inquiry—and their ultimate implication, however indirect, in the violent repressive sociopolitical practices of the American state.

This general antimetaphysical impulse in Heidegger's texts continued to matter after the Vietnam War, but in a more particularized form. The failure of Heideggerian existentialism to effect lasting and productive changes in American culture and sociopolitics precipitated the need to address the general metaphysics of the ontotheological tradition in terms of humanism: the historically specific post-Enlightenment allotrope of metaphysics, the discursive practices of which are determined by the anthropologos.[18] This narrowing of focus was concurrent with the emergence of the poststructuralist critique of the vestigial metaphysics of Heidegger's text, particularly Derrida's disclosure of the incompleteness of Heidegger's interrogation of the (self-present) subject (the problem of authenticity, or *Eigentlichkeit*) and Foucault's disclosure of the subject as the invention of post-Enlightenment bourgeois/capitalist humanism. Together they compelled me to take into account those gestures in Heidegger's texts that were politically retrogressive, which is to say, to stress, against them, those projective initiatives of his destructive hermeneutics amenable to appropriation for a viable oppositional and progressive transdisciplinary discourse. My disillusionment in the emancipatory possibilities of "Heideggerian Existentialism" and my encounter with poststructuralism did not lead me to reject Heidegger's discourse (for reasons I will elaborate shortly). Rather, it precipitated an effort to reconcile Heidegger's de-struction of the vicious circularity of metaphysics—what I will call his ontic/ontological project—with that aspect of poststructuralist discourse that addresses itself to the constituted origins of power relations in the so-called democratic societies, specifically with Foucault's genealogy of the "regime of truth."

Let me put this modification in another, more technical way that is closer to Heidegger's texts. The early essays in this book might suggest that my representation of his destruction gives priority to the ontological (originary) over the ontic (secondary or derivative). Despite the asymmetry of the weight I originally attributed to these terms in the relationship, however, an attentive chronological reading will show that my

interpretation of the destruction assumes from the beginning their simultaneity in the "circular" hermeneutic process. Given the finiteness of
Dasein, the interpretation of being is necessarily "never presuppositionless" (BT, 191–92). It is a project always already inscribed by the discursive: "Is there not, however, a definite ontical way of taking authentic
existence, a factical ideal of Dasein, underlying our ontological Interpretation of Dasein's existence? That is so indeed. But not only is this Fact
one that must not be denied and that we are forced to grant; it must also
be conceived in its *positive necessity*" (BT, 358). The destruction does not
disclose the presence occluded by everyday being-in-the-world, nor does
it unveil the nothingness of temporality (and the difference it disseminates) contained and repressed in the structure of Being (as it is understood in the ontotheological tradition) in its pure or primordial or transcendental form, as external to being-in-the-world. The temporality of
being is always already and necessarily contaminated by inscription (the
ontic). *Nevertheless*, this primal temporality is "revealed" in and by the
circular interpretive process (*Wiederholung*: repetition or retrieval) as that
which interpretation cannot interpret and bring-to-stand: always already
defers. To appropriate Althusser's neo-Marxist version of Lacan's understanding of the "real" (appropriated in turn from Heidegger?), the destruction reveals the temporality of being as "absent cause" and interpretation itself as always already an act of construction, or, in Fredric
Jameson's phrase, a "strategy of containment."[19]

In order to foreground the containing or repressive imperatives and
the distorting consequences of metaphysical structuration, however, I
gave, like Heidegger, an inordinate rhetorical emphasis in my early writing to the temporality disclosed by the destruction. In doing so, I inadvertently suggested a separation of the *ontological* (the temporality of
being) and the *ontic* (inscription or reification). Or rather, I put what was
actually *simultaneous* in such a way as to make it appear to be a hierarchized binary opposition in which the ontological acts as a base to the
ontic superstructure. This misleading emphasis will be found in chapters
2–4, though in diminishing degree.

In the wake of my encounter in the mid-1970s with Derrida's critique
of Heidegger's vestigial metaphysics, and with Foucault's interrogation
of the humanist subject and knowledge/power relations in the post-
Enlightenment disciplinary society (the "repressive hypothesis"), I re-
adjusted this hierarchical imbalance (which also characterizes Heidegger's
texts) to accommodate the posthumanist critique of disciplinarity or,
alternatively, hegemony. What emerged from this encounter was a revised version of destructive hermeneutics—also justified by Heidegger's
texts, most explicitly in his insistence in *Being and Time* on the "equiprimordiality" of *Dasein*'s occasion (*Befindlichkeit*), understanding (*Ver-*

stehen), and discourse (*Rede*) (BT, 169–72)—that represents being as always already ontic/ontological. According to this revision, being is understood as an indissoluble lateral continuum of forces that, however unevenly developed (and semiautonomous) at any particular historical conjuncture, includes all the sites or regions of being, from the ontological (being as such) through the cultural (textual production) to the sociopolitical (gender, class and race relations, sociopolitical formations, and so on).

This recapitulation of the history of my relationship to Heidegger's texts can be rephrased in a way that specifically addresses the question of their vulnerability to moral and political critique. In order to elaborate this transdisciplinary interpretive strategy precipitated by my encounter with Foucauldian genealogy, I had increasingly to disassociate my discourse from certain nostalgic—indeed, reactionary—discursive emphases in Heidegger's revolutionary texts, especially from those residual metaphysical gestures that culminated in his endorsement of National Socialism. But this distancing in no way constituted a judgmental act against or rejection of his philosophical discourse. Rather, it involved a fuller thematization of the projective implications of Heidegger's destructive hermeneutics. It involved the foregrounding, that is, of what was only latent and implicit in the early essays: the degree to which my own texts have been, from the beginning, de-structive readings of or "reciprocal rejoinders" to Heidegger's.

Given the increasing presence of post-Heideggerian politically left thinkers in the most recent phase of my work—especially Foucault and Said, though also Gramsci, Adorno, Althusser, Jameson, Laclau and Mouffe, and other neo-Marxists—it might be objected by oppositional critics that my insistence on the continuing viability of Heidegger's discourse for a radical oppositional criticism betrays a misguided and disabling nostalgia for a by-now-overcome origin. My response to this possible objection is twofold. The first is inscribed in my (implicit) narrative of the genealogy of contemporary theory—specifically, the dialogic relationship with Heidegger's texts that characterizes the new left discourses of the postmodern or posthumanist occasion. Put summarily, the "presence"—even as the object of critique—of Heidegger's radical interrogation of the founding (ontotheological) discourses that have "written" the discourse and practice of humanist/patriarchal/bourgeois/ capitalist modernity in these emancipatory discursive practices cannot be written off as accidental and irrelevant. It simply has been, as I have said, enabling.

The second and more specific response is spelled out at some length in "Heidegger and Foucault: the Politics of the Commanding Gaze." It will suffice here to suggest the following: If Foucault's brilliant genealogy of the microphysical power relations in the post-Enlightenment disciplinary society dramatizes the sociopolitical limitations of Heidegger's essentially ontological and thus rarefied destruction of the philosophical discourses of the ontotheological tradition, Heidegger's destruction of the philosophical discourse of the ontotheological tradition, in turn, dramatizes the ontological limitations of Foucault's genealogy of the microphysical power relations in the post-Enlightenment disciplinary society. Thinking Heidegger with Foucault thematizes the tendency of Heidegger's discourse to abstract history: to overlook (or distort) the historical specificity of modern power relations (the sociopolitical sites on the ontic continuum). But to think Foucault with Heidegger, on the other hand, thematizes the tendency of Foucault's discourse (and that of the "new historicism" it enabled) to limit the genealogical origins of the disciplinary society to the Enlightenment. Such a reading foregrounds Foucault's tendency (epitomized by the overwhelming bulk of his historically specific scholarship) to emphasize empirical science/technology as the source and determining agent of modern power relations at the expense of minimizing the complicity of the Western philosophical tradition at large: the "classical" tradition always invoked by modern "poetic" humanists since Matthew Arnold (including the New Critics) against modern science and technology. This reading (which points to the continuity of these last essays with the earlier ones, which attempt to disclose the complicity of New Critical discourse with the positivism it would oppose) suggests how Foucault's genealogical discourse can lend itself, however inadvertently, to the reinscription of the misleading, because essentially monologic, "two cultures" debate.

This is no small problem. As the subsequent history of Foucauldian genealogical criticism bears witness, such a reinscription of this spurious debate licenses "poetic" humanists—philosophers, literary and art critics, and historians (the custodians of the *litterae humaniores*)—to escape identification with the disciplinary society, and to perpetuate the discursive practices of truth/beauty as the *privileged adversary* of power and violence—precisely the discursive practices that Foucault's genealogy is intended to demystify. This inadvertent relegitimation of the "repressive hypothesis" also lends itself to the legitimation of the Western, primarily American, interpretation of the global events of 1989–90 in Eastern Europe. I mean the interpretation that represents these events as epochal: the final triumph of the founding humanist principles (the culture) of capitalist democracy (truth/beauty) over the "totalitarian" principles of socialism (power), which is to say, as the resolution of the Cold War narrative and the precipitation of a "new world order" determined by the United States.

This insight into the antithetical critical limitations of Heidegger's and

Foucault's (and other contemporary materialist or "worldly" critics') vestigial adherence to disciplinary boundaries and the consequent awareness of the transdisciplinary critical/emancipatory potentialities of a reconciliation of Heidegger's destruction and Foucault's genealogy marks the essential disclosure of the itinerary of my engagement with Heidegger's texts. It was, further, this moment of recognition that precipitated the imperative to respond, by way of retrieving that itinerary within this book, to the humanists—whether the French *nouveaux philosophes* or the American pluralists or the German neohumanist Marxists—who have appropriated the occasion of the publication of Victor Farías's biographical "disclosures" to discredit Heidegger's philosophical discourse by representing its antihumanist project to be fundamentally dehumanizing.

This introduction to the essays that follow was written from the end—from the theoretical and historical vantage point arrived at in the last essay. It thus constitutes a re-presentation of the errant history of my engagement with Heidegger's thought. Unlike those who still assume language to be transparent and thus write prefaces that make their books—the process of their research—superfluous, however, I have been conscious of the distortions endemic to retrospection and have tried, accordingly, to minimize them in the writing. But there is finally no succeeding in this task. Indeed, far from being a cause for lament, I take the historical materiality of language—its refusal to stand still—as a darkly absent cause of celebration. For it is not in the climactic moment of a development, but in the rift—which is to say, the *opening*—always already instigated by the resistance of historicity to the language of containment (worlding) that the "truth," as well as individual and collective freedom, is to be found. This preface is an interpretation or representation of a living and thus errant process which I openly acknowledge as finally undecidable. It is not intended to declare the truth of the history of my engagement with Heidegger's thought (let alone the truth of Heidegger's complex engagement with the question of being). It is not proffered to serve as an authority to follow, but as a provisional guide for the reader interested enough to undertake a repetition of my itinerary. It is intended as necessary "forestructure" that the circular temporal process of engagement in and with my texts will inevitably transform into something other: a "reciprocal rejoinder." To put it differently, I offer up this preface—as, I submit, Heidegger's revision of the interpretive theory and practice of the ontotheological tradition essentially demands of scholarship—to the finite act of destruction.

Chapter 2
Breaking the Circle:
Hermeneutics as Dis-closure

Those masterful images because complete
Grew in pure mind, but out of what began?
A mound of refuse or the sweepings of a street,
Old kettles, old bottles, and a broken can,
Old iron, old bones, old rags, that raving slut
Who keeps the till. Now that my ladder's
gone,
I must lie down where all the ladders start,
In the foul rag-and-bone shop of the heart.

W. B. Yeats, "The Circus Animals' Desertion"

Reality is the beginning not the end,
Naked Alpha, not the hierophant Omega,
Of dense investiture, with luminous vassals.

It is the infant A standing on infant legs,
Not twisted, stooping, polymathic Z,
He that kneels always on the edge of space

In the pallid perception of its distances.
Wallace Stevens, "An Ordinary Evening in New Haven"

*I have reached no conclusions, have erected no
  boundaries
shutting out and shutting in, separating inside
  from outside: I have
  drawn no lines:*

A. R. Ammons, "Corsons Inlet"

Martin Heidegger's destructive phenomenology has shown that modern philosophy, from Descartes through Kant and Hegel to the discourse of positive science, constitutes an "anthropology" that fulfills the imperatives of a metaphysical or logocentric concept of truth and thus brings "philosophy to its end."[1] Simultaneously, in dis-closing the temporality of being that the (anthropo)logos as Word or Presence encloses (covers over and forgets), Heidegger's destruction of the tradition points to a hermeneutics of being that is capable of surpassing metaphysics (*Überwindung*), to a postmodern hermeneutics of dis-covery, in which a disclosed temporality is given ontological priority over Being.[2] What I wish to suggest in this essay is that a destruction of the Western literary/critical tradition will reveal an analogous significance. In aestheticizing the literary text or (what is the same thing) in coercing the reading experience of the text into a metaphysical hermeneutic framework, American New Criticism (and its later extension in French structuralism) constitutes the completion of the Western literary tradition and thus "the end of criticism." Put more immediately, it will suggest that Modernist criticism, in fulfilling the traditional formal imperative, first articulated by Plato and Aristotle, to *see* the work of literary art from the end—as an autonomous and in-clusive object or, in the phrase adopted by most recent critics to characterize Modern literature, as a "spatial form"[3]—has accomplished the forgetting of the processual dynamics and thus the temporal/historical being—the be-ing—of the narrative it projects.

As Derrida has suggested in his deconstruction of Heidegger's thought, Heidegger's late quest for an originary language—"the one word"— tends to reappropriate the metaphysics he intended to overcome. His hermeneutic project in the essays on poetry, language, and thought therefore does not suggest a method of interpretation radical enough to accomplish the task of breaking out of the impasse—the enclosure—into which New Critical and structuralist formalism has driven modern literary studies. It is his existential analytic in *Being and Time*, by which he intends to gain access to being, that points to a hermeneutics of literary texts commensurate with the crisis of contemporary criticism. In retrieving or dis-covering the temporality of being that a recollective metaphysics covers over and forgets, the hermeneutic violence of this analytic points to a literary hermeneutics analogous to that inhering in post-modern literature. I mean here the *iconoclastic* literature that breaks the circle of closed form, and constitutes an attempt to release time from Form and being from Being and thus activate the being of the reader as being-in-the-world. The quest for a new literary hermeneutics, there-fore, requires a rethinking of Heidegger's existential analytic. This ana-lytic, it must be remembered throughout, is a project in fundamental ontology, not in ethics as such. It is not intended to reveal the moral limitations of human being as *das Man*, but to provide access to the *Seinsfrage*, the being-question, or what it means to be.

In drawing this analogy between Western literature and Western phi-losophy, I am in significant disagreement with Paul de Man's influential assumption—derived from Nietzsche's notion of art as will to power and Derrida's reduction of the traditional speech/writing (*parole/écriture*) op-position to "writing in general"—about the literary tradition: that liter-ary texts, unlike critical texts and myths, have never been self-deceived; that they have always been fictional, characterized by a conscious play that takes the void and the radical difference between sign and referent, language and empirical reality, for granted. Indeed, this essay is implic-itly an effort to bring this assumption, which might be called a mystifi-cation of literary texts in reverse, into question: not to revalorize the authorless, the logocentric myth, but to demystify the literary text and the text of the literary tradition in behalf of activating hermeneutic dialogue.

II

What Heidegger in *Being and Time* "wrests" from the "fallenness" (*Ver-fallensein*) of everyday being—the derivative or second-order existence of the "they" (*das Man*)[4]—is that *Dasein* is primordially a being-there as being-in-the-world or, to return to his source in Kierkegaard, as "inter-ested" being-between (*inter-esse*). In the "beginning," *Dasein* is an onto-logically free and careful being-toward-death, thrown *into the midst*—both spatially and temporally—of an open-ended and thus uncanny (*unheimliche*) world, in which, as the etymology suggests, it finds itself not-at-home. As primordially free and care-ful, *Dasein* is "being-ahead-of-itself" in the sense of "being-towards one's ownmost potentiality-for-being (BT, 237; SZ, 193). Its radical existential structure is thus its temporality.

The existential analytic also discloses that *Dasein* as being-in-the-world "is"—comports itself toward things as they are—in two broad ways. It can interpret the alien and uncanny world—the nothingness that its finitude, its being-toward-death, discloses—from a privileged logo-centric vantage point so as to objectify or *presence*, and thus neutralize or annul by gaining distance from (by "over-looking"), this world's most threatening possibility: its radically finite temporality. This is *Dasein*'s natural mode of being-in-the-world, how it comports itself "proximally and for the most part." It is the mode of inauthenticity (*Uneigentlichkeit*): the *derived* not-my-ownness of everyday life and public interpretation, which is in constant need of interpretation. Or it can acknowledge its finiteness and historicity and encounter or "meet" the things of the world as nothing or, what is the same thing, as temporality, in pursuit of the ultimate "meaning" of being-in-the-world. This mode of standing-in occurs primarily when the instrumentalized world breaks down, or, more appropriately, when a "rupture of reference" (*Störung der Verweisung*), a "break in the referential totality" (*Bruch der Verweisungszusammenhange*) takes place (BT, 105–6; SZ, 75–76). This is the mode of authenticity (*Eigentlichkeit*): the primordial my-ownness of individual life or of exis-tential interpretation. In contrast to the logocentric mode of inauthentic comportment, it may be called the ec-static stance, the stance, for example, of Watt in the house of Knott, in Samuel Beckett's great post-modern novel.[5]

This distinction between authenticity and inauthenticity (and its rela-tionship to the hermeneutic implications of the broken instrument) is at the problematic heart of Heidegger's phenomenological analysis of the nature of truth and the dynamics of its alternating concealment and dis-closure, but it is too complex a subject to be treated directly here.[6] I will instead examine the subsuming and enabling particular distinction within this general antithesis: the authentic mood of *Angst* (anxiety or dread)[7] and the mood of *Furcht* (fear), its "inauthentic" counterpart. Such a focus will suffice to suggest both the essential critical thrust of Heidegger's destruction of the ontotheological tradition (and its spatial hermeneu-tics), and the *projective* implications of his existential/phenomenological ontology (and the temporal hermeneutics it calls for). If, further, we keep in mind the remarkable similarity between Heidegger's interpretation of *Angst* and Aristotle's "pity and terror," which it is the purpose of the tragic form—the metaphysical form par excellence—to purge, this anal-ysis should also suggest the direction that the analogy with literature and literary criticism will take.

The "rupture of the referential totality" discloses *Dasein*'s primordial condition: its authentic *Befindlichkeit* (literally, "state of mind," but Heidegger's sense is more accurately "the discovery of self as already in the world").[8] This situation is one in which *Dasein* finds itself in an alien and uncanny temporal/spatial environment without fixed reference points and boundaries. In this original, radically temporal realm, the fundamental mood of *Dasein* is dread, which has no thing or nothing as its object. Echoing Kierkegaard's definition in *The Concept of Dread* ("Nothing begets dread"),[9] Heidegger writes:

> That in the face of which one has anxiety is characterized by the fact that what threatens is *nowhere*. Anxiety "does not know" [in terms of the propositional or derived knowledge of "calculative thinking"] what that in the face of which it is anxious is . . . [that] which threatens cannot bring itself close from a definite direction within what is close by; it is already "there," and yet nowhere; it is so close that it is oppressive and stifles one's breath, and yet it is nowhere. (BT, 231; SZ, 185)[10]

And again, in a passage from a later essay that sharply focuses both the *ungraspability* of the nothing (or mystery) that is the "object" of dread and the bewildered uncertainty of the authentic phenomenological standpoint:

> In dread, as we say, "one feels something uncanny [*unheimlich*]." What is this "something" [*es*] and this "one"? We are unable to say what gives "one" that uncanny feeling. "One" just feels it generally [*im Ganzen*]. All things, and we with them, sink into a sort of indifference. But not in the sense that everything simply disappears; rather, in the very act of drawing away from us everything turns towards us. This withdrawal of what-is-in-totality [this is the homogeneous world named and charted by the coerciv logocentric language of assertion], which then crowds round us *in dread*, this is what oppresses us. *There is nothing to hold on to*. The only thing that remains and overwhelms us whilst what-is slips away, is this "nothing."[11]

This dread that has no thing as its object and "nothing to hold on to" is, of course, a dread of being-in-the-world: "That in the face of which anxiety is anxious is nothing ready-at-hand within-in-the-world." But this

> "nothing" of readiness-to-hand is grounded in the most primordial "something"—in the *world*. Ontologically, however, the world belongs essentially to Dasein's Being as Being-in-the-world [the reference to belonging here is a reference to the *Dasein's* intentionality as care]. So if the "nothing"—that is, the world as such—exhibits itself as that in the face of which one has anxiety, this means that *Being-in-the-world itself is that in the face of which anxiety is anxious*. (BT, 231–32; SZ, 187)

The full ontological meaning of dread, and thus of its central import for Heidegger's destruction of the ontotheological tradition and his hermeneutics of being, does not become clear, however, until it is understood in the contrasting light of its inauthentic counterpart, fear. According to Heidegger (and in this he is virtually at one with every other existential phenomenologist since Kierkegaard), fear, unlike dread, *has* an object: "that in the face of which we fear is a detrimental entity within-the-world which comes from some definite region but is close by and is bringing itself close, and yet might stay away" (BT, 230; SZ, 185). Or again, in "What Is Metaphysics?": "We are always afraid of this or that definite thing, which threatens us in this or that definite way. 'Fear of' is generally 'fear about' something. Since fear has this characteristic limitation—'of' and 'about'—the man who is afraid . . . is always bound by the thing he is afraid of."[12] Because existence as such in the primordial not-at-home is intolerable, *Dasein* seeks to "flee in the face of death" and its ontological counterparts, time and nothingness, by "interpreting [these] publicly": by transforming dread into fear or, since fear has its source not in *no* thing, but in *some* thing, *by willfully objectifying* (finding objects for and referentially locating, that is, re-presenting) dread. They seek to transcend the uncanny not-at-home, in other words, by exerting the will to power over being, or, to use the term the postmodern occasion has called into question, by "humanizing" its nothingness.[13] This solidification of nothing thus domesticates (at-homes) the uncanniness of being-in-the-world (*die Unheimlichkeit*), rendering it accessible, apprehendable (capable of being taken hold of) by the mind. As Paul Tillich puts what Heidegger only hints at here, fear, as opposed to dread, "has a definite object . . . which can be faced, analyzed, attacked, endured. One can act upon it, and in acting upon it participate in it—even if in the form of struggle."[14] This coercive anthropomorphic representation of the nothing, it is worth observing, is what Keats refers to as the "irritable reaching after fact or reason" of the person who is incapable "of being in uncertainties, Mysteries, doubts." As Iris Murdoch's and Charles Olson's formal and thematic appropriation of the content of Keats's letter on negative capability testifies, this decentralizing motif becomes increasingly central for the postmodern literary imagination.[15]

If we recall that nothingness in Heidegger is synonymous with temporality, this reification of the primordial not-at-home suggests a further extension of his phenomenological distinction, one that points significantly to the analogy with the Western literary critical/tradition, especially to its culminating Modernist manifestation. The will to reify dread takes the form of imposing a *telos*, an end, upon the nothingness of temporality from the beginning. As such, this will to "take hold of nothing" is also more fundamentally a will to make the dreadful mystery visible and thus pleasurable. This is what Derrida means, despite the virtual absence of terms like "care," "dread," "mystery," and so on, in his discourse, when he refers insistently to "logocentrism" as a presencing of absence that brings "repose" or "peace."[16] Ultimately, the objectification of dread domesticates the not-at-home in the sense that it reduces by re-presenting the boundless and dread-provoking temporality of being-in-the-world into a tranquilizing "world picture": (1) a flattened-out, static, and homogeneous Euclidean space—a totalized and ontologically depthless grid of referents (a map)—if the objectifying consciousness is positivistic or realistic; or (2) a self-bounded or sealed-off and inclusive image (icon or myth), if the objectifying consciousness is idealistic or symbolistic. In either case, this reduction allows *Dasein* to *see* temporal existence from the beginning: all-at-once. In so doing, it distances *Dasein*; that is, disengages its care from the world. It renders *Dasein* an objective, disinterested or care-less, *observer* of an ultimately familiar or autonomous picture in which (the force of) temporality—its threat and its differential possibilities—has been pacified. To put this transformation in terms that extend Heidegger's thought (but are in keeping with its *élan*), what his existential/phenomenological analysis of the authentic/inauthentic structure of *Dasein* discovers is that the *objectification of nothingness is the spatialization (and thus covering up) of time and (by extension) of being.*

None of Heidegger's commentators has made explicit the relationship between his phenomenological interpretation of fear as the objectification of nothing (in the sense of the spatialization of time) and his interpretation of metaphysics as the perception of being from above or beyond "it." Nevertheless, this relationship enabled by the existential analytic is the fundamental disclosure of his destruction of the ontological tradition: both its concept of truth and its representation of being. Since the time of the classical Greek philosophers (but especially since the Romans' translation of the Greek *aletheia* to *veritas*: the adequation of mind and thing), the Western tradition, according to Heidegger, has increasingly represented the word *logos* in the sentence "man is the animal who is endowed with *logos* (ζῷον λόγον ἔχον)" "as 'reason,' 'judgment,' 'concept,' 'definition,' 'ground,' or 'relationship' " (BT, 55; SZ, 32). In so doing, this ontotheological tradition has covered up and, in the hardening process, eventually forgotten its origin in *legein* (to talk). *Legein*, or in Heidegger's translation, *Rede*, does not mean the "speech" informed by self-presence, which, according to Derrida, informs the logocentric tradition. In being *equiprimordial* with *Dasein*'s *Befindlichkeit* (its original and finally inescapable being-in-the-world as thrown) and its *Verstehen* (its authentic understanding of being-in-the-world as potentiality-for-being), it means, rather, a speech which is radically temporal.[17] In equating the *logos* as *legein* with temporality—nothingness or absence (of presence)—Heidegger, at least in *Being and Time*, interprets authentic oral discourse as a spontaneous and indeterminate existential act of an un-self-present self, as the "cry of its occasion,/Part of the *res* itself and not about it."[18] As such (and for other reasons I cannot elaborate here), it is a mode of discourse that transgresses the oral tradition, which, according to Derrida's representation, is identified with the *oracular* or *vatic* and thus with (self-)presence.

This metaphysical interpretation of *Dasein*, according to Heidegger, eventually resulted, by way of the mediation of the Roman reduction of *a-letheia*, in the naturalization of the derived notion of truth as correspondence (the agreement of the mind with its object of knowledge: Aristotle's *homoiosis*, St. Thomas's *adequaetio intellectas et rei*) and its hermeneutic corollary (the propositional language of assertion: judgment). It resulted, that is, in the acceptance of a constituted discourse as original and self-evident. Since judgment (correctness or accuracy of correspondence) is the goal of the subject/object relationship, it privileged an epistemology the essential imperative of which is to wrest the object (thing or human being) from its existential/temporal context—its occasion— to render it a pure and shareable presence. As interpreter, according to this epistemological imperative, *Dasein* must reduce its temporality to a measurable series of "now points," and its comportment as inquirer to an *"awaiting [gewärtigen] which forgets and makes present"* (BT, 389; SZ, 339). In terms of this essay, the traditional concept of truth requires *Dasein* to *suspend* and thus *spatialize* the always differentiating temporal process. In this way, it achieves "objectivity": a distance from the originally encountered object that allows it to become a privileged "observer," one who "looks at" or rather "overlooks" process synchronically (BT, 413; SZ, 361). It is in this sense that the "truth" of the traditional notion of truth as correspondence becomes in its hardened form a static and visual image (a metaphor) and the hermeneutic articulation of this truth a "disinterested" re-presentation (or, to anticipate, a recollection) of differential temporality from the end: calculative assertion.

This is ultimately the hermeneutic point Heidegger makes in *Being and Time* when he contrasts the sentence "The hammer is too heavy" with the derived proposition, "The hammer is heavy." With this latter assertion, which, according to Heidegger, is in the "self-evident" mode of "common sense" (Husserl's "natural standpoint," prior to the phenomenological reduction), the primordial significance of the hammer undergoes a subtle but radical transformation. Grounded on a "definite" and "developed way of conceiving"—the *logos* as presence—the assertion at the outset represents the lived situation involving the hammer in such a way as to make it fit into (enclose it within) its preestablished "logical" *structure*. The hammer is reduced to a neutral object with a definite and fixed character: "the unexplained presupposition is that the 'meaning' of this sentence is to be taken as: 'This thing—a hammer—has the property of heaviness'" (BT, 200; SZ, 152). Thus a concealment, a covering over, takes place. Something with which we act in the world (a tool) becomes a "what" about which we assert, or as Heidegger would say in amplifying Husserl's terminology, something "ready-to-hand" (*zuhanden*) becomes something "present-at-hand" (*vorhanden*). The "hermeneutic 'as'" dims into the "apophantic 'as.'" That is, something *lived* (experienced in circumspective concern) becomes something *observed* disinterestedly in the flattened-out realm of "superficiality" (*Ausserlichkeit*) (BT, 389; SZ, 339): in a timeless, static, and homogeneous space, "a worldless world." The absent cause—the temporal difference that makes a difference—which, if it can never be extricated from, nevertheless resonates in, inscription (the "hermeneutic 'as'"), is obliterated in inscription (the "apophantic 'as'"):

> When an assertion has given a definite character to something present-at-hand, it says something about it *as* a "what" [This is the "apophantic 'as'"]. . . . The [hermeneutic] as-structure of interpretation has undergone a modification. In its function of appropriating what is understood, the "as" no longer reaches out into a totality of involvements. . . . *The "as" gets pushed back into the uniform plane of that which is merely present-at-hand.* . . . *This levelling of the primordial "as" of circumspective interpretation* to the "as" with which presence-at-hand is given a definite character is the specialty of assertion. Only so does it obtain the possibility of exhibiting something in such a way that we *just look at it.* (BT, 200–201; SZ, 158; my emphasis)

In thus pointing to this "flattening" (*Einebnung*) or "leveling down" (*Nivellierung*) of the *Lebenswelt* of circumspective concern, Heidegger suggests that the traditional concept of truth as correspondence is both a derivative and a spatializing mode of truth. Indeed, he is suggesting that its derivative status is precisely defined by its spatialization of historicity, its transformation of an always already e-mergent temporality (*physis*) into a self-contained "referential surface" (map) or self-reflexive plane (icon):

> When space is discovered non-circumspectively by just looking at it, the environmental regions get neutralized to pure dimensions. Places—and indeed the whole circumspectively oriented totality of places belonging to equipment ready-to-hand—get reduced to a multiplicity of positions for random Things. The spatiality of what is ready-to-hand within-the-world loses its involvement-character [existentially situated condition], and so does the ready-to-hand. The world loses its specific aroundness; the environment becomes the

world of Nature. The "world," as a totality of equipment ready-to-hand, becomes spatialized [*verräumlicht*] to a context of extended Things which are just present-at-hand and no more. The homogeneous space of Nature shows itself only when the entities we encounter are discovered in such a way that the worldly character of the ready-to-hand gets specifically *deprived of its worldhood.* (BT, 147; SZ, 112; Heidegger's emphasis)[19]

Similarly, and by extension, Heidegger's destruction of the Western ontotheological tradition discloses that, despite its positivistic and idealistic variations, the essence of this tradition has been increasingly characterized by the willful impulse to close off and spatialize time as a means of transforming the mystery of being (*das Nichts* or, later, *die Erde*) into measurable (and useful) certainty. For the privileged and "self-evident" *logos*-as-*ratio* of the traditional notion of truth conceals a more fundamental and inclusive "self-evident" ontological concept: the *logos* as eternal essence. This is the *logos* variously represented in the history of Western ontology as "the Unmoved Mover," "the final cause," "the principle of causality," or, as Heidegger has focused it for us, as "permanent presence" (*ousia*).[20] What Heidegger's destruction discovers is that the ontotheological tradition, from Plato through St. Thomas and the church fathers to Descartes, Leibniz, Kant, Hegel, and the philosophers of classical modern science, has been essentially a metaphysical tradition, in which, according to its familiar formulation, essence precedes existence. This implies that the tradition has "grounded" the meaning of being *meta-ta-physika*—"beyond-what-is as such"[21] (the "what-is" being the realm of temporal/historical actuality), in the related senses of both *after* and *above*, from the distance of the end or *telos*. As such, it is a tradition that has reified being, reduced verbal be-ing to nominal Being, a super Thing (*Summum Ens*). It is a tradition that has "relegat[ed] becoming to the realm of the apparent."[22] In the final terms of Heidegger's destruction of the Platonic turn (the reference to understanding should be marked):

This transformation of unconcealment [*aletheia*] by way of distortion to undistortion and thence to correctness must be seen as one with the transformation of *physis* [e-mergent being] to *idea*, of *logos* as gathering to *logos* as statement. On the basis of all this, the definitive interpretation of being that is fixated in the word *ousia* now disengages itself and comes to the fore. *It signifies being in the sense of permanent presence, always-thereness.* What actually has being is accordingly what always is, *aei on. Permanently present* [according to the metaphysical tradition] *is what we must go back to in comprehending and producing*: the model, the *idea*. Permanently present is what we must go back to in *hypokeimenon, subjectum.* From the standpoint of *physis, emergence,* what was always-there is the *proteron,* the earlier, the a priori.[23]

This fundamental disclosure of Heidegger's phenomenological de-struction of the ontotheological tradition has often been noted. What needs to be thematized, however, especially in the context of the question of the relation between Heidegger's thought and the Western literary tradition and its hermeneutics, is that *this reification of existence is a spa-tialization of time. As the etymology suggests, it constitutes a willfully coerced metamorphosis of temporality into simultaneous image or picture: an aesthetic structure the model or prototype of which is the plastic or architectonic—visual— arts.* It is no accident, as Heidegger implies, that the Western tradition, both philosophical and literary, has privileged the visual sense ever since Plato gave the eye ontological priority over the other senses.

This extension of the meaning of the metaphysical reification of being to include the spatialization of time is implicit from the beginning in Heidegger's thought, especially in his pervasive identification of "inau-thentic" covering up with *sight.*[24] But it receives one of its most explicit and (because it recalls the phenomenological distinction between dread and fear in *Being and Time*) most suggestive expressions for my purposes in the essay entitled "Die Zeit des Weltbildes" ("The Age of the World Picture"). I am referring specifically to the section of the essay where Heidegger identifies the Cartesian *Umkehrung* (reversal) as the moment in Western history when "Man" becomes the relational center of that which is as such.[25] After this Cartesian turn, the divine Word of the medieval dispensation (the theologos) becomes increasingly the willfully aggressive *logos* of human subjectivity (the anthropologos) in Kant, Hegel, Nietzsche, and modern science, thus preparing for the "end of philosophy." The reification and domestication of temporal existence since Descartes, according to Heidegger, take the form of representation (*Vorstellung*): the placing of the *Ob-jectum* before or in front of the subject. In thus object-ifying the *Seinenden* (the existents or things-as-such), in thus replacing them in front of the subject's eyes as objective presence whose relationship to the subject is determined in advance by the subject, the strategy of re-presentation transforms time into picture, immobilizes be-ing and renders its differential and emergent force safe and utterly manageable. "This objectifying of whatever is," Heidegger writes, "is accomplished in a setting-before, a representing [*vorstellen*] that aims at bringing each particular being before it in such a way that man who calculates can be sure, and this means certain, of that being" (AWP, 127). (As I will show in the next chapter, Heidegger's analysis of post-Cartesian representation is remarkably similar to Søren Kierkegaard's decisive interpretation and critique of Platonic and Hegelian or, what for him is the same thing, "aesthetic" re-collection. It also reminds us not only of the retrospective orientation of realistic fiction, but of Wordsworth's, of Proust's, and by extension, the literary modernists' methodology of "remembrance."[26]

Under the aegis of the metaphysical *Vorstellung*, therefore, the temporal world at large becomes explicitly what it is implicitly in *Being and Time*: a flattened-out or depthless representation of the world in miniature, an in-clusive "world picture" (*Weltbild*), in which everything, including human being, has been reduced to the derived—timeless and "worldless"—mode of present-at-handness (*Vorhandenheit*). This means that the differential "things as such" are in fact *seen as* a systematized totality at a distance from their lived context—as located (identified and permanently fixed) within a hierarchized grid of mathematically or geometrically determined coordinates. Like the elements in the periodic table, for example, they are rendered fully certain, predictable, manipulable, and aesthetically pleasurable. The central passage from Heidegger's crucial essay deserves extended quotation, not only because it thematizes the optical metaphorics Heidegger's destructive project would call into question but also because it resonates with suggestive possibilities about the aesthetic/hermeneutic implications of the metaphysical spatialization of (temporal) being:

> What is a "world picture" [*Weltbild*]? Obviously a picture [*Bild*] of the world [*Welt*]. But what does "world" mean here? What does "picture" mean? "World" serves here as a name for what is, in its entirety [*der Seienden im Ganzen*]. The name is not limited to the cosmos, to nature. History also belongs to the world. Yet even nature and history, and both interpenetrating in their underlying and transcending of one another, do not exhaust the world. In this designation the ground of the world [*Weltgrund*] is meant also, no matter how its relation to the world is thought.
>
> With the word "picture" we think first of all of a copy of something. Accordingly, the world picture would be a painting, so to speak, of what is as a whole. But "world picture" means more than this. We mean by it the world itself, the world as such, what is, in its entirety, just as it is normative and binding for us. "Picture" here does not mean some imitation, but rather what sounds forth in the colloquial expression, "We get the picture" [*Wir sind über etwas im Bild*: literally, "we are in the picture"] concerning something. This means that matter stands before us exactly as it stands with it for us. "To get the picture" [literally, "to put oneself into the picture"] with respect to something means to set whatever is, itself, in place before oneself [*vor sich stellen*] just in the way that it stands with it, and to have it fixedly before oneself as set up in this way. But a decisive determinant in the essence of the picture is still missing. "We get the

picture" concerning something does not mean only that what is, is set before us, is represented to us, in general, but that what is stands before us—in all that belongs to it and all that stands together in it— *as a system.* "To get the picture" *resonates with the idea of knowing the answers, of having a preconceived framework, of being oriented towards the issues in question.* Where the world becomes picture, what is, in its entirety, is conceived and fixed as that on which *man is able to orient himself,* which, therefore, he wished to bring and to fix before himself and thus in a decisive sense to represent to himself. Hence world picture, when understood essentially, does not mean a picture of the world but the world *conceived and grasped* as picture. What is, in its entirety, is now taken in such a way that it first is in being and only is in being to the extent that it is set up by man, who represents and sets forth. Wherever we have the world picture, an essential decision takes place regarding what is, in its entirety. The Being of whatever is, is sought and found in the representedness of the latter [*Vorgesteltheit*]. (AWP, 129–30; my emphasis)[27]

To put it as succinctly as possible, Heidegger's destruction of the ontotheological tradition discovers that the metaphysical orientation manifests itself in a coercive "permanentizing" of being (*Bestandsicherung*), and this discovery reveals the Platonic reality to be appearance, *eidos* (idea), in fact, *eidolon,* an idol or image.[28] But we can be even more explicit than Heidegger and his commentators in thematizing the essential nature of this "permanentizing." In seeing existence *meta-ta-physika,* in grounding temporal existence in presence, the beginning and the middle in the end, being in Being, the tradition's spatialization of time, we may add, *assumes its ultimate iconic form in the auto-telic and in-clusive figure of the circle, whose center is the* logos *as invisible presence.* Put in terms of this extension of the destruction, the assumption by the tradition of the ontological priority of Being over temporality recalls Plato's abiding circular image of history (The Great Year); here described by Mircea Eliade:

> The myth of eternal repetition, as reinterpreted by Greek speculation has the meaning of a supreme attempt toward the "staticization" of becoming, toward annulling the irreversibility of time. If all moments and all situations of the cosmos are repeated *ad infinitum,* their evanescence is, in the last analysis, patent; *sub specie infinitatis,* all moments and all situations remain stationary and thus acquire the ontological order of the archetype. . . . From the point of view of eternal repetition, historical events are transformed into categories and thus regain the ontological order they possessed in the horizon of archaic spirituality [*in illo tempore, ab origine*].[29]

But this prioritization of Being over temporality also recalls the circular image of time and history privileged by Modernists such as W. B. Yeats,

James Joyce, Marcel Proust, Virginia Woolf, and T. S. Eliot (and the New Critics, who modeled their autotelic poetics on their practice)— and, by contrast, the essential strategy of the postmodern literary imagination. I mean the formal effort by postmodern writers such as Jean-Paul Sartre, Eugène Ionesco, Samuel Beckett, Jorge Luis Borges, Thomas Pynchon, William Carlos Williams, and Charles Olson (to name a few of the enabling practitioners) to break or break out of the symbolic circle. This foregrounding of the polyvalency of the privileged image of the centered circle makes explicit the logocentrism informing both the philosophic and literary traditions and, by way of the self-disclosure of the circle's limits, suggests in what sense both are "coming to their end."

The implications of the ontotheological tradition for the hermeneutics of understanding become clear. In transforming the always differential openness of temporal existence into a closed circle, which, emptied of time, can be "looked at" synchronically (object-ively), the metaphysical standpoint negates possibility, the originative interrogative (dialogic) mood, in favor of a derived indicative frame of reference in which the answer is ontologically prior to, and determines, the questions that can be asked of being. From the privileged transcendental vantage point of this "objective" distance from existence, interpretation takes the form of suspending the temporal process in favor of the identical whole: an operation that transforms the time of existential being-in-the-world (and text) into a "pure sequence of 'nows' . . . in which the ecstatical character of primordial temporality has been levelled off" (BT, 377; SZ, 329). Unlike the "anticipatory resoluteness" of authentic *Dasein*, which runs "ahead-of-itself" in care, interpretation from this objective standpoint thus becomes an "*awaiting* which *forgets and makes present* (BT, 389; SZ, 339; Heidegger's emphasis). It becomes a forgetful re-presenting that is now understood to mean "envisaging" (*Vergegenwärtigung*) (BT, 410, SZ, 359): a "deliberative" or, in Heidegger's later term, "calculative" awaiting that, on the basis of the *logos* and the visual gaze it privileges, *expects* all temporal and spatial phenomena to cohere eventually. Like the classical detective, such an interpreter *knows* he/she will "get the picture" in the end, because the end is ontologically prior to the process. Metaphysical interpretation is a visual practice of self-confirmation.

But this metaphysical frame of reference involves more than self-confirmation. Since the iconic circle becomes increasingly the representation of the subjective desire for certainty, hermeneutics gets subordinated to the anthropomorphic concept of correctness. It comes to be determined by the derived principle of truth as "*adequaetio intellectus et rei,*" which, in beginning from the end, inevitably results in the willful coercion of the vital minute particulars into the predetermined and comprehensive circle. In short, the self-confirming interpretive practice enabled by this metaphysical framework also becomes a will to power over the differences that temporality always already disseminates.

In spatializing time, the metaphysical perspective closes off the futural possibilities of differential existence and thus reduces the hermeneutic process to a vicious circle. The metaphysical is a *retrospective* perspective. As such, its circularity provides a spatial "insight" that at the same time shuts off—blinds—the interpreter to the more primordial and problematic temporality of being. This is the testimony of modernity itself. In fulfilling the metaphysical tradition and achieving an analogously absolute hermeneutic methodology, the modern period has (self-)disclosed the temporality to which the West has become increasingly blind, and reactivated—remembered—the question of being (as a question of the temporality of being) that it has forgotten. It has been the fulfillment of the inexorable binary logic of metaphysics in the modern "world picture" that has disclosed the contradictions informing this logic. In "coming to its end," the metaphysical tradition has ruptured the referential surface despite itself—thematized the "lack." In so doing, it has precipitated the need to "surpass" both the logic of metaphysics and the vicious circularity of the retrospective interpretive practice that has determined the meaning of the texts of particular moments of history and of the text of history at large.

III

The implications of my reading of Heidegger's destruction of the ontotheological tradition for Western literary history should by this time be explicit to anyone conversant with that history. It suggests that, despite the alternations between its idealistic and realistic manifestations—and the significant exceptions to its binary structure—the Western literary tradition from the post-Socratic Greeks, and especially the Roman Virgil to Balzac, Zola, and Dreiser, on the one hand, and Proust, Joyce, Yeats, and Eliot on the other, has also been, by and large and increasingly, a metaphysical tradition motivated by the will to power over temporal existence. It has been a tradition in which the monumentalized works of literary art, like their ontotheological philosophical counterparts, the global metaphysical systems of Plato, of Aquinas, of Descartes, of Leibniz, of Kant, of Hegel, constitute an increasingly willful reification of the "mystery" (of nothingness)—a spatialization of the temporality of being. It has been a tradition that has its ultimate raison d'être in the growing need (generated by increasingly recalcitrant historical breakdowns) to gain distance from the dreadful ambiguities, the uncanniness

(*Unheimlichkeit*), of the immediate situation of being-in-the-world. Indeed, it is precisely the historical hardening of the primordial temporality of the being of the literary text that constitutes the Western literary tradition. The essential validity of the analogy I am drawing between the philosophical and literary discourses of the Occidental tradition—and the enormously significant implications for literary history it discovers— may be suggested by invoking the broad, however uneven, continuity in literary theory and practice existing from Aristotle's poetics (which, we must not forget, governed or mirrored not simply the theorization but the making of serious literature from classical Greece to the beginning of the twentieth century) to the poetics of Modernism: more specifically, by exposing the "metaphysical" assumption that constitutes the ground both of Aristotle's poetics of mimesis and the iconic poetics and literary practice of Modernism.

When Aristotle says in the *Poetics* that "the plot is the first principle and, as it were, the very soul of tragedy," his structural model is the teleological universe of his *Metaphysics*. Despite his appeal to Sophocles' *Oedipus Tyrannos* as point of departure, the Aristotelean literary work, like the universe pictured in that philosophical text, is defined by a beginning that generates discords, a middle in which the discords intensify into crisis, and an end that not only resolves the discords (the differences) but, like an epiphany (the simultaneous perception of the unified totality), reveals that the discords are only appearance, the result of partial or immediate experience. Like Aristotle's metaphysical universe, the Aristotelean literary work is grounded in a *telos*, an unmoved mover, a *logos* as presence, that determines and gives intelligibility to the action—the event, the historicity, as it were—of the text from the end, *meta-ta-physika*.

Since the Being (or form) of the work is ontologically prior to its being (the temporal medium of words and the differential process it articulates), the essential formal imperative of Aristotelean mimetic theory is thus the spatialization of time. The structuralist demand to reduced time to an integral plot, "an action that is complete in itself, forming a whole of a sufficient magnitude or extent," is a demand to make an inclusive, self-bounded, or autotelic microcosm of the macrocosm: a "world picture" in miniature that mediates the apparent nothingness of immediate, of existential, experience. In thus transforming time into an inclusive spatial circle and allowing us to "see" the universe as a miniaturized ordered and intelligible whole, the Aristotelean work disengages the anxious being-in-the-world from the world. It generates aesthetic distance from the dislocating contradictions of life in time. In short, it transforms him or her into the beholder of a spectacle. As Heidegger might put it, *Dasein* as being-in-the-world is "disburdened" (BT, 165;

SZ, 127) of its existence and "volatized" (BT, 153; SZ, 117). It becomes, like Kierkegaard's infinitely negative ironist, a "free-floating" spectator of a scene of writing (BT, 160; SZ, 124).[30]

To translate the sedimented terminology of Aristotle's discourse into the language of Heidegger's phenomenological destruction, the Aristotelean poetics of mimesis imposes an end (in both senses of the word) on being-in-the-world and thus, in a prescient Hegelian dialectic, reconciles the opposing and dis-locating (or un-homing) motions of pity and terror: the dread of nothing (*Angst*), which is the basic existential mood of *Dasein*'s original situation (*Befindlichkeit*), its awareness of being thrown into the boundless and uncanny world, which is to say, the not-at-home. In reconciling the antithetical energies of dread (attraction and repulsion), in achieving equilibrium, as it were, the Aristotelean form then brings the "spectator's" restless soul into balanced repose. This aesthetic spatialization and transcendence of temporality—this at-homing that *arrests* the motion of the anxious consciousness of being-in-the-world—is what Aristotle called *catharsis*. It is also what the Modernist I. A. Richards called *irony* in his celebration of the healing effects of tragic form:

> What clearer instance of the "balance or reconciliation of opposite and discordant qualities" [Coleridge] can be found than Tragedy? Pity, the impulse to approach, and Terror, the impulse to retreat, are brought in Tragedy to a reconciliation which they find nowhere else. . . . Their union in an ordered single response is the *catharsis* by which Tragedy is recognized, whether Aristotle meant anything of this kind or not. This is the explanation of that sense of release, of repose in the midst of stress, of balance and composure, given by Tragedy, for there is no other way in which such impulses, once awakened, can be set at rest without suppression. . . .
>
> Irony [of which Tragedy is the highest form] consists in the bringing in of the opposite, the complementary impulses; that is why [the "exclusive" and "unstable"] poetry which is exposed to it is not of the highest order, and why irony itself is so constantly a characteristic of [the "inclusive" and "stable"] poetry which is.[31]

Understood in terms of the conventional (realist) interpretation of the Aristotelean literary tradition, Modernist literature—by which I mean the literature of the Symbolist/Imagist movement and the ironic critical theories modeled on the Symbolist poem—appears to constitute a significant literary revolution in its departure from the literature that imitates "nature." This appearance is enhanced by the pervasive Modernist reaction against the "Aristoteleanism" of the positivistic or "well-made" fiction (and drama) of the nineteenth century: what Virginia Woolf calls the "materialistic novel" in her famous essay "Modern Fiction," and T.

S. Eliot "the narrative method" in his equally famous review of Joyce's *Ulysses*.[32] Encountered from the standpoint of Heidegger's destructive interrogation of the ontotheological tradition, however, Modernism's revolutionary status takes on the lineaments of illusion. It comes to be understood as simply an allotrope of traditional "realism," another, though in many respects more aggressive, effort of the metaphysical will to power to repair the broken instrument or (to use the essential terms of this essay), to restore the referential surface ruptured by the breakdown of the logocentric tradition. Indeed, Modernism, especially its critical/hermeneutic counterpart (the New Criticism, and later, structuralism), comes to be seen as the fulfillment and exhausted end of the Western literary tradition just as modern philosophy, according to Heidegger, brings the Western philosophical tradition to its fulfillment and exhausted end. Exacerbated by the breakdown of the Judeo-Christian and humanist (both idealist and positivist) world pictures, that is, the Modernist literary impulse to spatialize temporality into the inclusive and closed eternal (iconic) circle becomes, like the philosophical impulse to perceive existence *meta-ta-physika* of Cartesian representation, Hegelian dialectics, and Nietzschean will to power, more or less absolute—and thus self-disclosive.

This "end" of the Western literary tradition, from its most elemental to its most inclusive articulations, is written in the following (by now famous but still to be understood) passages from the documentary history of Modernism:

    1. *T. E. Hulme* (representing Wilhelm Worringer's distinction between the "urge to empathy" of Western humanistic art and the "urge to abstraction" of "primitive," Egyptian, Byzantine, and Oriental art in behalf of the neo-abstractionism of the Modernist "revolution"):[33]

This art ["Greek art and modern art since the Renaissance"] *as contrasted with geometrical art can be broadly described as naturalism or realism. . . . The source of the pleasure felt by the spectator before the products of art of this kind is a feeling of increased vitality, a process which German writers on aesthetics call empathy* (Einfühlung) *. . . we can say that any work of art we find beautiful is an objectification of our own pleasure in activity, and our own vitality. . . . Putting the matter more simply we may say that in this art there is always a feeling of liking for, and pleasure in, the forms and movements to be found in nature. It is obvious therefore that this art can only occur in a people whose relation to outside nature is such that it admits of the feeling of pleasure in its contemplation.*

Turn now to geometrical art. It most obviously exhibits no delight in nature and no striving after vitality. Its forms are always what can be described as stiff and lifeless. The dead form of a pyramid and the suppression of life in a Byzantine mosaic show that behind their arts there must have been an impulse, the direct opposite of that which finds satisfaction in the naturalism of Greek and Renaissance art.

This is what Worringer calls the tendency to abstraction. . . . It can be described most generally as a feeling of separation in the face of outside nature.

While a naturalistic art is the result of a happy pantheistic relation between man and the outside world, the tendency to abstraction . . . occurs in races whose attitude to the outside world is the exact contrary of this. . . .

Take . . . the case of more primitive people. They live in a world whose lack of order and seeming arbitrariness must inspire them with a certain fear. . . . The fear I mean here is mental, however, not physical. They are dominated by what Worringer calls a kind of spiritual "space-shyness" in face of the varied confusion and arbitrariness of existence. In art this state of mind results in a desire to create a certain geometrical shape, which, being durable and permanent shall be a refuge from the flux and impermanence of outside nature. . . . In the reproduction of natural objects there is an attempt to purify them of their characteristically living qualities in order to make them necessary and immovable. The changing is translated into something fixed and necessary. This leads to rigid lines and dead crystalline forms, for pure geometrical regularity gives a certain pleasure to men troubled by the obscurity of outside appearance. The geometrical line is something absolutely distinct from the messiness, the confusion, and the accidental details of existing things. (Modern Art and Its Philosophy, Specula-tions: Essays on Humanism and the Philosophy of Art*)*

2. *Ezra Pound* (defining Imagism against the realistic art of *kinesis* of nineteenth-century Europe):

An "Image" is that which presents an intellectual and emotional complex in an instant of time. . . .

It is the presentation of such a "complex" instantaneously which gives that sense of sudden liberation: that sense of freedom from time and space limits. ("A Few Don'ts," Poetry 1: 6 [March 1913]*)*

3. *James Joyce* or, rather, *Stephen Dedalus* (explaining the cathartic effect of his "proper" "iconic" or "epiphanic" poetics of stasis):

You see I use the word arrest. *I mean that the tragic emotion is static. Or rather the dramatic emotion is. The feelings excited by improper art are kinetic, desire or loathing. Desire urges us to possess, to go to something; loathing urges us to abandon, to go from something. These are kinetic emotions. The arts which excite them, pornographical or didactic, are therefore improper arts. The esthetic emotion (I use the general term) is therefore static. The mind is arrested and raised above desire and loathing.* (A Portrait of the Artist as a Young Man [*1916*])

4. *T. S. Eliot* (extending the Image or the "objective correlative" to include myth):

In using the myth [of the Odyssey], *in manipulating a continuous parallel between contemporaneity and antiquity, Mr. Joyce is pursuing a method which others must pursue after him. . . . It is simply a way of controlling, of ordering, of giving a shape and a significance to the immense panorama of futility and anarchy which is contemporary history. It is a method already adumbrated by Mr. Yeats, and of the need for which I believe Mr. Yeats to have been the first contemporary to be conscious. It is a method for which the horoscope is auspicious. Psychology (such as it is, and whether our reactions to it be comic or serious), ethnology, and* The Golden Bough *have concurred to make possible what was impossible even a few years ago. Instead of narrative method, we may now use the mythic method. It is, I seriously believe, a step toward making the modern world possible for art.* ("Ulysses, Order, and Myth," The Dial [*1923*])

5. *Cleanth Brooks* (defining the ironic poetry of the "Metaphysical" tradition—the poetry, as he observes repeatedly [after I. A. Richards], in which "the structure of inclusion is the basic structure"):

Compare the "tough reasonableness" of Eliot's poetry of wit with the invulnerability to irony of Richards' poetry of synthesis; the "alliance of levity and seriousness" with Richards' unification of opposed impulses; Eliot's "sensibility which could devour any kind of experience" with Richards' statement that "tragedy . . . is perhaps the most general, all-accepting, all-ordering experience known. It can take anything within its organization." One may suggest one more definition of metaphysical poetry, a definition based on Richards' terms: it is a poetry in which the opposition of the impulses which are united is extreme. Or, to base oneself directly on Coleridge: it is a poetry in which the poet attempts the reconciliation of qualities which are opposite or discordant in the extreme.

*Such a definition of poetry places the emphasis directly on the poet as a maker. It is his making, his imagination that gives the poem its poetic quality, not some intrinsic quality (beauty or truth) of the materials with which he builds his poem. The metaphysical poet has confidence in the power of the imagination. He is constantly remaking his world by relating into an organic whole the amorphous and heterogeneous and contradictory. (*Modern Poetry and the Tradition [*1939*])*

6. *Joseph Frank* (summing up his definition of Anglo-American Modernism):

Allen Tate, speaking of the Cantos, *writes that Ezra Pound's "powerful juxtaposition of the ancient, the Renaissance, and the modern worlds reduces all these elements to an unhistorical miscellany, timeless and without origin"; and this is called the "peculiarly modern quality" of all the work we have before us—they all maintain a continual juxtaposition between aspects of the past and the present, in such a way that both are fused in one comprehensive view. . . . By this juxtaposition of past and present, as Allen Tate realized, history becomes unhistorical: it is no longer seen as an objective, causal progression in time, with distinctly marked out differences between each period, but is sensed as a* continuum *in which distinctions between past and present are obliterated. Just as the dimension of depth has vanished from the plastic arts [in the work of Modernist abstract painting and sculpture], so the dimension of depth has vanished from history as it forms the content of [the major works of Modernist literature]: past and present are seen spatially, locked in a timeless unity which, while it may accentuate surface differences, eliminates any feeling of historical sequence by the very act of juxtaposition. . . . The objective historical imagination, on which modern man has prided himself, and which he has cultivated so carefully since the Renaissance, is transformed in these writers into the mythical imagination for which historical time does not exist—the imagination which sees the actions and events of a particular time merely as the bodying forth of eternal prototypes. . . . And it is this timeless world of myth, forming the common content of modern literature, which finds its appropriate aesthetic expression in spatial form. ("Spatial Form in Modern Literature" [*1945*])*

7. *Claude Lévi-Strauss* (analyzing "the small-scale model or miniature . . . as the universal type of the work of art" from a point of view that becomes the ground of structuralist poetics):

What is the virtue of reduction either of scale or in the number of properties? It seems to result from a sort of reversal in the process of understanding. To understand a real object in its totality we always tend to work from its parts. The resistance it offers us is overcome by dividing it. Reduction in scale reverses this situation. Being smaller, the object as a whole seems less formidable. By being quantitatively diminished, it seems to us qualitatively simplified. More exactly, this quantitative transposition extends and diversifies our power over a homologue of the thing; and by means of it the latter can be grasped, assessed and apprehended at a glance. A child's doll is no longer an enemy, a rival or even an interlocutor. In it and through it a person is made into a subject. In the case of miniatures, in contrast to what happens when we try to understand an object or a living creature of real dimensions, knowledge of the whole precedes knowledge of the parts. And even if this is an illusion, the point of the procedure is to create or sustain the illusion, which gratifies the intelligence and gives rise to a sense of pleasure which can already be called aesthetic on these grounds alone. (La Pensée Sauvage [1962])

It has often been observed that the American New Criticism (and French structuralism after it) modeled its poetics on the Modernist literature of "spatial form," a literature which, in turn modeled its verbal structure on the abstract plastic or iconic arts of Paul Cézanne, Pablo Picasso, Amedeo Modigliani, David Bromberg, Wyndham Lewis, Henri Gaudier-Brzeska, Jacob Epstein, and Constantin Brancusi. When, however, we consider this relay of affiliations in the context of the disclosures of Heidegger's destructive hermeneutics, we begin to perceive the unexamined metaphysical assumptions that lie behind its fundamental commitment to the autotelic (self-bounded or self-enclosed and self-determinate) status of the literary work and thus also the spatializing imperatives of its exegetical frame of reference. We begin to understand that the New Critical (and structuralist) commitment to the "autonomous" poem—to the idea that "a poem should not mean / but be"[34]— is grounded in the assumption that such a poem is an inclusive object (*Seiendes*). It thus demands an interpretive practice that, in beginning from the end—*meta-ta-physika*—must suspend (overlook) the temporality of the text (its words): in short, a methodological *making present* or *presencing* similar to that demanded by the retrospective metaphysical orientation of the Western (ontotheological) philosophical tradition.

It will require only one reference to perceive that what Joseph Frank says unquestioningly about the exegetical imperatives demanded by the formal character of Modernist literature applies equally to the hermeneutics of the New Criticism (and of structuralism):

Aesthetic form in modern poetry, then, is based on a space-logic that demands a complete re-orientation in the reader's attitude towards language. Since the primary reference of any word-group is to something inside the poem itself, language in modern poetry is really reflexive: the meaning-relationship is completed only by the simultaneous perception in space of word-groups which, when read consecutively in time, have no comprehensible relation to each other. Instead of the instinctive and immediate [read "existential"] reference of words and word-groups to the objects or events they symbolize, and the construction of meaning from the sequence of their references, modern poetry asks its readers to suspend the process of individual references temporarily until the entire pattern of internal references can be apprehended as a unity.[35]

Like its philosophical allotrope, the "objective" or "disinterested" hermeneutics of Modernism inevitably becomes, in Heidegger's term, a privileged "awaiting which forgets": a "deliberative" or "calculative" bracketing of "temporal references," which, grounded in certain expectation that the "whole picture" will come into view before the reader as spectator, tends to coerce a temporal medium into an "in-clusive" object or a closed circle. Such a visually oriented interpretive practice closes off—becomes blind to—the possibility of a more original understanding of the text, whether a particular work or the tradition, an understanding in which meaning would be infinitely open and undecidable.[36] To be truer, perhaps, to *Being and Time*, the reification of language, the transformation of words into Image, by the mystified logocentric hermeneutics of objective Modernist criticism—the New Criticism, the myth criticism of Northrop Frye, the "phenomenological" criticism of consciousness of Georges Poulet and the Geneva school, and the structuralism of Tsvetan Todorov, Gérard Genette, and Roland Barthes— close off the possibility of *hearing* the temporality of words, in which the "real" being of a literary text inheres.

IV

In opposition to the derived and enclosed mode of (anthropo)logical interpretation, Heidegger calls for an originative and open phenomenological hermeneutics in *Being and Time*. What he means by this crucial distinction is fully articulated in his etymological analysis of the two components of the word "phenomenology": "phenomenon" (from φαίνω "to bring to light" and ultimately, φῶς "light": that which comes to light from hiddenness) and especially *logos* (from λέγειν [German: *Rede*, "to talk," "to hold discourse"]. It will suffice for my purposes to thematize the implications of Heidegger's existential analytic in *Being and Time* for literary interpretation: that it calls for an antimetaphysical, which is to say a phenomenological, hermeneutics of dis-closure, a hermeneutics in which temporality is ontologically prior to— is the condition for the possibility of—the Being (or spatial form) of the text. More specifically, it demands a phenomenological reduction (*epoché*) of the metaphysical perspective, a "return to the things themselves," not, as in Husserl, in the sense of uncovering a lost or buried logocentric origin, an *arché* as source, but of retrieving one's original status as situated being-in-the-world (*In-der-Welt-Sein*).

Here, we recall, *Dasein*'s occasion (*Befindlichkeit*: the primordial situation into which it is thrown) its understanding (*Verstehen*: that which reveals *Dasein*'s possibilities as being-in-the-world), and most important for my purposes, the e-mergent saying that makes this understanding explicit (*Rede*: the *logos* as *legein*), are understood as equiprimordial. And despite their forestructurality, they are *radically temporal*: un-grounded, or rather, grounded in nothing, which is to say, always already open. Here also—and because of its temporality—*Dasein*, as the hyphenated "being-in-the-world" suggests, is characterized not by disinterestedness, but by the interest precipitated by *anxiety* (*Angst*). In taking "away from *Dasein* the possibility of understanding itself . . . in terms of the 'world' and the way things are publicly interpreted," anxiety discloses *Dasein*'s "ownmost Being-in-the-world, which as something that understands, projects itself essentially upon possibilities" (BT, 232; SZ, 187). Anxiety, that is, discloses *Dasein*'s being as care (*Sorge*). This, of course, is Heidegger's radicalized version of Husserl's definition of intentionality as "consciousness of." The distinction between Husserl's phenomenology and the phenomenology of *Being and Time*—especially Heidegger's interpretation of speech (*Rede*) as an existentially temporal discourse "grounded" in nothingness—needs to be emphasized to counteract Derrida's, and especially his followers', too easy but influential structuralist identification of Heidegger's privileging of *Rede* (oral discourse) with oracular expression, and thus with the principle of presence and the logocentric tradition.[37]

In grounding itself on the ungrounded *logos* as *legein* in the sentence "Man is the Being who has *logos*," Heidegger's phenomenological hermeneutics retrieves a more primordial understanding of the "truth" of a text than that afforded by the derived or spatial notion of truth as judgment (the *adequaetio*). It retrieves the truth of *aletheia* (that which always already gets un-concealed or un-hidden):

The "Being-true" of the λόγος as αληθεύειν means that in λέγειν as ἀποθαίνεσθαι [Heidegger goes on to define "phenomenology" as

"ἀποφαίνεσθαι τὰ φαινόμενα: to let that which shows itself be
seen from itself in the very way in which it shows itself from itself"]
the entities *of which* one is talking must be taken out of their
hiddennness; one must let them be seen as something unhidden
(ἀληθές); that is, they must be *discovered*. (BT, 56–57; SZ, 33;
Heidegger's emphasis)

The Heideggerian phenomenological reduction, that is, dereifies the interpreter in the sense of retrieving his/her ec-static or ec-sistential temporality, his/her *openness* to being. In so doing, it also retrieves the primordial ontological difference from the structure of identity into which
the metaphysical eye has coerced it. In thus abandoning the will to power
over being, or, to put it positively, in letting being be as it shows itself
from itself,[38] the interpreter, in other words, *allows* the "object" of interpretation to undergo a liberating or, better, an e-man-cipating metamorphosis. The reified text, the text that the Medusan eye of the metaphysical interpreter "looks at" and petrifies[39]—turns into something present-
at-hand, or, to invoke a related metaphor, reduces to "graspable" icon
(or Euclidean map)—undergoes a sea change. It now emerges explicitly
as transitive verbal text—a text to be heard—from its context in the
realm of deposited or "monumentalized" knowledge. It becomes an *event*
in the interpreter's temporal horizon of circumspective care, an event he/
she experiences hermeneutically, *as* event, in the sense, as the crucial pri-
vitive prefix of *a-letheia* makes clear, of dis-covering the temporal being
that spatialization covers over or conceals.

According to a phenomenological hermeneutics, then, it is not, as it
has been "from ancient times," the static, presentational, uprooted—and
coercive—language of assertion that constitutes the "'locus' of truth"
(BT, 196; SZ, 154). It is, rather, the kinetic, explorative—and generous—language of human speech: not the mystified orality of the (self-
present) Word of mythic or Platonic Man with which Derrida identifies
Heidegger's understanding of *Rede*, but the always potential dialogic
process, which, in being temporal, precludes a definitive revelation of a
being.[40] This process "locates" the truth of being in the interpreter's continuous ecstatic awareness of the ontologically alternating rhythm of
concealment and disclosure, appearing and disappearing, inscription and
de-scription, truth and error, continuity and change, or, to appropriate
Paul de Man's antinomy for my purposes, blindness and insight.

To return to the spatial metaphor, in modeling itself on the *logos* as
legein, in assigning ontological priority to temporality over form in understanding, phenomenological hermeneutics becomes a process of dis-
covery in the sense of *dis-closing*—opening out, liberating—the hermeneutic possibilities that the inauthentic spatial impulse of the Western
literary consciousness closes off, conceals, and eventually forgets in

coercing the temporality of the text into a totalized circle. It is hardly accidental that, in contrast to the spatializing "awaiting which makes present and forgets," Heidegger's term for *Dasein*'s authentic (i.e., temporal and projective) hermeneutic comportment before being is "*vorlaufende Entschlössenheit*," which means simultaneously "anticipatory resoluteness" and, as its etymology suggests, a "running forward which dis-closes" (BT, 343 ff.; SZ, 297 ff.)[41] It is in this sense of a resolute opening out that remembers (repeats or retrieves) that phenomenological hermeneutics, unlike the amnesiac spatial memory, renders encounters with a literary text "fateful," that is, historically significant—and for "its time," that is, timely (BT, 434–39; SZ, 382–87).[42]

In putting into question the old, the habitual, metaphysical frame of reference, the phenomenological interpreter (as Heidegger understands this being) loses privileged status as "objective" observer of the sealed-off and familiar or "domesticated" (at-homed) world of modernity: the world as blueprint or formalized icon or, as Heidegger puts it, "useful chart by which we may find our way amid the various possible things and realms of things."[43] He or she becomes, rather, a care-ful *Dasein* "inquiring into the *extra*-ordinary";[44] becomes, that is, *Homo viator*, a human being always already on the way. The imperative to de-construct the metaphysical circle of the Western tradition, to retrieve the temporal/ explorative comportment toward being from representation, is not restricted to poststructuralist philosophy. It is also a felt need of the post-modern poet and novelist. I will explore this relationship at some length in the next chapter. It will suffice here to briefly invoke the testimony of the American poet Charles Olson, who voiced this destructive/ projective imperative in both his poetry and prose perhaps more insistently and succinctly than any other "postmodern" writer. Like Heidegger, who calls for the interpretive practice of a *Homo viator*, Olson calls for a poetics that reflects the horizontal vision of a "Figure Outward," a "Juan de la Cosa," who encounters the world as such, including the world of the literary text—even the most metaphysical or autotelic—as a being there, in the midst, and thus with "the old measure of care."[45]

As privileged observer beyond history, the metaphysical reader (whether positivist or idealist, historicist or New Critic) questions the text to achieve mastery over it. As destructive/phenomenological interpreter he/she becomes an interested participant. To radicalize Hans-Georg Gadamer's insight, such a reader risks his/her inscribed prejudices before the text in the sense of generously *letting* the text as historical utterance and event also ask questions about what he/she assumes to be the truth.[46] It makes possible the retrieval of the interpreter's historicity and thus also the retrieval of the temporality of the text from History. It enables the interpreter to render the temporal "structure" (the "structurality of structure," to appropriate Derrida's phrase) explicit: to *hear* the *logos* as *legein*, as always e-mergent speaking voice. It is this phenomenological/destructive imperative, in other words, that brings meaning, not as determinate truth, but *as* being-saying, out of concealment or oblivion into the opening/closing of finitude.

Further, the imperative to read particular texts temporally must constitute the first stage, the beginning, of a destruction of the Western literary tradition that would achieve the paradoxically liberating double retrieval (*Wiederholung*). This imperative should not be limited solely to discovering texts buried in and by the hardened tradition: their "timeliness," the "meaning" they bear for us in the present. It also demands the retrieval of a stance within the Western literary tradition (especially as it has been formulated and represented by the ontotheological New Critics and structuralists for the present age). I mean a postmodern history that, in substituting dis-closure for representation, both validates the inexhaustibility of the literary text (literary history as "misreading") and commits literary discourse to the difficult larger task of "overcoming metaphysics": a history, in other words, that puts literature at the service of being rather than being at the service of literature.[47]

The recent emergence of a felt need to rethink the past of Western literature in behalf of demystifying and overcoming metaphysics, it should be remembered, has been made explicit by the breakdown (selfdestruction) of this tradition in the modern period. It thus necessitates emphasizing that the temporal hermeneutics I have appropriated from *Being and Time* applies to the "text" of literary history as well as to particular literary texts. The appropriation of the Derridean or the de Manian version of Heidegger's destruction (i.e., deconstruction) by literary criticism has indeed yielded provocatively productive results concerning the question of literary history. However—and here my remarks apply equally, if in a different way, to the hermeneutic methodology underlying Heidegger's post-*Being and Time* exegetical dialogues with Friedrich Hölderlin, Georg Trakl, Stefan Georg, and Ernst Jünger (the National Socialist Heidegger)—this appropriation of Derrida's or de Man's deconstructive projects is subject to significant "error," or blindness, in interpretation and even lends itself to willful misreading. This is because, despite its interrogation of "spatial form," it too frequently begins the hermeneutic process from the end: to ground its deconstruction of the literary tradition in an unexamined tendency to read particular historical texts or oeuvres spatially. Committed to the ontology of absence/presence (or *différance*) in their critique and revision of the Western literary tradition, the literary deconstructors nevertheless reappropriate, in an unwarrantedly naïve way, the "objective" distance inscribed in and demanded by the interpretive methodology of metaphysics, which in turn inhibits the possibility of existential encounter with ("leap-ing wholly and primordially into") the text's temporality. This specta-torial comportment before the text, that is, blinds itself to the text's rep-resentation of being, to the question of how it stands with be-ing in the text.

This, despite his theoretical efforts to retrieve the temporality of the literary text, is even the case in Paul de Man's remarkable deconstruction of Jacques Derrida's deconstruction of Rousseau's *Essai sur l'origine des langues*. Derrida's, it will be recalled, concludes that Rousseau's blindness to what he in fact " 'knew,' in a sense" ("that his doctrine disguised his insight into something closely resembling its opposite")[48] was the con-sequence of the inscribed pressure of the Western tradition's ontology of presence. It is essentially by means of a reflexive reading, which tends to perceive Rousseau's text as a mosaic structure and thus to disregard (over-look) its process, or "time-structure," that de Man can "prove" with equal authority that, on the contrary, Rousseau consciously fiction-alized his affirmation of the priority of oral expression (*parole*) over writ-ing (*écriture*). De Man will assert against a structuralist such as Todorov that "prior to any generalization about literature, literary texts have to be read, and the possibility of reading can never be taken for granted."[49] But there is little evidence in his interpretation of Rousseau, or in the practice of his other essays in "interpretation," that reading, for him, is originative or exploratory, a temporal "inquiry into the *extra*-ordinary." There is little evidence, in other words, that he, any more than Todorov, is conscious of the ontological implications vis-à-vis being-in-the-world of the temporal structure articulated in a particular literary text. And it is this blindness to the temporal being of the text that despite the bril-liance of the argument, renders his account of Rousseau ultimately un-convincing and, in my mind, imposes limits on his extremely valuable Nietzschean project.

More important, this tendency to read historically specific texts spa-tially seems also to blind de Man to the essentially mystified character of the imaginative literature of the Western tradition: to the pervasive teleological structure of literary texts from Sophocles to the Modernist period. It thus leads him to conclude that Western literature has never been self-deceived about its constructedness, that it always begins with an awareness "that sign and meaning can never coincide,"[50] that it "knows and names itself as fiction." In the literary text, in other words, "the human self has experienced the void within itself and the invented fiction, far from fulfilling the void, asserts itself as a pure nothingness, our nothingness stated and restated by a subject that is the agent of its own instability" (CC, 19). Finally, in "knowing and naming itself as fic-tion," the literary text is "demystified from the start" (CC, 18) and thus is not in need of deconstruction. In short, this tendency to read spatially, and thus to contradict the interpretive imperative of deconstruction, in effect precludes the possibility of recognizing the complicity of imaginative literature with literary criticism (and history) in the formation and legitimation of the (repressive) ontotheological tradition.

Temporal reading, that is, dis-covers phenomenologically that, like the philosophical and historiological text in the ontotheological tradition, the literary text in the history of Western literature has by and large, and increasingly, until quite recently, been intent on holding a mirror up to one form of logocentric metaphysical universe or another. And it has done this not, as de Man insists, to produce "fiction" that, aware of the "presence of nothingness," "names this void with ever-renewed understanding" (CC, 18). Rather, its ultimate purpose, like that of myth, is to mediate—to spatialize immediate temporal experience for the purpose of securing its readers' always flagging faith in the logocentric order of that experience: to objectify the dread that has no thing (time) as its "object" in behalf of a (quiescent) repose. To put it another way, temporal reading discovers that Western literature has, however unevenly, existed to fulfill and confirm, to certify and strengthen, the inscribed teleological expectations (the logocentric interpretive habits) of the reader, not to demystify them. This is the *essential* testimony of postmodern literature at large: of the fiction of Samuel Beckett, Alain Robbe-Grillet, Donald Barthelme, and Thomas Pynchon; of the drama of Eugène Ionesco, Harold Pinter, and Bertolt Brecht; of the poetry of René Char, Wallace Stevens, William Carlos Williams, and Charles Olson, for example. In playing havoc with the sense of an ending in both the exclusive linear narrative of nineteenth-century "realism" and its twentieth-century allotrope, the inclusive circular narrative of Modernist symbolism, this self-consciously intertextual literature exists primarily to deconstruct and demystify the spatialized literary texts privileged (canonized) by the Occidental tradition. The ultimate purpose of this deconstruction of traditional literary forms is to dis-integrate by formal violence the inscribed logocentric or (as I prefer) spatial frame of reference of the modern reader.[51] This de-structive strategy of the postmodern writer is remarkably similar to de Man's Nietzschean account of Western literature at large. But in committing itself to deconstructing the "second nature" truth of the "fiction" of the tradition, this body of e-mergent literature throws de Man's and his followers' project into serious question.

The failure to give the temporality of the literary text its due as "other" has its source, perhaps, in the fact that the site of de Man's critical inquiry is almost exclusively the critical essay rather than imaginative literature. It is revealing that his exemplary "fiction" is Rousseau's philosophical *Essai sur l'origines des langues*, where temporality is more thematic than formal. Whatever its origins, this blindness inhibits—as it does in different ways in the later Heidegger and in Gadamer—the understanding and articulation of deconstruction's full potential for literary history. Only temporal reading can disclose "how it stands with being" in a literary text. Only the disclosure of "how it stands with being" in a historically specific text can disclose "how it stands with being" in the literary tradition. Paradoxically, it was J. Hillis Miller, a convert to the de Manian project, who concluded, in a paper commenting on the Yale Colloquium on Criticism in 1966, that

> the tradition in modern thought and art which rebels against dualism would also claim that spatial thinking is an abstraction from the concrete richness of experience. Human existence is fundamentally temporal, and even our experience of space is false if it is described in terms of geometrical abstractions. Among those forms which are falsified by spatialization, such thinkers would say, is literature. Literature is a temporal, not a spatial art, and should be described as such, in vocabulary proper to its temporality.[52]

It was also Miller who, with de Man's invocation of Heidegger's *Being and Time* in mind, looked forward to a new hermeneutics "on the basis of the swing to monism and temporality in twentieth-century thought."[53]

V

Having established the ontological priority of temporality over structure in human understanding, the "next stage" would have to account for the repeatability of reading, or to put it otherwise, for the whole, the Being or form of a literary text. This task—which requires analysis of the hermeneutic circle—will be undertaken in the next chapter. It will suffice here to address the objection that I have not accounted for the concept of "the whole" by pointing out that it has always been present in the argument, though held in abeyance, and needs only to be made explicit. As Heidegger says at the outset of *Being and Time*, and repeatedly in opposition to Husserl's commitment to a "presuppositionless philosophy," *all* inquiry, "as a kind of seeking, must be grounded beforehand by what is sought. So the meaning of Being must already be available to us in some way" (BT, 25; SZ, 57, 5); this is what Heidegger calls "the forestructure" of *Dasein*'s understanding. The effort to avoid circularity, therefore, is a futile gesture; it also does violence to the "truth" insofar as it naturalizes what is always already constituted. "What is decisive," Heidegger reiterates, "is not to get out of the circle but to come into it in the right way" (BT, 195; SZ, 153). And the right way, as we have seen, is through the ontic/ontological *Dasein*:

> This circle of understanding is not an orbit in which any random kind of knowledge may move; it is the expression of the existential *fore-structure* of Dasein itself. It is not to be reduced to the level of a vicious circle, or even of a circle which is merely tolerated. In the circle is hidden a positive possibility of the most primordial kind of knowing. (BT, 195; SZ, 153)

What I have hinted at throughout in referring to the New Critical and structuralist tendency to perceive the temporal text as "autotelic," "bounded," "sealed off," "inclusive"—as a centered circular space—is that this kind of privileged spatial understanding and hermeneutics begins with a commitment to the ontological priority of form (icon, image, model, myth, and so on) over the temporal process of reading the text. In so doing, it is subject to a vicious circularity. Contrary to its assumption of disinterestedness or objectivity, Modernist interpretive practice "finds," or confirms, what it already has or desires—*as a whole* in advance.

I have also tried to suggest, on the other hand, that in giving ontological priority to temporality (a temporality grounded in nothing), the circular process of a destructive hermeneutics becomes, paradoxically, dis-covering or disclosing. In grounding understanding in the existential intentionality, the care of *Dasein* as being-in-the-world, it *opens up* the infinite possibilities of the meaning of be-ing that reside in the reader/text (time/form) relationship, those possibilities which are *closed off*, covered over, and forgotten by the spatial/metaphysical imagination. In the terms Heidegger borrowed from Kierkegaard, entering the hermeneutic circle in the right way precipitates "repetition" (*Wiederholung*): a movement that, unlike Platonic or Hegelian (aesthetic) recollection which "repeats backwards," is a "recollection forward."[54] In distinguishing between the Cartesian/Hegelian methodology of systematic doubt and existential doubt (and extending this distinction to include disinterestedness and interest and recollection and repetition), Kierkegaard's (dis)seminal pseudonymous text, *Repetition* (unpublished in his lifetime), prefigures in a remarkable way Husserl's and especially Heidegger's interpretation of the phenomenological reduction: the principle of intentionality (care) and the hermeneutic circle.[55] Hermeneutics as repetition, in other words, "is the *interest* of metaphysics and at the same time the *interest* upon which metaphysics founders."[56] It discloses the difference in the text and the world that makes a difference.[57]

Chapter 3
Heidegger, Kierkegaard, and the Hermeneutic Circle

I argue thus. If it be true that painting employs wholly different signs or means of imitation from poetry,—the one using forms and colors in space, the other articulate sounds in time,—and if signs must unquestionably stand in convenient relation with the thing signified, then signs arranged side by side can represent only objects existing side by side, or whose parts so exist, while consecutive signs can express only objects which succeed each other, or whose parts succeed each other, in time.

Objects which exist side by side, or whose parts so exist, are called bodies. Consequently bodies with their visible properties are the peculiar subjects of painting.

Objects which succeed each other, or whose parts succeed each other in time, are actions. Consequently actions are the peculiar subjects of poetry.

Gotthold Lessing, *Laocöon*

The "Being-true" of the λόγος *as* αληθεύειν *means that in* λέγειν [*to talk*] *as* ἀποφαίνεσθαι [*letting-something-be-seen*] *the entities of which one is talking must be taken out of their hiddenness; one must let them be seen as something unhidden (*ἀληθές*); that is, they must be discovered.*

Martin Heidegger, *Being and Time*

In the previous chapter, I tried to show that Modernism in Western literature—and in the New Critical and structuralist hermeneutics to which it gave rise—is grounded in a representational strategy that spatializes the temporal process of existence as being-in-the-world. It is, in other words, a strategy that is subject to a vicious circularity that closes off the phenomenological/existential understanding of the temporal being of existence, and analogously, of the literary text: the sequence of words. It is no accident that the autotelic and in-clusive circle—the circle, that is, as image or figure, or, as I prefer, as icon—is inscribed in the literary discourse of high Modernism as its essential and enabling symbol: not only in the literary texts of novelists such as Marcel Proust (the recollection of things past) and James Joyce (the continuous parallel between antiquity and the present) and poets such as W. B. Yeats (the unity of being in the cyclical theory of time) and T. S. Eliot (the mythical method), but also in the autotelic poetics of New Critics such as W. K. Wimsatt and Cleanth Brooks and of structuralists such as Tzvetan Todorov and Gérard Genette.

My attempt to develop a theory of literary interpretation that would "surpass" Modernism, then, is analogous to Heidegger's attempt to articulate a philosophical hermeneutics that would surpass Western metaphysics: the discourse of the ontotheological tradition that, in fulfilling the *re-presentational* imperatives of a philosophical perspective that *sees* the temporal realm of finite things *meta-ta-physika* (all-at-once), has "come to its end" in the "age of the world picture." Like Heidegger's philosophical project, my purpose is to retrieve the temporal being of the literary text from a literary/critical tradition that, in fulfilling the spatializing imperatives of its end-oriented perspective, has contributed to the reification and exhaustion of the be-ing of being in modernity. The surpassing of criticism, like the surpassing of metaphysics, begins not in presence but in the absence of presence, in a temporality "grounded" in Nothing: the radical finitude of *Dasein* as being-in-the-world. It is this temporal, as opposed to spatial, orientation that enables an emancipatory reading not only of particular literary texts but also of the text of literary history.

Having reestablished the ontological priority of temporality over structure in human understanding by way of Heidegger's existential analytic of *Dasein*, we can now introduce explicitly into the hermeneutic process the "concept" of Being (or, to orient the discussion toward the literary argument, the "concept" of the whole, of form). This hermeneutic circle has in fact been present from the beginning, but has been held in abeyance until now. Indeed, it will have already been remarked that an existential/ontological hermeneutics, understood as a process of dis-covery or dis-closure, implies that being is somehow already known in advance by the interpreter, just as the being (or form) of a text that can be read again is "known" in advance: that the interpretive process is ultimately circular. This is precisely and explicitly what Heidegger says about the hermeneutics of *Being and Time*: "Inquiry, as a kind of seeking, must be guided beforehand by what is sought. So the meaning of Being must already be available to us in some way."[1] And again: "Any interpretation which is to contribute understanding, must already have understood what is to be interpreted" (BT, 32, 194; SZ, 152). Destructive hermeneutics, that is, does not discover anything radically new as such. It dis-covers what the interpreter (the inquirer) by his or her very condition as being-in-the-world already has as a whole (an inscribed "totality of involvements") in advance, but in his or her average "everydayness" is unaware of until the traditional interpretive instrument breaks down, that is, until a rupture occurs in the referential surface (what, in *The Structure of Scientific Revolutions*, Thomas Kuhn calls "the paradigm"). At this point the "hermeneutic *as* structure" (the something *as* something) that one has in advance but has forgotten *begins to achieve explicitness* (BT, 16, 104–7; SZ, 75–76).[2] "Whenever something is interpreted as something," Heidegger writes in opposition to Husserl's objectivity, "the interpretation will be founded essentially upon fore-having, fore-sight, and fore-conception. An interpretation is never a presuppositionless apprehending of something presented to us" (BT, 32, 191–92; SZ, 150).[3]

Does this overt appeal to presuppositions—indeed, this affirmation of circularity—justify leaping to the conclusion drawn by many deconstructive critics that the hermeneutics of *Being and Time* is ultimately no different from the logocentric hermeneutics of metaphysics—and, by extension, of the New Criticism and structuralism? It should be clear from Heidegger's equation of circularity and the positional forestructure of *Dasein*'s being-in-the-world (as well as from my argument in the previous chapter: that the existential analysis of *Dasein* guides the ontological quest) that the answer is an emphatic no. For Heidegger's temporal hermeneutics in *Being and Time* does not begin from the whole in the same way that the spatial hermeneutics of the metaphysical and New Critical or structuralist standpoint does: from the whole seen as *télos* or presence, as centered circle.

In the last instance, according to Heidegger, all human inquiry is necessarily circular. Indeed, as the passages quoted above suggest, the very notion of inquiry presupposes it, for the lack of a prior "awareness" of "what is sought" precludes the possibility of questioning. It is precisely this argument that Heidegger proffers at the outset of *Being and Time* (in the introductory section called "The Formal Structure of the Question of Being") as the ground for asking the question of what it means to be:

"Thus to work out the question of Being adequately, we must make an entity—the inquirer—transparent in his own Being. The very asking of this question is an entity's mode of *Being*; and as such it gets its essential character from what is inquired about—namely Being" (BT, 2, 27; SZ, 7). The effort to avoid the hermeneutic circle, to achieve objectivity, a presuppositionless stance, therefore, is not only a futile negative gesture; it also does positive violence to "the truth" by way of concealing that which it is supposed to reveal. "What is decisive," Heidegger reiterates, "is not to get out of the circle but to come into it in the right way."[4] And the right way is through the existential *Dasein*, the *Dasein* as being-in-the-world: "This circle of understanding is not an orbit in which any random kind of knowledge may move." It is not the closed or spatial circle of the metaphysical standpoint, in which everything that is, including human beings, is simply an object present-at-hand located in a totalized map or table. It is rather "the expression of the existential *fore-structure* of Dasein itself. It is not to be reduced to the level of a vicious circle, or even of a circle which is merely tolerated. In the circle is hidden a positive possibility of the most primordial kind of knowing" (BT, 32, 195; SZ, 153).

Heidegger's culminating reaffirmation of the existential nature of the hermeneutic circle is presented not only as a refutation of the Husserlian charge that, because it is not presuppositionless, the process constitutes a vicious circle. In so doing, he also implies a countercharge: that, despite its claims to objectivity—its desire to protect the autonomous purity of the object of investigation—the metaphysical standpoint that makes the charge ("common sense" or "public understanding," in the following quotation) becomes itself guilty of vicious circularity in being blind to its derivative or constituted status. Heidegger's interpretation of the hermeneutic circle is at the very heart of his version of the phenomenological return "to the things themselves," not to a lost Origin but to origins as "groundless ground," and is crucial to an adequate understanding of the distinction I wish to draw between an existential/temporal literary hermeneutics and the metaphysical/spatial interpretive methodology of Modernist (including structuralist and even reader response) criticism. This culminating passage, therefore, deserves quotation at length. In answering the charge of circularity made from the standpoint of "common sense," Heidegger first differentiates between the presuppositions of his existential analytic and the propositions of logical investigation:

> When it is objected that the existential Interpretation is "circular," it is said that we have "presupposed" the idea of existence and of Being in general, and that Dasein gets Interpreted "accordingly," so that the idea of Being may be obtained from it. But what does "presupposition" signify? In positing the idea of existence, do we

also posit some proposition from which we deduce further propositions about the Being of Dasein, in accordance with formal rules of consistency? Or does this pre-supposing have the character of an understanding projection, in such a manner indeed that the Interpretation by which such an understanding gets developed, will let that which is to be interpreted [*Dasein*] *put itself into words for the very first time, so that it may decide of its own accord whether, as the entity which it is, it has that state of Being for which it has been disclosed in the projection with regard to its formal aspects?* Is there any other way at all by which an entity can put itself into words with regard to its Being? (BT, 63, 362–63; SZ, 314–15; Heidegger's emphasis)

Despite "beginning" with a presupposition, the hermeneutic circle, Heidegger implies, is not ontologically spatial. It does not begin with derived and fixed propositions (public knowledge) that have become structural models. Rather it begins concretely and temporally (my-ownly, as it were).

Heidegger then goes on to assert that "circularity" in research is unavoidable and that the effort on the part of "common sense" to avoid it, to be "objective," is an implicit strategy to negate care (*Sorge*), the existential intentionality that, as he makes emphatically clear, is the basic structure of the inquirer as being-in-the-world and has its source in this inquirer's finite temporality, the temporality that, in making a difference, instigates projectivity:

We cannot ever "avoid" a "circular" proof in the existential analytic, because such an analytic does not do *any* proving *at all* by the rules of the "logic of consistency." What common sense wishes to eliminate in avoiding the "circle," on the supposition that it is measuring up to the loftiest rigour of scientific investigation, is nothing less than the basic structure of care [*Sorge*]. Because it is primordially constituted by care, any Dasein is already ahead of itself. As being, it has in every case already projected itself upon definite possibilities of its existence; and in such existentiell projections [i.e., on the level of ontic (or ordinary) as opposed to ontological being] it has, in a pre-ontological manner, also projected something like existence and Being. *Like all research*, the research which wants to develop and conceptualize that kind of Being which belongs to existence, *is itself a kind of Being which disclosive Dasein possesses*; can such research be denied this projecting which is essential to Dasein? (BT, 63, 363; SZ, 315; Heidegger's emphasis)

In fact, according to Heidegger, referring again to the interpretive imperative of "common sense" to level difference and annul care and the projective understanding it discloses, the "disinterestedness" of common sense is itself an interested—inscribed or constituted—point of view:

Yet the "charge of circularity" itself comes from a kind of Being which belongs to Dasein. . . . Common sense [grounded in "our concernful absorption" in the "they" (*das Man*), which interprets things as they are publicly] concerns itself, whether "theoretically" or "practically," only with entities which can be surveyed at a glance circumspectively. *What is distinctive in common sense is that it has in view only the experiencing of "factual" entities, in order that it may be able to rid itself of an understanding of Being* [my emphasis]. It fails to recognize that entities can be experienced "factually" only when Being is already understood, even if it has not been conceptualized. [This is a reference to the derivative or constituted nature of propositional understanding as opposed to the originary play of hermeneutic understanding.] Common sense misunderstands understanding. And *therefore* common sense must necessarily pass off as "violent" anything that lies beyond the reach of its understanding, or any attempt to go out so far. (BT, 63, 363; SZ, 315)

Thus, in his summation, Heidegger "concludes":

When one talks of the "circle" in understanding, one expresses a failure to recognize two things: (1) that understanding as such makes up a basic kind of Dasein's Being, and (2) that this Being is constituted as care. To deny the circle, to make a secret of it [as "common sense" or, more philosophically, the metaphysical standpoint does], or even to want to overcome it, means finally to reinforce this failure. We must rather endeavor to leap into the "circle," primordially and wholly, so that even at the start of the analysis of Dasein we make sure that we have a full view of Dasein's circular Being.[5] (BT, 63, 363; SZ, 52, 315–16)

What Heidegger's distinction between the circularity of traditional interpretation and the circularity of phenomenological hermeneutics implies throughout *Being and Time* is this: In beginning omnisciently or, to anticipate chapter 5, "panoptically" from the end—disinterestedly or care-lessly, as it were—the radically logocentric metaphysical standpoint (whether in its naturalistic or its idealistic modes) "rids itself of" Dasein's authentic being by "closing off" its temporal existence. It thus generates the vicious—which is also a reductively coercive—circle. In the process, the interpreter imprisons himself or herself and eventually forgets his or her differential being inside its erosive bounding line. The end of interpretation in the viciously circular metaphysical mode is the exhaustion of the interest that difference instigates. This reduction of the will to act to an enervated *accidia*, not incidentally, is invariably the fate of those characters in proto-postmodern and postmodern literature who would spatialize their temporal being-in-the-world: of Kierkegaard's aesthetes (everywhere in his pseudonymous writing), of Dostoevsky's "straightforward" gentlemen (*Notes from Underground*), of Conrad's Axel Heyst (*Victory*), of Tolstoy's Ivan Ilych (*The Death of Ivan Ilych*), of T. S. Eliot's Prufrock ("The Love Song of J. Alfred Prufrock") and Tiresias ("The Waste Land"), of Samuel Beckett's Vladimir and Estragon (*Waiting for Godot*) and Belacqua (*More Pricks than Kicks*), of Sartre's Autodidact (*Nausea*), of Eugène Ionesco's Mr. and Mrs. Smith (*The Bald Soprano*), and of Thomas Pynchon's "Whole Sick Crew," whose yo-yoing is an entropic motion toward inanimateness (*V.*).

On the other hand, in "leaping into the 'circle,' primordially and wholly," in beginning consciously in the limited and contextual temporal standpoint of being-in-the-world, the interpreter becomes an ek-sistent in-sistent *Dasein*: an interested or care-ful inquirer whose "understanding" of being in advance takes the form, not of a derived conceptual proposition—a finalized and spatial totality in which all "entities . . . can be surveyed at a glance," but of a dim "preontological" awareness of that which the truth of "common sense" has covered up and forgotten. The being "presupposed" in the forestructure of existential/ontological understanding is not a closed and static structure or form, a temporal existence re-collected in tranquillity, but, as we have seen, an always opening and closing horizon. The metaphysical perspective tends to understand, or rather misunderstand, being (and understanding) by interestedly negating the originary *interest* of the interpreter "on the supposition that it is measuring up to the loftiest rigour of scientific investigation." In contrast, the existential/ontological standpoint of destructive phenomenology is "*guided* and *regulated*" (BT, 63, 359; SZ, 312) by this vague primordial understanding of being, which, in belonging "*to the essential constitution of Dasein itself*" (BT, 2, 28; SZ, 8), makes "the idea of existence [temporal be-ing] . . . our clue [to] an ontologically clarified idea of Being" (BT, 63, 362; SZ, 314).

Phenomenological hermeneutics, as Heidegger understands it, is always already an *ontic/ontological* process. It is a mode of inquiry that partakes in a careful and interested double movement through time that both "destroys" the metaphysical standpoint (discloses its blindness, its impulse to spatialize time) and thematizes—brings out into the open—that which, to paraphrase T. S. Eliot, always "flickers in the corners of our eyes":[6] the vague and indefinite primordial understanding of being covered over and forgotten in and by *the tradition*. Ultimately, it discovers that being "resides" in the temporal process itself, that what it means to be is be-ing.

The hermeneutic circle is thus not a vicious circle, despite its presuppositions about being. For at the end of the temporal process of interpretive disclosure the whole, the form it discovers or retrieves, is quite different from the whole, the form, *as* object understood in the beginning.

The end turns out to be endless, or historical. Entering the hermeneutic circle wholly and primordially discloses being to be both richer and more problematic than the Being represented by metaphysics: a dynamic concealing/unconcealing, truthful/errant, process that, in always already disseminating difference or deferring presence, makes things make a difference. What Heidegger says about the hermeneutic circle in the language of destructive phenomenology will find its counterpart in the language of postmodern poetry, the purpose of which is to "surpass" the formalism, the closed or iconic form, of literary Modernism. This transdisciplinary relation is remarkably evident, for example, in A. R. Ammons's "Corsons Inlet," a poem that echoes the (dis)seminal Poundian *periplus*:

> the walk liberating, I was released from forms,
> from the perpendiculars,
>   straight lines, blocks, boxes, binds
> of thought
> into the hues, shadings, rises, flowing bends and blends
>   of sight:
>   I allow myself eddies of meaning:
> yield to a direction of significance
> running
> like a stream through the geography of my work:
>   you can find
> in my sayings
>   swerves of action
>   like the inlet's cutting edge:
>   there are dunes of motion
> organizations of grass, white sandy paths of
>   remembrance
> in the overall wandering of mirroring mind:
>
> but Overall is beyond me: is the sum of these events
> I cannot draw, the ledger I cannot keep, the accounting
> beyond the account . . . [7]

As in Heidegger's *Being and Time*, time, in this synecdochal instance of the postmodern poetic understanding of the circle of interpretation, is ontologically prior to—is the condition for the possibility of—Being or form (the "Overall"), but not different from it. [8]

The hermeneutic circle is paradoxically a liberating movement, an opening toward being. It is, finally, to give this movement the name Heidegger borrows from Kierkegaard, a repetition or retrieval (*Wiederholung*): [9] a process of discovering and remembering the primordial temporality of being and thus of the truth as *a-letheia*. I mean, more specifically, the truth as unhiddenness, which metaphysical understanding and interpretation (re-presentation or, to anticipate, re-collection), in closing time off by coercing temporality into spatial icon (the circle), has always over-looked, covered over, and, in hardening this closure into the "Tradition," finally forgotten.

The full significance for literary hermeneutics of the Kierkegaardian movement I will develop later in this essay. Here it will suffice merely to point provisionally to its ground in existential care and to the paradoxical *forwarding* of remembrance. Repetition or retrieval is not (as it is, for example, in E. D. Hirsch's hermeneutics) a process of re-cognizing a (historical) text in the tradition for its own sake;[10] nor does it signify, as it does for traditional humanist critics, a process of re-collecting an absolute or privileged origin (the *logos* as presence) as the measure for evaluating a historically specific text. It is rather a discovering of beginnings in the sense of rendering the contemporary interpreter, as in the cases of Heidegger and Ammons, a projective *Homo viator*. Repetition as retrieval brings the reader into an originary—a care-ful, exploratory, and open-ended—relationship with the being of a text: a relationship, in Heidegger's term, of "anticipatory resoluteness." In short, the hermeneutic circle as repetition involves the abandonment of a calculative and coercive *methodology* in favor of an unmethodical and generous *comportment* toward the text, in which the interpreter puts his or her prejudices (presuppositions) at risk. It involves the my-ownly (*eigentliche*) speech act undertaken by the interpreter in the spirit of *Gelassenheit*: a negative capability that simultaneously *lets* the being of a text be, lets it *say* how it stands with being, and *challenges* its saying, that is, offers it a "reciprocal rejoinder." To enter the hermeneutic circle primordially and wholly is to enter into antagonistic dialogue with the text. "The repeating of that which is possible," we recall, "does not bring again [*wiederbringen*] something that is 'past,' nor does it bind the 'Present' back to that which has already been 'outstripped.' Arising, as it does, from a resolute projection of oneself, repetition does not let itself be persuaded of something by what is 'past,' just in order that this, as something which was formerly actual, may recur. Rather, the repetition makes a *reciprocal rejoinder* to the possibility of that existence which has-been-there."[11]

Heidegger does not explicitly apply the distinction between the hermeneutic circle of destructive phenomenology and the vicious circle of metaphysics to literary production or to literary exegesis as such in *Being and Time*. That it is applicable, however, can be demonstrated by further analysis of the fundamental, though too often overlooked, Kierkegaardian category to which I have just referred: the existential "concept" of repetition, which he opposes to the Hegelian concept of recollection (*Er-innerung*). This seminal distinction, along with Schleiermacher's and Dilthey's versions of the hermeneutic circle,[12] clearly influenced Heidegger's thinking about hermeneutics in a decisive way. And it sheds important light on the significance of the hermeneutics of *Being and Time* for aesthetics and, more specifically, for literature and literary exegesis.

Kierkegaard's distinction goes back as far as his important but neglected master's thesis, *The Concept of Irony*,[13] to which I will return. But it is given its fullest and, for my purposes, most accessible formulation in *Repetition*, his strange, "indecisive" novella about the violent—Jobian— dislodging of a young man from the "aesthetic stage" into something like authentic existence (the "ethico-religious stage"). In this pseudonymous text, the "author," Constantine Constantius, is the "constant" and "steady" detached observer, who therefore, despite his sympathy for his subject, cannot undergo repetition. Near the beginning of his account of the young man's experience, nevertheless, he writes, perhaps better than he knows: "Repetition and recollection are the same movement, only in opposite directions; for what is recollected has been, is repeated backwards, whereas repetition properly so called is recollected forwards."[14] Somewhat later, in a remarkable prevision not only of Mircea Eliade's analysis of the myth and metaphysics of the eternal return[15] but also of the postmodern critique of the Richardsian/New Critical doctrine of ironic inclusiveness (the fundamental structural principle of Modernist poetics), he amplifies this distinction by giving its terms historical specificity. He equates the Hegelian recollection with "the pagan life-view" and ultimately with Greek—especially Platonic—metaphysics, and repetition with the "new" existential movement in philosophy:

> The dialectic of repetition is easy; for what is repeated has been, otherwise it could not be repeated, but precisely the fact that it has been *gives to repetition the character of novelty*. When the Greeks said that all *knowledge* is recollection [the reference is clearly to Plato's logocentric concepts of *anamnesis* (un-forgetting) and the preexistent soul] they affirmed *that all that is has been*; when one says that life is a repetition one affirms *that existence which has been now becomes*. When one does not possess the categories of recollection or of repetition the whole of life is resolved into a void and empty noise. Recollection is the pagan life-view, repetition is the modern life-view; repetition is the *interest* of metaphysics, and at the same time the *interest* upon which metaphysics founders; repetition is the solution contained in every ethical view, repetition is a *condition sine qua non* of every dogmatic problem.[16]

The difficulty posed by these passages resides in the unfamiliarity of Kierkegaard's valorization of the italicized word *"interest"* in the last sentence of the second. Inscribed by the metaphysical imperative to spatialize time (to represent Being as substance), the Western consciousness assumes the naturalness and thus the absolute epistemological value of *disinterest*. In opposition, Kierkegaard understands the word "interest"—which he emphasizes to distinguish it from metaphysical "disinterestedness"—in its etymological sense. "Reflection ['knowledge' in the above quotation] is the possibility of relationship," he says elsewhere. "This can also be stated thus: Reflection is disinterested. Consciousness ['life' in the above quotation] is relationship, and it brings with it interest or concern; a duality which is perfectly expressed with pregnant double meaning by the word 'interest' (Latin *interesse*, meaning (i) 'to be between,' (ii) 'to be a matter of concern')."[17] Kierkegaard's "interest" is the *difference* that being-in-the-midst of time, and the difference it always already disseminates, makes. As such it is fundamentally similar to the existential/ontological care (*Sorge*) of Heidegger's *Dasein* as being-in-the-world.

When Kierkegaard's "interest" is understood in this way, the apparently difficult passage from *Repetition*—indeed, the whole apparently unintelligible novel itself (which Constantius "writes" "like Clemens Alexandrinus in such a way that the heretics cannot understand what he writes")[18]—becomes manifestly clear. The distinction Kierkegaard is making between recollection and repetition is, if we secularize his "eternity" as Heidegger's "being" (*Sein*), precisely the distinction Heidegger works out in *Being and Time* between *logos* as Word or presence or *ratio* and *logos* as *legein* (*Rede*: e-mergent discourse); ontic and ontic/ontological inquiry; metaphysics and destructive phenomenology. Kierkegaard's differentiation of repetition from recollection is fundamentally the same as Heidegger's between the hermeneutic circle of the temporal or existential consciousness (which discloses difference) and the vicious circle of the essentialist spatializing consciousness (which reduces and levels difference and confirms identity). There must be a prior understanding—a presupposition—of being, since, if there were not, "the whole of life" would resolve "into a void and empty noise," a sound and fury signifying nothing.

As in Heidegger, what is of primary importance for Kierkegaard, however, is how one enters and remains in the circle. Recollection and repetition are both grounded in *interest*—in the primordial need (desire) of the finite individual, the existential human being, for continuity and meaning. But in "recollecting backward"—in remembering (in the sense of re-collecting) differential temporal experience from a point of view that is ontologically prior to the contingency of the lived world (as in the case of Plato's *concept* of Being as realm of ideal Forms or Hegel's ideal dialectical system)—the recollection resolves the contradictions. The recollection brings the disseminations of time to a re-collected presence and annuls the very interest—the difference the deferral of presence makes in the world—that originally generates the metaphysical question of what it means to be. In achieving "dis-interestedness" ("objectivity," or in-difference), recollection also achieves the peace of repose or, to invoke the term privileged by literary Modernism, *stasis*. But it finally mistakes a distanced knowledge *about* (possibility) for authentic understanding. The recollective eye, that is, loses sight of, blinds itself to, the essential question concerning the "true" meaning of being: the question of the existence (ek-sistence) of the interpreter. By aesthetically reconciling and internalizing the contradictions of worldly possibility in the inclusive identical whole, recollection neutralizes the existential imperative to choose resolutely *in situation*. "Hang yourself, you will regret it; do not hang yourself, and you will also regret that; hang yourself or do not hang yourself, you will regret both; whether you hang yourself or do not hang yourself, you will regret both. This, gentlemen, is the sum and substance of all philosophy. It is not only at certain moments that I view everything *aeterno modo*, as Spinoza says, but I live constantly *aeterno modo*": this is how the desperate metaphysical aesthete of *Diapsalmata* who will outdo Spinoza puts his "triumphant" transcendence of the ethical-existential either/or of temporal existence.[19] Aesthetic recollection, in other words, like the circularity of assertion in Heidegger's critique of metaphysics, is paradoxically a willful over-looking and forgetting of being. And the end of the logical economy of this recollective process is in-difference. It is in thus achieving the perspective *sub specie aeternitatis*, or, as Kierkegaard puts it, *aeterno modo*, that metaphysics "founders" on interest: self-destructs.

On the other hand, in "recollecting forward," repetition relies pre-cisely on the interest, the intentionality, of *interesse*, of the existential self *as* being-in-the-world, for its access to the "meaning" of being. It is not an objective mode of perception, which contemplates or reflects on things-as-they-are from beyond or after or above them: *aeterno modo*. Repetition is an interested, a care-ful, mode, in which the singular or, in Kierkegaard's preferred term, the *exceptional* interpreter (as opposed to a universal observer like Constantius himself) is guided beyond the present by the intimation of "spirit" (the primordial question of being) "resid-ing" as a trace in his memory. As such, repetition is both a mnemonic and an anticipatory—a de-structive and pro-jective—movement. Though it presupposes a meaning of being, it does so not tautologically, but in such a way as to ground authentic understanding in "novelty" or "be-coming," that is, in openness and anxious freedom, which is to say, in differential temporality. Thus, in a passage from the appended letter of explanation to "this book's real reader" that recalls Heidegger's hermeneutic quest for the "meaning" of being in and through *Dasein*, Kierke-gaard writes:

> The exception thinks also the universal [read: the question of being] when it thinks itself, it labors also for the universal when it elaborates itself, it explains the universal when it explains itself. If one would study the universal thoroughly, one has only to look for the justified exception, which manifests everything more clearly than does the universal itself. . . . There are exceptions. If one cannot explain them, neither can one explain the universal. Commonly one does not notice the difficulty because one does not think even the universal with passion but with an easygoing superficiality. On the other hand, the exception thinks the universal with serious passion.[20]

In thus entering the circle in the right way, leaping into it "primordially and wholly"—interestedly, Kierkegaard's repetition, like Heidegger's presuppositional (ontic/ontological) hermeneutics, becomes in the last analysis a *remembering as dis-covering*, a dis-closing of closure, a retrieval of the difference of identity. This, in fact, is precisely how Kierkegaard puts it in his unpublished polemic against the Hegelian J. L. Heiberg, who in praising Kierkegaard's *Repetition* in a review had utterly and, given his "metaphysical" problematic—his thinking about the universal with "an easygoing superficiality"—inevitably misunderstood the itali-cized "*interest*": "So step by step [the young man] discovers repetition, being educated by existence."[21]

My reason for invoking Kierkegaard's distinction between recollec-tion and repetition is not simply to draw attention to a supporting par-allel with Heidegger's distinction between the hermeneutic and the vi-cious circle. In *Being and Time*, Heidegger restricts his overt theorization of the distinction to the site of philosophical discourse, and his critique of the vicious circularity of traditional Western thought primarily to "common sense": the scientific tradition. As Vigilius Haufniensis's equa-tion of the "disinterestedness" of (Hegelian) metaphysics and (Kantian) aesthetics in the extended quotation from *Repetition* in *The Concept of Dread* suggests,[22] Kierkegaard, on the other hand, explicitly subsumes the philosophical distinction under the wider and more radical sphere of the creative imagination. In so doing, he also subsumes the critique of the vicious circularity of "common sense" under the broader category of metaphysics, which in turn is subsumed under the even broader category of aestheticism. In Heidegger the literary implications of the distinc-tion between recollection and repetition would seem on the surface to point to a critique restricted to the well-made plot, the map structure of positivistic literature. In Kierkegaard they focus explicitly on a critique of the spatial or iconic form of Romantic or symbolist literature.

It is this subsumption of metaphysics under aesthetics that renders the parallel between Kierkegaard's and Heidegger's versions of repetition useful for my purposes. It points toward the applicability of the destruction to both allotropes of modern metaphysics: to idealism as well as to positive science, and analogously, to symbolist as well as to realist or naturalist literature. It reminds us that, despite its disarming critique of positivism and positivistic poetics, literary Modernism, especially the New Criticism's doctrine of ironic inclusiveness and its spatial exegetical methodology, is a structuralism in the metaphysical tradition which it is the purpose of a Heideggerian destructive hermeneutics to surpass.

As both volumes of *Either/Or* make especially clear, recollection— whether it takes the form of metaphysics or that of the literature of Romantic irony (i.e., symbolism)—is the fundamental hermeneutic mode of the "aesthetic" stage. In contradistinction to the "ethical" and "religious" stages on life's way, the aesthetic, we recall, is a perspective in the "eternal mode": a perspective, as Kierkegaard knew from his own experience as an artist, based on the metaphysical will to neutralize the dread of existential time in a totalized and de-differentiated present, the timeless moment, the *epiphany* of full presence. In an entry in his *Diapsalmata*—utterly infused by Kierkegaard's irony—the aesthete A observes:

> The life in recollection is the most complete life conceivable, recollection satisfies more richly than all reality, and has a security that no reality possesses. A recollected life-relation has already passed into eternity and has no more temporal interest.[23]

Or again, this time in the words of the aesthete William Afham of *Stages on Life's Way*, whom Louis Mackey calls "the most explicit champion . . . [of recollection]—its theorist, so to speak":[24] "Memory is immediacy . . . whereas recollection comes only by reflection. Hence it is an art to recollect." It "seeks to assert man's eternal continuity in life and to insure that his earthly existence shall be *uno tenore*, one breath, and capable of being expressed in one word"—which is, of course, the *logos* as the Word, the Omega—and thus "consists in removing, putting at a distance" the immediate and contingent existence that is recalled. Thus "recollection is ideality."[25] Like the anthropological metaphysics of Hegel, the *art* of recollection, in other words, is a logocentric art that internalizes and reflectively purifies actuality—the differential essence of the existential occasion. It reduces the kinetic, erratic, and open-ended process of temporal events into a static, unerring, unified, and inclusive spatial image. For to bestow this "consecrating" ideality on existence and to achieve the reposeful distance it affords, the art of recollection must begin from the *end*. Beginning any other way, from the Alpha in the sense of *interesse*, is the rock, so to speak, upon which ideality founders. "Properly speaking," Afham writes,

> only the essential is the object of recollection. . . . The essential is not simply essential in itself, but it is such by reason of the relation it has to the person concerned. He who has broken with the idea cannot act essentially, cannot undertake anything essential. . . . Outward criteria notwithstanding, everything he does is unessential.[26]

These representative passages on the underlying aestheticism of recollection are freighted with ironic echoes of logocentric philosophies of presence extending from Plato through St. Augustine and St. Thomas to Descartes, Kant, and Hegel, and point even to Nietzsche's will to power. As such, they recall the teleological thrust of hermeneutic theory and practice throughout the entire history of metaphysics as Heidegger discloses it in his destruction of the ontotheological tradition. But they also allude to Sophocles' *Oedipus*, to Aristotle's *Poetics*,[27] to Virgil's *Aeneid*, to Schiller's *On the Aesthetic Education of Man*, to Friedrich Schlegel's *Lucinde*, and perhaps even to Wordsworth's "Preface to the Lyrical Ballads" and Coleridge's definition of the imagination as an "esemplastic power." In so doing, they point proleptically to the essential principle informing the poetics (both theory and practice) of literary Modernism at large. I mean the recollective/spatializing principle that functions to "arrest," to achieve "stasis" (a plenary circularity), not only in the Modernist discourse of Wilhelm Worringer (*Abstraction and Empathy*), of T. E. Hulme ("Modern Art"), of Marcel Proust (*À la recherche du temps perdu*), of W. B. Yeats (the poetry of *A Vision*), of James Joyce (*Ulysses*), of T. S. Eliot ("The Waste Land"), of Virginia Woolf (*To the Lighthouse*), but also in the structuralist poetics of the *nouveau roman*, of Roman Jakobson, Gérard Genette, and Tzvetan Todorov.

Besides evoking the logocentric thrust of the hermeneutics of the Western philosophical tradition at large, that is, these representative passages from Kierkegaard's texts also lay bare the essentialist thrust of interpretive theory and practice throughout Western literary history. I mean, more specifically, its defining impulse to objectify and thus annul the dread of being-in-the-world that has no-thing as its object or, to put this philosophical language in literary terms, to spatialize time in order to gain aesthetic distance from the dislocating differences it disseminates.[28] In so doing, these passages proleptically make explicit the complicity of the ironic/inclusive mode of the neo-Kantian New Criticism (and its extensions in the myth criticism of Northrop Frye and the miniaturizing imperatives of Lévi-Straussian structuralist interpretation) with this literary tradition. Indeed, they suggest that this highly self-conscious Modernist mode brings the literary hermeneutics of the tradition to its logical fulfillment and end in becoming an absolutely (self-) reflective practice intended to bring the text and the reader into the repose of essential stasis.

It is worth invoking at this juncture Stephen Crites's brilliant essay on Kierkegaard's pseudonymous writing for the light it throws on the connection I am making between the philosophical and literary traditions and between traditional and Modernist hermeneutics. Commenting on Kierkegaard's characterization of recollection as the essential aesthetic category in a section titled "Aesthetic Rest vs. Existential Movement," he writes words that should strike familiar chords:

> The ideality bodied forth in a work of art is always an abstraction from experience. It arises out of the temporality of experience, but it achieves a purified form as a self-contained possibility, free of temporality. That is why both artist and his audience are able to come to rest in it. At least for this ideal moment of experience a man achieves integration, his consciousness drawn together by its concentration on a single purified possibility. Kierkegaard speaks of this moment of repose in ideal possibility as a recollection, in a sense of the term derived from Plato: here temporal reality is recollected, assimilated to atemporal forms that are logically prior to it. The recollected possibilities are logically prior in the sense that they give intelligible meaning to the reality of experience.
>
> This important function of art is also performed by other operations of the mind and the Imagination. Therefore Kierkegaard sometimes employs the term "aesthetic" in an extended sense that includes science and philosophy as well as art. For the cognitive grasp of an object, whether a purified object of experience or an ideal, logico-mathematical object, also enables consciousness to suspend its bewildering temporal peregrinations and to come to a satisfying moment of clarity: All knowledge is recollection.[29]

As the reference to Plato suggests, the aesthete, or what for Kierkegaard is the same thing, the ironist who "lives poetically,"[30] achieves "rest" by irrealizing temporal existence, by transforming the differential force of finite time into plenary cyclical space—that is, by entering into an inclusive and in-closed circle from the beginning.

In the above passage Crites is simply defining aesthetic recollection. What is left out of his account of Kierkegaard's analysis of the ironic transcendence of time or, as he usually puts it, of "actuality," is his insistence on the terrible consequences of this kind of circularity. As we see everywhere in the pseudonymous works, far from achieving an authentically liberating *stasis*, the aesthete, who by definition enters a completed circle from the beginning, enters an inexorable erosive process. It is a deadly process that not only estranges him or her from existence but eventually brings on despair and melancholy: that *accidia* or spiritual sloth in which rest is defined by an achieved timelessness that has atrophied the desire that difference activates. It is a process that, in annulling the memory of (the temporality of) being, ends in the enervation of the bodily and spiritual will to act. (This, of course, is a more radical version of Heidegger's *Seinsvergessenheit*: the oblivion of being consequent on the reduction of *Dasein* to *das Man*.)

Kierkegaard makes this point especially clear in his stunning portraits of the aesthetes in *Either/Or*: "How terrible tedium is—terribly tedious," A writes in *Diapsalmata*. "I know no stronger expression, none truer, for only the like is known by the like. If only there were some higher, stronger expression, then there would be at least a movement. I lie stretched out, inactive; the only thing I see is emptiness, the only thing I move about in is emptiness. I do not even suffer pain. The vulture constantly devoured Prometheus' liver; the poison constantly dripped down on Loki; that was at least an interruption, even though a monotonous one. Even pain has lost its refreshment for me."[31] But it receives its most significant expression, at least for my purposes, in his critique of the *Künstlerroman* of Friedrich Schlegel, *Lucinde*, which, according to his description of its essential formal characteristics, makes it precisely a forerunner of the Modernist (poetic) novel of spatial form. "At the very outset," Kierkegaard observes,

> Julian [the narrator] explains that along with the other conventions of reason and ethics he has also dispensed with chronology. He then adds: "For me and for this book, for my love of it and for its internal formulation, there is no purpose more purposive than that right at the start I begin by abolishing what we call order, keep myself aloof from it, and appropriate to myself in word and deed the right to a charming confusion." With this he seeks to attain what is truly poetical.[32]

Kierkegaard is not unaware, of course, that what is "confusion" to the vulgar materialist is for the elitist Julian and Schlegel the "charming"— pleasurably spellbinding—aesthetic order of the eternal imagination.

After thus describing Schlegel's novel in terms that might apply equally to any number of detemporalized Modernist (and structuralist) novels from Huysman's *À Rebours* through Virginia Woolf's *To the Lighthouse* to the "structuralist" fiction of Alain Robbe-Grillet and the "metafiction" of William Gass, Raymond Federman, and Ronald Sukenick, Kierkegaard comments witheringly: "When the imagination is allowed to rule in this way it prostrates and anesthetizes the soul, robs it of all moral tension, and makes of life a dream. Yet this is exactly what *Lucinde* seeks to accomplish."[33] And again, after his brilliant analysis of the character of the "poetical" and melancholic Lisette, who, like young Stencil in Thomas Pynchon's *V.* (the postmodern allotrope of Henry Adams's narrative of entropy) objectifies and distances her dread of life by referring to herself in the third person (as a character in a completed narrative), Kierkegaard underscores the enervating consequence of spatializing temporal existence from the aesthetic perspective of *aeterno modo*: "Throughout the whole of *Lucinde*, however, it is this lapsing into an aesthetic stupor which appears as the designation for what it is to live poetically, and which, since it lulls the deeper ego into a somnambulant state, permits the arbitrary ego free latitude in ironic self-satisfaction."[34]

In thus tracing the moral history of circularity as recollection in the progress of the "ironic"—the inclusive and indifferent—aesthete, Kierkegaard also prophesies the essential moral history of circularity as recollection both in modern philosophy (from Hegel's annunciation of the saving circuitous journey of the spirit toward *Wissenschaft* to Heidegger's destruction of it) and in modern literature, at least as this history has been read by the postmodern avant-garde. It is precisely this devastating "progression" we witness, for example, in the transition—generated by the foundering of metaphysics (and its aesthetic counterpart) on the rocks of contemporary history—from W. B. Yeats's celebration of ourobouric time (the mythic time of the phases of the moon) to Samuel Beckett's grim recognition of its erosive horror.

For the Modernist Yeats, we recall, the epiphanic moment—when time has come around full circle (has become space)—integrates dispersion—or, to use his own vocabulary, *unifies being*. It transforms the finite existential self into Image, and history into Byzantium, the timeless *polis* of (iconic) art:

> and after,
> Under the frenzy of the fourteenth moon,
> The soul begins to tremble into stillness,
> To die into the labyrinth of itself!
> . . . .
> All thought becomes an image and the soul
> Becomes a body: that body and that soul
> Too perfect at the full to lie in a cradle,
> Too lonely for the traffic of the world:
> Body and soul cast out and cast away
> Beyond the visible world.[35]

And again (the contrast with Kierkegaard, which is manifest even in the language [of "breaking"], is startling in its absoluteness):

> Astraddle on the dolphin's mire and blood,
> Spirit after spirit! The smithies break the flood,
> The golden smithies of the Emperor!
> Marbles of the dancing floor
> Break bitter furies of complexity,
> Those images that yet
> Fresh images beget,
> That dolphin-torn, that gong-tormented sea.[36]

For the postmodern Beckett, on the other hand, Yeats's aesthetic-metaphysical circle of plenary beauty and perfection has become Clov's "zero zone." Far from being a space of fulfillment, it is an empty and exhausted zone, where, as Gogo and Didi despairingly observe, there is "Nothing to be done."[37] Having "achieved" aesthetic *stasis*, the Belacqua figure of *More Pricks than Kicks*, of *Murphy*, of the *Molloy* novels—who is invariably a (Modernist) artist and/or metaphysician—is thus doomed to wallow eternally, like "Sloth our own brother," in his willed willessness. This, the postmodern Beckett implies, is the "freedom" from the "messiness" of existence, and the "desire and loathing" activated by its differential force, that Yeats and Joyce (in *A Portrait of the Artist as a Young Man*) would achieve by iconizing temporality: "Being by nature sinfully indolent, bogged in indolence [Belacqua asked] nothing better than to stay put."[38] And despite their "art," the ground-down tramps of *Waiting for Godot* are doomed to move in endless circles until the entropic process, in running its course, utterly annuls their memory of being:

> *ESTRAGON*: Well, shall we go?
> *VLADIMIR*: Yes, let's go.
> *They do not move*
>
> Curtain, Act I
>
> *VLADIMIR*: Well, shall we go?
> *ESTRAGON*: Yes, let's go.
> *They do not move*
>
> Curtain, Act II[39]

On the other hand, Kierkegaard does not—indeed he refuses to—define and systematize the literary significance of the existential movement of repetition. And the reason for this is fundamental: whereas

recollection is a mode of knowledge—understands existence theoretically—and thus is accessible to the methodical or conceptual language of
analysis or aesthetics, repetition is essentially a mode of existential *praxis*,
of unsayable human being-in-the-world. But Kierkegaard does suggest
what repetition implies about literary form and hermeneutics in the very
"method" of indirect communication that characterizes his pseudonymous works. And it turns out to be remarkably like Heidegger's in *Being
and Time*. I mean his revolutionary transformation of the traditional literature of recollection, in which the economy of language *as tautology*
stills the motion and force of temporality and thus neutralizes both the
author's and the reader's will to act, into a literature of "action," in which
a language *as always already dialectical movement* (repetition) liberates the
moving force of temporality and the "selfhood" of the Self: that is, it
activates dialogue between author and reader. In the pseudonymous
works, in other words, Kierkegaard rejects, or deconstructs, the traditional sense of an ending, the poetic or ironic principle of closure. More
specifically, he refuses to resolve, sublate, and internalize the conflicts of
the historically specific occasion; refuses to reduce the irreducible existential either/or to the free-floating aesthetic neither/nor—to what I. A.
Richards would call the "inclusiveness" or "balanced poise" and Cleanth
Brooks and W. K. Wimsatt the "ironic equilibrium" and Northrop Frye
the "total mythic structure"—of the aesthetic perspective, the perspective *aeterno modo*.

The creative process in Kierkegaard's pseudonymous texts is energized by a "mastered irony" that masters irony.[40] It takes the anti-
Hegelian form of a "dialectic of revocation."[41] In the Heideggerian terms
of this essay, it becomes an icon-oclastic, a de-structive act, in which an
existential movement collides irreconcilably with the aesthetic frame of
the book. This collision "ruptures the referential surface" of the "spatial
form" recollected from the super-visory perspective of aesthetic vision;
that is, it destructures its "objective" and inclusive/conclusive (ironic)
structure. About *Repetition*, where Kierkegaard's strategy is most representative, Crites remarks:

> There are occasional hints about the meaning of repetition, but we
> are never permitted to see the movement itself [as it is made by the
> young man] except in the distorting mirror of the aesthetic.
> Constantine [the "objective" author, who recollects the story *aeterno
> modo*] speaks of the affair as a "wrestling match" or a "breaking"
> (*brydning*): "the universal breaks with the exception, breaks with it in
> strife, and strengthens it by this breaking." This break is what we are
> permitted to see in the book, but as it occurs the young man breaks
> out of the aesthetic frame of the book as well, and is lost from
> view. . . . The pseudonym and his book constitute a mirror

reflecting from its angle and within its frame the existential movement as it breaks away. . . . The aesthetic medium is purely dialectic: it is simultaneously presented and obliterated.[42]

In thus breaking the aesthetic frame, which, for Yeats "break[s] the bitter furies of complexity," the existential movement also breaks the reader's (interpreter's) privileged logocentric perspective. It undermines any certain expectation of an aesthetic resolution: the "awaiting" (*Gewärtigens*) an "end," which, unlike the "anticipatory resoluteness" of the interested interpreter, according to Heidegger, manifests itself psychologically as a calculative impulse to suspend the differentiating temporal process, to reduce the conflictual forces it disseminates to "a pure sequence of 'nows' " (BT, 65, 377; SZ, 329 and BT, 68, 389; SZ, 339). It destroys the reader's spatializing perspective, which would annul the strife between world and earth for the sake of the satisfying repose that fulfillment promises. In so doing, this movement leaves the reader unaccommodated, alone with the existential movement itself and whatever claim it may make on him.[43] The "resolution," if there is to be one at all, must be achieved by the reader as such in an existential decision of his or her own. In *Guilty/Not Guilty?*, the diary of a young man who has undergone something like an existential movement in the process of a love affair in which, like Kierkegaard, he abandons his beloved, the diarist expresses his utter uncertainty about the meaning of his act:

> I have never been able to understand it in any other way than this, that every man is essentially assigned to himself, and that apart from this there is either an authority such as that of an apostle—the dialectical determination of which I cannot comprehend, and meanwhile out of respect for what has been handed down to me as holy I refrain from concluding anything from non-understanding— or there is chatter.[44]

Commenting on this crucial passage about the interpretive/practical imperatives of *interesse*, Crites concludes about Kierkegaard's narrative method:

> That, in the end, represents the standpoint of Kierkegaard's authorship as a whole . . . the pseudonymous writings are designed to throw every reader back on his own resources. There is not even an actual author to lay claim on him. They assign him to himself.
> The pseudonymous works present their life-possibilities in this elusive form in order to evoke in the reader a movement that is entirely his own. They are not cookbooks that he could follow in concocting a novel but pretested pattern for life. . . . But each work is in its own way designed to create a quiet crisis in the life of a reader that can be resolved by his own decision.[45]

I would supplement Crites's "cookbook" (the positivist model) with the "icon" (the idealist model) in characterizing that interpretive practice that annuls the imperative to engage the "voice" of the text and, by extension, the historically specific world. Any effort, according to Kierkegaard, to explain the existential movement in discursive language or to "re-present" it in a literary art grounded in the traditional Western circular strategy of recollection is doomed to negate it.

Given his commitment to the existential structures, it was inevitable that Kierkegaard should make the effort to reaffirm the ontological priority of temporality over form in language. For him literature becomes, in the last analysis, "anti-literature" in the same way that the Heideggerian destruction is anti-metaphysical: an effort to surpass the Western philosophical tradition. To put it in terms of the hermeneutic argument of this essay, Kierkegaard withstands the enormous pressure of—and the security offered by—the Western metaphysical/aesthetic tradition to write authorially (from a privileged origin) about existence. He chooses, rather, to write, with all the risks this choice entails, within the human, temporal/contemporary situation of openness and uncertainty. Unlike his aesthetes (who, in their "objective" comportment toward the world in which they live, bear a remarkable resemblance not only to the aesthetic metaphysician par excellence, G. W. F. Hegel, but, as we have seen, to the French and Anglo-American Modernists), Kierkegaard chooses to write in *temporali modo*: in the exploratory or errant mode demanded by being *interesse*. He writes, in other words, to alienate the inscribed perspective *aeterno modo*, to activate an *interest* (care) that engages his reader dialogically. He writes, that is, in such a way as to transform the interpreter's impulse to objectify into an interest (care) that engages her or him dialogically with the text and with the ambiguous and anxiety-provoking either/or of the temporal being the text is exploring. In short, Kierkegaard's "dialectic of revocation," in which the universal "breaks with the exception" in strife, becomes for aesthetics what repetition, "the interest on which metaphysics founders," is for reflective thought. As such an iconoclastic practice it anticipates the differential circularity of Heidegger's destructive hermeneutics, the hermeneutics that would overcome, by "breaking" it, the *circulus vitiosus* of metaphysical inquiry.

In exploring the dialogic and ethical possibilities of open, temporal, and existential form released by his interrogation of the distancing aestheticism of a closed or spatial form, Kierkegaard takes his place, along with the Dostoevsky of *Notes from Underground*, the Pirandello of *Six Characters in Search of an Author*, the Kafka of *The Trial*, and the Sartre of *Nausea*, as an important literary forebear of open form in postmodern literature. For postmodern literature not only thematizes the temporality (and the difference it disseminates) disclosed by the breakdown of the problematic of metaphysics following the "death of God" (or at any rate the death of God as Omega) but also makes the medium itself the message. Its function is to perform a Heideggerian destruction of the traditional metaphysical frame of reference, to accomplish the phenomenological reduction of the spatial perspective by formal violence. Like the dialectics of revocation of Kierkegaard's pseudonymous texts, that is, this de-structive movement of postmodern literature leaves the reader *interesse*—a naked and unaccommodated being-in-the-world, a *Dasein* in the place of origins, where time, despite its implication in structure, is ontologically prior to Being rather than the other way around.[46] Kierkegaard's formal experiments, like Heidegger's experimental philosophy in *Being and Time*, are ultimately grounded in a profound and inaugural intuition: that, as the postmodern poet Wallace Stevens puts it,

> we live in a place
> That is not our own and, much more, not ourselves[47]

and that the "spiritual" health of human being depends not on getting out of the circle but coming into it in the right way—that is, existentially.

To return again to Heidegger, it is true that the Kierkegaardian repetition is a fictional strategy intended to engage the reader ethically, and is not, as in Heidegger, a theory of textual interpretation. But the difference (if we bracket the religious dimension) is a matter of their respective historical occasions. Whereas Kierkegaard feels compelled to adopt a narrative strategy of hermeneutic violence against an age still "innocent" about metaphysics, Heidegger feels that "the rupture of the referential surface" of the metaphysical world picture has taken or is taking place, and thus that the modern reader has been prepared historically to accept this originative stance as a hermeneutic imperative: has "come of age," as it were. Seen in the light of the foregoing discussion, then, the relationship of Kierkegaard's repetition to a Heideggerian literary hermeneutics based on the phenomenological/existential analytic of *Being and Time* should now be obvious. It suggests that the hermeneutic circle as repetition or retrieval (*Wiederholung*) finally translates into a demystification of the Modernist, especially the New Critical and structuralist, representation of the hermeneutic situation. It entails, in other words, an undermining of the privileged status of the "objective" interpreter, which, grounded on the unexamined (derived) assumption that end is ontologically prior to temporal process, justifies a supervisory or mastering interpretive practice in the name of disinterestedness and the autonomy of the text.

More specifically, this translation enables a literary hermeneutics that is capable of revealing the "objectivity" of Modernist interpretive practice to be a strategy of willful accommodation intended to reduce the temporal being of the text to spatial form: to a vicious circle, a circle that closes off temporality and erodes one's memory of the being of the text, its contemporaneity—and ultimately, insofar as language is the house of being, of being itself. Just as Kierkegaard's (anti)narrative strategy of repetition is a dialectics of revocation that, in denying the reader an authorial ground, breaks the metaphysical circle of interpretation and "assigns him to himself," so also the Heideggerian hermeneutic circle is a process of de-struction that dismantles the metaphysical/spatial frame of reference and assigns the interpreter to him- or herself: makes the reader a historical *Dasein*, a temporal being-in-the-world, in original and careful (interested and dialogic) relationship to the being of the text and ultimately to (differential) being itself. Just as the Kierkegaardian repetition is "the interest on which metaphysics founders," so the Heideggerian hermeneutic circle is the care on which spatial form founders.

Unlike recollection (the vicious circle), which is "repeated backwards," repetition in Heidegger's and in Kierkegaard's texts is finally a "recollecting forwards." Although Heidegger, in the following passage, is referring to the history of the Western philosophical tradition, what he says about retrieval (*Wiederholung*) applies as well to the encounter with a particular literary text, since, as Lessing's distinction between the verbal and the plastic arts suggests, a literary text, by virtue of the temporality of its words, is itself a history in little:

> To ask "How does it stand with being?" means nothing less than to recapture, to repeat (*wieder-holen*), the beginning of our historical-spiritual existence, in order to transform it into a new beginning. This is possible. It is indeed the crucial form of history, because it begins in the fundamental event. But we do not repeat a beginning by reducing it to something past and now known, which need merely be initiated; no, the beginning must be begun again, more radically, with all the strangeness, darkness, insecurity that attend a true beginning. Repetition as we understand it is anything but an improved continuation with the old method of what has been up to now.[48]

It is this Kierkegaardian understanding of the hermeneutic circle that enables one to appropriate the destructive/phenomenological hermeneutics of Heidegger's existential analytic for a contemporary literary hermeneutics of discovery or disclosure. This literary hermeneutics is simultaneously and *always already* a dis-covering or dis-closing (present) of what has been covered over or closed off and forgotten by the metaphysical imagination (past), and a care-ful exploration of or opening to *terra incognita* (future). To put it more literally, I mean a hermeneutics that makes the interpreter a being-in-the-world in dialogic relationship simultaneously with a particular literary text and (since the text enters history on being written) with the "text" of literary history, and, beyond that, with the "text" of the history of Western humankind. It is by thus interpreting Heidegger's hermeneutic circle in terms of Kierkegaard's distinction between recollection and repetition that we are enabled to conceive a new literary hermeneutics of disclosure that is post-Modernist (or poststructuralist) and thus commensurate with the postmodern occasion.

In one of the epigraphs of this essay, I invoked Gotthold Lessing's famous distinction between poetry and painting by way of orienting the reader toward the analogy I wished to develop between the literary text and the phenomenological/existential analytic of *Being and Time*. I also was implying that, whatever his intention, in defining the limits of poetry in terms of its temporal medium and the limits of painting in terms of its spatial medium, Lessing prepared the way for an enormously important, if still to be fulfilled, dis-seminal development in literary criticism. Since the justification of this view depends on perceiving the transformation of meanings that it has undergone in the process of the ensuing discussion, the passage bears repetition:

> If it be true that painting employs wholly different signs or means of imitation from poetry,—the one using forms and colors in space, the other articulate sounds in time,—and if signs must unquestionably stand in convenient relation with the thing signified, then signs arranged side by side can represent only objects existing side by side, or whose parts so exist, while consecutive signs can express only objects which succeed each other, or whose parts succeed each other, in time.
>
> Objects which exist side by side, or whose parts so exist, are called bodies. Consequently bodies with their visible properties are the peculiar subjects of painting.
>
> Objects which succeed each other, or whose parts succeed each other in time, are actions. Consequently actions are the peculiar subjects of poetry.[49]

In his influential essays on spatial form in modern literature, Joseph Frank dismisses the critical judgment informing Lessing's distinction in favor of its importance "solely as instrument of analysis."[50] In the light of the foregoing interpretation of Heidegger's destructive version of Husserl's phenomenological call to return "*zu den Sachen selbst*," it can now be seen why Lessing's distinction between the plastic and temporal arts constitutes a (dis)seminal insight. However at odds his existential intuition was with his conscious classical intentions, Lessing was engaged in an act of hermeneutic destruction bent on recovering the ontological priority of temporality in the understanding of literature from the derivative (constituted) and spatial/metaphysical critical consciousness. To use the original and more precise terms of this discussion of hermeneutics, he was engaged in an act of iconoclasm intended to discover the *logos* as *legein* (*Rede*) buried deeply and eventually forgotten by the Western spatial imagination when it interpreted Man, the ζῷον λόγον 'έχον, as "rational animal." In insisting, against the traditional (essentially Roman) representation of poetry as *ut pictura poesis*, that words as temporal phenomena ("sounds in time") are the media of the articulation of human actions ("objects which succeed each other, or whose parts succeed each other, in time"), Lessing was ultimately saying that the essential existential structure of human life is language as human speech. He was, that is, anticipating Heidegger's interpretation of human being: that "Dasein, man's Being, is 'defined' as . . . that living thing whose Being is essentially determined by the potentiality for discourse" (BT, 6, 41; SZ, 20; see also BT, 7, 55; SZ, 32). In putting the Word under erasure, he was reasserting, against the grain of Western culture (and his own neoclassical inclinations), that literature, though not to be confused with life, is as radical medium *equiprimordial* with the temporal occasion of *Dasein* (*Befindlichkeit*) and the ek-static understanding (*Verstehen*) of that occasion.

In reading Lessing's aesthetic distinction in terms of Heidegger's destructive hermeneutics, a postmodern generation discovers with a shock of recognition that a literary text is not (like) a painting. Despite its repeatability, it cannot simply *be* (present to itself), as Archibald MacLeish puts it in his poem "Ars Poetica" and the New Critics (and the structuralists after them) represented it in their brilliantly superficial (ontic as opposed to ontic/ontological) exegetical practice. To affirm that a poem "should not mean but be," we can now know, betrays the fatal spatial logic of the ontotheological tradition, the fulfillment of which has precipitated the crisis of modernity. It is to read *logos* not as *legein*—the disseminal or emergent "act of an instant," as the postmodern American poet Charles Olson puts it[51]—but as the Word, and thus to *see* literary form as Western metaphysics *sees* being: as Being (*Summum Ens*), as totalizing image that in-closes time within the bounding line of an inclusive and comprehendable space. We discover that modern literary criticism has concealed the primordial essence of literature: *that it uses words*, and not pigments, to represent experience, and that words, "as consecutive signs," are not only intrinsically differential, as Jacques Derrida has shown, but also—and prior to their differentiating/deferring dynamics—radically temporal, especially when they are "the act of an instant."

In thus covering over the temporal/differential essence of language, modern literary criticism has also forgotten that, if a poem must "be," as the New Critics insisted, it must "be" in the way that Heidegger's destructive phenomenology discloses being to be: as always already e-mergent temporal process.[52]

If we allow the analogy that Lessing and Heidegger jointly suggest, in giving equiprimordial and indissolubly affiliated status to the human occasion (*Befindlichkeit*), understanding (*Verstehen*), and discourse (*Rede*), then the destructive/phenomenological stance demands a reorientation of perception in the reading process and thus a revision of the interpretive act similar to and as radical as that which Heidegger calls for in *Being and Time* in the encounter with temporal existence. For if a literary text is fundamentally a temporal phenomenon, if, that is, this temporality is ontologically prior to (is the condition for the possibility of) the form of a text, then literary hermeneutics must abandon, or must *de-inscribe*, the prevailing and by now culturally inscribed habit of suspending the temporal dimension, and the similarly inscribed attitude of dis-interest, in favor of the ontologically prior dynamic differential *process* conveyed by words in sequence. Literary interpretation, that is, must lay itself bare before the differential experience of language: the ongoing ek-static instants that, in always already deferring presence, engage the reader's *interest* as care. It must, in other words, put its inscribed prejudices at risk before the being of the text, which in always already deferring presence, always already defamiliarizes temporal perception: not simply one's present expectation of the future and understanding of the past, but also one's present understanding of one's own historical occasion as it is lived in the mind and body or, as Merleau-Ponty would say, in the fingertips. A postmodern interpreter must bracket the arrogant anthropomorphic frame of reference of the metaphysical consciousness, the *Wille zum Wille*, and its synchronic (retro)spective standpoint in favor of a situated or historical imagination and its diachronic perspective: the interested standpoint of ek-static *Dasein*.

To return to the term that finally emerges as the inevitable definition of the hermeneutic act, the postmodern literary interpreter must become an explorer, a *Homo viator*, in the place of origins. Here the author and the "world" of the literary text—whether it is Homer's *Odyssey* or Dante's *Divine Comedy* or Shakespeare's *King Lear* or Yeats's "Sailing to Byzantium" or Pound's *Cantos* or Eliot's "Four Quartets" or Beckett's *Malone* or Olson's *Maximus Poems*—undergo a profound metamorphosis. The god, *meta-ta-physika*, indifferently paring fingernails in the aftermath of creative labor, comes down into the arena of free play, into the zero zone, as it were. Here, however violent his/her hermeneutic act may seem to those adhering to the principle of "disinterest" or "objectivity," he/she becomes a dialogic partner, a sharer. And what was conceived as an artifact to be read from a printed page, an image to be looked at from a distance, an It to be mastered, becomes oral speech to be heard immediately in time, a Thou. When we ask the question of its being in care, the work of literature becomes in turn a voice that asks us not simply the question of being, but the question as it pertains to our present historical occasion. In the place of origins, as Hans-Georg Gadamer has persuasively reminded us, literature, ancient and modern, once more becomes fraught with risk—and possibility.[53]

Chapter 4
The Indifference of *Differance*:
Retrieving Heidegger's Destruction

"To be convinced of this, go with me for a moment into the Prisons of the inquisition." [God help my poor brother Tom] . . . *"Behold this helpless victim delivered up to his tormentors,—his body so wasted with sorrow, and confinement."—[Oh! 'tis my brother, cried poor* Trim *in a most passionate exclamation, dropping the sermon upon the ground. . . . Why,* Trim, *said my father, this is not a history—'tis a sermon thou art reading;—pri'thee begin the sentence again.]*

Laurence Sterne, Tristram Shandy

Levelling is not the action of one individual but a reflective-game in the hand of an abstract power.

Søren Kierkegaard, Two Ages

I

In an essay entitled "Nothing Fails Like Success," Barbara Johnson, one of the ablest apologists for deconstruction, attempts to defend it against attacks from the literary right and left.[1] In the process, she betrays the "blindness of (over)sight" of most, if not all, of the American exponents and practitioners of this method of interpretation deriving more or less from the authority of Jacques Derrida.[2] Like them, she all too characteristically *overlooks* the fact that deconstruction as articulated and practiced by Derrida himself has its source in and constitutes a calculated *re-vision* (as much as a deconstruction) of Martin Heidegger's destruction (*Destruktion*) of the metaphysics of the "onto-theo-logical tradition." This characteristically metaphysical oversight is the result of archivalizing Derrida's Nietzschean text, of making it the original Book of the Deconstructed Word. It minimizes an adequate reply to the countercritique of conservative and liberal humanists such as Meyer Abrams, Wayne Booth, Gerald Graff, Denis Donaghue, Eugene Goodheart, John Ellis, and, most seriously, Jürgen Habermas, who all, in defense of "their belief in the basic communicability of meaning and value," according to Johnson, accuse deconstructive criticism of "relativism, nihilism, or self-indulgent love of meaninglessness."[3] It also precludes an adequate defense against the criticism of those literary and political radical critics such as Edward Said, Fredric Jameson, John Brenkman, Frank Lentricchia, Paul Bové, Jonathan Arac, Donald Pease, and Jim Merod, who "accuse [deconstruction] of not living up to its claim of radicality, of working with too limited a notion of textuality, and of applying its critical energy only within an institutional structure that it does not question and therefore confirms."[4] It is this oversight rather than "success" that has made deconstruction susceptible to domestication and institutionalization. It is this forgetful looking from above—through the eyes, that is, of the archivalized Derridean Text—that has also, if inadvertently, rendered it an instrument contributing to the legitimation of the spirit of what Heidegger aptly calls the technological "age of the world picture"[5] and the disciplinary consumer society that spirit elaborates.

In what follows, I intend to explore some important aspects of this critical oversight. I want to suggest by way of a disclosive remembering that the Heideggerian *destruction*, whatever Heidegger's specific sociopolitical application, is inherently more adequate than deconstruction to the radical emancipatory task of contemporary oppositional intellectuals: not simply to the defense of the discourse of difference against the charge of nihilistic relativism made by its traditional humanistic critics, but to the effective critique of the metaphysical binary logic of mastery— "culture or anarchy" as Matthew Arnold codified it—that informs the humanistic discourse and the cultural and sociopolitical institutions it reproduces.[6] I want to suggest that insofar as it is multisituated—that is, understands the being into which it inquires as an indissoluble, however asymmetrical, continuum between language and sociopolitics—the Heideggerian destruction is more amenable than deconstruction to the literary, cultural, and sociopolitical adversarial purposes of the decentered postmodern countermemory.

I cannot assume even at this late date that my readers, both humanists and deconstructors, are conversant with Heidegger's destruction as such (beyond its crude representation as an instrument of fascist violence in the aftermath of the publication of Victor Farías's *Heidegger and Nazism* in 1987) or with its differential relationship to deconstruction (beyond that articulated in various texts by Derrida). I will therefore begin by recalling at some length Heidegger's definition in the second part of the introduction of *Being and Time*, a definition that the oversight of deconstructors has relegated to oblivion:

> If the question of Being is to achieve clarity regarding its own history, a loosening of the sclerotic tradition and a dissolving of the concealments produced by it is necessary. We understand this task as the *de-struction* of the traditional content of ancient ontology which is to be carried out along the *guidelines of the question of Being*. This de-struction is based upon the original experiences in which the first and subsequently guiding determinations of Being were gained.
>
> This demonstration of the provenance of the fundamental ontological concepts, as the investigation which displays their "birth certificate," has nothing to do with a pernicious relativizing of ontological standpoints. The de-struction has just as little the *negative* sense of disburdening ourselves of the ontological tradition. On the contrary, it should stake out the positive possibilities of the tradition, and that always means to fix its *boundaries*. These are factually given with the specific formulation of the question and the prescribed demarcation of the possible field of investigation. Negatively, the de-struction is not even related to the past: its criticism concerns "today" and the dominant way we treat the history of ontology, whether it be conceived as the history of opinions, ideas, or problems. However, the de-struction does not wish to bury the past in nullity; it has a *positive* intent. Its negative function remains tacit and indirect. . . .
>
> In accord with the positive tendency of the de-struction *the question must first be asked whether and to what extent in the course of the history of ontology in general the interpretation of Being has been thematically connected with the phenomenon of Time. We must ask whether the range of problems concerning Temporality which necessarily belongs here was fundamentally worked out or could have been.*[7]

To understand the relationship between Heidegger's destruction and Derrida's deconstruction, it will first be necessary to define the latter in its generality. What should be marked at the outset, however, is that the "beginning" that Heidegger wishes to retrieve from the ontotheological tradition is absolutely related to the question of temporality that this sclerotic speculative/recollective tradition, in all its manifestations, has also forgotten in forgetting the question of being. This disclosed "beginning" is not an absolute origin that reproduces a genetic (or strictly circular) representational model of interpretation, as it seems often to be understood both by Derrida (and assumed by his progeny) and by Heidegger's orthodox disciples, existentialists, or humanists. As the "Existential Analytic of *Dasein*"—the analytic of being-in-the-world— in *Being and Time* bears insistent witness, it is, rather, always already an ontic/ontological beginning: a (constituted) ground that is groundless. It is a condition in which structure is simultaneously articulated and undermined, in which a temporality "grounded" in nothing (word*s*) is an "absent cause" of the destruction of structure (the Word) and the dissemination of difference. As such it is clearly similar to Derrida's *differance*, but more inclusive, and more corrosive. That is, it contains *differance* as one (textual instance) of several instances in an indissoluble relay encompassing the totality of being.

II

According to Derrida, especially in *Of Grammatology*, language use in the logocentric tradition, whether it takes the form of writing (*écriture*) or speech (*parole*)—the mode of discourse the tradition since Plato has privileged over writing as agency of self-presence (or the "proper self")— has its origin in a *logos* or "transcendental signified" or "center," "which itself is beyond the reach of play."[8] It is thus essentially Adamic. Because of the foundational genetic model it rests on, language is assumed to be capable of naming (re-presenting, bringing back to presence) the temporally situated referents it intends, and thus of grounding "the play of substitutions,"[9] of assimilating differences, of locating and fixing them within the structure of the totalized and differentiated dedifferentiated circle of identity or sameness on which determinative meaning depends. Logocentrism thus valorizes a concept of truth as *adequaetio intellectus et rei* (the adequation of mind and object). In so doing, it mystifies a binary logic—the inclusive anthropomorphic either/or of the true and false as the "proper" mode of inquiry—and the constituted metaphysical rhetoric (metaphorics) of *enlightenment* that the genetic model silently inscribes and naturalizes as truth in the inquiring consciousness.[10] The primary function of deconstructive criticism, therefore, is to demystify the (humanist) discourse of truth by pressing this binary logic to its contradictory limits. It involves the disclosure of its metaphorical—differential—essence, or alternatively, the exposure of the *mise en abîme* between signifier and signified, the groundless ground of *mimesis* as representation. Its primary function is to show that language, written as well as spoken, is not self-identical but differential: it doubles or supplements the signifier and in thus always already substituting one signifier for another always already differentiates and defers the presence it would bring to stand.

More specifically, Derrida, and especially those such as Paul de Man, Jonathan Culler, Christopher Norris, J. Hillis Miller, Joseph Riddel, Eugenio Donato, Barbara Johnson, Cynthia Chase, and others who have applied Derrida's deconstructive practice to literary theory or to the reading of literary texts, assume from the beginning that *all* texts, past and present, veridical or literary, no matter what they *intend* to signify, are subject to deconstruction or, as in the case of de Man and his students, deconstruct themselves. They are, by the very nature of "writing in general," duplicitous: aporetic in essence and thus transgressive and subversive of the totalization intended by logocentric discourse. Because all texts necessarily lack a center that enables the totalization, self-identity, and determinative meaning called for in the "classical hypothesis," they are, in Derrida's rhetoric, subject to the "structurality of structure," to the infinite "play of difference," to the "movement of *supplementarity*" of writing:

> If totalization no longer has any meaning, it is not because the infiniteness of a field cannot be covered by a finite glance or a finite discourse, but because the nature of the field—that is, language and a finite language—excludes totalization. This field is in effect that of *play*, that is to say, a field of infinite substitutions only because it is finite, that is to say, because instead of being an inexhaustible field, as in the classical hypothesis, instead of being too large, there is something missing from it: a center which arrests and grounds the play of substitutions. One could say . . . that this movement of play, permitted by the lack or absence of a center or origin, is the movement of *supplementarity*. One cannot determine the center and exhaust totalization because the sign which replaces the center, which supplements it, taking the center's place in its absence—this sign is added, occurs as a surplus, as a *supplement*.[11]

Since its finite doubling nature renders language duplicitous, the writer, no matter who he or she is or when he or she writes, and no matter what the historical occasion, can therefore never say what he or she wishes to say (*vouloir dire*). Thus the essential function of the interpreter is not, as it is for traditional critics, to "interpret" the writer's plenary intention and, by thus totalizing it, to "master" the text, to take "command" over it. Rather, in Paul de Man's phrase, it is to disclose the blindness (to the aporias) of the writer's logocentric insight. The writer, Derrida says (echoing Nietzsche) in *Of Grammatology*,

> writes *in* a language and *in* a logic [the binary logic of logocentrism] whose proper system, laws, and life his discourse by definition

cannot dominate absolutely. He uses them only by letting himself, after a fashion and up to a point, be governed by the system. And reading must always aim at a certain relationship, unperceived by the writer, between what he commands and what he does not command of the patterns of the language that he uses.[12]

In order to guard against the possibility of "say[ing] almost anything" about the text, Derrida acknowledges the necessity of proceeding tentatively but rigorously according to the interpretive imperatives of the classical or humanistic strategy: to re-present and recuperate the "conscious, voluntary, intentional relationship that the writer institutes in his exchanges with the history to which he belongs."[13] But such traditional "doubling commentary," devoid of any awareness of the dissimulations of writing in general, closes off rather than opens up a reading. A text reveals its deferring supplementarity, the "undecidability" that is its opening, only to the ironic deconstructive reader of the commentary:

> If reading must not be content with doubling the text, it cannot legitimately transgress the text toward something other than it, toward a referent (a reality that is metaphysical, historical, psychobiographical, etc.) or toward a signified outside the text whose content would take place, could have taken place outside of language, that is to say, in the sense that we give here to that word, outside of writing in general. That is why the methodological considerations that we risk applying here to an example [Rousseau] are closely dependent on general propositions that we have elaborated above; as regards the absence of the referent or the transcendental signified. *There is nothing outside of the text* [there is no outside-text; *il n'y a pas de hors-texte*].[14]

In this notorious passage, Derrida in fact repeats Heidegger's version of the hermeneutic circle: the deconstructive reader necessarily begins inquiry with preconceptions (a forestructure) that the temporal process of reading (words) will always already deconstruct. But there is a crucial difference in emphasis, if not in essence, one that has contributed to the fixation of the essentially textual character of deconstructive practice in America. "Il n'y a pas de hors-texte:" this formula means that there is no transcendental signified, no structuring *logos* or center beyond the reach of the free play of language, as traditional interpretive theory and practice assume. It also means, therefore, that there is only textuality, that what is traditionally understood as the referent of the sign, whether this referent "is metaphysical, historical, psychobiographical, etc." is itself textual through and through, the sign of a sign of a sign. . . . There is no "outside reality" that is free of material inscription. Thus the deconstructive reader "cannot legitimately transgress the text towards something other than it, towards a referent." For Derrida, as both his insistence on the "deferring" operation of *differance* (implicitly, that writing/reading takes time) and his later "politically" oriented texts make clear,[15] this does not mean that the text *cannot* be historical; it means, rather, that one can invoke being, history, and personhood only as these come to us as a text. Nevertheless, in *Of Grammatology* and other early texts that introduced deconstruction to American critics, Derrida identifies the deferring operation of *differance* with (Saussurean) "textuality," a system of linguistic differences without positive terms, rather than with the temporality that subsumes not simply specifically textual differentiation but a relay of other differentiations as well. Further, he does not in practice differentiate historically between the writings he addresses in these early texts: Plato, Rousseau, Hegel, Saussure, and others.

These emphases in Derrida's text, as a consequence, lent themselves to a construal of this sentence that represents the text as an autonomous "intertextual" or "self-citational" or "re-iterative"—that is, *freefloating*—play of self-destructive signs alienated from historically specific actuality and divested of discursive signification.

Those who construed Derrida's meaning in this way were the American literary critics who, under the influence of de Man's substitution of allegory for grammatology, reduced Derrida's heuristic insight into the multivalent historicity of textuality to an antitranscendental transcendental literary rhetoric—and, not incidentally, established deconstruction as the dominant oppositional discourse in the academy. J. Hillis Miller characteristically lays out this (inadvertent?) reduction of the Derridean resonance:

> The relation between one text and its "sources," like the relation among the elements in a single text, is an ambiguous interplay of sameness and difference. . . . Moreover, the "sources" (Plato, St. Augustine, or whoever) are no more simple than their progeny. Like the "derived" texts, the primary texts contain their own contradictory elements and have ambiguous relations to their own sources. They can therefore never serve as unequivocal principles of explanation for the meaning of the later texts they have engendered. In all their relations within the text and between the text and what is outside it, the interaction is never between signs and something safely outside their enigmatic play, but always a relation between one sign and another, between one text and another, the relation Paul de Man has termed "allegorical."[16]

What I have said above hardly constitutes an adequate summary of a dense, complex, resonant, brilliantly articulated, and, in my mind, irrefutable "methodology" of reading. But it is enough to suggest what is both valuable and problematic about it from the perspective of the Heideggerian destruction. In its inscribed obsession with a *mon*-archic certainty, the logocentric tradition, in all its substitutions or supplementations of center for center, privileges an amnesiac memory. It exists to make us forget our "thrown" occasion: not simply the finally unbridgeable abyss between words, between texts, and between texts and the "reality" of the world to which they refer, but also the groundlessness of the privileged hierarchical/binary discourse of metaphysics and the totalizing and ultimately dedifferentiating genetic model it elaborates. This privileged tradition, that is, exists to make us forget that language cannot name and dominate *physis* in general—the de-centering, e-mergent temporality of being—but always fictionalizes and defers (differentiates) the being it would bring to presence. In short, it exists to obliterate our preontological awareness that language *as* (objective) truth constitutes a violence against the earth and its processes. To put it in terms that Derrida's literary followers have characteristically overlooked in their successful effort to institutionalize deconstruction, "The concept of centered structure is in fact the concept of play based on a fundamental ground, a play constituted on the basis of a fundamental immobility and a reassuring certitude, which is itself beyond the reach of play. *And on the basis of this certitude anxiety can be mastered.*"[17] To the degree that the (non)concept of *differance* reminds us of these forgotten or repressed actualities, the deconstructive criticism of Derrida is useful to a "critical theory" of reading that would be simultaneously a sociopolitical activity or counter-*praxis*. In insisting on the "structurality" of language, on the fact that difference is the condition for the possibility of identity (and not the other way around), it suggests the possibility of thematizing the logocentric language of re-presentation as a reification, of activating the reader's awareness of the "normalizing" power inscribed (and hidden) in the metaphysical—structuralist—imperative of the binary logic of humanistic discourse.

However, insofar as deconstruction refuses to acknowledge the intentionality of discursive practice or, what is the same thing, insists on the autonomy of (inter)textuality and on the consequent interpretive imperative that "our reading must be *intrinsic* and remain with the text,"[18] it tends to textualize the *differance* disseminated by the nothing or by temporality. As such, it constitutes a reduction of the Heideggerian destruction, which, as a mode of destructive/projective being-in-the-world, is radically historical and demands historical specification, even if Heidegger does not adequately meet this demand. In a way reminiscent of the American New Criticism, to which I will return, it tends to dehistoricize or "unworld" both the text and the reading process: to "idealize" them according to a reversed ideality. Whereas the Heideggerian destruction is simultaneously a destructive/projective practice, deconstruction takes the secondary purpose of demystifying textuality to be the primary and only one. It becomes, that is, a purely negative ironic process of disclosing the unintended (or intended) aporias that always already breach *all* writing—literary or veridical—whatever its historically specific occasion.

As Barbara Johnson observes, deconstruction "at its best . . . undoes the very comforts of mastery and consensus that underlie the illusion that objectivity is situated somewhere outside the self."[19] But this characteristic emphasis on the purely textual character of *differance*—the "writerly" or "grammatological" or "rhetorical" or "allegorical" essence of writing—overlooks the insistent historical fact that, as Foucault will remind us, the discourse of objectivity is enabled by historically specific discursive practices, by socially constituted and regulated rules of discursive formation. If it is true that the essence of language has been misunderstood and mystified in the logocentric tradition at large, it is also true that texts have always had and continue to have real and very serious worldly consequences; that they have made and continue to *make a difference in the world*. As Michael Sprinker puts it in calling attention to Derrida's inattention to the historically specific regularities of Rousseau's discourse in his deconstructive reading of "Rousseau":

> Brilliant and dazzling as, for example, Derrida's reading of Rousseau can often be, it is fair to ask of Derrida how the mere chain of supplements in a text can not only theorize a social structure such as Rousseau produces in *The Social Contract* and *The Second Discourse*, but can also have the effective force that Rousseau's texts achieved in the late eighteenth and early nineteenth centuries. Derrida is simply unable to account for the power that texts acquire and deploy in the political and cultural sphere, where the play of signification becomes a deadly serious game in which human subjects are at stake.[20]

To say that Derrida "is simply unable to account for the power that texts acquire and deploy in the political and cultural sphere" is certainly to overstate the case against his version of deconstruction. But Derrida does in practice (especially in the early texts) subordinate the possibilities of a historically specific critique of power to an analysis of an inverted universal textuality. He does go far to make this inverted universal textuality a base for superstructural sites such as culture and sociopolitics, in which the latter are treated more or less epiphenomenally. It is in thus lending itself to a certain representation and practice of deconstruction that limits its critical project to a monophasic pursuit of textual contradictions—to the disclosure of the "double, aporetic logic" of all logocentric discourses, as Jonathan Culler puts this limitation in his influential "guide" to Derridean deconstruction—that Derrida's discursive practice opens itself exactly to the critique of Sprinker and other worldly critics of the left:

> The question that now arises, especially for literary critics who are more concerned with the implications of philosophical theories than with their consistency or affiliations, is what this [disclosure of "structural inconsistencies" in "theories grounded on presence"] has to do with the theory of meaning and the interpretation of texts. The examples we have examined so far [from Rousseau and Saussure] permit at least a preliminary reply: deconstruction does not elucidate texts in the traditional sense of attempting to grasp a unifying content or theme; it investigates the work of metaphysical oppositions in their arguments and the way in which textual figures and relations, such as the play of the supplement in Rousseau, produce a double, aporetic logic. The examples we have considered give no reason to believe, as is sometimes suggested, that deconstruction makes interpretation a process of free association in which anything goes, *though it does concentrate on conceptual and figural implications rather than on authorial intention.*[21]

In the terms of this essay, deconstruction minimizes precisely what the Heideggerian destructive mode takes to be the "first" of the always and simultaneous twofold operation of this hermeneutic practice. If the destructive mode of inquiry is understood not simply as the critique of structuration but also as the retrieval by violence (releasement) of the temporality of being from structuration, be-*ing* from Being, the lived futural possibilities of *Dasein*'s understanding from permanent presence, it is also and simultaneously a *pro-jective* mode of inquiry. In accordance with the dis-closive imperatives of the hermeneutic circle, it thus invites us, even if Heidegger himself failed decisively to accept the invitation or, in accepting it, misrepresented its imperatives, to open up our horizonal interpretive focus on the question of being to the "world": to take into "interested" or "careful" consideration the linguistic and, through the linguistic, the cultural, economic, and sociopolitical sites that constitute being-in-the-world. I mean Heidegger's insistence on the ontic/ontological equiprimordiality of *Befindlichkeit*, *Verstehen*, and *Rede* (*Dasein*'s occasion, understanding, and discourse).

The Heideggerian destruction retrieves the domain of knowledge as a historical and material field of forces from the disciplinary compartmentalization to which it has been subjected by the universalizing metaphysical tradition. In thus retrieving knowledge as a diachronic and, at any historically specific moment, indissoluble relay, the destruction instigates a mode of inquiry in which, wherever one situates the question—whether at the site of ontology, language, psychology, history, ecology,

gender, economics, culture, or politics—one is always already addressing the other *topoi* in the kinetic field: always and necessarily discovering
their affiliative relationship, however assymetrical and temporary it may
be, to the chosen site. The circle of destructive understanding thus makes
explicit what the traditional compartmentalization of knowledge into
disciplines, and the "advanced" deconstructive textualization of *differance*,
tends to preclude: the historical materiality of language and the worldliness of the text.

The destructive mode invites a critical engagement with the tradition
that occurs all along the indissoluble continuum of being: not simply at
the site of ontology or of textuality as such, but also and simultaneously
at those cultural, racial, social, and political sites that are the specific genealogical concerns of contemporary neo-Marxist critics of late capitalist
semiotic systems; of other "worldly critics" of Enlightenment logic and
the hegemonic discursive practices, disciplines, and institutions it has
elaborated; of black critics of Occidental racism; and of feminist critics
of modern patriarchal power relations. To appropriate the term Edward
Said adapts from Gramsci's and Foucault's revision of the traditional
Marxist base/superstructure model, the destruction activates an intertextuality that makes explicit the ideological *affiliation* between texts and
historically specific contexts, the usually invisible "network of peculiarly
cultural associations . . . between forms, statements, and other *aesthetic*
elaborations on the one hand, and, on the other, institutions, agencies,
classes, and fairly amorphous social forces": in short, the unseen and
silent ideologies that, in the name of free inquiry, enable and determine—
permit or interdict—discursive practice:

> Affiliation [in contrast with homology and filiation, which, "so far
> as humanists are concerned, have created the homogeneously
> utopian domain of texts connected serially, seamlessly, immediately
> only with other texts"] is what enables a text to maintain itself as a
> text and this is covered by a range of circumstances: status of the
> author, historical moment, conditions of publication, diffusion and
> reception, values drawn upon, values and ideas assumed, a
> framework of consensually held tacit assumptions, presumed
> background, and so on and on. In the second place, to study
> affiliation is to study and recreate the bonds between texts and
> world, bonds which specialization and the institutions of literature
> have all but completely effaced. Every text is an act of will to some
> extent, but what has not been very much studied [and
> deconstruction, too, tends to overlook] is the degree to which—and
> the specific cultural space by which—texts are made permissible. To
> recreate the affiliative network is therefore to make visible, to give
> materiality back to, the strands holding the text to the society, the
> author, and the culture that produced it. In the third place, affiliation

releases a text from its isolation, and imposes upon the scholar or critic the presentational problem of historically re-creating or re-constructing the possibilities out of which the text arose. Here is the place for intentional analysis, and for the effort to place a text in homological, dialogical or antithetical relationships with other texts, classes, institutions, etc.[22]

In his reading of *Being and Time*, Derrida locates the remnant of meta-physics in Heidegger's thought in the *Seinsfrage*. This reading not only deflects attention away from the essential disclosure of Heidegger's re-trieval of the question of being: the radical temporality and historicity of being that has been reified in and by the ontotheological tradition. In representing the *Seinsfrage* as vestigially metaphysical and putting it out of play—*hors texte*—in his revision of Heidegger's destruction, Derrida also minimizes the potential of the *differance* to disclose the hidden, spe-cifically articulated ideologies and will to worldly power over the "other" that inform the canonical or archival logocentric texts: both the historically specific origins, determinations, representations, and affilia-tions of this logocentric violence and its historically specific cultural and sociopolitical effects. Deconstructive criticism, as Derrida brilliantly demonstrates in "White Mythology" and elsewhere is, of course, acutely capable of demystifying (Western) philosophy *in general*, of disclosing the metaphoricity of "white"—"reduced" or "effaced"—veridical proposi-tions: the play of supplementarity that dis-seminates Occidental philo-sophical (but also literary) discourse, that renders the "truthfulness" of its syntax an agency of dissimulation:

> To metaphors. The word is written only in the plural. If there were only one possible metaphor, the dream at the heart of philosophy, if one could reduce their play to the circle of a family or a group of metaphors, that is, to one "central," "fundamental," or "principial" metaphor, there would be no more true metaphor, but only, through the one true metaphor, the assured legibility of the proper. Now, it is because the metaphoric is plural from the outset that it does not escape syntax; and that it gives rise, in philosophy too, to a *text* which is not exhausted in the history of its meaning (signified concept or metaphoric tenor: *thesis*), in the visible or invisible presence of its theme (meaning and truth of Being). But it is also because the metaphoric does not reduce syntax, and on the contrary organizes its divisions within syntax, that it gets carried away with itself, cannot be what it is except in erasing itself, indefinitely constructing its destruction.[23]

Indeed, deconstruction, in Derrida's hands at least, is also capable of dis-closing the political complicity between "proper" philosophy's reduction of the play of metaphoricity and its reduction and domination of the "figural" and thus "improper" Oriental "other": the "white-man-ness" of philosophy as "white mythology," that is, the continuous dialectical operation of the Platonic *anamnesis*/Hegelian *relève* [*Aufhebung*] in *both* the linguistic and geopolitical spheres:

> Philosophical discourse—as such—describes a metaphor which is displaced and reabsorbed between two suns [the rising sun as "sensible" and the falling sun as "sense"] This *end* of metaphor is not interpreted as a death or dislocation, but as an interiorizing anamnesis (*Erinnerung*), a recollection of meaning, a *relève* of living metaphoricity into a living state of properness. This is the irrepressible philosophical desire to summarize-interiorize-dialecticize-master-*relever* the metaphorical division between the origin and itself, the Oriental difference. In the world of desire, metaphor is born in the East as soon as the latter sets itself to speak, to work, to write, suspending its pleasures, separating itself from itself and naming absence: that is, what is. Such at least is the philosophical proposition in its geotropic and historico-rhetorical enunciations. "As man's first motives for speaking were of the passions, his first expressions were tropes. Figurative language was the first to be born. Proper meaning was discovered last." And "the genius of the Oriental languages" is to be "vital and figurative."[24]

However, because deconstruction is methodologically committed to the "irreducible secondarity" of the speaking subject and his or her speech,[25] its "political" disclosures must remain at a very high level of abstraction. In privileging the project of freeing the signifier from any form of the transcendental signified (a relation, according to Derrida, that remains vestigially in Heidegger's representation of language from *Being and Time* to his last writing—a view I will presently contest), it inhibits, if it does not entirely preclude, the possibility of historically situating and differentiating between *the particular syntaxes of violence* that the privileged (reconciling) metaphorical impulse to spatialize or reify difference—to reduce particulars to sameness, to assimilate the dissimilar—does to *physis*, to emergent things-as-they-are. What Derrida in "White Mythology" says, for example, about the constellation of metaphors radiating from the primal metaphor of the Sun (light, vision, circle, wester[n]ing, and so on) inscribed in the philosophical discourse of Descartes's *Meditations* applies *equally* to *all* the syntaxes of metaphor he deconstructs in his discourse, whether it is the syntax of "Aristotle," of "du Marais," of "Fontanier," of "Hegel," of "Bachelard":

> This metaphorics is of course articulated in a specific syntax; but as a metaphorics it belongs to a more general syntax, to a more extended

system that equally constrains Platonism; everything is illuminated by this system's sun, the sun of absence and of presence, blinding and luminous, dazzling.[26]

The slide from the particular to the general in this otherwise remarkably resonant passage may signal a contradiction in Derrida's discourse, but it is finally no accident. Derrida's commitment to the irreducible secondarity of the subject and to (free-floating) "textuality" precludes precisely the analysis of this admitted, but rarely explored, qualification. "Descartes" (and all the other historical writers around whose names Derrida insistently puts quotation marks to distance "their" discourses from the historically specific subjects who produced them) produced a (historically) *"specific syntax."* In putting the quotation marks of textuality around the names of these historically situated beings-in-the-world, in generalizing if not exactly universalizing their specificity, Derrida reduces them all, *indiscriminately*, to predetermined logocentric (Western) metaphorizers. In so doing, he neutralizes the historical occasion—the particular historicity, the particular discursive practice, the particular worldliness of their texts.[27] From the perspective of this more or less global or panoramic *over-view* of the different metaphorical syntaxes of the metaphysical tradition, Plato's *"eidos,"* Descartes's "clear and distinct ideas," Hegel's "Sun of self-consciousness,"[28] Husserl's "phenomenology," even Heidegger's "lighting" (*Lichtung*), and, one is led by this "logic" to presume, Jeremy Bentham's "panoptic gaze," for example, become paradoxically identical. And, as I have suggested, what is after all a contradiction or a tendency in Derrida, becomes formulaic and doctrinaire in the literary critical discourses of his American followers.

Nor, by extension, since form itself is an extended metaphor, can deconstructive criticism differentiate between and historically situate the specific syntaxes of ideological power that the different historical structures within the logocentric tradition have authorized or legitimated: the historically specific circular structures, for example, of philosophic texts such as Plato's *Republic* (the monologic dialogue), Hegel's *Phenomenology of Spirit* (the circuitous dialectical journey toward *Wissenschaft*), or Bentham's *Panopticon* (the calculative/disciplinary scientific "project"); or of literary texts like Virgil's *Aeneid*, Fielding's *Tom Jones*, James's *The Princess Casamassima*, Joyce's *Ulysses*, or Conrad's *Heart of Darkness*. On the other hand, insofar as the Heideggerian destruction of the ontotheological tradition acknowledges that language is "the house of being"— which is to say that texts, as "representations," make a difference, whether for good or ill, in "worlding" the world—it can, if pursued beyond the ontological site to which Heidegger chose by and large to delimit his investigations, be appropriated for sociopolitical analysis and criticism. No matter how riddled by grammatological aporias the logocentric texts it addresses are, the destruction can historically locate and ideologically discriminate between the historically specific *"supplements"*—"the different forms or names" the "center receives" in "the history of the West." To put this in terms of the power relations that Derrida's rhetoric elides, the Heideggerian destruction, insofar as it is the ontic/ontological practice of a being-in-the-world, can differentiate between the specific recuperative formal syntaxes of power—the "discursive regularities," in Foucault's more appropriate rhetoric—precipitated by and constituting the logocentric tradition.

Heidegger, admittedly, chose to explore the specific effects of the will to power informing the philosophical discourses of the ontotheological tradition at the site of ontology. He thus reinscribed a base/superstructure model on discourse: the very disciplinary model his destructive hermeneutics was intended to dismantle. It was a focus that blinded him to the positive—projective—sociopolitical possibilities of the destruction, however acute and persuasive his critique of the general relay between ontology and sociopolitical formations of the onto-theo-logical tradition.[29] Substantial as the limitations of Heidegger's own practice are, they do not preclude the possibility of appropriating a salient motif of his destructive hermeneutics that takes his thought in a more worldly (and contemporary), if not radically different, direction from that pursued by Derrida and his followers. The direction I am projecting, to be specific, does not lead simply to a generalized disclosure of the "structurality of structure," or alternatively of the "textuality" of "writing in general" ending in, as Barbara Johnson puts it, the "radicality" of deconstruction, the accompanying "surprise" of ignorance: "What the surprise of encounter with otherness should do is lay bare some hint of an ignorance one never knew one had."[30] It also leads to a textual criticism that is sociopolitically emancipatory: in Foucault's terms, to a *critical* "history of the present." Heidegger's historically specific distinctions between the three phases of the metaphysical (Western) tradition that comes to its end in the modern age of the world picture—the onto- (Greco-Roman), theo- (Medieval), logical (post-Enlightenment humanist)—clearly suggests this potential of destruction, however abstractly these distinctions are formulated. It can, for example, demonstrate the continuity of and differentiate between literary texts located anywhere in the Western tradition: for example, Virgil's *Aeneid*, the *télos* (the insistent prophecy/fulfillment structure) of which is complicitous with the Metropolis (the divinely sanctioned Augustan imperial project); Fielding's *Tom Jones*, the mathematically well-made plot of which attributes causality to accident—the condition of the human occasion—and thus affiliates its self-present structure with the disciplinary social goals of the deistically sanctioned and empirically oriented humanist discourse of the Enlightenment; and Conrad's *Heart of Darkness*, the essentially sane and normal recollective or re-presentational narrative structure of which, in naturalizing excess, mystifies, normalizes, and legitimates the hegemonic purposes of Western (British) technological/capitalist colonialism.[31]

Further, the destruction lends itself to a kind of intertextual criticism capable of discriminating between "marginal" texts in the tradition like Euripides' *Orestes*, Rabelais's *Gargantua and Pantagruel*, Cervantes's *Don Quixote*, Sterne's *Tristram Shandy*, Diderot's *Jacques le fataliste*, Melville's *Moby-Dick*, and Tolstoy's *Death of Ivan Ilych*. I mean texts that the literary tradition has accommodated, but that have their *raison d'être*, as their enabling influence on postmodern fiction suggests (Thomas Pynchon's *Gravity's Rainbow*, John Barth's *Letters*, Robert Coover's *Public Burning*, Donald Barthelme's *The Dead Father*, E. L. Doctorow's *Ragtime*, Umberto Eco's *The Name of the Rose*, Milan Kundera's *The Unbearable Lightness of Being*, Don DeLillo's *White Noise*, etc.) in an adversarial effort to de-stroy specific canonical texts or canonical forms of the Western tradition, and also to delegitimate the historically specific forms of cultural and sociopolitical power that the canonical monuments have been invoked to support and confirm.

Practiced in terms of the imperatives of this kind of intertextuality, destruction can disaffiliate Cervantes's *Don Quixote* from the monumental tradition that has pacified its multisituated revolutionary force. The custodians of the European literary tradition have represented *Don Quixote* as the text that brings the humanist novel form into being. A destructive reading will show, on the contrary, that Cervantes's novel exists, in fact, to interrogate the epistemological and sociopolitical ideology informing the emergent humanism. By parodying Don Quixote's assumed identity—that is, by pushing its anthropological logic to its grotesque narrative end—the novel thematizes the continuity of this (anthropo)logic and its sociopolitical value system with the (theo)logic and sociopolitical value system of the Spanish Inquisition. The destruction is inherently capable of showing that the structural errancy of Cervantes's novel is intended to demystify or "dis-enchant" not only the interwoven, highly wrought, and enchanting "tapestry"—a privileged figure of textual deconstruction—of the archival medieval romance of, say, Ariosto's *Orlando Furioso*, but also the end-oriented epistemological/narrative principle of the "enchanter." I mean what, according to critical convention, might be emptily called the *deus ex machina*, but which a destructive hermeneutics addressing Cervantes's parodic (intertextual) text would facilitate our calling more accurately and tellingly the ontotheological "principle of last resort" in the face of the exorbitant mystery of difference: the absolute Other invented and recurrently reconstructed by the metaphysical tradition to establish its identity and guarantee its worldly authority. In *Don Quixote*, it takes the ludicrous form of the ubiquitous "enchanter," who, no matter how destructive the force of contradiction, always serves to confirm the Don's visionary humanistic narrative of the Golden Age. It is, in other words, the paradoxical principle of magic that normally remains hidden behind or hovers out of sight (and out of play) above the "objective" narrative (and interpretive practice) of the custodians of empirical reality and the causally oriented *polis* it enables. In short, it is, if we recall the transitional historical context of Cervantes's novel, the supplementary ideological principle that naturalizes and reinscribes the supernatural principle of absolute evil that visibly informs the providential history (and interpretive practice) of the church fathers. I mean the theological principle of last resort that confirms the prefigurative narrative of medieval Christianity—the narrative that coerces the differential spatial and temporal force of historicity into a continuous, seamless, and proper system of correspondences—and gives rise to the Spanish church's inquisitorial practices vis-à-vis heresy. Here Quixote laments to Sancho, whom the doubly malicious "enchanters" have allowed to behold the extraordinary beauty of Dulcinea, after his dis-enchanting encounter with the ugly country girl he had expected to be his "Princess and world-famous lady of El Toboso":

> Do you see now what a spite the enchanters have against me, Sancho? See to what extremes the malice and hatred they bear me extend, for they have sought to deprive me of the happiness I should have enjoyed in seeing my mistress in her true person. In truth, I was born a very pattern for the unfortunate, and to be a target and mark for the arrows of adversity. You must observe also, Sancho, that these traitors were not satisfied with changing and transforming my Dulcinea, but transformed her and changed her into a figure as low and ugly as that peasant girl's. And they have deprived her too of something most proper to great ladies, which is the sweet smell they have from always moving among ambergris and flowers. For I must tell you, Sancho, that when I went to help Dulcinea on her hackney—as you say it was, though it seemed a she-ass to me—I got a whiff of raw garlic as stank me out and poisoned me to the heart.[32]

Because of its commitment to the textuality of texts—the absolute absence of reference in the signifier—the deconstructive mode, on the other hand, must, as Michel Foucault says of Derrida's textualization of Descartes's discourse, necessarily end in "reducing discursive practice [read "the materiality of discourse"] to textual traces":

> It's not because of carelessness that classical interpreters, before Derrida and like him, have erased this passage from Descartes. It's systematic. It's a system of which Derrida today is the most decisive representative: reduction of discursive practices to textual traces; elision of events they produce that retains only the traces of reading; invention of voices behind texts in order not to analyze the modes of implication of the subject in discourse; assigning the originary as the said and nonsaid in order not to replace discursive practices in the field of transformations where they take place.[33]

Foucault's critique of Derrida's discourse reduces deconstruction to system, pure and simple, and reduces the ambiguous relation between signifier and signified to a certain and easily institutionalized textual emptiness. It is therefore perhaps more appropriately applied to his American followers. But insofar as Derrida's emphasis falls heavily on the signifier/signified distinction (an emphasis that continues even into the later essays, which attempt to thematize the sociopolitical implications of his deconstructive discourse), it does indeed minimize the historicity—the occasion—of discourse. And in so doing, it lends itself to appropriation by, if it does not sanction, a deconstructive discourse that represents intertextuality as a free-floating (transcendental) system of differential signs and ends in an "*élision*"—a dedifferentiation—"*des événements.*" Insofar as it commits itself to a systematic separation of text and referent, deconstructive criticism must, then, *overlook* such material relationships between text and world, between fiction and discursive formation, and such historical discriminations between texts that confirm and texts that destroy the various historically specific ideological economies of discursive power. In short, insofar as it sees its primary and only legitimate purpose to be making explicit the necessary transgressiveness—the play of *differance*, the "double, aporetic logic"—that always already disrupts the "inscribed" totalizing impulse of the "author" in the broad logocentric tradition, deconstruction must remain an ahistorical discourse that implicates its practitioners in the hegemonic institution.

As in the case of the microtextual metaphor, deconstructive criticism's summary and global textualization of discursive practice elides all texts in the logocentric tradition and disengages them from the specific syntaxes of history. In thus leveling difference, it disables a sociopolitical interrogation of their concealed affiliations with the various *epistémés* (historically specific ideologies) that have supervised the cultural and sociopolitical life of Western men and women in the name of rationality. As Edward Said puts it:

> All of Derrida's work has magnificently demonstrated that such a contract exists, that texts demonstrating logocentric biases are indications that the contract [between bodies of knowledge, institutions, power] exists and keeps existing from period to period in Western history and culture. But it is a legitimate question, I think, to ask what keeps that contract together, what makes it possible for a certain system of metaphysical ideas, as well as a whole structure of concepts, praxes, ideologies derived from it, to maintain itself from Greek antiquity up through the present. What forces keep all these ideas glued together? What forces get them into texts? How does one's thinking become infected, then get taken over, by those ideas? Are all these things matters of fortuitous coincidence, or is there in fact some relevant connection to be made, and *seen*, between the instances of logocentrism and the agencies perpetuating it in time? . . .
>
> The answers to these questions cannot be found by reading the texts of Western thought *seriatim*, no matter how complex the reading method and no matter how faithfully followed the series of texts. Certainly any reading method like Derrida's—whose main ambition is both to reveal undecidable elements in a text in lieu of some simple reductive message the text is supposed to contain and to shy away from making each reading of a text part of some cumulatively built explicit thesis about the historical persistence of and the agencies for Western metaphysical thought—certainly any method like that will finally be unable to get hold of the local material density and power of ideas as historical actuality. For not only will these ideas be left unmentioned, *they cannot even be named*— and this, any reader of Derrida will know, is highly consonant with the entire drift of Derrida's antinomianism, his dedefinitional philosophy, his desemanticizing of language. In other words, the search *within* a text for the conditions of textuality will falter and fail at that very point where the text's *historical presentation* to the reader is put into question and made an issue for the critic.[34]

In its tendency to dehistoricize discursive *praxis*, to put Said's critique positively, Derrida's emphasis on the textuality of texts points to a disciplinary methodology, especially of literary criticism. Despite Derrida's protests to the contrary and his more recent efforts to draw out the political implications of deconstruction, this emphasis ends in a practice that transforms all texts into self-canceling, free-floating signifying systems that hover above time, which is to say, if temporality makes (the) difference, into identical texts, or into an undifferentiated global anti-Book.

Understood in these terms, the deconstructive discourse of *differance* becomes a universalist discourse in reverse: an antiidealist idealism that leaves the ideological power of the texts and the tradition it would interrogate intact.

It is not, therefore (as apologists for Derrida's textuality such as Barbara Johnson, Jonathan Culler, and Christopher Norris, claim), "an oversimplified understanding of certain aspects of deconstructive theory"[35] that lies behind the massive institutionalization of deconstruction. Its failure in practice (with the exception of a certain feminist/Marxist deconstruction exemplified by Gayatri Spivak) to cross over the disciplinary boundary line of literary criticism into the cultural, economic, and sociopolitical sites it hedges[36] is the consequence, rather, of this methodological or systemic refusal to encounter language as the *historical* "house of being": as a temporal and, however asymmetrical, indissoluble relay of material articulations between ontological representation and sociopolitical formations.

This theoretical necessity has rendered deconstructive criticism, like the New Criticism it repudiated as a new orthodoxy, a determining academic *discipline*, which transforms the indissoluble lived relations of being-in-the-world into a hierarchical *structure* whose base is writing, the "foundation" of an "edifice," that, if it acknowledges the materiality of these other "worldly sites" at all, reduces them to epiphenomenal superstructural status:

> [Derrida's] argument can be stated most simply in the following terms. If writing is the very *condition* of knowledge—if, that is to say, it can be shown to precede and articulate all our working notions of science, history, tradition, etc.—then how can writing be just one object of knowledge among others? What Derrida is using here is the form of "transcendental" reasoning which Kant first brought to bear upon the central problems of philosophy. . . . What philosophy had much better do, [Kant] argued [against philosophers who "challenged the claims of epistemological skepticism"], was examine the inbuilt presuppositions of their own and (implicitly) of *all* cognitive enquiry, the intellectual ground-rules in the absence of which our thinking would have no sense, no logic or purpose. And then, according to Kant, they could start to rebuild the whole edifice of human knowledge on the rational foundations that were placed beyond doubt by the fact that they belonged to a simply inescapable, *a priori* structure of concepts.
>
> Derrida's version of this Kantian argument makes writing (or "arche-writing") the precondition of all possible knowledge. And this not merely by virtue of the fact—the self-evident fact—that writing is the form in which ideas are passed down, preserved in a

constantly expanding archive, and thus made available to subsequent debate. His claim is *a priori* in the radically Kantian sense: that we cannot *think* the possibility of culture, history, or knowledge in general without also thinking the prior necessity of writing.[37]

Indeed, what Raymond Williams says about the base/superstructure model in his critique of the discursive practices of orthodox Marxism applies as well, despite the reversed ontological representation, to deconstruction as it has come by and large to be practiced in North America:

> In the transition from Marx to Marxism, and then in the development of expository and didactic formulations, the words used in the original arguments were projected, first, as if they were precise concepts, and second, as if they were descriptive terms for observable "areas" of social life. The main sense of the words in the original arguments had been *relational*, but the popularity of the terms tended to indicate either (a) relatively enclosed categories or (b) relatively enclosed areas of activity. These were then correlated either temporally (first material production, then consciousness, then politics and culture) or in effect, forcing the metaphor, spatially (visible and distinguishable "levels" or "layers"—politics and culture, then forms of consciousness, and so on down to "the base"). The serious practical problems of method, which the original words had indicated, were then usually in effect bypassed by methods derived from a confidence, rooted in the popularity of the terms, in the relative enclosure of categories or areas expressed as "the base," "the superstructure."
>
> It is then ironic to remember that the force of Marx's original criticism had been mainly directed against the *separation* of "areas" of thought and activity (as in the separation of consciousness from material production—real human activities—by the imposition of abstract categories). The common abstraction of "the base" and "the superstructure" is thus a radical persistence of the modes of thought which he attacked.[38]

It is too strong to say, with Foucault, that Derrida's deconstructive method is a *petite pedagogie* that,

> historically well-determined, hides in this "textualization" of discursive practices, that manifests itself in a quite visible manner. A pedagogy teaching the student that there is nothing outside the text, but rather that in it, in its interstices, in its blanks and nonsaids [*nondits*], there reigns the reserve of the origin; that it is therefore not at all necessary to seek elsewhere, that right here, not in the words, of course, but in the words put under erasure, in their grid, that the "meaning of being" articulates itself.[39]

But it can be said that, in textualizing the ontological difference—in reducing the difference that temporality disseminates all across the indissoluble continuum of being to *differance*—deconstruction "after" Derrida has precluded itself from becoming a historically material transdisciplinary *praxis*. In the hands of Derrida's American followers, in other words, deconstruction has closed off the possibility of disclosing and analyzing the affiliative bonds between texts and other worldly sites, let alone "its institutional underpinning, and economic and social relations with the world."[40] Indeed, in becoming such a "literary" discipline, deconstruction, despite Derrida's clearly radical intention, has become paradoxically a calculative practice reminiscent of the logocentric practice it would call into question: a violent panoptic *methodology of leveling*.

III

Derrida's insistence on the textuality of the "non-word" or "non-concept" *differance* renders deconstruction essentially a monophasal—a privative or negative—interpretive activity. This is not only because it is, despite J. Hillis Miller's rhetorical maneuver to disarm the naïve objectivist critique, parasitic on canonized texts. In translating its possibilities into the empty, free-floating realm of a rhetoric or textuality that always already destroys itself, deconstruction also, and more importantly, blinds its practitioners to that which is released—I am tempted to say "liberated" or "decolonized"—from the imperial bondage of structure. Indeed, in some fundamental sense, its privative orientation—the limitation of its project to the exposure of aporias that always already deconstruct structure—undermines agency: the desire and will to "self"-activation, to pro-jective *praxis* in the context of a dedifferentiated difference. Thinking gets *dissociated* from a doing motivated by the difference that difference makes (in-the-world).

Derrida has from the beginning—and in an increasingly self-conscious and deliberate way in the wake of the American appropriation of deconstruction—tried to minimize the disabling sociopolitical consequences of the irreducible "gap" between the critique of philosophical discourse and the critique of the institutional orders it supports. But this double bind is, finally, the point that he admits in *Digraphe 8*:

> If the deconstruction of institutional structures . . . if this
> immediately political deconstruction is indispensable, then we must
> take into account certain gaps and try to reduce them, *even if for*
> *essential reasons it is impossible to efface them*: for example, between the
> discourses and practice of this immediately political deconstruction

and a deconstruction with a theoretical and philosophical aspect. These gaps are sometimes so great that they dissimulate the relays or render them, for many, unrecognizable.[41]

If for Derrida the impossibility of effacing the gap between a theoretical and a political deconstruction produces a disturbing double bind, it is this abyssal gap and the "uncanniness" it instigates that his American followers have sanguinely (rhetorically) affirmed. In their hands, deconstruction has become, in practice if not in theory, *theory*: a negatively transcendent and visually oriented speculative method that observes the undecidable scene in the "theater" of *praxis* from a panoptic height. The word "theory," as Aristophanes reminded his audience by suspending the theoretical philosopher (Socrates) in a basket hovering above the rout (*The Clouds*), comes from the Greek *theoria* (contemplation, speculation, sight), which itself derives from *theoros* (spectator) and further back, from *thea* (sight) and *theasthai* (look upon),[42] all of which have their ultimate source, perhaps, in *theos*, the omniscient and always hidden deity who looks down indifferently on the totality of an emergent *physis*—all at once, or spatially—from the separated and distanced vantage point of the sky. Put this way, one cannot but be reminded of the image of the author represented by Stephen Dedalus and, whatever Joyce's intention, appropriated and privileged by the Anglo-American Modernists, above all, by the New Critics. I mean the impersonal and ruthlessly authoritarian omniscient (metaphysical) author who brings the development of Occidental literary structure to its generic end in the recuperated purity of the "spatial form" of *rendered* drama:

> The personality of the artist, at first a cry or cadence or a mood [the lyric] and then a fluid and lambent narrative [the epic], finally refines itself out of existence, impersonalises itself, so to speak. The esthetic image in the dramatic form is life purified in and reprojected from the human imagination. The mystery of esthetic like that of material creation is accomplished. The artist, like the God of the creation, remains within or behind or beyond or above his handiwork, invisible, refined out of existence, indifferent, paring his fingernails.[43]

The negative image of the deconstructive critic and his or her look suggested by the etymology of "theory" is absolutely antithetical to the "grasping gaze" of Dedalus, the New Critics, and their philosophical (Kantian) and theological (Aquinian) precursors. For that very reason, however, it is absolutely the same.

For Heidegger, it will be recalled, the destruction is intended to retrieve (*wiederholen*) the question of being (or rather, as I shall presently insist, of be-*ing*) from the oblivion to which sclerotic metaphysical

thinking has, in its retrospection, relegated it. The purpose of this retrieval is, as Heidegger reiterates in *Being and Time*, to "free" human
being—"especially . . . that [ontological] understanding (and its possible
development) which is rooted in the proper Being of Dasein"—from the
"world in which it is": the "tradition" (the historically various supplementary semiotic systems inscribed in the cultural memory) in which it
is (always already) "ensnared."[44] In privileging a visually oriented epistemology that perceives *meta-ta-physika* from after or above things-as-
they-are (*physis as* "e-mergence"),[45] this tradition spatializes or reifies the
radical temporality of being by "over-looking" the differences it disseminates in favor of its essential figure. It reduces a primordially temporal
(originative) mode of inquiry—as always already *dis-covering* or *dis-closing*
(*a-letheia*)—to a secondary or derivative method. Under its aegis, inquiry
becomes theoretical: a distanced, authoritative, and super-visory activity
of confirmation that "deprives Dasein of its leadership in questioning
and choosing."[46] To appropriate Foucault's archeological rhetoric, the
tradition becomes an *arch*ive that exists, as the etymology suggests, to
re-form *Dasein*'s essentially errant being-in-the-world in the glaring light
emanating from a hidden absolute origin, a first (and last) Word beyond
the reach of the free play of criticism.

Admittedly, Heidegger's discourse was focused too insistently on the
ontological implications of this "ontotheological" tradition. And when
he did intervene at the site of sociopolitics it was to align his discourse
with a certain reactionary politics, if not, as it is too crudely represented
by his humanist critics, the historically specific German National Socialism. This is not the appropriate place to enter the debate over Heidegger's politics precipitated by the publication of Victor Farías's biograph-
ically determined study of Heidegger's affiliation with Nazism. This
extremely complex question will be addressed at length in chapter 6. It
will have to suffice for this context to suggest, too summarily, that Heidegger's failure to fulfill the practical (sociopolitical) emancipatory imperatives of his destructive ontological project in the context of his own
historically specific occasion—to make thinking overtly a *critical* theory,
as it were—had in some fundamental sense to do with a resistance to
thinking the forgetting or, conversely, the thought of retrieval, to its
"end."[47] More specifically, it could be attributed to a combination of his
vestigial nostalgic loyalty to the separation of *theoria* and *praxis* inscribed
by the Socratics into the philosophical tradition and an unexamined nationalism that reinscribed, *against his destructive discourse*, the principle of
ethnic (*not* racial) identity. Whatever the source, it is possible to claim
that this failure (or, to read his practice during the period of the Third
Reich in its worst light, this misrepresentation of his sociopolitical occasion) was more complex and shorter lived than it is now being repre-

sented by his humanist critics. As his destruction of the official National Socialist version of Nietzsche in the Nietzsche lectures (1937 and 1939–41) and of his own adherence to National Socialism in the *Parmenides* lectures (winter semester 1942-43) suggest, it is possible to claim that his apparent intellectual complicity with Nazism after his resignation of the rectorate was the result of a disabling tension precipitated by the historical occasion: between the political circumstances in which he was teaching and writing (circumstances that demanded an indirect rather than overt confrontation of the brutal excesses of the Nazi regime), on the one hand, and his abiding and overdetermined commitment to the critique of Western technological imperialism, on the other. To read Heidegger's texts after the brief period of the rectorship (April 1933-February 1934) in the "light" of the accomplished enormities of the Nazis would terminate in the repression of the voice of one of the greatest thinkers in the history of Western philosophy. More important, it would constitute a tacit acknowledgment and confirmation of the Western metaphysical tradition: the tradition, according to Heidegger's essential thought, that has come to its end in the globalization of *Technik*. It would, in short, tacitly reprieve the West's essential complicity in the making of the Nazi machine and the horrors it perpetrated.

This is not intended to apologize for Heidegger's practice in behalf of Nazism, nor for his silence in the postwar period about the extermination of the Jews. These commissions and omissions are not finally rationalizable. Rather, it is intended to counter the effort of his present humanist critics—and the inadvertent support they have received from some quarters of the oppositional intellectual community (poststructuralists, neo-Marxists, feminists)—to delegitimate not simply Heidegger's "anti-humanist" thought but also the posthumanist thought it has enabled by way of appealing to biographical anecdote rather than to the texts he actually wrote.

Above all, it must not be overlooked, as both his critics as well as too many of his admirers have done, that Heidegger's ontologically situated destruction of the Western philosophical tradition, especially of the anthropologos and its modern allotrope technology, and its "devastation of language,"[48] can be—indeed, has been transcoded—into a profound interrogation of the Eurocentric and hegemonic/imperial implications of the technological superstructure of modern democratic/capitalistic societies. However limited as such by its generalized ontological focus, Heidegger's interrogation has become acutely essential to an oppositional discourse that would counter the prevailing representation of contemporary Western history in the aftermath of the "end" of the Cold War. I mean the representation that grossly mystifies the epochal events of 1989 in Central and Eastern Europe as the "fall of socialism" or, conversely, the "triumph of the principles of democracy," which projects these events narrationally as the "end of history" or, alternatively, as the advent of a "new world order" presided over by the spirit of the "free subject."

In leveling language, in emptying it of its ontological content in the name of enlightenment, this technological "end" of Western philosophy, according to Heidegger, has also reduced thinking to representation/ calculation (*Vorstellung*). It has become a global disciplinary cybernetic instrument positively capable of "enframing" being. In its violent leveling of the difference that temporality disseminates, it has, in fact, rendered our time the "age of the world picture" (*Weltbild*).[49] In turn, this disciplinary spatialization of time (and its "regulated-regulating" institutional agencies of global transmission) undertaken in the name of (Western) Man threatens to level *physis* (the emergent dynamics of being), including human being—not only men and women in the Occident but men and women beyond its geographical circumference—into an indifferent and thus purely docile and useful "standing reserve" (*Bestand*):

> This science [cybernetics, from *kybernetes*, "steerer"] corresponds to the determination of man as an acting social being. For it is the theory of the steering of the possible planning and arrangement of human labor. Cybernetics transforms language into an exchange of news. The arts become regulated-regulating instruments of information. . . .
>
> The sciences are now taking over as their own task what philosophy in the course of history tried to present in part, and even these only inadequately, that is, the ontologies of the various regions of beings (nature, history, law, art). The interest of the sciences is directed toward the theory of the necessary structural concepts of the coordinated areas of investigation. "Theory" means now: supposition of the categories which are allowed only a cybernetic function, but denied any ontological meaning. The operational model character of representational calculative thinking becomes dominant. . . .
>
> The end of philosophy [in cybernetics] proves to be the triumph of the manipulable arrangement of a scientific-technological world *and of the social order proper to this world.* The end of philosophy means: *the beginning of the world civilization based upon Western European thinking.*[50]

Understood in terms of its resonant disclosure of the imperial dynamics informing the logic of modernity ("the end of philosophy"), Heidegger's destruction comes, in fact, to bear a striking resemblance to Foucault's and Said's more "political" critical genealogies. However more abstract (ontological), his disclosure of the filial complicity between anthropological inquiry and the planetary technology/cybernetics of European modernity parallels Foucault's disclosure of the disciplinary panopticism inscribed in the structure of modern Western (humanist) societies and Said's disclosure of the will to cultural dominance inscribed in the Occidental archival discourse he calls "Orientalism":

> Taking the late eighteenth century as a very roughly defined starting point Orientalism can be discussed and analyzed as the corporate institution for dealing with the Orient—dealing with it by making statements about it, authorizing views of it, describing it, by teaching it, settling it, ruling over it: in short, Orientalism as a Western style for dominating, restructuring, and having authority over the Orient. . . . My contention is that without examining Orientalism as a discourse one cannot possibly understand the enormously systematic discipline by which European culture was able to manage—and even produce—the Orient politically, sociologically, militarily, ideologically, scientifically, and imaginatively during the post-Enlightenment period.[51]

However unrealized in Heidegger's practice, the destruction or disclosure of the metaphysical, or specifically, the anthropological circle is informed by the theoretical imperative to activate an opening of the horizon of understanding—in Gadamer's terms, of understanding to horizonality,[52] to include the "worldliness" of the world: the indissoluble relationality of the sites of being. It is essentially informed by the imperative to liberate the awareness or the remembrance that the prison house of the logocentric archive exists to confine and subdue not only at the site of philosophy (metaphysical thought per se), but, because language is the house of being, all along its indissoluble continuum from language through culture to sociopolitics.[53] The destruction is not, therefore, a nihilistic activity of thought, whether that of metaphysics or a certain deconstruction, that neutralizes its active emancipatory force by leveling difference to one or another form of identity. Rather, it is paradoxically a positive or pro-jective interpretive activity in which thinking (*theoria*) *is* doing-in-the-world (*praxis*). It is a "self"-activity or *praxis* that always already *destroys* the reified determinations (the re-presentations) inscribed in the subject by metaphysics (and its linguistic, cultural, and political elaborations) and simultaneously *discloses* the understanding's radical and multisituated temporality. If *Dasein* as being-in-the-world is inscribed— is never "presuppositionless," as Heidegger everywhere acknowledges— it is also ek-static: temporality is, as it were, always already an absent cause. The measure of Heidegger's "proper self" (*Eigentlichkeit*) is not the measure of full presence, but of its own (historical) occasion. The disclosure of the "origins of the fundamental ontological concepts," we should recall, "has nothing to do with a pernicious relativizing of ontological standpoints. The destruction has just as little the *negative* sense of disburdening ourselves of the ontological tradition. On the contrary, it should stake out the positive possibilities of the tradition. Negatively, the destruction is not even related to the past: its criticism concerns 'today' and the dominant way we read the history of ontology, whether it is conceived as the history of opinions, ideas, or problems. However, the destruction does not wish to bury the past in nullity; it has a *positive* intent. Its negative function remains tacit and indirect."

Thus understood as a retrieval or remembering of the radical temporality of *Dasein*'s occasion that a recollective or archival metaphysics forgets, the Heideggerian *Destruktion* becomes a historical/dialogic (not dialectic) activity: an *Auseinandersetzung*, which, as its etymology suggests, is simultaneously and *always* (interminably) destructive and projective. Like Foucault's and Said's genealogical projects, it activates critical consciousness of ideology: the " 'representation' of the imaginary relationship of individuals to the real conditions of their existence,"[54] if one takes Althusser's resonant definition to mean the recognition of and resistance to the relay of power that, however asymmetrically, traverses the ontological, cultural, and sociopolitical sites on the continuum of being as that continuum has been discursively represented and realized in the "benign" historically specific *epistemes* successively elaborated by the supplementary centered metaphorics of the ontotheological tradition. In destroying (destructuring) the intended totalized structures and the circular geo-metries of these panoptic discourses, however, the destruction also discloses, activates, and energizes "self"-activity, a will to *praxis* that is not a commanding. In breaching any of the various panoptically inscribed structures of the ontotheological tradition, the destruction thematizes the ontological difference: opens up and remembers the forgotten question of being as it was originally posed: as a question of the (temporal) *be-ing* of being.

This "step back," which is intended to retrieve the question of being as the question of the be-*ing* of being, is the essential gesture of Heidegger's destructive hermeneutics, despite his failure to clearly elaborate and practice its worldly implications. It thus needs to be retrieved from the oblivion to which it has been relegated in the wake of the deconstructive turn. For in representing Heidegger's phenomenological retrieval of the *Seinsfrage* as a recuperation in the last instance of a philosophy of presence or re-presentation, Derrida (among others) has, however unwittingly, authorized his belated American followers to identify Heidegger's discourse with the "speech" privileged by the ontotheological tradition, and thus to render the reading of Heidegger's texts superfluous, and, above all, to institutionalize an extremely narrow representation of difference as pure textuality. It has also, not incidentally, abetted those humanists who would discredit Heidegger's thought by identifying his invocation of "Being" with the *Führerprinzip*.

An example of this curious oversight on Derrida's part comes ready to hand in an important early essay, "The Ends of Man" ("Les fins de l'homme"), that Derrida delivered in the United States in October 1968 before an international philosophical congress on "Philosophy and Anthropology."[55] In this essay, Derrida mounts a massive inaugural critique of Heidegger's phenomenological hermeneutics, a critique that focuses on what he takes to be Heidegger's logocentric commitment, however vestigial, to the "concept of proximity" inscribed in his "existential analytic" of *Dasein*, the agency of retrieving the question of being. According to Derrida:

> It is in the play of a certain proximity, proximity to oneself and proximity to Being, that we shall see constituted, against metaphysical humanism and anthropologism, another insistence of man, one which relays, relieves, supplements that which it destroys, along pathways on which we are, from which we have hardly emerged—perhaps—and which remain to be examined.[56]

Derrida's critique of Heidegger's "recuperative" phenomenology of representation is complex and cannot be fully developed in this limited space. It is also just, insofar as he thematizes a tendency in Heidegger's discourse that seems to reaffirm the *anthropologos* by reinscribing the Hegelian *Aufhebung* (*relève*): by sublating the contradiction he has exposed in the discourse of humanism. Nevertheless, two related and characteristic passages from his text, which articulate the essence of Derrida's reiterated reservations about Heidegger's destructive hermeneutics, will perhaps suffice to suggest my point about its problematic deflection of the critique of anthropologism away from temporality to textuality:

> The analytic of *Dasein*, as well as the thinking which, beyond the *Kehre*, will pursue the question of Being, will maintain itself in the space which separates and relates to one another such a proximity and such a distance. The *Da* of *Dasein* [here] and the *Da* of the *Sein* [there] will signify as much the near as the far. Beyond the common closure of humanism and metaphysics, Heidegger's thought will be guided by the motif of Being as presence—understood in a more originary sense than it is in the metaphysical and ontic determinations of presence or of presence as the present—and by the motif of the proximity of Being to the essence of man. *Everything transpires as if one had to reduce the ontological distance* acknowledged in *Sein und Zeit* and to state the proximity of Being to the essence of man.[57]

And again, amplifying the critique of the Heideggerian representation:

> The restoration of the essence [of man] is also the restoration of a dignity and a proximity: the co-responding dignity of Being and man, the proximity of Being and of man. . . .
>   The ontological *distance from* Dasein *to what* Dasein *is as ek-sistence and to the* Da *of* Sein, *the distance that first was given as ontic proximity, must be reduced by the thinking of the truth of Being.* Whence, in Heidegger's discourse, the dominance of an entire metaphorics of proximity, of simple and immediate presence, a metaphorics associating the proximity of Being with the values of neighboring, shelter, house, service, guard, voice, and listening. As goes without saying, this is not an insignificant rhetoric; on the basis of both this metaphorics and the thinking of the ontico-ontological difference, one could even make explicit an entire theory of metaphoricity in general.[58]

This is an acute observation that points to what is sociopolitically disabling in Heidegger's discourse vis-à-vis being. But it is an observation that must be read in the context of Derrida's primary purpose. It emphasizes Heidegger's representation of the ontological difference (the "concept of proximity") which will justify Derrida's substitution of the difference of "writing in general" for the difference of temporality. As such, it is an emphasis that has led his American followers—and other poststructuralists—prematurely to bypass Heidegger's discourse as finally an overcome logocentrism, and more important, to institutionalize a form of deconstruction that privileges *differance* over the ontological difference, the temporality of being and its disseminations; which is to say, a form of deconstruction that limits deconstruction to "literary" textuality: the printed words on a page.[59] What is significantly, and surprisingly, missing in this critique—and everywhere in Derrida's text where he accuses Heidegger's discourse of recuperating a philosophy of presence—is any reference to Heidegger's insistence in *Being and Time* on the *radical* and *irreducible* temporality—the be-*ing*—of Dasein and, by extension, of the *Sein* that this inaugural existential/hermeneutic analytic aims to bring out of concealment.

> In accord with the positive tendency of the destruction, the question must first be asked whether and to what extent in the course of the history of ontology in general the interpretation of Being has been thematically connected with the phenomenon of Time. We must also ask whether the range of problems concerning Temporality which necessarily belongs here was fundamentally worked out or could have been. Kant is the first and only one who traversed a stretch of the path toward investigating the dimension of Temporality—or

allowed himself to be driven there by the compelling force of the phenomena themselves. Only when the problem of Temporality is pinned down can we succeed in casting light on the obscurity of his doctrine of the schematism. Furthermore, in this way we can also show *why* this area had to remain closed to Kant in its real dimensions and in its central ontological function. . . . What it is that Kant shrank back from . . . must be brought to light thematically and in principle if the expression "Being" is to have a demonstrable meaning. Ultimately the phenomena to be explicated in the following analysis under the rubric "Temporality" are precisely those that determine the *most covert* judgments of "common reason," analysis of which Kant calls the "business of philosophers."[60]

What is also, in a related way, left unsaid in Derrida's critique—and here I am invoking "*Ousia* and *Grammé*," where Derrida *does* attempt to implicate Heidegger's understanding of temporality with Aristotle's and Hegel's teleological notion of time as line/circle[61]—is any reference to "the compelling force" of that which "drove" Kant towards "it," but which in the end he "shrank back from." Let us not, in the face of the deconstructionist cool, overlook the shudder that Heidegger attributes to his Enlightenment predecessor. For it is this "phenomenon"—this "non-concept," we might call it—that instigated Kant's shudder—and the supplemental philosophies of the ontotheological tradition that, in the process of annulling the anxiety "it" provoked, reified/technologized being and eventually forgot it *as a question*. I mean the *nothing* that Heidegger insistently acknowledges as the "origin" and "end" of temporality, the an-archic, uncanny (*unheimliche*), or groundless ground that activates the anxiety or dread (*Angst*) that, in having *no thing* as its object, in turn provokes the question of being:

> In anticipating the indefinite certainty of death, Dasein opens itself to a constant *threat* arising out of its own "there" [/"here"]. In this very threat Being-towards-the-end must maintain itself. So little can it tone this down that it must rather cultivate the indefiniteness of the certainty. How is it existentially possible for this constant threat to be genuinely disclosed? All understanding is accompanied by a state-of-mind [*Befindlichkeit*]. Dasein's mood brings it face to face with the thrownness of its "that it is there." *But the state-of-mind which can hold open the utter and constant threat to itself arising from Dasein's ownmost individualized Being, is anxiety.* In this state-of-mind, Dasein finds itself *face to face* with the "nothing" of the possible impossibility of its existence. Anxiety is anxious *about* the potentiality-for-Being of the entity so destined, and in this way it discloses the uttermost possibility.[62]

Understood as a temporality "grounded" in nothing, therefore, Heidegger's *Sein* does not mean, as Derrida says in "*Ousia* and *Grammé*," where he implicates "time in general" with "metaphysical conceptuality,"[63] an absolute and abiding origin or *telos*, a "now-point" that reinserts Heidegger's thought into the tradition extending from Aristotle to Hegel, that reifies time by way of the restricted economy of the *Aufhebung*. It does not signify an unfallen or primordial presence that, like the "soul" of the plot in Aristotle's schema in the *Poetics*, gathers up the other ekstasies of time, past and future, into a certain and cathartic permanent present. It is not, in Derrida's terms, a center or transcendental signified beyond the reach of free play that comprehends the essential difference of temporality into a line/circle, a dedifferentiated, re-presented, proper, determinate, and determinable identity and, in so doing, imposes the imperial peace that brings peace. As irreducibly temporal "being," Heidegger's *Sein* implies, rather, a permanent absence, or absenting, which does what Derrida says only writing can do. In "always already" (Heidegger's phrase, by the way) destroying presence, it always already disseminates being: disperses and defers what in the metaphysical tradition is taken to be eternal, identical, proper, and thus plenary—certain and graspable—into indeterminate and ineffable (uncanny) temporal difference. "The indeterminateness of that in the face of which and for which we become anxious [the nothingness of temporality]," according to Heidegger, "is no mere lack of determination but rather the essential impossibility of determining it."[64] As such, it activates anxiety (*Angst*) and care (*Sorge*), which is to say, the question of the be-*ing* of being. As temporal difference—as that which is the condition for the possibility of identity and not, as in the discourse of metaphysics, the other way around—*being as that which disseminates difference makes a difference.*

This, according to my reading—or mis-reading—of Heidegger's text, is in part the point of his reiteration of the ontological difference. In insistently "differentiating" between *Seiende* and *Sein*, entities and being, Heidegger's purpose is not, as Derrida implies in the passages quoted above and elsewhere, to point to the *spatial distance* between the ontic and the ontological that *Dasein* has totally to reduce in order to achieve authenticity (*Eigentlichkeit*: my-ownness), to become a truly "proper self." Indeed, Heidegger insistently refers to inquiry—the hermeneutic circle—not as a movement that would close the gap separating the ontic and ontological, but as a process that is *always already* ontic/ontological:

> Is there not . . . a definite ontical way of taking authentic existence,
> a factical ideal of Dasein, underlying our ontological Interpretation
> of Dasein's existence? That is so indeed. But not only is this Fact one
> which must not be denied and which we are forced to grant; it must
> also be conceived in its *positive necessity*, in terms of the object which

we have taken as the theme of our investigation. Philosophy will never seek to deny its "presuppositions," but neither may it simply admit them. It conceives them, and it unfolds with more and more penetration both the presuppositions themselves and that for which they are presuppositions. (BT, 358, SZ, 310)[65]

Heidegger's "distinction," rather, is intended to retrieve the play between the ontic and ontological annulled by the collapsing of the ontological *into* the ontic in and by the tradition that culminates in the humanist/technological "age of the world picture." In other words, it is intended to facilitate the destruction and demystification of the traditional metaphysical and, particularly, anthropomorphic spatialization or reification of being (*ousia*). I am referring to the Being that, whether as Unmoved Mover, the One, Presence, God, Telos, the Word, Causality, and so on, has in an increasingly hardening way guided (*super*vised) not only philosophical inquiry into the nature of being and humankind, but also (in the form of Form) of cultural production and interpretation ever since the Romans translated *aletheia* to *veritas*, or *pseudos* to *falsum*.

Heidegger insists on the ontological difference to disclose the now closed archival concept of Being-as-thing—the concept that has enabled knowledge as comprehension or "grasping" (*Begriff*)—to open out the in-terminable, differentiating, and uncanny free play of the temporality of be-ing, and the language that "refers" to it. Understood in this destroyed sense, as Derrida, in circumventing the question of the ungrounded temporality of being, apparently does not, Heidegger's destructive hermeneutic project to retrieve the *Seinsfrage* need not be interpreted as a recuperation of a philosophy of presence and an anthropology of self-presence, of the "proper self." The concept of "proximity" informing the existential analytic of *Being and Time* is not necessarily to be understood as a spatial metaphor involving the separation of objects. To bring into proximity need not mean to bring a distanced alienated presence into immediate presence, to "reduce the ontological distance from *Dasein* to what it is as eksistence and the *Da* [the there] of *Sein*." "To bring being near" could mean, as I read Heidegger's text, the activation of the reified "self." It could, that is, mean *to activate awareness*, against an inscribed (ontic) understanding of being as always present Thing (*Summum Ens*), of the always already absent/absenting presence (what Derrida calls "the trace") within the ontic, of the groundless being of being, and above all, of the difference that its always deferring temporal "essence" (this now has to be put under erasure) disseminates. I do not mean difference as such, but the difference that *makes a difference* to *Dasein* as being-in-the-world. To put this in terms of Barbara Johnson's rhetoric, the "surprise" she insists on as that which the deconstructive project must always already precipitate as its "end"—this being overtaken by that which the exegete would take over (comprehend), this unexpected reversal of the inscribed narrative of knowledge production as mastery—is an existential/temporal structure of which the *differance* of textuality is but one in a relay of manifestations.

Despite his acknowledgment of Heidegger's solicitation of the question of Man, Derrida finally implicates Heidegger's discourse at large with metaphysics on the basis of his insistence on the proximity of *Dasein* to itself and, because of its privileged status vis-à-vis the *Seinsfrage*, to being. More specifically, the concept of proximity in *Being and Time* and other texts justifies Derrida's identification of Heidegger's destruction with "a hermeneutics of unveiling," with a mode of inquiry that, as the very etymology of the word "phenomenology" suggests, takes as literal the constellation of metaphors radiating from the central and centralizing "eye" of the subject's mind (including geometrics and archeology/genealogy, i.e., emergence-and-descent), the eye that has determined the discourse of truth throughout the logocentric tradition:

> Doubtless this proximity, this identity or self-presence of the "entity that we are"—of the inquirer and of the interrogated—does not have the form of subjective consciousness, as in transcendental phenomenology. Doubtless too, this proximity is still prior to what the metaphysical predicate "human" might name. The *Da-* of *Dasein* can be determined as a coming presence only on the basis of a rereading of the question of Being which summons it up. Nevertheless, the process of disengaging or of elaborating the question of Being, as a question of the *meaning* of Being, is defined as a *making explicit* or as an interpretation that makes explicit. The reading of the text *Dasein* is a hermeneutics of unveiling or of development. . . . If one looks closely, it is the phenomenological opposition "implicit/explicit" that permits Heidegger to reject the objection of the vicious circle, the circle that consists of first determining a being in its Being, and then of posing the question of Being on the basis of this ontological predetermination. . . . This style of a reading which makes explicit, practices a continual bringing to light, something which resembles, at least, a coming into consciousness, without break, displacement, or change of terrain.[66]

The force of Derrida's argument seems irresistible, until one notices the slippage in the appositive structure in the first sentence of the passage, which identifies "proximity" with "identity" and "self-presence." As I have suggested, the words in Heidegger's texts that Derrida represents as "proximity" (as well as "proximity" itself) do not mean "identity." They mean, rather, "nearness."[67] What, then, accounts for this insistently uncharacteristic slippage in Derrida's rigorously articulated discourse? Is it that Derrida's problematic compels him to overlook or repress what, in Heidegger's discourse, would disrupt his rigorous *reading* as such, a reading that would legitimate a textual understanding of difference? More important, in overlooking or repressing the temporality that always already precipitates the difference that makes a difference (to *Dasein*), doesn't Derrida, despite his intentions, pave the way for a determination of difference in which difference manifests itself as an indifferent difference? And thus the domestication of the "surprise of otherness," of "ignorance"?

Similarly, one can, by extension, read Heidegger's "phenomenology" (and the "whole metaphorics of proximity"—"neighborhood, shelter, house, service, guard, voice and listening"—to which, as Derrida has observed, it gives rise) in this destroyed sense.[68] For Derrida, of course, Heidegger's phenomenology is in the last instance continuous with Husserl's. Insofar as it privileges the "authentic" (*eigentliche*) voice/speech that, as "*s'entendre parler*," brings presence to light against the "secondarity" or "fallenness" of writing, it betrays the complicity with logocentrism that disables Husserl's phenomenology. If, however, the metaphorics of the *phoné/phos* that determine Heidegger's discourse are understood in their erased sense—and it is, as I have observed, surprising that one as acutely attuned to textual erasure as Derrida should render Heidegger's text representationally ("mimetologically")—Heidegger's phenomenology cannot finally be taken as a "photology" in the sense that it privileges *theory*: an *all*-seeing and grasping (panoptic), *all*-speaking eye/voice that is beyond the reach of free play. It could just as well be understood as a situated *horizonal* eye/voice that sees/speaks/hears, not *the* Same/*the* Word, but difference/words, whose measure is the always uncanny (*unheimliche*) measure of *Dasein*'s radically finite and errant being-in-the-world, of the groundless beginning- and end-less temporality that is its occasion. "The nature of language," Heidegger says, "does not exhaust itself in signifying, nor is it merely something that has the character of sign or cipher."[69] A word "does not and never can re-present anything: but signifies something, that is, shows something as abiding into the range of its expressibility."[70] As the scientist in the "Conversation on a Country Path" puts it in the process of thinking the essence of thinking, "I tried to release myself of all re-presenting, because waiting moves into openness without re-presenting anything. And, released from re-presenting, I tried to release myself purely to that-which-regions *because that-which-regions is the opening of openness*."[71] In short, Heidegger's phenomenology is not a methodology of re-presentation grounded in a concept of truth as adequation, but an activity of *aletheia*, precipitated by the existential experience of truth as errancy, an *always already* (not once and for all) bringing out of hiddenness of that which, because it is inextricably temporal, *always already* (not once and for all) conceals itself. And what I have said about phenomenology as such applies as well to the metaphorics of light embedded in the term and the discourse it elaborates.

This "occasioning" occasionality[72] is not restricted to *Being and Time*. It is the case after the *Kehre*, which most commentators, including Derrida, interpret as Heidegger's abandonment, after *Being and Time*, of the question of temporality in favor of an explicit commitment to the nostalgic historical (and politically reactionary) quest for the epochal Being of metaphysics.[73] Although his discourse, as Derrida rightly observes, focuses more and more on the question of the epochality of being at the expense of the theme of temporality, it is still the unrepresentable temporality—the differential dynamics—of being that is, now implicitly, at stake in and the measure of Heidegger's later discourse. This is suggested in part (and in a way that contradicts Derrida's spatialization of Heidegger's "proximity") by his insistent evocation of the occasioning "rift" between world and earth that it is the imperative of language as *poiesis* to always instigate and preserve:

> In setting up a world and setting forth the earth, the work [of art] is an instigating of this striving. This does not happen so that the work should at the same time settle and put an end to the conflict in an insipid agreement, but so that the strife *may remain* a strife. Setting up a world and setting forth the earth, the work accomplishes this striving. The work-being of the work consists in the fighting of the battle between world and earth.[74]

It is also suggested by Heidegger's reiterated critique of language as technological/cybernetic instrument of representation that brings philosophy to its totalized closure—and end—in the "enframement" (*Gestell*) of being or, alternatively, in the reduction of the modern occasion to the "age of the world picture." For the age of the world picture is precisely an age that, in totalizing representation, has bridged the rift between world and earth (*Welt* and *Erde*), the distance between the here of *Dasein* and the there of *Sein*. In accomplishing the spatialization, the "enframement," of time, it has also accomplished the detemporalization of the being—the disruptive and differentiating temporality—of being and thus the subjection of the ineffable mystery of the earth (*die Erde*) to mastery:

> "We get the picture" concerning something does not mean only that what is, is set before us, is represented to us, in general, but that what is stands before us—in all that belongs to it and all that stands together in it—as a system. "To get the picture" throbs with being acquainted with something, with being equipped and prepared for it. Where the world becomes picture, what is, in its entirety, is

juxtaposed as that for which man is prepared and which, correspondingly, he therefore intends to bring before himself and have before himself, and consequently intends in a decisive sense to set in place before himself. Hence world picture, when understood essentially, does not mean a picture of the world, *but the world conceived and grasped as picture.* What is, in its entirety, is now taken in such a way that it first is in being and only is in being to the extent that it is set up by man, who represents and sets forth. Whenever we have the world picture, an essential decision takes place regarding what is, in its entirety. The Being of whatever is, is sought and found in the representedness of the latter.[75]

Being and time in Heidegger's discourse at large are not incommensurable horizons. They are relational. The difference between the discourse of *Being and Time* and the discourse after the so-called *Kehre* is a matter, not of a separation and a rejection, but of a refiguring of emphasis of the terms in the relationship. If in *Being and Time* Heidegger dwelled on the project of retrieving the temporality of being from metaphysical Being, in post-*Kehre* essays such as "The Origin of the Work of Art" or "The Age of the World Picture" or "The Question Concerning Technology" or "Discourse on Thinking," he dwells on the epochal representations of Being (especially that of the anthropological post-Enlightenment) and the institutional agencies that were devised to annul the dislocating force of temporality.

In retrieving the *Seinsfrage*—the "original experience on which the first and subsequently guiding determinations of Being were gained"— the Heideggerian destruction retrieves, not the centeredness, but the eccentricity, the ex-orbitance or, in Heidegger's preferred term, the errancy of being understood in its temporal modality: the be-ing that always already precipitates care or interest, the awareness of the difference that difference makes. If this is a recuperation of humanism, as Derrida claims, it is a humanism put under erasure. It is a disappropriated humanism. It is a humanism that both divests "Central Man" of his "proper" and "proprietary" authority—of the empowering anthropologos—and enables "him" to act in the world.

IV

The destruction of the metaphorics of circularity inscribed in the canonical texts of the tradition retrieves the idea of language as the "house of being." This does not mean, as it is frequently assumed, the recuperation of an at-home from the not-at-home (*die Unheimliche*): a house ruled by the sovereign word. Heidegger's discourse, especially his analysis of the enabling "equiprimordiality" of *Befindlichkeit* (the *Dasein*'s occasion), *Verstehen* (*Dasein*'s understanding), and *Rede* (*Dasein*'s discourse),[76] demands a reading of this notorious phrase that puts it under erasure. In retrieving the differential be-*ing* of being from the metaphysical tradition, the destruction also retrieves the idea of language as word*s*—as, that is, a temporal deferring/differentiating medium—from what Kierkegaard, in his *Auseinandersetzung* with Hegel, calls the re-collective tradition of the archival Word. Which is to say, with Nietzsche, from the prison house of metaphysical discourse. Thus destroyed, this problematic metaphorical phrase—language as "the house of being"—discloses a function of textual interpretation quite different from what both his followers and critics attribute to Heidegger. On the one hand, it activates the possibility of exposing and defusing the panoptic power and authority not simply of metaphysical discourse at large, but also, as I will show more fully in the next chapter, the affiliated semiotic elaborations of what I will call provisionally a "Roman" civil and political society grounded in the geo-metry of a logocentric measure. I mean precisely those "disciplinary" and "imperial" cultural and sociopolitical formations that are the objects of the critical genealogy of Foucault or Said, among others. On the other hand, it retrieves the possibility of a postmodern or, more specifically posthumanist discourse the measure of which is the measure of *Gelassenheit*, a measure that, at home in the not-at-home (*unheimliche Welt*), lets the endless be-ing of being be. In the poet Robert Creeley's resonant phrase, the measure retrieved by the destruction is "the measure of its occasion": a measure not of (anthropo-)logocentric mastery but of negative capability.

As I have said elsewhere,[77] the meaning of a measure that is "the measure of its occasion" is implicit in the etymology of the word "occasion," immediately from *occasus* ("to fall," "to drop," as in the setting of the sun; and "to fall," "to perish," "to die," as in *de casibus virorum illustrium*: "of the fall of great men"). An interpretive activity that is the measure of its occasion, that is, is not a constraining, masterful, and transcendent "geometry" having its ultimate model in the Platonic *mousiki* (of the spheres). It is not, to appropriate Yeats's Modernist (and "Orientalist") rhetoric in "Sailing to Byzantium," the "oriental" measure of a golden bird singing "of what is past, passing, or to come" from the infinitely negative distance of eternity. It is the measure of "Those dying generations / at their song": a measure that acknowledges human beings' "mortal dress" as the case. It is the falling measure, the *cadence* of finite being-in-the-world, of *Dasein* (being here/there) "caught" in what passes: in the domain of the not-at-home (*Unheimlichkeit*), of *accident*, of *incident*, of *coincidence*.[78] It is the decentered or ec-centric measure of mortality, of dwelling in the rift between the world and the earth. It is finally (if, like Nietzsche and Foucault, we carnivalize the binary opposition between West and East that has served both to validate the West's identity and justify its domination of the East) a "westerning" measure. For another etymological source of "occasion" is, of course, the cognate *occidere* (which means "to fall," especially "to set"; and "to die, to perish") from the present participle of which (*occidens*) the English word "Occident" comes.[79] This resonance, not incidentally, is, as Heidegger frequently indicates, more overt in the German *Abendland*.

Understood in its destroyed sense, language as the house of being opens up a diacritical discourse, a "westerning" *poiesis* free of its ethnocentric determination, and negatively capable of rewriting and rebuilding the *polis* on the groundless ground of a differential measure. I mean a measure that allows men and women to "dwell poetically": not in the "proximity of Being," where difference is, in the last instance, gathered up into the "we" of (Occidental) Mankind, but in the rift occasioned by the strife that temporality always already activates between world and earth. The "gathering" or "housing" of dispersion *which simultaneously resists structuration and lets the difference that temporality disseminates be*, which precipitates *Auseinandersetzung*: this renewed possibility of language is finally the occasional *witness* (as opposed to the panoptic prophecy of super-vision inscribed in the mastering discourse of logocentrism) of Heidegger's texts at large.

> To write poetry is measure-taking, understood in the strict sense of the word, by which man first receives the measure for the breadth of his being. Man exists as a mortal, he is called mortal because he can die. To be able to die means: to be capable of death as death. Only man dies—and indeed continually as long as he stays on this earth, so long as he dwells. His dwelling, however, rests in the poetic. . . . The nature of the "poetic" [is seen] in the taking of the measure by which the measure-taking of human being is accomplished. . . . A strange measure [this measure that transforms man as a measure into the measure of man], perplexing it would seem to the common notion of mortals, inconvenient to the cheap omniscience of everyday opinion, which likes to claim that it is the standard for all thinking and reflection. . . . A strange measure for ordinary and in particular also for all merely scientific ideas, certainly not a palpable stick or rod [note the identity of calculative measure and power] but in truth simpler to handle than they, provided our hands do not abruptly grasp but are guided by gestures befitting the measure here to be taken. This is done by a taking which at no time clutches at the standard but rather takes in a concentrated perception, a gathered taking-in, that remains a listening.[80]

This renewed possibility of language, not incidentally, is also, I would argue against Fredric Jameson's identification of (dis)seminal postmodernism at large with "the logic of late capitalism,"[81] the occasional witness of the postmodern artist. William Carlos Williams, for example, would rewrite and rebuild Paterson on the *groundless* ground—the divisions—of a renewed measure:

> Without invention nothing is well spaced,
> unless the mind change, unless
> the stars are new measured, according
> to their relative positions, the
> line will not change, the necessity
> will not matriculate: unless there is
> a new mind there cannot be a new
> line, the old will go on
> repeating itself with recurring
> deadliness: without invention
> nothing lies under the witch-hazel
> bush, the alder does not grow from among
> the hummocks margining the all
> but spent channel of the old swale,
> the small foot-prints
> of the mice under the overhanging
> tufts of the bunch-grass will not
> appear; without invention the line
> will never again take on its ancient
> divisions when the word, a supple word
> lived in it, crumbled now to chalk.[82]

And Charles Olson would destroy the regulative representational measure of an archival humanism and the dedifferentiated—and indifferent—"pejorocracy" it has elaborated in behalf of a renewed *polis* ("Gloucester") founded on the groundless ground of "the old measure of care."[83]

Despite Heidegger's interrogation of "the limit that has always constrained us, that always constrains us—we who inhabit a language and a system of thought—to form the sense of being in general as presence or absence, in the categories of being or beingness (*ousia*),"[84] his insistence on the "ontic-ontological difference," according to Derrida, betrays his nostalgia for a lost Origin. This, he claims, is because Heidegger grounds the difference in the self-present voice, the *phoné*, which, as simultaneous hearing/understanding (*s'entendre*), brings being into proximity with the speaking self. Derrida thus revises Heidegger's text by appropriating Saussure's semiotic analysis of the inaudible difference of writing ("in general"). Saussure, he says in his influential essay "Differance," had only to remind us that the play of difference was the functional condition, the condition of possibility, for every sign; and it is itself silent. The difference between two phonemes, which enables them to exist and to operate, is inaudible. The inaudible opens the two present phonemes to hearing, as they present themselves. If, then, there is no purely phonetic writing, it is because there is no purely phonetic phone. The difference that brings out phonemes and lts them be heard and understood [*entendre*] itself remains inaudible.[85]

And again:

It was Saussure who first of all set forth the *arbitrariness of signs* and the *differential character* of signs as principles of general semiology and particularly of linguistics. And, as we know, these two themes—the arbitrary and the differential—are in his view inseparable. Arbitrariness can occur only because the system of signs is constituted by the differences between the terms, and not by their fullness. The elements of signification function not by virtue of the compact force of their cores but by the network of oppositions that distinguish them and relate them to one another. "Arbitrary and differential" says Saussure "are two correlative qualities."[86]

Derrida insists repeatedly that *differance* is a "non-concept": "Such a play [of differences], then—differance—is no longer simply a concept, but the possibility of conceptuality. . . . For the same reason, differance, which is not a concept, is not a mere word; that is, it is not what we represent to ourselves as the calm and present self-referential unity of a concept and sound [*phonie*]."[87] As its differentiating/deferring dynamics suggest, *differance* is ultimately temporal. Nevertheless, Derrida's appropriation of Saussure's assertion that "in language there are only differences *without positive terms*" in effect translates the temporal difference that Heidegger locates in material being (understood as an indissoluble lateral continuum between the ontological and sociopolitical occasions of human being) into a transcendental/universal that operates in the free-floating, leveled-out space of textuality. In this tendency to restrict the application of the "non-concept" *differance* to textuality, Derrida enables, if he himself does not finally perform, the absolute separation of the differential—temporalizing and spacing—measure of language (speech and writing) from the world to which it putatively refers.

Derrida's *differance* "without positive terms" reveals its historically specific origins in the cultural and sociopolitical occasion leading up to and through the events of May 1968; in the hands of his American followers it is reduced to a methodology of reading that precludes the perception of the question of language as simultaneously and equiprimordially a question of temporal being. Thus limited to a nonreferential textuality, deconstruction must eschew interpretation (what it pejoratively calls "hermeneutics") in favor of an ironic or self-reflexive comportment that observes and delights in the "spectacle" of the undecidable play occurring simultaneously throughout history, which is to say, universally: no*where*/no *time*. This metamorphosis of language as positive material *praxis* into free-floating theatrical performance and of the dialogic reader into spectator suggests that deconstruction understands the dismantling process, not as an opening up, a releasement (or decolonization) of the radical temporality of being that metaphysical structuration closes off and forgets, but an ironic remarking of the baselessness of canonical logocentric texts everywhere and every time in history. Guided by such a metaphorics of theatricality, the deconstructive criticism of Derrida's American followers, especially those who have appropriated deconstruction for literary criticism, becomes in essence a negative, indeed, a deterministic nihilist critical movement. The deconstructive gesture remembers the "dangerous" supplementarity and thus the duplicity, the absolute undecidability, of "writing in general," *but it is blinded by its oversight both to the worldliness of the text under scrutiny and to the positive, the pro-jective, that is, worldly possibilities it dis-closes*: to that which, despite the admittedly significant limitations of Heidegger's own discursive practice, the Heideggerian destruction enables.

Although deconstruction as it is practiced in North America calls into question the privileged status of the dominant (post-Enlightenment) philosophical discourse and its metaphorics of presence or center and light, its ironic "liberation" of the reader from the prison house of metaphysical language—what Nietzsche called the nihilism of teleological seriousness—reincarcerates him/her in the prison house of an essentially similar, violently leveled, nihilistic space. After all, the Daedalean labyrinth that Derrida appropriates in *Glas* to characterize and celebrate the scattered center of "the scene of writing"[88] was a prison designed by Daedalus to contain the Minotaur who would destroy the disciplinary city of anthropomorphic Man.

At best, as in Derrida, deconstruction calls into question the dominant anthropological institutional discursive practices of the contemporary occasion and activates the Nietzschean affirmation: "the joyous affirmation of the play of the world and of the innocence of becoming, the affirmation of a world of signs without fault, without truth, and without origin which is offered to an active interpretation. *This affirmation then determines the noncenter otherwise than as a loss of the center.* And it plays without security. For there is a *sure* play: that which is limited to the *substitution* of *given* and *existing, present,* pieces. In absolute chance, affirmation also surrenders itself to *genetic* indetermination, to the *seminal* adventure of the trace."[89]

At worst, however, as even the best practitioners of deconstruction have come to realize, it becomes a sterile textual game emptied of the awful existential/historical (genealogical) resonances of the Nietzschean affirmation of play. I mean emptied of the "self-activating" dread or anxiety in the face of the abyssal nothing that Heideggerian destruction identifies as *die Unheimlichkeit* or, on another related register, of those "actual intensities and creations of life," to which, according to Foucault's critical genealogy, the "suprahistorical" or "monumental" history of the humanist historians "bar[red] access."[90] In the hands of Derrida's belated American literary disciples—the institutional critics and teachers whom J. Hillis Miller curiously calls the "critics of uncanniness" to distinguish them from the "canny critics" (the structuralists, including the New Critics)[91]—deconstruction is reduced to purely formal, and quite comfortable observational exegesis of the aporetic "scene of writing." However brilliant the results, they all too often betray little, if any, awareness of the historically specific origins of deconstruction in the effort to expose the violence inherent in the discourse of humanist modernity. Nor do they reflect consciousness of the dislocating profundity of the abyss— the decentered and uncanny temporal realm of radical difference—over which Derrida's (and de Man's) pyrotechnical interpretive practice is willing to dance.

As such, this exegetical writing reminds us of a tradition of critical aestheticism that extends from the mannered interpretive ingenuity of the Alexandrian exegetes of the Old and New Testaments to the New Critics. Here, for example, is Miller's ironic and acutely witty observations on the abyssal ambiguities of the word "host" in his response to M. H. Abrams's and Wayne Booth's simplistic assertion that "the 'deconstructionist' reading of a given work 'is plainly and simply parasitical' on the obvious or univocal reading." I quote this representative passage of "explication" at some length to convey both its exegetical brilliance and its mannerism: its reduction of historicity to a methodical and free-floating play of verbal surfaces, what Fredric Jameson would rightly call postmodern and late capitalist "pastiche":

> If the host is both eater and eaten, he also contains in himself the double antithetical relation of host and guest, guest in the bifold sense of friendly presence and alien invader. The words "host" and "guest" go back in fact to the same etymological root: *ghos-ti*, stranger, guest, host, properly "someone with whom one has reciprocal duties of hospitality." The modern English word "host" in this alternative sense comes from the Middle English (*h*)*oste*, from Old French, host, guest, from Latin *hospes* (stem *hospit-*) guest, host, stranger. The "pes" or "pit" in the Latin words and in such modern English words as "hospital" and "hospitality" is from another root,

pot, meaning "master." The compound or bifurcated root *ghos-pot* meant "master of guests," "one who symbolizes the relationship of reciprocal hospitality," as in the Slavic *gospodi*, lord, sir, master. "Guest," on the other hand, is from Middle English *gest*, from Old Norse *gestr*, from *ghos-ti*, the same root as for "host." A host is a guest, and a guest is a host. A host is a host. The relation of household master offering hospitality to a guest and the guest receiving it, of host and parasite in the original sense of "fellow guests," is inclosed within "host" itself. . . . The uncanny antithetical relation exists not only between pairs of words in this system, host and parasite, host and guest, but within each word in itself. It reforms itself in each polar opposite when that opposite is separated out. This subverts or nullifies the apparently unequivocal relation of polarity which seems the conceptual scheme appropriate for thinking through the system. . . .[92]

The domestication of undecidability—the "uncanniness" of language (which for Heidegger and even Derrida and de Man means the dreadful not-at-homeness [*Unheimlichkeit*] of being-in-the-world as thrown) is self-evident in this passage. But what is equally important is that the aporias Miller ironically observes in the single word "host" are exactly (indifferently) and predictably the same aporias he ironically observes in all of Shelley's poetry, indeed, in all the texts he deconstructs. So, too, finally, is the rhetoric he uses to remark them. Thus, in summation of his exegesis of a number of passages from several poems in Shelley's oeuvre he writes:

All these projects fail at once. They fail in a way which *The Triumph of Life* makes clearest in showing that the conjunction of lovers, clouds, wave and shore, or words both destroys what it conjoins and always leaves a remainder. This genetic trace starts the cycle of lovemaking, attempts by the self to possess itself, self-destructive political tyranny, and poetry-writing all over again: Shelley's poetry is the record of a perpetually renewed failure. It is a failure ever to get the right formula and so end the separate incomplete self, end lovemaking, end politics, and poetry, all at once, in a performative apocalypse in which words will become the fire they have ignited and so vanish as words, in a universal light. The words, however, always remain, there on the page, as the unconsumed traces of each unsuccessful attempt to use words to end words. The attempt must therefore be repeated. *The same scene, with the same elements in a slightly different arrangement, is written by Shelley over and over again* from *Queen Mab* to *The Triumph of Life*, in a repetition ended only with his death. This repetition mimes the poet's failure ever to get it right and so end the necessity of trying once more with what remains.[93]

In passing over the differential discursive practice of historically situated texts in favor of "looking at" them as objects at the scene of writing, deconstructive critics like Miller annul the historical specificity of the texts they address: the difference that makes a difference for good or ill in the world. But this is not all. Whatever deconstruction's claim to opposition, the systematic dedifferentiation of difference by the American practitioners of deconstruction is itself symptomatic of the indifference to politics and the sociopolitical quiescence *produced* by a discourse that privileges textuality as a kind of base to cultural and sociopolitical superstructural epiphenomena.[94] It is this reduction of the "worldliness of the text" to an indifferent object of explication that affiliates the American version of deconstruction with the New Criticism and more than anything else accounts for its institutional success: its all too easy accommodation to the ideologically informed "value-free" space of the late capitalist university.

In her defense of deconstruction, Barbara Johnson (among others) criticizes the tendency of these American "critics of uncanniness" to reduce Derrida's abyssal exegetical dance to an assured and dedifferentiating methodology—a *machine Derridienne*—and recalls them to the Nietzschean affirmation of radical uncertainty and surprise:

> Much has been made of the fact that "knowledge" cannot be taken for granted. But perhaps rather than simply questioning the nature of knowledge, we should today reevaluate the static, inert concept we have always had of ignorance. Ignorance, far more than knowledge, is what can never be taken for granted. If I perceived my ignorance as a gap in knowledge, instead of as an imperative that changes the very nature of what I think I know, then I do not truly experience my ignorance. The surprise of otherness is that moment when a new form of ignorance is suddenly activated as an imperative. If the deconstructive impulse is to retain its vital, subversive power, we must therefore become ignorant of it again and again.[95]

But even this welcomed rehabilitation of ignorance, this revitalization of the dynamics of sur-prise (being taken over by otherness) cannot, as Geoffrey Hartman implies in his differently stated but similar recommendation in his review of Derrida's *Glas*,[96] finally answer "the critique of deconstruction, which," we recall, "accuses it of not living up to its own claims of radicality, of working with too limited a notion of textuality, of applying its critical energy only within an institutional structure that it does not question and therefore confirms." For this limitation of deconstructive criticism to the exposure of the general mastering impulse behind the binary logic of logocentric discourse at large for the sake of reaffirming ignorance (undecidability) and surprise is *purely* ne-gational. As such, it is a stance before and away from the text that finally remains blind not only to the historically specific ways that knowledge produces power but also to the "negative *capability*," the relay of positive projective possibilities *disclosed* by, if not adequately thematized in, Hei-degger's version of the destruction. It thus does little to inhibit the re-duction of the imperative of ignorance to an empty and quiescent anti-formalist formalism, as in the case of J. Hillis Miller's texts, where the uncanny of the "criticism of the uncanny" is reduced to a theoretical play on a undecidable word.

Insofar as deconstruction continues to subordinate the analysis of the relations between knowledge production and power to the general ne-gational function of calling into question the "exclusive" either/or of logocentric logic in general, it cannot resist its momentum to end, as Kierkegaard insistently reminds the hovering speculative philosopher, in the enervating "inclusive logic" of the self-canceling "neither/nor." The "self-determined indetermination" that Geoffrey Hartman appropriates from Coleridge's definition of Cartesian doubt to characterize Derrida's deconstructive methodology[97] will terminate in a willed willessness that transforms the projective measure disclosed by the destruction—the measure of which is the measure of the relational human occasion—into the certain, regulative, empty, finally timeless—and productive—meth-odology (read "institutional discipline") of the textual double bind, which is to say with Kierkegaard, of "unmastered irony."[98]

In *Principles of Literary Criticism*, the authorizing text of the New Crit-icism, I. A. Richards denigrates the poetry of the engaged imagination, which according to his reductive binary definition of this imagination as a positivism, *excludes* the opposite and discordant qualities of human ex-perience from the poem. In opposition, he privileges the poetry of the ironic imagination. In the name of seeing "[things] as they really are," this poetry includes and reconciles their differences in a textually auton-omous "equilibrium," an equilibrium that lends itself inevitably to ("dis-interested" and "detached") transcendent descriptions. I quote the fol-lowing familiar passage at some length not only because it enabled the poetics and interpretive practice of the New Criticism, but also because its rhetoric is informed by the (effaced) constellation of metaphors that the discourse of deconstruction both demystifies *and* reinscribes:

> The structures of these two kinds of experiences are different, and the difference is not one of subject but of the relations *inter se* of the several impulses active in the experience. A poem of the first group is built out of sets of impulses which run parallel, which have the same direction. In a poem of the second group the most obvious feature in the extraordinary heterogeneity of the distinguishable

impulses. But they are more than heterogeneous, they are opposed. They are such that in ordinary, nonpoetic, non-imaginative experience, one or other set would be suppressed to give as it might appear freer development to the others. . . .

The difference comes out clearly if we consider how comparatively unstable poems of the first kind are. They will not bear an ironical contemplation. . . . Irony in this sense consists in the bringing in of the opposite, the complementary impulses; that is why poetry which is exposed to it is not of the highest order, and why irony itself is so constantly a characteristic of poetry which is. . . .

. . . *The equilibrium of opposed impulses, which we suspect to be the ground-plan of the most valuable aesthetic responses,* brings into play far more of our personality than is possible in experiences of a more defined emotion. We cease to be oriented in one definite direction; more facets of the mind are exposed and, what is the same thing, more aspects of things are able to affect us. To respond, not through one narrow channel of interest, but simultaneously and coherently through many, is to be disinterested in the only sense of the word which concerns us here. . . . *We seem to see "all around" them,* to see them as they really are; *we see them apart from any one particular interest* which they *may have for us. Of course without some interest we should not see them at all, but the less any one particular interest is indispensable,* the more *detached* our attitude becomes. . . .

These characters of aesthetic experiences can thus be shown to be very natural consequences of the diversity of their components. But that so many different impulses should enter in is only what may be expected in an experience whose ground-plan is a balance of opposites. For every impulse which does not complete itself in isolation tends to bring in allied systems. The state of irresolution shows this clearly. *The difference between any such welter of vacillating impulses and the states of composure we are considering* may well be a matter of mediating relations between the supporting systems brought in from either side. One thing only is certain; what happens is the exact opposite to a deadlock, *for compared to the experience of great poetry every other state of mind is one of bafflement. . . .*

. . . *The consciousness which arises in these moments of completed being* lends itself inevitably to transcendent [read epiphanic] descriptions.[99]

One of the essential purposes of deconstructive criticism as practiced in North America has been to undermine the imperviousness to irony that the New Critical spatializing hermeneutics achieves by way of an inclusive and autotelic poetics that privileges "the equilibrium of opposing impulses" in behalf of the wider panoramic and plenary perspective of detached observation. But in translating the signifiers emerging from and addressing *different* American historical/cultural situations into one timeless, however undecidable, intertexual (ironic) text, deconstruction ironically betrays its affiliation with the "disinterested"—and indifferent—"ironic" formalism of the New Criticism and its structuralist allotrope. In the wake of Derrida's overdetermination of the metaphorics of the theater, the deconstructive reader, like the New Critic and structuralist, has become a distanced and disengaged ironic observer of the global "scene of writing," beyond the reach of the free play of criticism. Like the New Critic, this reader has become an aesthete in Kierkegaard's sense of the term: one who perceives the free-floating textuality of the text from the infinitely negative ("hovering") distance of the spatializing ironic mode, and who thus levels all texts, no matter how different they are and what differences they have made or make in the world, to the same text. Under the "disinterested" scrutiny of his or her panoptic gaze, they all become *one*, indifferent and pacified. In thus coercing the difference within and between the texts into a paradoxically totalized differential identity, American deconstructive criticism, despite its commitment to the play of *differance*, has trapped itself in precisely what at its origins it would call into question by way of the interrogation of the tradition of presence. Despite its differentiating intentions, its general economy has become, in tendency at least, the obverse face of the same currency: a negative leveling violence that mirrors the positive leveling violence of metaphysical (and New Critical) specular inquiry.

It is not, therefore, as Barbara Johnson claims, the institutional success of American deconstructive criticism that in the last analysis has rendered it a timeless, self-replicating, predictable, indifferent, and self-defeating professional activity that confirms by reproducing the institution it would call into question. On the contrary, its institutional success is the consequence and not the cause of this condition. What has guaranteed the institutional hegemony of deconstruction is its universalization of difference: its methodological refusal or failure, aided and abetted by Derrida's (and de Man's) domesticated revision of Heidegger's destruction, to *situate* itself and the text in-the-world. It is this successful de-situation of language as engaged discursive practice into the theoretical "scene of writing" that also accounts for the reduction of deconstruction to an indifferent instrument immune to dialogue. It is this transformation of the materiality of words into a transcendental that affiliates deconstruction with, and in so doing lends legitimacy to, the institutions that the "disinterested" anthropological discourse of humanism authorizes.[100]

Understood from the perspective of a radicalized Heideggerian destruction that thematizes its understanding of being as an indissoluble continuum, the deconstructive project that has come to dominate the "advanced criticism" of our American time reminds us of Kierkegaard's recognition (which is also Gramsci's, Althusser's, and Foucault's, among many other posthumanist critics on the left side of the sociopolitical spectrum) that the "present [Hegelian] age of reflection" is positively capable of producing the illusion among its speculative (theoretical) intellectuals that they are active adversaries of the dominant culture and of the power structures that lie behind it:

> A passionate, tumultuous age wants to *overthrow everything, set aside everything.* An age that is revolutionary but also reflecting and devoid of passion changes the expression of power into a *dialectical tour de force: it lets everything remain but subtly drains the meaning out of it; rather than culminating in an uprising, it exhausts the inner actuality of relations in a tension of reflection that lets everything remain and yet has transformed the whole of existence into equivocation that in its facticity is— while entirely privately a dialectical fraud interpolates a secret way of reading—that it is not.*[101]

As a speculative mode of reflection that, according to Edward Said, is "dominated by the spirit of refinement,"[102] the deconstructive "play of mind" celebrated by American deconstructionists becomes an exemplary instance of the kind of passionless revolutionary thinking that Kierkegaard attributes to the "revolutionary" intellectuals in the age of Hegel: the thinking of a "representative" or "universal" intellectual (in Foucault's resonant term) that transforms the contestatory domain of history into an infinite free-floating space and the positive inner impulse to revolt against the old repressive order into a "dialectical tour de force," an infinitely negative and ineffectual rhetoric of undecidability. Further, in emptying out the "inner actuality of relations in a tension of reflection that lets everything remain," it has become, however brilliant its speculative discourse, perilously similar, again in the terms Kierkegaard employs to characterize the Hegelian moment, to the garrulous and uninterruptible "chatter" of an industrious wit industry that, like the New Criticism before it, ultimately if unwittingly validates and serves the leveling and dedifferentiating hegemonic sociopolitical purposes of the present age, the new world order.[103]

I do not wish to suggest, with the grave humanist heirs of Matthew Arnold (F. R. Leavis, Lionel Trilling, and more recently M. H. Abrams, Wayne Booth, E. D. Hirsch, and Gerald Graff, not to say Walter Jackson Bate, Allan Bloom, William Bennett, Hilton Kramer, Roger Kimball, and Dinesh D'Souza) who advocate the recuperation of "high seriousness," that the play of wit is essentially a trivializing gesture of the understanding. For, as Rabelais or Sterne or Kierkegaard or Nietzsche or Foucault reminded the grave "great wigs" of their respective occasions, its errant measure is radically grounded in *this* world. Indeed, this awareness informs, if it does not clearly define, Derrida's texts from the outset, and increases under the pressure of the mounting critique of "American" deconstruction by the political left. When, however, the play of wit forgets that the play of difference has its source in the be-ing of being, when wit becomes a textual/institutional industry, as it has in the hands of many of Derrida's American followers, its "occasional measure" becomes paradoxically the regulating, paralyzing, and blinding *rule* of an always high noon. As such a reinscribed and commodified negative Apollonianism, deconstruction calls for destruction.[104]

V

Nietzsche's Dionysian violence inaugurates both Heidegger's destructive and Derrida's deconstructive projects:

> Every concept originates through our equating what is unequal. No one leaf ever equals another, and the concept "leaf" is formed through an arbitrary abstraction from these individual differences, through forgetting the distinctions; and now it gives rise to the idea that in nature there might be something besides the leaves that would be "leaf"—some kind of original form after which all leaves have been woven, marked, copied, colored, curled, and painted, but by unskilled hands, so that no copy had turned out to be a correct, reliable, and faithful image of the original form.[105]

As Nietzsche insistently suggests, it is the task of critical genealogy to remember the difference that the Western tradition, especially in its post-Enlightenment or anthropological phase, has strategically dedifferentiated and forgotten in inscribing the simplifying and coercive Platonic *Idea* into language, and into the discourses, institutions, and sociopolitical formations this language authorizes and elaborates. But the difference he wrests by violence here and elsewhere in his discourse—in *The Genealogy of Morals* and *The Untimely Meditations*, for example—is not simply a matter of textual traces to be retrieved for their own sake. It is also and simultaneously a phenomenon of be-ing. Nietzsche's interrogation of metaphysical language and the Apollonian intellectual disciplines it continuously reproduces is essentially a critical exposure of their worldly will to power over the disseminating and de-viating differences—the (Dionysiac) *force*, as Derrida put it in an important essay neglected by his American followers, of being.[106] In remembering and insisting on the individual differences, the differentiating qualities, of the leaf that the assimilative metaphysical language ("the idea 'leaf' ") forgets or represses, Nietzsche does not construct an instrument for the recuperation of a lost Origin. He enables a contemporary critical counter-memory. In Foucault's Nietzschean term, he makes possible a critical genealogy that, aware of the constructed character of the "real," always already destroys the authoritative discursive practices privileged by the metaphysical impulse to recuperate identity. In so doing, it activates awareness of the *differance* informing textuality, and also—simultaneously—of the ontological difference, which, as even Derrida implies in focusing the temporal deferring of *differance*, is its coeval, if not its source. In short, Nietzsche enables an adversarial discourse that, in retrieving the "actual intensities and creations of life" from the imperial Identity, makes a difference in the world, a discourse that *as genealogy* energizes an always dedifferentiating theory into an always differentiating *praxis*.

The Derridean deconstruction has served and continues to serve an important disruptive function in the postmodern effort to problematize the coercive canonical discourse of traditional humanistic anthropologism. But insofar as it textualizes *differance* and renders it indifferently, insofar, that is, as it remains willess *theoria* at the ever-present scene of writing, deconstruction cannot adequately accomplish the whole multi-situated adversarial task of criticism in our belated time. Indeed, as we have seen, the "pessimism or impotence" incumbent on its neither/nor logic lends itself to the recuperative hegemonic strategy of the dominant (late capitalist) culture. In referring to "our belated time," I do not simply mean the Occidental time that, in becoming the inclusive "age of the world picture," has self-disclosed the relay of others that its frame cannot finally contain. I also mean specifically the time that, in transforming the discourse of the sovereign self into an inclusive hegemonic and neoimperialist discourse during the Vietnam decade, self-disclosed the violence against the multiple relay of others that it would contain. That active task, the most difficult of all tasks not impossible, I submit, remains to the "Heideggerian," if not to Heidegger's, destruction. For its differentiating circular logic of repetition makes a difference, not simply at the scene of writing, but at every site on the indissoluble continuum of being from ontology (Heidegger, Gadamer) through language (Derrida, de Man) and cultural formations (Williams, Said) to gender relations (Irigaray, Spivak) and sociopolitical institutions (Foucault, Laclau and Mouffe).

Chapter 5
Heidegger and Foucault: The Politics of the Commanding Gaze

Since the imperial epoch, the Greek word "politics" signifies something Roman. Of the Greek therefore there is nothing but an empty resonance.

Martin Heidegger, *Parmenides*

The Roman reference that accompanied [the Napoleonic regime and the form of state that was to survive it] certainly bears with it this double index: citizens and legionaries. While jurists or philosophers were seeking in the pact a primal model for the construction or reconstruction of the social body, the soldiers and with them the technicians of discipline were elaborating procedures for the individual and collective coercion of bodies.

Michel Foucault, *Discipline and Punish*

I

In the preceding essays, I situated my destructive inquiry into the operations of humanist discursive practices at the site of ontology. My purpose in doing so was to suggest the underlying continuity between the various historically specific representations of reality in the onto-theological tradition, the tradition that has come to be called "the West" or "the Occident": that these representations constitute, in Derrida's terms, "a series of substitutions of center for center, . . . a linked chain of determinations of the center."[1] My limitation of inquiry to the site of ontology was intended to thematize the metaphysics informing the dominant order in the present historical conjunction, and the metaphorics of the centered circle it enables: the metaphorics all too invariably discounted, overlooked, or minimized by both neo-Marxists and other "worldly critics" in their interrogation of the hegemony of what has been variously called "humanism," "bourgeois capitalism," "the consumer society," "*la société de la spectacle*," "late capitalism," "the age of the world picture," or "the disciplinary society." I do not want to suggest that a destructive hermeneutics renders the historically specific conjuncture irrelevant or minimally significant, as Heidegger unfortunately did with dire consequences. On the contrary, this relative indifference to the historical occasion constitutes the essential limitation of Heidegger's version of the destruction and, in a different way, of Derrida's (and de Man's) deconstruction. Heidegger's tendency to limit his interrogation of the ontotheological tradition to the question of being (*die Seinsfrage*) overlooks the affiliation between philosophy and sociopolitical formations. And, as I have suggested in chapter 4, Derrida's tendency to limit inquiry to the site of textuality—as a transhistorical "base" to epiphenomenal superstructural phenomena (especially the sociopolitical)—paradoxically reduces the text's historically specific difference, and the difference for good or ill it makes in the world, to an indifferent *différance*. In this essay I want to suggest that, whatever the political limitations of Heidegger's hermeneutics—and they are substantial—it nevertheless lends itself to appropriation in behalf of an emancipatory discursive practice that overcomes the limitations of deconstructive textuality, classical Marxist essentialism, and the genealogical criticism that tends to understand history as a discontinuous series of epistemic ruptures.[2]

In order to justify what may seem an arbitrary leap, however, it will be necessary to amplify the critical imperatives of my appropriation of Heidegger's destruction of the ontotheological tradition beyond the parameters to which I have more or less limited it in the previous essays: parameters, not incidentally, within which those who have adopted Heidegger's version of the *Destruktion* in *Being and Time* continue to restrict their commentary. This limitation of its inquiry to the site of ontology renders the destruction justly vulnerable to countercritique by the discourse of humanism, which it was in large part Heidegger's purpose to delegitimate.

At present, several theoretical discourses are competing for authority in the interrogation of the dominant culture and the (discreetly) repressive sociopolitical formations it legitimates: the discourses of textuality, of psychoanalysis, of ontology, of feminism, of black criticism, of Marxism, and so on. Each of these interpretive strategies *tends* to assume a base/superstructure model in which the particular base determines in the last instance the superstructural sites and thus represents the latter as more or less epiphenomenal. Understood in terms of the questions they have raised in their common demystification of the problematic of the dominant culture—questions about consciousness, language, culture, gender, race, the ecos, society, and politics, to which this "value-free" problematic is necessarily blind—a different understanding of base and superstructure suggests itself.

According to my appropriation of the destruction—a reading I believe is latent in Heidegger's destructive hermeneutics—the field of inquiry is not divided according to the imperatives of the base/superstructure model. Its sites are not in essence hierarchically ordered, but *laterally* equiprimordial: they constitute an indissoluble and interpenetrating continuum or force field of lived discursive practices, although unevenly developed at any historically specific moment. The destruction understands the constituted history of "the Occident"—the onto-theo-logical tradition—as a *process of reconstitutions*, a process characterized by periods of relative stability all along the lateral field of discursive forces that undergo destabilization when their internal contradictions surface as disruptive events or, in Foucault's phrase, "discursive explosions,"[3] which in turn are *accommodated* by the substitution of another socially constituted and comprehensive center. In this process of accommodation to the "new" center, particular historical conjunctures will overdetermine one or more discursive sites at the expense of the visibility of the others. (It is in this sense that one could say that the lateral discursive field of forces is always unevenly developed at any historically specific moment in the tradition.) As a consequence of this historical overdetermination, it *appears* that the overdetermined site (or sites) is determinant in the last instance of the less visible ones: that it constitutes the base that shapes its superstructural manifestations.

With the rise of capital in the Western industrial nations in the late eighteenth and early nineteenth centuries, for example, the economic site became overdetermined. It thus seemed to Marx and Engels (and to the theoreticians of capitalism) that the economic site constituted the base of the superstructural sites. However insistent their qualifications, it was finally the ownership of the means of production that determined the structural characteristics of language, culture, gender, law, politics, and so on:

> According to the materialist conception of history, the *ultimately* determining element in history is the production and reproduction of real life. More than this neither Marx nor I have ever asserted. Hence if somebody twists this into saying that the economic element is the *only* determining one, he transforms that proposition into a

meaningless, abstract, senseless phrase. The economic situation is the basis, but the various elements of the superstructure—political forms of the class struggle and its results, to wit: constitutions established by the victorious class after a battle, etc., juridical forms, and even the reflexes of all these actual struggles in the brains of the participants, political, juristic, philosophical theories, religious views and their further development into systems of dogma—also exercise their influence upon the course of the historical struggles and in many cases preponderate in determining their *form*. There is an interaction of all these elements in which, amid all the endless host of accidents (that is, of things and events whose inner interconnection is so remote or so impossible of proof that we can regard it as non-existent, as negligible) the economic movement finally asserts itself as necessary. Otherwise the application of the theory to any period of history would be easier than the solution of a simple equation of the first degree.[4]

This historically constituted assumption of the priority of the economic site led to "Marxism": the determination of history grounded in the means of production that privileged a "social realist" discursive practice that spatialized, factored, and hierarchized lived experience and thus profoundly minimized the active role played by the subject, culture, language, and social, political, racial, and gender formations in the dominant order's effort to achieve hegemony.

In the twentieth century, however, following the collapse of imperialism during World War I, the new and essentially disruptive knowledge released by this collapse was accommodated by the dominant order within the inclusive network of information theory and retrieval technologies. As a result of this accommodation, the economic site as defined by Marx and Engels and more rigidly by the discourse of social realism (i.e., Stalinism) lost its privileged status to the newly overdetermined discursive site. This "crisis of Marxism" explains the massive and essentially positive efforts on the part of neo-Marxists—from Gramsci and the Frankfurt School through Althusser, Poulantzas, Macherey, Jameson to Laclau and Mouffe—and other "worldly critics" of the postwar West—Foucault, Kristeva, Lyotard, Baudrillard, Habermas, Williams, and Said—to readjust the Marxist base/superstructure model to accommodate itself to this overdetermined site.[5] One recognizes this strategy of accommodation, for example, in the productive revisionist Marxism of Gramsci and Althusser (and those they influenced), which criticizes Marxist "economism" as an essentialism or, in Althusser's terms, an "analytico-teleological" interpretive theory that recuperates Hegelianism in favor of giving "semi-autonomy" to the superstructural overdeterminations. But the metaphysics of even an Althusserian anti-Hegelian

Marxism is betrayed by its insistence on the determination of superstructural overdeterminations by the modes of material production "in the last instance."[6] It is this determinist essentialism inhering in the base/superstructure model, this pyramidal representational strategy, that recent theorists on the left such as Raymond Williams and in a more radical way Ernesto Laclau and Chantal Mouffe find in the discourse of "vulgar" Marxists, and also, however vestigially, in that of revisionist Marxists such as Althusser and even Gramsci. As Williams puts it in *Marxism and Literature*:

> In the transition from Marx to Marxism, and then in the
> development of expository and didactic formulations, the words
> used in the original arguments were projected, first, as if they were
> precise concepts, and second, as if they were descriptive terms for
> observable "areas" of social life. The main sense of the words in the
> original arguments [of Marx and Engels] had been relational, but the
> popularity of the terms tended to indicate either (a) relatively
> enclosed categories or (b) relatively enclosed areas of activity. These
> were then correlated either temporally (first material production,
> then consciousness, then politics and culture) or in effect, forcing the
> metaphor, spatially (visible and distinguishable "levels" or
> "layers"—politics and culture, then forms of consciousness, and so
> on down to the "base").[7]

Like the model of *Homo economicus* of classical capitalism, the classical Marxist base/superstructure model abstracts social life, reduces its dynamic differential relationality, to reified counters in a spatialized totality. It would not be an imposition to say, appropriating Heidegger's critique of modernity at large, that like capitalism, the discourse of classical Marxism transformed being-in-the-world into *reine Technik*; transformed an always already temporal process into a re-presented totality in what he calls "the age of the world picture."

Williams's awareness of the disabling, because disciplinary, aspect of the Marxist critique of capitalism, including that of neo-Marxists who have given far more prominence to cultural production (the superstructural sites), precipitates his own more radical revision of the Marxist project: one that collapses the hierarchical and temporally sequential distinction between base and superstructural sites in favor of the absolute *indissolubility* of the relationship between them. It is a revision (also marking the discourse of Laclau and Mouffe) that rejects the base/superstructure model (and its essentialist—i.e., secondary or derivative—interpretive practice) precisely because it *spatializes* (and disciplines) temporal phenomena: appropriated, that is, the reductive metaphysical principle that identity (economy) is the condition for the possibility of difference (the individualized superstructural sites). This revision retrieves a historical materialism understood as "specific indissoluble real processes":

> What is fundamentally lacking, in the theoretical formulations of this important period, is any adequate recognition of the indissoluble connections between material production, political and cultural institutions and activity, and consciousness. . . . What is wrong with [these formulations] is [their] description of these "elements" as "sequential," when they are in practice indissoluble: not in the sense that they cannot be distinguished for purposes of analysis, but in the decisive sense that these are not separate "areas" or "elements" but the whole, specific activities and products of real men. That is to say, the analytic categories, as so often in idealistic thought, have, almost unnoticed, become substantive descriptions, which then take habitual priority over the whole social process to which, as analytic categories, they are attempting to speak. Orthodox analysts began to think of "the base" and "the superstructure" as if they were separable concrete entities. In doing so they lost sight of the very processes—not abstract relations but constitutive processes—which it should have been the special function of historical materialism to emphasize.[8]

The parallel I am pointing to between certain neo-Marxist critiques of classical Marxism and Heidegger's more generalized critique of classical Westernism (the "technologization" or "Europeanization" of the planet),[9] both grounded in the concept of *Homo economicus*, is not incidental. It suggests a reading of Heidegger's critique of modernity that problematizes the politically negative conclusions drawn by those humanists, whether the French *nouveaux philosophes* or American pluralists, who now identify Heidegger's philosophical discourse—indeed, "Heideggerianism" at large—with fascist politics. In putting this parallel into play, I want to suggest that Heidegger's *Sein* is significantly other than the transcendental authority to be followed blindly, which, according to his humanist critics' representation, utterly implicates Heidegger's pursuit of the question of being with the politics of the *Führer*. I will address this misleading representation in the last chapter of this book. Here it will suffice to pursue the parallel. If we understand "continuum" as a lateral relationship of forces and "being" as be-*ing*, as temporality (or, more specifically, the differences that temporality disseminates), rather than as a transcendental (or derived) category (a base to superstructural epiphenomena), Heidegger's notion of the continuum of being provides a context for thinking the materiality of history in a way that is more adequate than available discourses to the conditions of the postmodern occasion. To think the continuum of being in this way, that is, suggests a material theory of historical inquiry capable of reconciling the ontological and the sociopolitical critique of the dominant order without either recuperating a teleological or metaphysical Origin or discounting the repressive power inhering in the spatial metaphorics privileged by the ontotheological tradition at large. I mean the perennial metaphorics constellated around the privileged figure of the centered circle—the panoptic eye, light and darkness, re-presentation, grasping (comprehension)—which continues (even in the attacks on Heidegger) to exert its silent and invisible power everywhere in the present (anthropological) historical conjuncture: not only in the classical physical and social sciences, where Foucault tends to locate it, but also—and most discreetly—in the discursive practices of the so-called *litterae humaniores*. Because critique is interested, must be guided by a point of view or by a "forestructure" in advance, it must focus on the overdetermined site that generates interest (makes a difference): in the case of the present conjuncture, on the positivist technology of information retrieval. But to do so, as so many contemporary worldly critics, whether neo-Marxists, feminists, or genealogists, or new historicists tend to, without recognition or acknowledgment of the ideological relay that saturates all the sites on the continuum, is to weaken the effectiveness of critique.

Understood in the context of this destructive reading of history, then, the temporal "progress" of Western civilization, including the cultural and political narrative paradigms it has elaborated to legitimate its particular allotropes, has in a general, however uneven, way involved the eventual recognition and exploitation of the indissoluble relationship between visual (spatial) perception of things-as-they-are and cultural, economic, and sociopolitical power. What from the beginning of the Western tradition was a tentative, discontinuous, and unevenly developed intuition of this relationship coalesced in the *epistéme* variously called the Enlightenment, the age of reason, or bourgeois capitalism, (and, not incidentally, the Augustan Age). According to Heidegger, this is the historical conjuncture that bore witness to the triumph of "re-presentation," the thinking of being as "world picture": the hardening of metaphysical speculation into a calculative technology of "enframing" (*Gestell*), in which being (including *Dasein* [being-in-the-world]) has been reduced to "standing reserve" (*Bestand*). According to Foucault's remarkably analogous, if more decisively concrete diagnosis, it is the *epistéme* that bore witness to the emergence of the "panoptic" schema, the microphysics of power that constituted the subject (the sovereign individual) to facilitate the achievement of sociopolitical consensus (identity) in the volatile social context precipitated by a rapidly changing demography.

To anticipate the affiliative relationship between Heidegger's and Foucault's discourses that I will treat more fully, this "progress" has involved the eventual recognition and exploitation of the integral relationship between the perennially and increasingly privileged figure of the centered circle *as the image of beauty and perfection and the centered circle as the ideal instrument of a totalized sociopolitical domination.*

Post-Renaissance Man intuited the inherent "strength" (which from a destructive perspective discloses the essential weakness) of metaphysical epistemology: its ability to *see* or re-*present* the differential temporal process as *integral* and *inclusive* picture (table, blueprint, grid, design, strategic map, etc.) or, negatively, to lose *sight* of and forget difference, in the pursuit of the certainty (distance) of logocentric order. This intuition, in turn, enabled the transformation of the over-sight of the metaphysical overview (survey) into a pervasive methodological or disciplinary instrument for the discreet coercion of difference into identity all through the field of forces that constitute being, from the ontological and epistemological sites through language and culture to economics and sociopolitics (gender, race, family, state, etc.). In the "age of the world picture," more accurately, metaphysical speculation was transformed into a disciplinary instrument positively capable of colonizing the "other," of harnessing difference (the individual entity) in behalf of normalization and utility: that is, exploitation. This centered "speculative instrument," which has inscribed its recollective/visual interpretive imperatives into all phases of Western culture, was and continues to be defined by that dominant social formation that benefits most from the circumscription and colonization of the earth. It therefore also serves, however inadvertently in some instances, to legitimate the dominant political/economic power structure (and its hegemonic purposes)—now become the computerized late capitalist establishment—that has largely determined the societies of Europe (including, until recently, the Soviet bloc) and America and their extraterritorial (colonial) ends since the Enlightenment. The difference between past and present is not ontologically substantive: whereas before the Enlightenment the center or eye that dominated was visible, in the age of the world picture or, alternatively, of panoptics, it has become "a center elsewhere . . . beyond the reach of [free] play": in Gramsci's term, "hegemonic."

Heidegger limited his destructive hermeneutics by and large, though not entirely, to the philosophical discourses of the ontotheological tradition. As a consequence, he minimized its potential application to the site of sociopolitics, a minimization, needless to say, that had unfortunate consequences for his understanding of the overdeterminations of his historically specific occasion. For him, in general, the destruction of the priority accorded to the spatializing eye by the Western philosophical tradition took the form of disclosing its ontological *limitations*: that metaphysical inquiry resulted in the global ("planetary") distortion of "truth," in an "overlooking," "leveling," and "forgetting" of the ontological difference, the difference that temporal being always already disseminates. However, his insistence on the equiprimordiality of the indissolubly constitutive structures that make up being-in-the-world, specifically *Dasein*'s state of mind (*Befindlichkeit*), understanding (*Verstehen*), and discourse (*Rede*), suggests that the temporality of being-in-the-world, which is coerced or accommodated to structure by the metaphysical gaze, is not a base to superstructural epiphenomena: "The phenomenon of the *equiprimordiality* of [these] constitutive items," he writes, "has often been disregarded in ontology, because of a methodologically unrestrained tendency to derive everything and anything from some simple 'primal ground'."[10] Heidegger's insistence on the equiprimordiality of this triad of existential structures suggests, rather, that the temporality of being-in-the-world is an always transforming, unevenly developed lateral field of constituted and domesticated forces encompassing all the "regions" between ontology and sociopolitics. It thus becomes possible to recognize, even though Heidegger himself failed to, that wherever (and whenever) one situates destructive inquiry, whether at the site of being (ontology), of the subject, of gender, of race, relations, of the law, of nature, of cultural production, of education, of the economy, or of sociopolitical relations, one is, in some degree or other, also always already interrogating all the other constituted sites.

II

Indeed, this possibility of destructive hermeneutics is reflected, however minimally thought in terms of its historical specificity, in several crucial, albeit largely overlooked, moments in Heidegger's texts, especially after his realization that the Nazi project to which he had committed his energies in the period of the rectorship was itself "caught up in the consummation of nihilism."[11] Thus, for example, in "Letter on Humanism," written in 1947, Heidegger extends his ontological/epistemological genealogy of the "truth" of modernity—the truth of disinterested inquiry—in *Being and Time* to encompass its affiliative relationship to sociopolitics. In this essay, Heidegger shows that the epochal Roman translation of the Greek *aletheia* to *veritas* enabled not only the truth of the ontotheological tradition at large but also—and contrary to its modern apologists, who trace its origins to Greek thought—the truth of humanist modernity. In so doing, he implicates the discourse of humanism and the sociopolitical practice of modern democratic/humanist states with Rome's imperial project.

According to Heidegger's genealogy of humanist truth, we recall, the decisive event in the historical process of the Occident's self-representation occurred when the Romans translated the Greek understanding of truth as *aletheia* (unconcealment) to *veritas* as *adequaetio intellectus et rei*, which, whether understood as " 'the correspondence of the matter to knowledge' or 'the correspondence of knowledge to the matter' has continually in view a conforming to . . . and hence think[s] truth as *correctness* [*Richtigkeit*]."[12] The epochal turning point occurred when the Romans began to think temporal phenomena "technologically": on the basis of a *ground* achieved by originary Greek thinking. The "translation of Greek names into Latin," Heidegger writes, "is in no way the innocent process it is considered to be to this day. Beneath the seeming and thus faithful translation there is concealed, rather, a *translation* of Greek experience into a different way of thinking." Roman thought emphatically and insistently "*takes over Greek words without a corresponding, equally original experience of what they say, without the Greek word. The rootlessness of Western thought begins with this translation.*"[13] Henceforth and increasingly, "the ontology which . . . has thus arisen has deteriorated to a tradition in which it gets reduced to something self-evident—merely material for reworking, as it was for Hegel." Greek ontology thus uprooted becomes "a fixed body of doctrine,"[14] a "free-floating" discourse that, remote from the historicity of being-in-the-world, nevertheless *determines* history from that remoteness.[15]

Truth as *veritas* involves the transformation of the uncentered—originary and errant—thinking of the Greeks into a secondary and derivative—and calculative—technology, in which the end determines the process of inquiry. To invoke the visual metaphorics underlying Heidegger's differentiation between *aletheia* and *veritas*—the metaphorics that brings Heidegger's interrogation of modernity into convergence with Foucault's—the Greek *aletheia* Heidegger would retrieve enables the always already de-*structuring* process of inquiry that he calls "repetition" (*Wiederholung*). This is the paradoxical circular movement that always already dis-closes (brings to light/liberates) the difference ordinarily closed off and concealed (by being "spoken for") by the identical discourse of "structure." It is the movement that precipitates an *Erwiderung*: a "reciprocal rejoinder" (which is a "disavowal") of what has been handed down (now understood as "forestructure," as opposed to "presupposition," that necessarily begins inquiry).

> Repetition, [we recall], *is handing down explicitly*—that is to say, going back into the possibilities of the Dasein that have-been-there. But when one has, by repetition, handed down to oneself a possibility that has been, the Dasein that has-been-there is not disclosed in order to be actualized over again. The repeating of that which is possible does not bring down again [*Wiederbringen*] something that is "past," nor does it bind the "Present" back to that

which has already been "outstripped." . . . Rather, the repetition
makes a *reciprocative rejoinder* to the possibility of that existence
which has-been-there. But when such a rejoinder is made to this
possibility in a resolution, it is made *in a moment of vision*
[*Augenblick*]; *and as such* it is at the same time a *disavowal* of that
which in the "today" is working itself out as the "past."[16]

The Roman *veritas* as *adequaetio intellectus et rei* involves a derivative
mode of inquiry in which the principle that identity is the condition for
the possibility of difference is determinative. It is a logocentrism that
begins inquiry into the differential phenomena (objects and events) disseminated by a temporality "grounded" in nothing (*das Nichts*) from the
end. To emphasize its visual orientation, inquiry understood as adequation of mind and thing proceeds from *above* (*meta-ta-physika*): from a
fixed transcendental vantage point—a "Transcendental Signified" or
"center elsewhere," in Derrida's terms, which is beyond the reach of free
play. In thus privileging the surveying and globalizing eye of vision, it
has as its ultimate purpose the coercion of difference into the circumference of the identical circle. The center spatializes and reifies the disseminations of temporality in order to "comprehend" them: not simply
to know but to "take hold of" or "manage," that is, dominate and use
them. The comportment toward phenomena the center enables is thus
that of the *commanding* eye, that is to say, the panoptic gaze. It is a visual
comportment that represents the force of difference as that which truth is
not, as *false* (*falsum*) and thus as a threat to truth that must be domesticated or pacified, willfully reduced to the same in the name of this justice.

From this genealogy of the concept of the "truth" of modernity—of
the humanist post-Enlightenment—which discloses its origins in the Roman translation of the Greek *aletheia* to *veritas*, the hermeneutic circle
(repetition) to the *circulus vitiosus* (recollection) that would pacify the
force of difference (of that which is "outside" the boundary of the centered circle), Heidegger proceeds to implicate this Romanized "truth"
explicitly with modern cultural production—specifically humanist *paideia*—and implicitly with the modern Western state:

> *Humanitas*, explicitly so called, was first considered and striven for in
> the age of the Roman Republic. *Homo humanus* was opposed to *homo
> barbarus*. *Homo humanus* here means the Romans, who exalted and
> honored Roman *virtus* through the "embodiment" of the *paideia*
> [education] taken over from the Greeks. These were the Greeks of
> the Hellenistic age, whose culture was acquired in the schools of
> philosophy. It was concerned with *eruditio et institutio in bonas artes*
> [scholarship and training in good conduct]. *Paideia* thus understood
> was translated as *humanitas*. The genuine *romanitas* of *homo romanus*
> consisted in such *humanitas*. We encounter the first humanism in

> Rome: it therefore remains in essence a specifically Roman
> phenomenon which emerges from the encounter of Roman
> civilization with the culture of late Greek civilization. The so-called
> Renaissance of the fourteenth and fifteenth centuries in Italy is a
> *renascentia romanitatis.* Because *romanitas* is what matters, it is
> concerned with *humanitas* and therefore with G.·eek *paideia.* But
> Greek civilization is always seen in its later form and this itself is
> seen from a Roman point of view.[17]

In this very resonant, but largely neglected, passage from "Letter on
Humanism," Heidegger ostensibly restricts the genealogy of modernity
to the complicity between humanist ontology and humanist pedagogy:
the logocentrism (and its will to power) informing Roman *veritas* also
informs the Roman *paideia.* Truth and knowledge production in the
anthropological tradition, according to Heidegger, are, however unevenly developed, coextensive. But if we read this essay in the historically specific context in which it was written—the catastrophe of Europe
precipitated by the Third Reich—a further extension in the relay of
power disclosed by the discourse and practice of humanist modernity
announces itself, one that implicates truth and knowledge with the politics of imperialism. For clearly, what Heidegger is saying here is not
simply that the "disinterested truth" and the "liberal" cultural apparatuses of the post-Enlightenment tradition (humanism) have their origins
in a pedagogical technology designed to produce "Romans," a "manly"
citizenry, which, as the embodiment of a *paideia* that "exalted and hon-
ored Roman *virtus*," would constitute a disciplined and dependable (or in
Foucault's terms, "useful and docile") collective of individuals. As the
resonant opposition between *homo humanus,* which "here means the
Romans," and *homo barbarus* makes clear, the ultimate purpose of the
logocentric Roman *veritas* and its *paideia* was the production of a disciplined and dependable citizenry committed to the achievement of the
hegemonic empire, an efficient army of citizens, as it were.

To put this relay of knowledge/power relations in terms of the metaphorics of the centered circle privileged by the humanist tradition, the
self-present subject as citizen/soldier produced by the discourse of *veritas*
and its *paideia* became the structural model of the *Civitas.* Just as the
humanist anthropologos justifies the domestication by "cultivation" of
the differential "provincial" energies of immature and deviant youth, so
the self-present Capitol, or the Metropolis, justifies the colonization of
the barbarian energies of the provincial peoples, who, as "other,"
threaten its civilized space. It is no accident, I would add to Heidegger's
genealogy of humanism, that the English words "cultivate" and "culture" privileged by this tradition, especially since the Enlightenment, are
cognates of "colonize" (from the Latin *colonus,* "tiller," "cultivator,"

"planter," "settler") and *colere* (to cultivate or plant). Nor is it accidental that these privileged counters have their ideological origin not in ancient Greek words referring to such agents and practices, but in the Latin *circulus*: the figure appropriated from the Greek words κὄκλος (cycle) or κίρκος (ring) to represent and symbolize beauty, truth, and perfection. In sum, the Roman ideological reduction and codification of the "errancy" and "prodigality" of originary (aletheiological) Greek thinking—their *circumscription, cultivation*, and *colonization* of truth-as-always-already *aletheia*—gave rise to its disciplinary educational project, and also legitimated the Romans' will to power over the peripheral and lowly—provincial—"barbarians." In short, the Roman translation of Greek thinking enabled in some fundamental way the Roman *"imperium sine fini"* (as Virgil puts it in the *Aeneid*), which goes by the duplicitous name of the *Pax Romana*.

It is, according to Heidegger's genealogy, this relay of repressions at the sites of the subject, cultural production, and the City, and enabled by the idealization of the circle, the center of which is both inside and outside (above) that constitutes the origins of the discourse and practice of the modern West.[18] The circle and the affiliated metaphors constellated around its center—the polarities of light/darkness, high/low, prelapsarian/fallen, and so on—are *polyvalent* in their material applications. To put Heidegger's genealogy of the discourse, cultural institutions, and sociopolitical practices of humanist modernity in terms of the legacy of imperial Rome is to indicate how near, however more generalized, it is to Michel Foucault's genealogy of the modern disciplinary society. I mean specifically the panoptic society eventually precipitated by an Enlightenment that deliberately appropriated the Roman model (specifically, the diagram of the military camp structure) to articulate its disciplinary epistemology, pedagogy, cultural agenda, and internal and external politics.

In this interpretation of the philosophically and historically resonant passage from Heidegger's "Letter on Humanism" quoted above, I have admittedly drawn a political thematic that is in excess of what he actually says concerning the origins of humanism and what he implies about the historical conjuncture his text addresses. It may be objected, therefore, that it constitutes an apologetic reading of Heidegger's postwar text. That it is not, that the political content I have thematized is justified by Heidegger's discourse in this period—indeed, with the exception of the period of the rectorship, in his discourse at large—is further verified by a course given in 1942–43, significantly after his resignation from the rectorship but considerably before the "Letter on Humanism"—indeed, before Hitler and the Nazis mounted their genocidal racist project against the Jews (and the "Bolsheviks").[19] I am referring to the *Parmenides* lectures, which, according to Eliane Escoubas in a crucial recent essay, constitutes the *"texte-charnière"* of Heidegger's "'explication' avec"—his "reciprocal rejoinder to"—German National Socialism.[20] This is not the occasion for a full analysis of what is surely one of the central theses of Heidegger's *Parmenides* and its implications concerning his adherence to Nazism: "Wir denken das 'Politische' romisch, d.h. imperial. . . . Das griechische Wort 'politisch' bedeudet etwas 'Romisches,' seit der Zeit des Imperiums. 'Griechisch' is daran nur noch der blosse Wortschall [We think the political in a Roman fashion. . . . Since the imperial epoch, the Greek word "political" means something Roman. Of the Greek, therefore, there is nothing but an empty resonance]."[21] Such an analysis would, in any case, duplicate Escoubas's reading. Given what I have said above about the *Homo romanus/Homo humanus* nexus, it will suffice for my general purposes simply to quote at some length a passage from this text that traces the origins of the "imperial" politics of Western modernity—and, as the "we" suggests, of Nazi Germany?—back to the "translation" of the Greek *aletheia* to Roman *veritas*, or more precisely, of the Greek *pseudos* to Roman *falsum*. For this synecdochical passage from Heidegger's *Parmenides* lectures implicates all three sites of the indissoluble relay I have thematized: the discourse of *veritas* (the true versus the false), the pedagogy devoted to scholarship and training in good conduct, and the imperial project. It also brings into play the visual metaphorics encoded in them—the panoptic gaze, light, spatialized time, heights on the one hand and the figure of the centered circle on the other—that are privileged over the constellation of metaphors associated with the other bodily senses (darkness, temporality, lowness, fallenness, etc.). In so doing, it constitutes, as we shall see, a remarkable if highly generalized prefiguration of Foucault's genealogy of the relationship between truth and power in modernity, specifically his analysis of the "repressive hypothesis," which underlies the discursive practices of the post-Enlightenment disciplinary society:

> The essential domain which prevails for the deployment of the
> Roman *"falsum"* is that of the *"imperium"* and of the "imperial." We
> take these words in their strict and original sense. *Imperium* means
> "command" [*Befehl*]. We understand here the word "command," of
> course, in its later, namely Roman-Romanistic meaning. Originally,
> *Befehl* (the *h* is written after the *l*: *befelh*) meant the same thing as
> *bergen* (to shelter): "to entrust" [*befehlen*] the dead to the earth or to
> fire, to entrust to sheltering. . . . In passing through French, *befehlen*
> became "to command"; more precisely, it became the Roman
> *imperare*—*im-perare* = to install [*enrichten*], to take preliminary
> measures, that is, *prae-cipere*, to occupy in advance and by that to
> have the "possessed" as domain [*Gebiet*], to dominate over it [*darüber*

gebieten]. The *imperium* is the domain that founds itself on the basis of the order [*Gebot*], and under whose dominion the others are subject. The *imperium* is the command [*Befehl*] in the sense of the disposing order. The command, thus understood, is the essential ground of sovereignty [*Herrschaft*], not at all only its consequence, and not only a form of its exercise. Thus, the god of the Old Testament is a "commanding" God: "You must not," "you must" is his word. This duty is inscribed in the Tables of the Law. No god of the Greeks, on the other hand, is a god who commands, but rather a god who shows, who indicates. The Roman "*numen*," by which the Roman gods are characterized, signifies by contrast "injunction" [*Geheiss*] and "will" [*Wille*] and has the character of command. The "numinous," in the strict sense, never concerns the essence of the Greek gods, that is, the gods who have their essence in the realm of *aletheia*. In the essential domain of "command" belongs the Roman "justice," *ius*. The word is attached to *jubeo*: to enjoin [*heissen*], by injunction [*Geheiss*] to have done and to determine acts and gestures. Command is the essential ground of dominion [*Herrschaft*] and of "being in the right" and "to have the right," understood in the Roman sense. As a result *iustitia* has an altogether different essential ground than *dike*, which has its essence in *aletheia*.

To commanding as the essential foundation of sovereignty belongs "being on high" [or "above," *Obensein*]. That is only possible through constant surmounting [*Überhöhung*] in relation to others, who are thus the inferiors [*Unteren*]. In the surmounting, in turn, resides the constant ability to oversee [super-vise and dominate, *Übersehen-können*]. We say "to oversee something," which means "to master it" [*beherrschen*]. To this commanding view, which carries with it surmounting, belongs the "always-being-on-the-lookout" [*Auf-der-Lauer-liegen*]. That is the form of all action that oversees [dominates from the gaze], but that holds to itself, in Roman the *actio* of the *actus*. The commanding overseeing is the dominating vision which is expressed in the often cited phrase of Caesar: *veni, vedi, vici*—I came, I *oversaw* [*übersah*], I conquered. Victory is already nothing but the consequence of the Caesarian gaze that dominates [*Übersehens*] and the seeing [*Sehens*] which has the character of *actio*. The essence of the *imperium* reposes in the *actus* of constant action [*Aktion*]. The imperial *actio* of the constant surmounting over others implies that the others, in the case where they raise themselves to a comparable or even identical height to command, are fallen [*gefällt werden*]—in Roman: *fallere* (participle: *falsum*). The "bringing-to-fall" [*das Zu-Fall-bringen*: "the occasioning of an ac-cident"] belongs necessarily to the domain of the imperial. The "bringing-to-fall" can be accomplished in a "direct" assault [*Ansturm*] and an overthrowing [*Niederwerfen*: literally, "throwing down"]. But the other can also be brought to fall by being outflanked [*Um-gehung*] and tripped up from behind. The "bringing-to-fall" is now the way of deceptive circumvention [*Hinter-gehen*], of the "trick"—a word which not accidentally comes from the "English." Considered from the outside, going behind the back is a complicated, circumstantial and thus mediate "bringing-to-fall" as opposed to an immediate overthrowing [*Niederwerfen*]. In this way, what is brought to fall [*Zu-Fall-Gebrachte*] does not thereby become annihilated, but in a certain manner redressed within the boundaries [*in den Grenzen*] which are staked out by the dominators. This "staking out" [*Abstecken*] is called in Roman *pango*, whence the word *pax*, peace. This, thought imperially, is the firmly established condition of what has been brought to fall. In truth, the bringing-to-fall in the sense of deception [*Hintergehens*] and outflanking [*Umgehens*] is not the mediate and derived imperial *actio* but the imperial *actio* proper. It is not in war, but in the *fallere* of deceptive outflanking [*hintergehenden Umgehens*] and its appropriation to the service of dominion that the proper and "great" trait of the imperial reveals itself. . . . In the Roman *fallere*—to bring-to-fall [*Zu-Fall-bringen*]—as a going around [*Hintergehen*] resides the deceit [*Tauschen*]; the *falsum* is the insidiously deceptive: "the false."

What happens when the Greek *pseudos* is thought in the sense of Roman *falsum*? The Greek *pseudos* as what dissimulates and thereby also deceives is now no longer experienced and interpreted in terms of concealment [*Verbergen*], but from the basis of deception [*Hintergehen*]. The Greek *pseudos*, through its translation into the Roman *falsum*, is *trans*ferred [*über*gesetzt] into the imperial Roman domain of the bringing-to-fall [*Zu-Fall-bringens*].[22]

The relay in this extraordinary passage between Roman truth (and falsehood), Roman cultural production, and Roman politics determined by the metaphorics of the supervisory gaze and the transcendental center is obvious. What should not be overlooked, however, is the historically specific context Heidegger's *Parmenides* addresses. At its most general level, it constitutes a genealogy of *modern* power relations. More specifically, it demonstrates that the "strong" discursive practices of what he calls "humanism" in his postwar "Letter on Humanism" have their origins, not in Greek thought, as it is assumed in modern Europe at large, but in the circular (anthropo)logic, the disciplinary pedagogy, and the imperial practice of Rome. It is no accident that in the latter half of the passage Heidegger carefully distinguishes between two kinds of domination that have a single origin. One kind of power over the fallen "other" operates directly (is immediate) and is thus visible; the other operates by indirection or detour (*Hintergehung*), is mediate, and is thus invisible. The "bringing-down-to-ground" can be accomplished in a direct assault (*Sturm*) or repressive conquest; or it can be achieved by discursive practices that are deceptively benign. But what is crucial is not simply that they are both determined by a fixed center that is above or beyond the reach of free play—of "reciprocal rejoinder," as it were—but also, and above all, that it is the latter—specifically, the discourse enabled by the Roman *veritas/falsum* opposition—that characterizes the developed form of "imperial" domination: "It is not in war, but in the *fallere* of deceptive outflanking and its appropriation to the service of dominion that the proper and 'great' trait of the imperial reveals itself." However generalized Heidegger's formulation, we are not far here from the post-structuralist and neo-Marxist interrogation of power relations in modernity: Foucault's analysis of the repressive hypothesis determining the practices of the disciplinary society, Gramsci's analogous analysis of capitalist hegemony, Althusser's analysis of the ideological state apparatuses,[23] and Said's analysis of the effects of the "strong languages" of the West vis-à-vis the "weak languages" of the "Third World," all of which implicate the "truth" of the dominant discursive practices with power and domination over the threatening "other."

Indeed, if, as there is every justification to do, we conflate the passages from the lectures on the *Parmenides* and the "Letter on Humanism" addressing the Roman reduction of Greek thinking, we arrive at the following proposition: Truth and power, knowledge production and repression, according to Heidegger, are not external to each other (as they are assumed to be in the discursive practices of humanism), but continuous and complicitous with each other. To put it in terms of the figure informing this relation, the circle of truth/beauty/perfection is also the circle of domination. The violence that accompanies overt imperialism is not incommensurate with but latent in the truth of humanism. Remarkably like Foucault, the benign discursive practices of humanism collectively constitute a "regime of truth."

In the historically specific context in which Heidegger is writing—and which he is implicitly addressing—what this disclosure concerning the origins of humanism suggests is that the *Parmenides* lectures and the "Letter on Humanism" constitute Heidegger's acknowledgment of the culpability of his political discourse during the rectorship, without succumbing to the judgment of his accusers. That is, they acknowledge its complicity with the dreadful practices of the Nazis, *and* they also constitute his decisive dissociation from the Nazis' grotesque imperial project, without, at the same time, subscribing to the compelling but dubious binary (ideo)logic (which, since Victor Farías's "revelations" in *Heidegger et le nazisme*, has been used against him) that radically distinguishes between the democracy of Western Europe (including the United States) and the fascism of the Third Reich. What Heidegger indirectly seems to be saying in these texts, at least in part, is that the nihilistic Nazi imperial project (which was about to culminate in Auschwitz) was not an aberration from the circular humanist logic of the Occident but its concrete and horribly explicit fulfillment. Heidegger indeed failed later to discriminate between the civilized barbarism of "Europe" and the Nazis' unspeakable project to exterminate the Jews, and for this he is profoundly culpable. But this (as I shall argue at length in the last chapter) is not reason enough to write off his resonant equation. As Philippe Lacoue-Labarthe puts it against those recent detractors of Heidegger's thought at large, who represent the horror perpetrated by the Nazi regime as the triumphal vindication of humanist democracy:

> Nazism is a humanism, insofar as it is grounded on a *humanitas* that in its view is more powerful, that is to say more effective, than any other. The subject of absolute auto-creation, even if it transcends all the determinations of the modern subject in a position that is immediately natural (the specificity of race), gathers and concretizes these same determinations, and constitutes itself as *the* absolute speaking subject in absolute terms. That this subject lacks the universality that apparently defines the *humanitas* of humanism in a received sense does not mean that Nazism is antihumanist. This subject simply inscribes humanism in the logic, of which there are many examples, of the realization and becoming concrete of abstractions.[24]

And, though Lacoue-Labarthe insists that Heidegger's "fault" was precisely his failure to think Auschwitz, "this event, the Extermination, is for the West, the terrible revelation of its essence."[25]

I shall address the question of the historically specific politics of Heidegger's philosophical discourse at large in the last chapter. Here, what concerns me is precisely his disclosure of the essential complicity of truth as *veritas* and the idealized figure of the circle informing it with the domination of the marginal "other": the disclosure enabled by his genealogical analysis of the "disinterested" discourse of Western (i.e., humanist) modernity, specifically its re-presentation of being and time, identity and difference, as hierarchized binary opposites in which the first term is empowered (as *principium* or center or truth) over the second (as accident—from *cadere*, to fall or perish—or periphery or falseness). For whatever the degree to which Heidegger appropriated his philosophical thought in behalf of the ends of Nazi practice—and I am not at all convinced that the anecdotal or circumstantial and retrospective strategy employed by his humanist detractors is adequate to the task of determining it—the fact remains that Heidegger's philosophical texts as such insist fundamentally on precisely this dis-closure vis-à-vis the philosophical discourse of the Occident. As such, they have enabled or at least catalyzed a number of contemporary discursive practices committed to the emancipation or emergence of a variety of cultural and sociopolitical subject positions hitherto spoken for and colonized by the hegemonic discursive practices of Occidental modernity.

It is true that Heidegger focused his interrogation of the dominant discourse of modernity on the most rarefied site on the indissoluble continuum of being: i.e., the ontological understood as *Technik*, the global enframing (*Gestell*) that has reduced being in all its manifestations to standing reserve (*Bestand*). It is also true that this focus blinded him to the other more "concrete" or "worldly" sites, most notably—and it must be conceded, irresponsibly—the site of European politics, where the Nazis perpetrated their murderous totalitarian practice. But, however consequential, this failure to de-structure his own historically specific sociopolitical occasion does not invalidate his ontological disclosure vis-à-vis the representation of being and difference or of difference in the light of Being by the Occident at large and by humanist modernity in particular. Nor, finally, does it disable *a* destructive hermeneutics that could interrogate the representations of those more "practical" and historically overdetermined sites, especially the sociopolitical, which Heidegger himself neglected or overlooked or misread. Indeed, such a passage from ontological to sociopolitical critique of Western modernity, despite the misguided ultranationalist twist of the rectorate period and his continuing identification of the German language with the ancient Greek, is latent in Heidegger's destructive effort, beginning with *Being and Time*, to retrieve being *as* historicity from Being as re-*presentation*. This is clearly suggested in the following unremarked moment in "Letter on Humanism," a text, it should be not forgotten, written in the aftermath of the destruction of the Third Reich, and at the outset of the Cold War:

> Homelessness is coming to be the destiny of the world. Hence it is necessary to think that destiny in terms of the history of Being. What Marx recognized in an essential and significant sense, though derived from Hegel, as the estrangement of modern man has its roots in the homelessness of modern man. This homelessness is specifically evoked from the destiny of Being in the form of metaphysics and through metaphysics is simultaneously entrenched and covered up as such. Because Marx by experiencing estrangement attains an essential dimension of history, the Marxist view of history is superior to that of other historical accounts. But since neither Husserl nor—so far as I have seen till now—Sartre recognized the essential importance of the historical in being, neither phenomenology nor existentialism enters that dimension within which a productive dialogue with Marxism first becomes

possible. . . . No matter which of the various positions one chooses to adopt toward the doctrines of communism and to their foundations, from the point of view of the history of Being it is certain that an elemental experience of what is world-historical speaks out in it.[26]

In the specific terms of my thematization of the political implications latent in Heidegger's destructive hermeneutics, the recognition of the temporality of being as a lateral, however unevenly developed, continuum or field of forces makes explicit the relay between the residual "humanities" and the overdetermined disciplinary technologies of Western modernity, a relay that the disciplinary compartmentalization of knowledge has made invisible. It exposes, in Edward Said's apt term, the "affiliation"[27] between the negative and inactive epistemological oversight, leveling, and forgetting of difference issuing from "inquiring" *meta-ta-physika* (from after or above temporality) and the positive and active (if largely rarefied, i.e., hegemonic) repression, territorialization, and colonization of the relay of sociopolitical "others" enabled by the super-visory panoptic machinery of the post-Enlightenment disciplinary society. In other words, such a recognition makes possible, indeed necessary in the present historical conjuncture, a productive dialogue between Heidegger's interrogation of the ontological ground of modernity—which includes both capitalism and Stalinism—and the recent, more "worldly" critics' interrogation of its sociopolitical practices, especially Foucault's analysis of the knowledge/power nexus: between Heidegger's de-struction of the ontotheological tradition at large and Foucault's genealogy of what he calls the modern "disciplinary society" or the "regime of truth."

I am suggesting the following narrative about the course of Western history: The inscribed tendency of the grave metaphysical eye to *over-look* distracting or disconcerting "deviations"—what William Blake called the "minute particulars," Heidegger "ontological difference" (the temporality of being), Derrida "*differance*," and Foucault "the singular event"— from the vantage point of a Transcendental Signified (the logocentric One) on behalf of truth, inevitably, however erratically and unevenly, became in time completely internalized. In the age of the Enlightenment, it took the form of a willful, indeed *mono*-maniacal and totalizing obsession of rationality to name, classify, comprehend, and control the disruptive mystery of difference. This movement, in turn, precipitated the generalized calculative reformist cultural and sociopolitical strategy of *sur-veillance* or *super-vision* that, according to Foucault, constitutes the essence of modernity. To put this narrative into the analogous terms of geometry, the centered circle—the figure of truth/beauty/perfection theorized by the post-Socratics and practiced by the Romans, according to Heidegger—came to be understood and utilized in and by the modern world as the *discreet and productive* figure not only of cultural but of sociopolitical power.

This is not to say that, in overdetermining the (scientifically and technologically organized) sociopolitical site, the history of the West has rendered Heidegger's ontological destruction of modernity irrelevant for critique in favor of Foucault's genealogy of discipline. However uneven the distribution of power, the ontological and the sociopolitical constitute an indissoluble relay. Insofar as Heidegger's destruction emphasized the ontological construction of modernity (its philosophical ground) it was, as we have seen, a limited agency of critical practice. But insofar as Foucault (and other contemporary worldly critics) emphasizes its sociopolitical construction (its scientific/technological ground), his genealogy too constitutes a limited agency of critique. The circular/panoptic technology of power that characterizes modernity is both ontological and sociopolitical. And it has as its calculative end the coercive re-formation— in the name of the logocentric/sociopolitical norm (the guardian eye)— of "de-formed" or "de-viant," or "fallen," ec-centric, or erratic forces all along the indissoluble continuum of being: temporal, ecological, linguistic, sexual, racial, and sociopolitical. What needs to be emphasized provisionally is that the planetary technology of power informing the discourse and practice of Western modernity is not simply the consequence of the rise of the scientific/technological *epistémé* of the Enlightenment, as Foucault's genealogy might suggest. Nor, on the other hand, is it simply the consequence of philosophy, as Heidegger's discourse all too insistently affirms. It is, as a reading of Heidegger with Foucault or Foucault with Heidegger will suggest, the consequence of both. A dialogue between their discourses will show that the overdetermined sciences and the "residual" humanities—the "two cultures" that the dominant culture represents as adversaries—are, in fact, different instruments of the *anthropo-logos*, the discourse of Man, and thus complicitous in the late capitalist West's neoimperial project of planetary domination.

III

It is not the explicit intention of Foucault's genealogical analysis of the theory and practice of humanist society to extend the scope of Heidegger's destructive hermeneutics. Indeed, Foucault seems to reject an understanding of Western history as a continuous narrative—an ontotheological tradition—seeing it rather as characterized by ruptures. But in his last interview before his untimely death, Foucault said this about his relationship to Heidegger's thought:

For me Heidegger has always been the essential philosopher. I began by reading Hegel, then Marx, and I set out to read Heidegger in 1951 or 1952; then in 1952 or 1953—I don't remember any more—I read Nietzsche. I still have here the notes that I took when I was reading Heidegger. I've got tons of them. And they are much more important than the ones I took on Hegel and Marx. My entire philosophical development was determined by my reading of Heidegger. I nevertheless recognized that Nietzsche outweighed him. I do not know Heidegger well enough: I hardly know *Being and Time* nor what has been published recently. My knowledge of Nietzsche certainly is better than my knowledge of Heidegger. Nevertheless, these are the two fundamental experiences I have had. It is possible that if I had not read Heidegger, I would not have read Nietzsche. I had tried to read Nietzsche in the fifties but Nietzsche alone did not appeal to me—whereas Nietzsche and Heidegger: that was a philosophical shock. But I have never written on Heidegger, and I wrote only a very small article on Nietzsche. . . . In the end for me there are three categories of philosophers: the philosophers that I don't know; the philosophers I know and of whom I have spoken; and the philosophers I know and about whom I don't speak.[28]

This statement in and by itself says nothing about the specific relationship between Foucault's and Heidegger's discourses. But if it is remembered that Foucault's "very small article on Nietzsche" was "Nietzsche, Genealogy, History" (1971), this teasing aside in his discourse activates a resonance that has not received adequate attention. For this pivotal essay in the itinerary of Foucault's discourse locates Nietzsche's critique of modernity at precisely the site where Heidegger's does: the "suprahistorical" perspective from which humanist historiography re-presents the differentiality of historicity:

Nietzsche's criticism, beginning with the second of the "Untimely Meditations," always questioned the form of history that reintroduces (and always assumes) a suprahistorical perspective: a history whose function is to compose the finally reduced diversity of time into a totality fully closed upon itself; a history that always encourages subjective recognitions and attributes a form of reconciliation to all the displacements of the past; a history whose perspective on all that precedes it implies the end of time, a completed development. The historian's history finds its support outside of time and pretends to base its judgments on an apocalyptic objectivity. This is only possible, however, because of its belief in eternal truth, the immortality of the soul, and the nature of consciousness as always identical to itself. Once the historical sense is mastered by a suprahistorical perspective, metaphysics can bend it

to its own purpose and, by aligning it to the demands of objective
science, it can impose its own "Egyptianism."[29]

In focusing on Nietzsche's exposure of the "Egyptianism"—the will to
power over difference—inscribed in the *suprahistorical* perspective of
the humanists' historiography, Foucault's essay also enables his epoch-
making genealogy of modern knowledge/power relations, *Surveiller et
punir* (1975), which disclosed the origins of modernity's disciplinary/
hegemonic "microphysics of power" in the panoptic technology precipitated by the quest for "enlightenment."

A reading of Foucault's *Discipline and Punish*[30] in the context of Heidegger's interrogation of the founding metaphorics of the Western philosophical tradition (I mean the light/darkness metaphoric opposition, or,
what has always been another version of the same figural constellation,
the centered circle/periphery, which privileges the first term as the symbol of the beautiful and utopian) will go far to establish the affiliation
between Heidegger's destruction of the philosophy of the ontotheological tradition and Foucault's genealogy of post-Enlightenment power relations. More important, such a reading will also suggest a theory of
knowledge/power relations that overcomes the disciplinary tendencies of
each discourse that minimize its critical potential, a theory that is more
adequate than either for a critique of modernity, of what Foucault calls
the "regime of Truth" and Gramsci, "hegemony": the totalizing discursive practice that has internalized visible power not simply at particular
sites, but throughout the continuum of being-in-the-world, by putting
the "truth" of "disinterested inquiry" in a binary adversarial opposition
against it.

Those commentators Foucault has influenced have represented as ax-
iomatic what in his genealogy of the disciplinary society is only an emphasis, a matter of overdetermination: that its origins lie in an epistemic
rupture that precipitated the Enlightenment:

> This business about discontinuity has always rather bewildered me.
> In the new edition of the *Petit Larousse* it says "Foucault: a
> philosopher who founds his theory of history on discontinuity."
> That leaves me flabbergasted. No doubt I didn't make myself
> sufficiently clear in *The Order of Things*. . . . It seemed to me that in
> *certain empirical forms of knowledge* like biology, political economy,
> psychiatry, medicine, etc. the rhythm of transformation doesn't
> follow the smooth, continuist schemas of development which are
> normally accepted. . . . These are not simply new discoveries; there
> is a whole new "regime" in discourse and forms of knowledge. And
> all this happens in the space of a few years. This is something which
> is undeniable, once one has looked at the texts with sufficient

attention. My problem was not at all to say, "*Voila*, long live discontinuity, we are in the discontinous and a good thing too," but to pose the question, "How is it that at certain moments and in certain orders of knowledge, there are these sudden take-offs, these hastenings of evolution, these transformations which fail to correspond to the calm, continuist image that is normally accredited?"[31]

In thus interpreting Foucault's apparent rejection of the continuist understanding of Western history as an affirmation of historical discontinuity, Foucault's commentators have also gone far to crystallize as dogma a related tendency—one on which he, in fact, focuses in the above passage—in Foucault's discourse: the separation of traditional "philosophy" (the discourses of classical humanism) and the post-Enlightenment empirical sciences. As a result, they have missed or denied the affinities between his genealogy of the disciplinary society and Heidegger's destruction of the ontotheological tradition. In order to retrieve these critically resonant affinities, therefore, it will be necessary to reread *Surveiller et punir* at some length, focusing on what is overlooked by commentary grounded in the unexamined assumption that modernity begins with an epistemic break occurring in the eighteenth century. I mean those marginal but insistently recurrent moments in Foucault's text that point to a history of the centered circle/panoptic gaze (and the will to power over difference inscribed in them) that long precedes its consummation (overdetermination) in the Enlightenment and after. These moments suggest the affiliative relationship between Heidegger's and Foucault's discourses; also, and more important, they implicate the "two cultures" split in the establishment, legitimation, and reproduction of the disciplinary society.[32]

Foucault is remarkably persuasive in suggesting that the supervisory schema emerging as something like an epistemic break during the Enlightenment has determined and continues increasingly to invest every facet of life in the modern West, from the everyday lives of ordinary men and women through material and cultural production to the history-making agendas of those who administer civil and political societies. What I am suggesting by way of contextualizing Foucault's historically specific discourse within the larger framework of Heidegger's interrogation of "philosophy" (the ontotheological tradition at large), however, is that this practically polyvalent schema long precedes the historical juncture in which Foucault apparently locates it. It is a latent possibility of the metaphysical or logocentric mode of inquiry, of the circle that has its "center elsewhere," of the binary light/darkness opposition privileged by the post-Socratic Greek philosophers (Plato, for example, in the

"Allegory of the Cave")[33] and above all by the republican and imperial Romans. I am also suggesting, by way of thematizing what Heidegger left unsaid, that this disciplinary super-visory schema came to be theorized and practiced considerably earlier, however experimentally, however underdeveloped in execution, than the Enlightenment.

It can be seen, as I have suggested elsewhere,[34] to be operative in the Utopian discourses of the Renaissance, in Campanella's ideal Platonic/Roman/Christian *City of the Sun* (1623), for example, the circular and radial geometry of which was theoretically intended not simply to represent in microcosmic form the self-identical beauty, the harmony, the integration, and the permanence of a heliocentric macrocosm supervised by a transcendental deity or being, but also to produce a private and collective form of life that reflected this ideal: an *urbis* mirroring the *orb*. But the supervisory schema was not restricted to the utopian discourses of Renaissance "poetic" humanists. Through the rediscovery and mediation of the Roman Vitruvius's *Ten Books of Architecture* (first century B.C.) in the fifteenth century, an architectural and city-planning tradition, both theoretical and practical, was inaugurated in Europe based on the first book, which posits radially organized circularity as the ideal design not only for defense but for the health of its citizens.[35] This architectural initiative led inevitably, however unevenly, from the circular city modeled on the Christian/humanist figure of beauty, order, perfection (Filarete, 1400–1469; Giocondo, c. 1435–1515; Cerceau the Elder, 1500–1584; Daniel Speckle, 1536–1589; etc.) through the circular fortress cities of the seventeenth and eighteenth centuries (Sardi; Errard de Bar-le-Duc, 1554–1610; and, above all, Vauban, 1633–1707) to the overdetermined manufactory (Claude-Nicholas Ledoux's Arc-et-Senans, 1775–1779) and city (Ledoux's Chaux). These last, according to Foucault, are the immediate predecessors of Jeremy Bentham's Panopticon. (This tradition is discernible in the radial geometry of Baron Haussmann's Paris.)

This synecdochical history thematizes a process in which the humanist figure of beauty par excellence gradually and inexorably however unevenly, manifests the practical potential for domination latent in it—paralleling at the site of architectural design a process that occurs at the sites of philosophy and literature. It thus suggests a significant modification of Foucault's genealogy of the disciplinary society, which, according to his emphasis, is given its enabling impetus by the "sudden take-off" of the empirical sciences (most notably, "biology, political economy, psychiatry, medicine, etc.") and the technological apparatuses developed in the Enlightenment. There is an affiliative relationship, however diminished in visibility by the rapid historical accretion of detail in the eighteenth century, between the panoptic *polis* of the post-Enlightenment and the circular cities of the Renaissance humanists—cities that drew their inspiration not only from the Roman Vitruvius's text on architecture, but also from the medieval theologians (St. Augustine, for example) and from the ontologians of classical antiquity (Plato, for example, whose texts are the focus of Heidegger's interrogation). The microphysical technologies of power enabled, according to Foucault, by the emergence of the panoptic schema in the Enlightenment are more scientific, more complex, more ordinary, more pervasive, and above all less visible than the obviously crude mathematical technique of supervision and discipline enabled by the "poetic" humanist Tommaso Campanella's circular/cosmic City of the Sun. And the effects of power—the uniform life of docile and useful bodies—produced by the geometry of panopticism are far more various and muted than the monochromatic uniformity of social life envisaged by the geometry of Campanella's Platonic/Christian heliocentrism. But they are both inscribed in a fundamental way by the polyvalent diagram of the centered circle and, as the following passage on genetics from the *City of the Sun* makes clear, by the supervisory procedures and disciplinary end that this perennially ideal figure is intended to produce:

> Since both males and females, in the manner of ancient Greeks, are completely naked when they engage in wrestling exercises, their teachers may readily distinguish those who are able to have intercourse from those who are not and can determine whose sexual organs may best be matched with whose [e quali membra con quali si confanno]. Consequently, every third night, after they have all bathed, the young people are paired off for intercourse. Tall handsome girls are not matched with any but tall brave men, while fat girls are matched with thin men and thin girls with fat men, so as to avoid extremes in their offspring. On the appointed evening, the boys and girls prepare their beds and go to bed where the matron and senior direct them. Nor may they have intercourse until they have completely digested their food and have said their prayers. There are fine statues of illustrious men that the women gaze upon. Then both male and female go to a window to pray to the God of Heaven for a good issue. They sleep in separate neighboring cells until they are to have intercourse. At the proper time [when the most favorable astronomical conditions obtain], the matron goes around and opens the cell doors.[36]

This brief retrieval of the history of the disciplinary uses to which the figure of the circle was put in architecture and urban planning, which, according to Foucault's emphasis, has its origins far more recently in Claude-Nicholas Ledoux's construction of the salt plant at Arc-et-Senan near Besançon (1775–79), is therefore important for my purposes. On the one hand, Heidegger fails adequately to perceive the possibility of a *sociopolitical* critique of the modern technological city because he puts the emphasis of his critique at the ontological site of the continuum of being. On the other, Foucault (and especially those sociopolitical critics he has influenced) fails adequately to perceive the possibility of an *ontological* critique of the disciplinary society: the degree, that is, to which the model of the circle as beauty/power has been already inscribed in the discursive practice of the disinterested humanitarian reformers. I mean the practice culminating in Jeremy Bentham's *Panopticon; or, Inspection House.*

To locate the disruptive emergence of the supervisory schema in the Enlightenment as such is to suggest that the repressive ideology inform-ing its ostensibly benign purposes is coincidental with the emergence of empirical science, applied technology, the bourgeois class, and capital-ism. It is, as the so-called two cultures debate in the 1960s bears witness, a context in which liberal humanists can all too easily disengage their "poetic" anthropology from complicity in the production of the disci-plinary society. However, the fulfilled supervisory schema can be traced back through the idealized circular cities of the Renaissance to the gen-eralized polyvalent image of beauty/perfection privileged by Augustine and, before that, by Plato and the post-Socratics and, as I have suggested by way of Heidegger's "Letter on Humanism" and his *Parmenides*, har-nessed politically in the form of the opposition between metropolis and provinces, *homo romanus* and barbarian, to the Roman pursuit of empire. To recognize the always reconstituted "continuity" of this schema, there-fore, is not simply to realize the profound degree to which the relation-ship between the spatial perception of temporal difference and sociopo-litical power is inscribed in the Occidental consciousness at large. It also suggests the continuing complicity of modern humanism—its "classical" mode of "disinterested" inquiry, the philosophical and literary texts it privileges, and its cultural apparatuses—with the disciplinary technology on which such sociopolitical thinkers as Gramsci, Althusser, Foucault, Adorno, Said, Laclau and Mouffe, and others focus their critique.

According to Foucault's emphasis in his genealogy of the disciplinary society, then, the relationship between the spatializing eye—"the disci-plinary gaze" (DP, 170)[37]—and power, supervision and discipline, as-sume overt theoretical articulation and practical implementation during the Enlightenment or *Aufklärung* (the metaphorics are not accidental). This theoretical and practical reality became increasingly prominent thereafter, when, it is important to remember, the "universal" (Occiden-tal) possibilities of humanistic (i.e., disinterested, liberal) cultural prac-tices began to become manifest.[38] The reformers of the brutal aristocratic punitive machinery were not essentially committed to humanitarian principles. They were more interested in the formulation and elaboration of a more efficient and economical penal system:

> It was not so much, or not only, the privileges of justice, its arbitrariness, its archaic arrogance, its uncontrolled rights that were criticized; but rather the mixture of its weaknesses and excesses, its exaggerations and its loopholes, and above all the very principle of this mixture, the "super-power" of the monarch. The true objective of the reform movement, even in its most general formulations, was not so much to establish a new right to punish based on more equitable principles, as to set up a new "economy" of the power to punish, to assure its better distribution, so that it should be neither too concentrated at certain privileged points, nor too divided between opposing authorities; so that it should be distributed in homogeneous circuits capable of operating everywhere, in a continuous way, down to the finest grain of the social body. The reform of criminal law must be read as a strategy for the rearrangement of the power to punish, according to modalities that render it more regular, more effective, more constant and more detailed in its effects; in short, which increase its effects while diminishing its economic cost . . . and its political cost. (DP, 80–81)

What the early reformers of the Enlightenment were ultimately searching for was not a penal system that acknowledged the otherness of the antisocial others. It was a system that would diminish the economic wastefulness of the indiscriminate irregularities and, equally important, the political visibility of power, one that would internalize, distribute, and saturate power in and throughout society (what Heidegger calls being-in-the-world) in order to increase productivity (of "knowledge" as well as capital goods) and to decrease the threat of revolt to which an identifiable power—a *visible* sovereign center—is necessarily exposed. They were groping toward a *generalized and generalizable system*, in short, capable of annulling the "force" of the alienated "other" and producing "docile and useful bodies." Foucault states the fully developed agenda of the post-Enlightenment:

> The historical moment of the disciplines was a moment when an art of the human body was born, which was directed not only at the growth of its skills, nor at the intensification of its subjection, but at the formation of a relation that in the mechanism itself makes it more obedient as it becomes more useful, and conversely. What was then being formed was a policy of coercions that act upon the body, a calculated manipulation of its elements, its gestures, its behaviour. The human body was entering a machinery of power that explores

it, breaks it down and rearranges it. . . . Thus discipline produces subjected and practised bodies, "docile" bodies. Discipline increases the forces of the body (in economic terms of utility) and diminishes these same forces (in political terms of obedience). In short, it dissociates power from the body; on the one hand, it turns it into an "aptitude," a "capacity," which it seeks to increase; on the other hand, it reverses the course of the energy, the power that might result from it, and turns it into a relation of strict subjection. If economic exploitation separates the force and the products of labour, let us say that disciplinary coercion established in the body the constricting link between an increased aptitude and an increased domination. (DP, 138)

In their search for such a "new 'economy' of the power to punish," the reformers, according to Foucault, were inevitably guided by the photological semiotic network privileged by the Enlightenment. The *episteme*'s overdetermined valorization of the eye and its light and the discriminating technology of optics to which it gave rise made these reformers increasingly aware of the relationship between enlightenment—the making visible, particular, knowable, and measurable of the obscure, amorphous, and always wasteful and threatening "other"—and power. They thus sought after a sophisticated design/apparatus the economy of which could organize and apply visible space for the purpose of achieving optimal production and disciplinary supervision of the individualized multiplicity enclosed within its well-lighted parameters:

The exercise of discipline presupposes a mechanism that coerces by means of observations; an apparatus in which the techniques that make it possible to see induces effect of power, and in which, conversely, the means of coercion make those on whom they are applied clearly visible. Slowly, in the course of the classical age, we see the construction of those "observatories" of human multiplicity for which the history of the sciences has so little good to say. Side by side with the major technology of the telescope, the lens and the light beam, which were an integral part of the new physics and cosmology, there were the minor techniques of multiple and intersectional observations, of eyes that must see without being seen; using techniques of subjection and methods of exploitation, an obscure art of light and the visible was secretly preparing a new knowledge of man. (DP, 170–71)[39]

There is no doubt that the "obscure art of light and visibility was preparing a new knowledge of man" which was to culminate in the disciplinary society. But the historically specific density of Foucault's genealogy—especially its emphasis on the science of optics and its technology—should not obscure the legacy these humanist reformers inherited from the ontotheological tradition, above all that variation of optics inscribed in the theology of Calvinist Protestantism. It is no accident that the reformatories—from the Rasphuis of Amsterdam (1596) through the penitentiary at Gloucester (England) to the Walnut Street Prison (in Philadelphia, 1790) that provided architectural models for the disciplinary prison culminating in Bentham's Panopticon—were largely Protestant in origin (the latter instituted "under the direct influence of the Quakers," DP, 124). For it is quite clear, despite Foucault's minimization of significant reference, that the Enlightenment's war of reason against "wastefulness" (and deviance) in behalf of sociopolitical and economic economy (duty and utility) coincides with the Calvinist/Protestant work ethic, which, according to Max Weber, gave rise to the "spirit of capitalism." I mean more specifically the ethic rationalized and enabled by the circular doctrine of predestination, by the austere providential history represented, as the etymology suggests, in the image of the absolutely hidden, inscrutable, and supervisory eye of the Calvinist God. This was, in Weber's telling words, the "transcendental being," "beyond the reach of human understanding," who, by his "quite incomprehensible decrees has decided the fate of every individual and regulated the tiniest details of the cosmos from eternity."[40] Foucault, in fact, alludes to this resonant continuity between the eye of the Protestant theo-logos that, in accounting even for the fall of a sparrow, makes every singular thing and event accountable, and the later anthropo-logos that, in the surveillance of detail (difference), makes it serve the hegemonic purposes of the dominant culture (identity):

> There is a whole history to be written about such "stone-cutting"—
> a history of the utilitarian rationalization of detail in moral
> accountability and political control. The classical age did not initiate
> it; rather it accelerated it, changed its scale, gave it precise
> instruments, and perhaps found some echoes for it in the calculation
> of the infinitely small or in the description of the most detailed
> characteristics of natural beings. In any case, "detail" had long been
> a category of theology and asceticism: every detail is important
> since, in the sight of God, no immensity is greater than a detail, nor
> is anything so small that it was not willed by one of his individual
> wishes. In this great tradition of the eminence of detail, all minutiae
> of Christian education, of scholastic or military pedagogy, all forms
> of "training" found their place easily enough. For the disciplined
> man, as for the true believer, no detail is unimportant, but not so
> much for the meaning that it conceals within it as for the hold it
> provides for the power that wished to seize it. (DP, 140)

What lay more immediately to hand as architectural/methodological models for these "observatories," according to Foucault, were, significantly, the hospital, the insane asylum, the workshop, the elementary classroom, and above all the military camp. For in these spaces, as in the medieval plague town (DP, 147), time was enclosed, partitioned, serialized, functionalized, and thus immobilized or frozen. It was arranged to achieve optimal supervision under "the scrupulously 'classificatory' eye of the master" (DP, 17)[41] of a prolific and proliferating temporal world assumed to be naturally deviant—or, on another level, "prodigal" or "fallen" and "dispersed." It was an economy of space/time designed to eliminate confusion and waste and to rechannel the force of living bodies from the vantage point of a preestablished judgmental norm: a center elsewhere.[42] The model for the perfect military camp, for example, was that of the Roman legions:

> Power would be exercised solely through exact observation; each gaze would form a part of the overall functioning of power. . . . The geometry of paths, the number and distribution of tents, the orientation of their entrances, the disposition of files and ranks were exactly defined; the network of gazes that supervised one another was laid down. . . . The camp is the *diagram of a power* that acts by means of *general visibility*. For a long time this model of the camp *or at least its underlying principle* was found in urban development, in the construction of working-class housing estates, hospitals, asylums, prisons, schools: the spatial "nesting" of hierarchized surveillance. The principle was one of "embedding" (*"encastrement"*). The camp was to the rather shameful art of surveillance what the darkroom was to the great science of optics. (DP, 171–72; my emphasis)

Thus, according to Foucault, a whole "new" spatial problematic emerges, of an architecture that would assure the domesticating ends of discipline by rendering those on whom power acted visible to the supervisory gaze. It was to be

> an architecture that is no longer built simply to be seen (as with the ostentation of palaces), or to observe the external space (cf., the geometry of fortresses),[43] but to permit an internal, articulated, and detailed control—to render visible those who are inside it; in more general terms, an architecture that would operate to transform individuals: to act on those it shelters, to provide a hold on their conduct, to carry the effects of power right to them, to make it possible to know them, to alter them. Stones can make people docile and knowable. (DP, 172)

"The camp is a *diagram* of power": I emphasize provisionally what Foucault's rhetorical focus on the effects of the military camp's structure might deflect attention from. Read in the context of Heidegger's destruction of the ontotheological tradition—specifically his thematization of the will to power informing the perennially privileged centered circle—Foucault's analysis of the historically specific sociopolitical conjuncture that gave rise to such disciplinary architectural experiments suggests, in fact, how deeply the affiliation between spatial perception—perception *meta-ta-physika*—and power, center and circle, was inscribed as an "underlying principle" in the Western consciousness by the time of the Enlightenment. It was inevitable, therefore, however ironic, that the quest of a demographically volatile age for such a functional economy of space—a productive economy that served as agency of both surveillance and correction (reformation) according to the anthropological norm—would culminate at the end of the century in an architectural model of the ideal prison that epitomized in practice the spatial perspective of logocentrism: precisely the distancing panoramic perspective that, according to Heidegger, informs the ontotheological philosophical tradition at large, its ontology (metaphysics), its epistemology (truth as *adequaetio intellectus et rei*), and its symbolic figuration (the centered circle and the commanding gaze). It was inevitable, in other words, that the Enlightenment, as the very name of this age suggests, should "discover" an architectural model for reforming or normalizing sociopolitical "deviants" in which "the spatial 'nesting' " of military surveillance becomes *sur*-veillance, supervision, *super*-vision.

Nor is it accidental that this structural model—this trope—inscribed as a deep structure in the Western consciousness by the ancient will to power over being should have been inferred from the philosophical tradition by a humanist who contributed significantly to the triumph of technology and to rendering the modern period what Heidegger calls the "age of re-presentation" or the "age of the world picture": a thinker, that is, who brings the tradition beginning with Plato's privileging of the eye, the recollective memory, and, by extension, the hierarchized *polis* supervised by the encompassing ("synoptic") gaze of the guardians, to its fulfillment—and, according to Heidegger, to its end. I mean the English philosopher Jeremy Bentham, whose Panopticon, or "inspection house," laid the ground for the production of the disciplinary society. This is the architectural design that, according to Foucault, draws the visual/disciplinary machinery (the "taxonomic table," the " 'evolutive' time of genesis," the "examination," etc.) and the spatializing models (the plague town, the hospital, the insane asylum, the military camp, etc.) articulated during the eighteenth century into absolute symmetry with the supervision enabled by the metaphorics that privileged space and light over time and darkness. Despite its familiarity, Foucault's description is worth quoting at length for the sake of retrieving the polyvalent sedimented

metaphorics—the relay between centered circle and vision privileged by
the ontotheological tradition—which have hitherto been overlooked by
Foucault's commentators:

> We know the principle on which it was based: at the periphery, an
> annular building; at the center, a tower; this tower is pierced with
> wide windows that open onto the inner side of the ring, the
> peripheric building is divided into cells, each of which extends the
> whole width of the building; they have two windows, one on the
> inside, corresponding to the windows of the tower; the other, on the
> outside, allows the light to cross the cell from one end to the other.
> All that is needed, then, is to place a supervisor in a central tower
> and to shut up in each cell a madman, a patient, a condemned man,
> a worker or a schoolboy. By the effect of backlighting, one can
> observe from the tower, standing out precisely against the light, the
> small captive shadows in the cells of the periphery. They are like so
> many cages, so many small theatres, in which each actor is alone,
> perfectly individualized and instantly visible. The panoptic
> mechanism arranges spatial unities that make it possible to see
> instantly and to recognize immediately. In short, it reverses the
> principle of the dungeon; rather of its three functions—to enclose, to
> deprive of light and to hide—it preserves only the first and
> eliminates the other two. Full lighting and the eye of the supervisor
> capture better than darkness, which ultimately protected. Visibility is
> a trap. (DP, 200)

But Bentham, according to Foucault, intended more than a generalized supervision per se by this individualizing and normalizing circular
architectural ordering of space. He also wished to eliminate communication between inmates and thus to annul their potentially disruptive
force and to facilitate their correction. "The individual cell, opposite the
tower, was arranged to impose on it an "axial invisibility," but the separated cells within the peripheric building implied "a lateral invisibility."
Thus, from the point of view of the guardian (the center), this double
arrangement transformed "the crowd, a compact mass, a locus of multiple exchanges, individualities merging together, a collective effect,"
into "a multiplicity that can be numbered and supervised," in other
words, "*a collection of separated individualities.*" From the point of view of
the incarcerated (the periphery), it was reduced to "a sequestered and
observed solitude" (DP, 201, my emphasis).

Further, Bentham "envisaged not only venetian blinds on the win-
dows of the central observation hall, but, on the inside, partitions that
intersected the hall at right angles and, in order to pass from one quarter
to another, not doors but zig-zag openings; for the slightest noise, a
gleam of light, a brightness in a half-opened door would betray the pres-

ence of the guardians." In this way the Panopticon would accomplish in practice Bentham's "guiding principle": "that power should be visible and unverifiable." It would induce in the errant inmates as its primary effect

> a state of conscious and permanent visibility that assures the automatic functioning of power. So to arrange things that the surveillance is permanent in its effects, even if it is discontinuous in its action; that the perfection of power should tend to render its actual exercise unnecessary; that this architectural apparatus should be a machine for the creating and sustaining a power relation independent of the person who exercises it; in short, that the inmates should be caught up in a power situation of which they are themselves the bearers. (DP, 201)

According to Foucault, Bentham intended a disciplinary transformation or re-collection of amorphous and threatening deviation into unitary conformity—a collective of discreet and thus knowable individuals in their *proper* places in the identical and self-present whole—in which the individuals themselves become subjected subjects. Like Heidegger's *das Man*—the collective "they" that acts according to "the way things are publicly interpreted"—Bentham's deviants would themselves become the tautological transmitters of the normative power that renders them docile and useful instruments of the dominant cultural and sociopolitical orders. Behind this post-Enlightenment disciplinary practice, it should now be evident (even though Foucault does not overtly refer to them), lies the enabling principle and figurative corollaries of Western metaphysics: (1) *the principle that identity is the condition for the possibility of difference and not the other way around*; (2) the transcendental Eye (and its light) which this principle must necessarily privilege; and (3) the metaphorics of the centered circle it precipitates to do its discreetly coercive work. This is precisely the constellation thematized by Heidegger's destruction of the ontotheological tradition. What I am suggesting in this rereading of Foucault's *Surveiller et punir* is that Bentham's Panopticon brings to momentary fulfillment the coercive potential latent in metaphysical "oversight" *and*, by way of this specified excess, makes explicit (visible) the disciplinary genealogy of the "disinterested" discursive practices of modern liberal democratic (humanist) societies.

An inattentive reading of Foucault's text might raise the objection that Bentham's Panopticon represents a historically specific institution—the reformatory prison—or an appropriate architectural model for the establishment of future historically specific institutions of reformation. But such an interpretation is what Foucault's genealogy insistently denies. This is suggested by several passages I have quoted from *Surveiller et punir*, which relate the metaphorics of vision/power inscribed in the disciplinary technology of the emergent penal institution to the metaphorics of vision/power inscribed in the discourse of truth/beauty of the ontotheological tradition at large. They disclose (often against themselves) the degree to which the generalized disciplinary model—the *figure* of the centered circle—had been inscribed, prior to Bentham's historical occasion, in the institutions of Western culture. As I have provisionally remarked, it is also suggested by Foucault's insistent, however muted, reference to the *principle* underlying the concrete architectural instance: the military camp, we recall, is a "*diagram* of power that acts by means of general visibility." But this affiliation between Bentham and the metaphysical tradition at large is most clearly thematized in Foucault's analysis of Bentham's Panopticon itself, where he shows that Bentham himself conceived of his "inspection house" as a *generalized* structural model that was separable from any concrete and particular practice:

> [The Panopticon] is the *diagram of a mechanism of power reduced to its ideal form; its functioning, abstracted from any obstacle, resistance or friction, must be represented in a pure architectural and optical system*: it is in fact a *figure* of political technology that may and must be *detached* from any specific use.
>
> *It is polyvalent in its application*; it serves to reform prisoners, but also to treat patients, to instruct school children, to confine the insane, to supervise workers, to put beggars and idlers to work. . . . Whenever one is dealing with a multiplicity of individuals on whom a task or a particular form of behaviour must be imposed, the *panoptic schema* may be used. It is—necessary modifications apart— applicable "to all establishments whatsoever, in which, within a space not too large to be covered or commanded by buildings, a number of persons are meant to be kept under inspection." (Bentham, 40; DP, 205–6; my emphasis)

And again, letting Bentham's rhetoric itself do his critical genealogical work, Foucault writes of the panoptic schema:

> It is a way of obtaining from power "in hitherto unexampled quantity," "a great and new instrument of government . . . ; its great excellence consists in the great strength it is capable of giving to *any* institution it may be thought proper to apply it to" (Bentham, 66). . . .
>
> Bentham's Preface to *Panopticon* opens with a list of the benefits to be obtained from his "inspection-house": "*Morals reformed—health preserved—industry invigorated—instruction diffused—public burthens lightened*—Economy seated, as it were, upon a rock—the gordian knot of the Poor-Laws not cut, but untied—all by a *simple idea* in architecture!" (Bentham, 39; DP, 206–7; Bentham's emphasis)

Despite his references to technology and machinery, moreover, Foucault is not finally limiting the polyvalency of the spatial/visual diagram to scientific uses. That he is also, however marginally, thinking the uses to which it has been and can be put by "poetic" humanists becomes clear in an interview entitled "The Eye of Power" (which followed the publication of *Surveiller et punir*), where he identifies Bentham's "liberal scientific" (technological) project with Rousseau's liberal "lyrical" project: the pedagogy of self-fulfillment:

> I would say Bentham was the complement to Rousseau. What in fact was the Rousseauist dream that motivated many of the revolutionaries?
> It was the dream of a transparent society, visible and legible in each of its parts, the dream of there no longer existing any zones of darkness, zones established by the privileges of royal power or the prerogatives of some corporation, zones of disorder. It was the dream that each individual, whatever portion he occupied, might be able to see the whole society, that men's hearts should communicate, their vision be unobstructed by obstacle, and that opinion of all reign over each. . . .
> Bentham is both that and the opposite. He poses the problem of visibility, but he thinks of a visibility organized entirely around a dominating, overseeing gaze. He effects the project of a universal visibility which exists to serve a rigorous, meticulous power. Thus Bentham's obsession, the technical idea of the exercise of an "all-seeing" power, is grafted onto the great Rousseauist theme which is in some sense the lyrical note of the Revolution. The two things combine into a working whole. Rousseau's lyricism and Bentham's obsession.[44]

Bentham's Panopticon is not a historically specific manifestation of an emergent empirical scientific worldview as such. It represents, rather, an overdetermined instance of the multiple practical uses to which the traditional panoptic diagram was put in the post-Enlightenment. Eventually, as Bentham prophesied, it would come to be fully applied to institutions as diverse as medicine, psychiatry, and education and other modes of cultural production. In the end, it would utterly obscure all its material signs and become, in Foucault's terms, the generalized, all-encompassing, and comprehensive—the hegemonic—"panopticism" of the "disciplinary society":

> There are two images . . . of discipline. At one extreme, the discipline-blockade, the enclosed institution, established on the edges of society, turned inwards towards negative functions: arresting evil, breaking communications, suspending time. At the other extreme, with panopticism, is the discipline-mechanism: a

functional mechanism that must improve the exercise of power by making it lighter, more rapid, more effective, a design of subtle coercion for a society to come. The movement from one project to the other, from a schema of exceptional discipline to one of generalized surveillance, rests on a historical transformation: the gradual extension of the mechanisms of discipline throughout the seventeenth and eighteenth centuries, their spread throughout the whole social body, the formation of what might be called in general the disciplinary society. (DP, 209)

To return to the sociopolitical terms latent in Heidegger's too-rarified ontological interrogation of modernity, the inscription of the humanist figure of truth/beauty/perfection will culminate in the "age of the world picture": the age in which anthropological re-presentation, however unevenly developed at any particular site, traverses the entire lateral continuum of being, from the representation of being itself through language and cultural production to sociopolitical formations.

IV

Let me summarize Foucault's historically specific analysis of the transformation of power relations that took place between the period of the *ancien régime* and the post-Enlightenment in the terms he develops in *The History of Sexuality, Vol. I*, which follows *Surveiller et punir*. The humanist "reformers" of the Enlightenment took the opportunity afforded by the delegitimation and eventual collapse of monarchical uses of power—the arbitrary, overt and visible employment of force that was economically wasteful and politically vulnerable (in the sense that its visibility made it resistable)—to elaborate a far more subtle system of coercion grounded in the "repressive hypothesis." This new view of power relations, according to Foucault, represents power in essentially negational terms: as "prohibition, censorship and denial," "repression" pure and simple.[45] In so doing, it authorizes and instigates, rather than restricts, the discourse of truth (the will to knowledge). Indeed, it renders (the production of) "truth" (its light) the essential agency of deliverance from power's negative effects (its darkness). As Hubert Dreyfus and Paul Rabinow put it in their succinct analysis of Foucault's genealogy of "the relations of sex, truth, power, the body, and the individual" in modernity:

> The repressive hypothesis is anchored in a tradition which sees power only as constraint, negativity, and coercion. As a systematic refusal to accept reality, as a repressive instrument, as a ban on truth, the forces of power prevent or at least distort the formation of

knowledge. Power does this by suppressing desire, fostering false consciousness, promoting ignorance, and using a host of other dodges. Since it fears the truth, power must suppress it.

It follows that power as repression is best opposed by the truth of discourse. When the truth is spoken, when the transgressive voice of liberation is raised, then, supposedly, repressive power is challenged. Truth itself would not be totally devoid of power, but its power is at the service of *clarity*, nondistortion, and one form or another of higher good, even if the higher good is nothing more substantive than *clarity*. . . . Foucault calls this view of power the "juridico-discursive." It is thoroughly negative; power and truth are entirely external to each other. Power produces nothing but "limit and lack." It lays down the law, and the juridical discourse then limits and circumscribes. Punishment for disobedience is always close at hand. Power is everywhere the same: It operates according to the simple and endlessly reproduced mechanism of "law, taboo, and censorship." Power is domination. All it can do is forbid, and all it can command is obedience. Power, ultimately, is repression; repression, ultimately, is the imposition of the law; the law, ultimately, demands submission.[46]

Foucault's point is that the "repressive hypothesis" on which the relations between truth and power in modernity rests is a deception—a construction of the dominant culture and sociopolitical order that is given the semblance of being naturally derived—and thus to be exposed. In representing power as purely negative, outside and in opposition to truth, the post-Enlightenment humanist reformers also represented the discourse of truth as essentially benign: disinterested and thus "liberal," "emancipatory," "ameliorative." But in fact this humanist discourse of truth is—precisely in its ability to produce knowledge (of the other)—complicitous with power. It is, in Gramsci's phrase, a compelling ruse intended to gain "spontaneous consent" by those differential constituencies on which power is practiced:

> We must cease once and for all to describe the effects of power in negative terms: it "excludes," it "represses," it "censors," it "abstracts," it "masks," it "conceals." In fact, power produces; it produces reality; it produces domains of objects and rituals of truth. The individual and the knowledge that may be gained of him belong to this production. (DP, 194)

To put it in a way that Foucault's commentators, including Dreyfuss and Rabinow, tend to obfuscate by generalizing truth and power, the "repressive hypothesis" elaborated in the Enlightenment put the *anthropologos* that replaced the *theologos* out of reach of the free play of criticism without at the same time annulling its power to dominate those differential constituencies that were the targets of the humanist discourse of truth. Despite Foucault's emphasis, the break with the *ancien régime* accomplished by the Enlightenment humanists was not finally a radical rupture. It was rather, to recall Derrida's Heideggerian discourse, the substitution of one center for another. In the age of monarchs the determining and repressive center elsewhere or "eye of power" (the *theologos* that sanctioned the sovereign king's direct use of force to punish or prohibit deviation) was *visible* and thus subject to resistance (as the French Revolution testifies). In the post-Enlightenment, the center elsewhere and its commanding/supervisory gaze (the *anthropologos*) of the humanist reformers became increasingly *invisible* (internalized) as the effects of its power increasingly spread throughout the social body. If one thinks the terms according to their Roman/Latin origins, it might be said that the "colonialism" of the *ancien régime* became the "neocolonialism" of the post-Enlightenment. This difference-in-continuity is, in fact, the enabling thesis of Foucault's genealogy of truth/power relations inscribed in the related discursive practices of sexuality in modernity:

> At bottom, despite the differences in epochs and objectives, the representation of power has remained under the spell of monarchy. In political thought and analysis, we still have not cut off the head of the king. Hence the importance that the theory of power gives to the problem of right and violence, law and illegality, freedom and will, and especially the state and sovereignty (even if the latter is questioned insofar as it is personified in a collective being and no longer a sovereign individual). To conceive of power on the basis of these problems is to conceive of it in terms of a historical form that is characteristic of our societies: the juridical monarchy.[47]

In thus bringing to explicitness the sedimented and naturalized metaphorics of the centered circle and the supervisory gaze informing what we can now call the humanist "ruse of the repressive hypothesis," we are compelled to retrieve Heidegger's genealogy of truth/power relations as these have been increasingly elaborated in and by Western civilization. I am referring not simply to his disclosure of the origins of the humanist discourse of truth in the Roman reduction of the originary thinking of the Greeks (*aletheia/pseudos*) to a derivative thinking intended to serve the imperial project (*veritas/falsum*) ("We think the political in a Roman fashion, that is, in its imperial sense"). I am also and primarily recalling his related distinction between an older immediate imperialism that applied force directly and its developed and fulfilled form, a mediate or neoimperialism that accomplished the hegemonic ends of empire by means of the ruse of the discourse of truth as *veritas*. Since the affiliations between Heidegger's and Foucault's genealogical discourses I want to foreground are crucial to my argument, the relevant part of the passage from the *Parmenides* lectures quoted earlier bears repeating:

> The "bringing-to-fall" [*das Zu-Fall-bringen*] belongs necessarily to the domain of the imperial. The "bringing-to-fall" can be accomplished in a "direct" assault [*Ansturm*] and an overthrowing [*Niederwerfen*: literally, "throwing down"]. But the other can also be brought-to-fall by being outflanked and tripped from behind. The "bringing-to-fall" is now the way of deceptive circumvention [*Hinter-gehen*: "going behind"]. . . . Considered from the outside, going behind the back is a complicated, circumstantial and thus mediate "bringing-to-fall" as opposed to an immediate overthrowing [*Niederwerfen*]. In this way, what is brought-to-fall [*Zu-Fall-Gebrachte*] does not thereby become annihilated, but in a certain manner redressed within the boundaries [*in den Grenzen*] which are staked out by the dominators. This "staking out" [*Abstecken*] is called in Roman: *pango*, whence the word *pax*, peace. This, thought imperially, is the firmly established condition of what has been brought-to-fall. In truth, the bringing-to-fall in the sense of deception [*Hintergehens*] and outflanking [*Umgehens*] is not the mediate and derived imperial *actio*, but the imperial *actio* proper. It is not in war, but in the *fallere* of deceptive outflanking [*hintergehenden Umgehens*] and its appropriation to the service of dominion that the proper and "great" trait of the imperial reveals itself.

It is this mediate *hintergehenden Umgehens*—the "trick" or ruse enabled by the naturalization of the imperial center and the enabling commanding gaze (the *Übersehen-können*) in the "truth discourse" of humanist modernity—that, according to Heidegger, has facilitated the "Europeanization of the planet"[48] in the "age of the world picture." Despite Heidegger's generalization of its sociopolitical implications, this *hintergehenden Umgehens* enabled by the invisible commanding gaze bears a striking resemblance to the "repressive hypothesis," which, according to Foucault, was enabled by the Enlightenment's rendering invisible the visible center elsewhere / panoptic gaze of monarchy. Is not this conquest by detour or circumvention, which represents the end of imperial violence as a universal *"pax,"* precisely the ruse of the discourse of truth, which calls the globalization of disciplinary society—the "regime of truth"—a space of freedom (the "new world order")?

Should this convergence I am suggesting sound like a perverse imposition, let me retrieve a dimension largely overlooked in most accounts of Foucault's genealogy; one which, however rightly subordinated to his immediate focus on the emergent technologies of discipline (the discourse of detail, the table, the examination, anatomy, etc.), nevertheless informs them through and through. I am referring to what Foucault calls "the Roman reference" (briefly remarked above in my citation of the military camp as a source of the panoptic diagram): the fact that the Enlightenment was also an age that modeled its cultural, military, and sociopolitical self-image on Roman (not Greek) antiquity. "One should not forget," Foucault writes, in remarking the "pyramidal" supervisory structure of the French Jesuit colleges, "that, generally speaking, the Roman model, at the Enlightenment, played a dual role; in its military aspect, it was the ideal schema of discipline. The Rome of the eighteenth century and of the Revolution was the Rome of the Senate, but it was also that of the legion; it was the Rome of the Forum, but it was also that of the camps." If, "up to the Empire, the Roman reference transmitted, somewhat ambiguously, the juridical ideal of citizenship and the technique of disciplinary methods" (DP, 146), in the Napoleonic era, these aspects coalesced in an "Augustan" imperial project that prepared the way for the "neoimperialism" of the humanist disciplinary society:

> Historians of ideas usually attribute the dream of a perfect society to the philosophers and jurists of the eighteenth century; but there was also a military dream of society; its fundamental reference was not to the state of nature, but to the meticulously subordinated cogs of a machine, not to the primal social contract, but to permanent coercions, not to fundamental rights, but to indefinitely progressive forms of training, not to the general will but to automatic docility.
>
> "Discipline must be national," said Guibert ["Discours preliminaire," *Essai général de tactique, I*, 1772]. "The state that I depict will have a simple, reliable, easily controlled administration. It will resemble those huge machines, which by quite uncomplicated means produce great effects; the strength of this state will spring from its own strength, its prosperity from its own prosperity. Time, which destroys all, will increase its power. It will disprove that vulgar prejudice by which we are made to imagine that empires are subjected to an imperious law of decline and ruin." . . . The Napoleonic régime was not far off and *with it the form of state that was to survive it* and, we must not forget, the foundations of which were laid not only by jurists, but also by soldiers, not only by councillors of state, but also junior officers, not only the men of the courts, but also the men of the camps. The Roman reference that accompanied this formation certainly bears with it this double index: citizens and legionaries, law and manoeuvres. (DP, 169, my emphasis)[49]

As in Heidegger's texts, so in Foucault's: it is the Roman model—the disciplinary training enabled by the commanding gaze (supervision of detail), a dependable citizenship (docile and useful bodies), and the "*imperium sine fini*" (Virgil)—that constitutes the ultimate, however distant, origins not only of the overtly imperial state but also the invisibly neoimperial modern state—the hegemonic disciplinary society—that survived the Napoleonic empire. And, however strained it may seem to both Foucauldians and anti-Foucauldians (the *nouveaux philosophes*, for example) it is the *homo humanus*—whose origins, according to Heidegger, reside in *homo romanus*—who, according to an underlying, if unremarked, motif in Foucault, provides the principle of continuity between both sociopolitical regimes. It is no accident, Foucault reiterates, that the world regulated by the "supervision of the smallest fragment of life and the body" envisaged by the Romanized intellectuals of the Enlightenment should bring us, first,

> at the end of the century, to the man who dreamt of being another Newton, not the Newton of the immensities of the heavens and the planetary masses, but a Newton of "small bodies," small movements, and small actions. . . . Napoleon did not discover this world; but we know that he set out to organize it; and he wished to arrange around him a mechanism of power that would enable him to see the smallest event that occurred in the state he governed; he intended, by means of the rigorous discipline that he imposed, "to embrace the whole of this vast machine without the slightest detail escaping his attention" (Treilhard, 14). (DP, 141)

and then, through Napoleon's political mediation of knowledge production, to the age of discipline determined by the concept of "Man":

> A meticulous observation of detail, and at the same time a political awareness of these small things, for the control and use of men, emerge through the classical age bearing with them a whole set of techniques, a whole corpus of methods and knowledge, descriptions, plans and data. And from such trifles, no doubt, the man of modern humanism was born. (DP, 141)[50]

And if, in *Disciple and Punish*, Foucault does not tell us explicitly what he means by "the man of modern humanism," he does elsewhere, in such a way as to identify this "invention" not simply with the ruse of the "repressive hypothesis," but with the entire chain of representational deceptions that Heidegger thematizes in his destruction of the anthropological discourse of Occidental modernity:

> By humanism I mean the totality of discourse through which Western man is told: "Even though you don't exercise power, you can still be a ruler. Better yet, the more you deny yourself the exercise of power, the more you submit to those in power, then the more this increases your sovereignty." Humanism invented a whole series of subjected sovereignties: the soul (ruling the body, but subjected to God), consciousness (sovereign in a context of

judgment, but subjected to the necessities of truth), the individual (a titular control of personal rights subjected to the laws of nature and society), basic freedom (sovereign within, but accepting the demands of an outside world and "aligned with destiny"). In short, humanism is everything in Western civilization that restricts *the desire for power*: it prohibits the desire for power and excludes the possibility of power being seized. The theory of the subject (in the double sense of the word) is at the heart of humanism and this is why our culture has tenaciously rejected anything that could weaken its hold upon us.[51]

V

To think Foucault's genealogy of the truth/power relations characterizing modernity in the context of this subordinated "Roman reference" is to perceive the continuity of his historically specific interrogation of the panopticism of post-Enlightenment modernity with Heidegger's generalized interrogation of the metaphysics of the ontotheological at large: more specifically, the perception of *physis*, the difference that temporality disseminates, from above. It is also to clarify the fundamental limitations of each discourse vis-à-vis the critique of modernity and to suggest, by way of reconciliation, a *critical theory* adequate to the complex conditions of power relations in a world in which the (Occidental) truth rather than overt force is the normal agency of oppression.

I have in the foregoing reading of Heidegger with Foucault suggested the weakness of Heidegger's discourse as an instrument of sociopolitical critique: its tendency, despite its essence, to separate theory from practice, thinking from politics, or, at worst, to distort the representation of the latter. It will be the purpose of this concluding section, then, to suggest the weakness of Foucault's discourse disclosed by a reading of Foucault with Heidegger. To put it provisionally, what is missing or underdeveloped in Foucault's genealogy of modern power relations is explicit and sustained reference to the ultimate ontotheological origins of "panopticism" or "the regime of truth": this historically specific and concrete technology of discreet power in which the subject (the individual) is constituted in order to better serve a privileged sociopolitical identity. To thematize and thus bring to bear on the critique of modernity what his discourse more or less leaves unsaid in what I take to be a disabling way, it will be necessary to repeat Heidegger's more inclusive, if rarefied, but finally not radically different thematization of the metaphorics of the centered circle informing the philosophical discourse of the ontotheological tradition. This time, however, I will emphasize the consequences of this inscribed figural complex for the modern age, which, after all, no less than Foucault's genealogy, is the primary concern of Heidegger's destruction of the ontotheological tradition.

According to Heidegger, we recall, the metaphysical mode of inquiry decisively inaugurated by the Roman translation of the Greek *a-letheia* to *veritas* extends through the Patristic theologians and exegetes not only to modern empirical philosophers like Descartes, Locke, and Bentham but also to idealists like Leibnitz, Kant, and Hegel. In the process of this history, it eventually hardened into a derivative or secondary discursive practice, a viciously circular *thinking about* temporal phenomena, that reduced being, including *Da-sein*, being-in-the-world, to the status of a thing that is present-to-hand (*vorhanden*). What this process of reification means in terms of Western history is that the hardening culminates—has its fulfillment and end (in both senses of the word)—in the complete "technologization" (understood in a broader sense than merely the empirical scientific) of the continuum of being: not only the earth but also human being in its individual and social capacity. Put figuratively, it ends in the re-presentation of being as totally spatialized object in the modern period. For Heidegger, in other words, the triumph of humanism—or alternatively, of "anthropology"—in the post-Enlightenment (what Foucault analogously refers to as the triumph of "panopticism") precipitates "the age of the world picture" (*die Zeit des Weltbildes*):

> The interweaving of these two events, which for the modern age is decisive—that the world is transformed into a picture and man into *subjectum*—throws light at the same time on the grounding event of modern history. . . . Namely, the more extensively and the more effectually the world stands at man's disposal as conquered, and the more objectively the object appears, all the more subjectively, i.e., the more importunately, does the *subjectum* rise up, and all the more impetuously, too, do observation of and teaching about the world change into a doctrine of man, into anthropology. It is no wonder that humanism first arises where the world becomes picture. . . . Humanism, therefore, in the more strict historiographical sense, is nothing but a moral-aesthetic anthropology. The name "anthropology" as used here . . . designates that philosophical interpretation of man which explains and evaluates whatever is, in its entirety, from the standpoint of man and in relation to man. . . .
> The fundamental event of the modern age is the conquest of the world as picture. The word "picture" [*Bild*] now means the structured image [*Gebild*] that is the creature of man's producing which represents and sets before [*des vorstellenden Herstellens*]. In such producing, man contends for the position in which he can be that particular being who gives the measure and draws up the guidelines for everything that is.[52]

Like Foucault's analysis of the panopticism of the disciplinary society, Heidegger's analysis of the "age of the world picture" exposes the "calculative thinking" (*rechnende Denken*) of anthropological representation (*Vorstellung*) to be a problematic that constitutes ("produces") the subject as "technological" consciousness. In turn, this subject, as Heidegger puts it elsewhere, "enframes" (*Ge-stell*) the temporality of being in its own (anthropological) image. And by thus achieving such a deceptive representational technique of mastery over *physis* in the modern age, this subjected subject has come perilously close to reducing "its" dynamic and "proliferating"—its differential—processes, including human being, into not simply knowable objects, but objects as "standing reserve" (*Bestand*), as "docile and useful bodies," as it were. This technological "achievement" of humanistic retro-spection or, what is the same thing, re-collection, is not simply the blindness of the anthropological version of metaphysical *oversight*. It is a *forgetting* of the be-ing of being (the ontological difference) with a vengeance: an amnesia, no less repressive than the super-vision that, according to Foucault, is the essential agent of discipline in the "regime of truth."

This retrieval of Heidegger's version of the origins of the modern age of the world picture suggests that Foucault's limitation of his genealogy of the disciplinary society to the site of a historically specific politics obscures and minimizes what in Heidegger's interrogation of the ontotheological tradition constitutes a persuasive enabling disclosure, however limited in the opposite direction, about the essence of modernity. I mean the prominence of the ideal figure of the centered circle and its discreetly repressive operations in the discursive practices of modernity at large. The disclosure of the complicity between knowledge and power enabled by Heidegger's interrogation of the ontotheological tradition, that is, is not finally limited to the site of the positive sciences precipitated in and by the Enlightenment as the predominant documentary evidence Foucault brings to bear on the question in *Madness and Civilization*, *The Birth of the Clinic*, *Discipline and Punish*, and *The History of Sexuality, Vol. I* seems to suggest. It also includes the site of the so-called *litterae humaniores*—philosophy, literature, the arts, and so on—privileged by the cultural memory of modern humanism.

More specifically, Foucault situated the articulated form of the panoptic diagram, if not exactly its genealogical origins, in the Enlightenment, the *episteme* that bore witness to the rise and overdetermination of the positive sciences and their pervasive methodological application to the human sciences at large—to *poiesis* as well as to the so-called social sciences. In this emphasis, his genealogy obscures the very ideality and polyvalency of the figure of the centered circle (and the correlative supervisory gaze it enables). In so doing, Foucault's discourse also obscures a deeper, if not prior, ideological structure informing the disciplinary ideology of the sociopolitical formation overdetermined by a model of knowledge production having its immediate source in scientific/technological investigation. I am referring to that ancient and abiding *meta-physical* ideology that, since Plato, according to Heidegger, has privileged the centered circle and its affiliated optics.

It is this practically polyvalent (idealized) spatial diagram that is inscribed both in the discourses of the physical and human sciences and in the institutional practices of the dominant sociopolitical order that I want to thematize. For it is this ideological relay concealed behind the figure of truth/beauty/perfection that is all too often (and, I submit, disablingly) overlooked by contemporary secular critics of modern power relations, even as their critical discourses, like Foucault's, circle more or less unthought around this metaphysics, this imaginary real: I mean primarily those critical genealogists and new historicists whom Foucault has influenced (Jacques Donzelot, Edward Said, Mark Poster, Paul Bové, Jonathan Arac, Frank Lentricchia, Stephen Greenblatt, and Donald Pease, for example), but also those neo-Marxist critics of the discourse and practice of hegemony (Raymond Williams, Jean Baudrillard, Fredric Jameson, Terry Eagleton, Jürgen Habermas, Stuart Hall, Ernesto Laclau, and Chantal Mouffe, for example), and those otherwise diverse feminist critics of the discursive practices of Western patriarchy (Julia Kristeva, Hélène Cixous, Juliet Mitchell, and Pamela McCallum, for example), whose oppositional discourses are directed against the hegemony of contemporary bourgeois capitalist culture.

To be sure, the "Heideggerians" he influenced, whether practitioners of deconstruction such as Maurice Blanchot, Derrida, and Lyotard, or practitioners of hermeneutics such as Hans-Georg Gadamer, Emmanuel Lévinas, and Paul Ricoeur, have, like Heidegger, if in different ways, failed to theorize adequately the *practical* implications of the polyvalent logo-center. They thus tend to restrict their critical discourses to the generalized site of ontology at the expense of sociopolitical critique. On the other hand (though their blindnesses are less disabling), neo-Marxist and genealogical critics of modern power relations have failed to theorize adequately the *theoretical* implications of the practical application of the panoptic mechanisms. They thus tend to restrict their critical discourses to the sites of sociopolitics at the expense of ontological critique. In both cases, in short, the *polyvalency* of the privileged figure of the circle and its optics remains insufficiently thought.

Let me be more specific. Despite Nietzsche's and Heidegger's disclosure of the origins of modern empirical science in the *ressentiment* of ascetic/speculative philosophy,[53] Foucault's unevenly developed discourse inadvertently reinscribes, or allows the reinscription of, the false opposition between the natural sciences and the humanities (*le querelle des anciens et modernes*) which has determined cultural discourse in the West at least since the Renaissance (of *Roman antiquity*). I mean the discourse on knowledge production epitomized in Anglo-American modernity by the "two cultures" debate, which has extended from Matthew Arnold and Thomas Henry Huxley through F. R. Leavis and C. P. Snow to the present.

It is true, of course, that Foucault's interrogation of the classical Marxist base/superstructure model of interpretation, in which the means of material production is determinative "in the last instance" (constitutes the base of superstructural, cultural, epiphenomena), led him to refocus the critique of modernity on the production of (cultural) discourse. This revision, no doubt, constitutes his greatest contribution to contemporary political thought. Nevertheless his interpretive practice reinscribes, in some degree, a base/superstructure model.[54] His genealogical discourse, in other words, has made it too easy for many of his academic followers to further separate the "lyrical" humanist discourse of the ontotheological tradition from the "hard" humanist discourse of post-Enlightenment science: to think the present historical conjuncture essentially in terms of a scientific base to the superstructural discursive practices of the *litterae humaniores*. As a consequence of this reductive separation and hierarchization, politically left-oriented critics of modernity, neo-Marxists and even those influenced by Foucault's genealogy of the disciplinary society, continue in practice to identify the "regime of truth" with the scientific/ technological/capitalist establishment. In so doing, they also continue to minimize the large role that philosophy, literature, and the arts (and the institutions that transmit their "truth") play in the repression-by-accommodation of the relay of sociopolitical "others" that constitutes being-in-the-world.[55] This tacitly enables contemporary humanists, especially professors of literature, both liberal and conservative, not only to deny the complicity of the humanities with the "science-based" disciplinary society. This minimizing of the repressive role of the humanities also tends to legitimate the rehabilitation of the interested liberal discourse of "disinterestedness"—the discreetly repressive logocentric, patriarchal, and ethnocentric ("colonialist") ideological agenda—which, no less than the "objectivity" of the discourse of empirical science, is grounded in the principle of the sovereign subject: the discourse, that is, which discreetly enacts repression in the name of freedom.

As the foregoing comparative destructive analysis has shown, both Heidegger's destructive hermeneutics and Foucault's genealogy of modernity have three related critical insights in common. (1) They have their fundamental point of departure in the de-centering of the *anthropologos*. (2) They interpret modernity, *in theory*, not in terms of the base/

superstructure model, but as an indissoluble, however uneven, lateral continuum of discreet oppressions enabled by a discursive practice that, far from being disinterested, is determined by the will to power informing a constellation of constructed and archivalized metaphors emanating from the polyvalent principle of presence or center. (3) They understand modernity as planetary, however asymmetrical, in its hegemonic reach. But both fail *in practice* to fulfill the implications of these profound insights for critique. On the one hand, insofar as Heidegger overemphasizes the site of ontology in his destruction of the ontotheological tradition, he minimizes or leaves unsaid or even distorts the relay of historically specific sociopolitical sites that are indissolubly affiliated with the ontological. On the other, insofar as Foucault overemphasizes the historically specific sociopolitical sites in his genealogy of the disciplinary society, he minimizes or leaves unsaid or distorts the perennial ontological site. However residual in the context of a modernity that has overdetermined a cultural production and sociopolitics informed by the discourse of scientific truth, the ontological site nevertheless remains, like the Dead Father in Donald Barthelme's novel, a potent agent of repression in modernity: not simply within the West, to which Foucault's discourse tends to delimit it, but, as Edward Said has shown in amplifying Foucault, far beyond its periphery. Both discourses, then (though Foucault's practice is clearly more satisfactory than Heidegger's in this respect), remain in some disabling degree inscribed in the disciplinary framework it is their intention to overcome.

This is why, despite or because of the enormously enabling contributions that Heidegger and Foucault have made to the critical discourse of the contemporary occasion, it is necessary to rethink Heidegger's destruction of the ontotheological tradition in terms of Foucault's genealogy of the disciplinary society *and* to rethink Foucault's genealogy in terms of Heidegger's destruction. To put this agenda in terms of the metaphoric constellation it has been the purpose of this essay to thematize, it is because Heidegger's and Foucault's critical insights into modernity are limited by the vestigial disciplinarity of their discourses that they failed to think what the other disclosed about the ideology informing the privileged figure of the centered circle and its related optics. This is why it remains a crucial project of "theory" to thematize Heidegger's underdeveloped understanding of the ontological circle of beauty/truth/perfection as the diagram of the will to power over difference (domination) in terms of Foucault's historically specific analysis of the Panopticon. This is why the rethinking of Foucault's underdeveloped understanding of the Panopticon as a "diagram of a mechanism of power reduced to its ideal form" in terms of Heidegger's analysis of the circle of beauty/truth/perfection as the diagram of the will to power over ontological difference is also a crucial project of "theory." No less than a Heideggerian critique of the ontotheological tradition that fails to recognize or misreads its historically specific worldly manifestations in the contemporary conjuncture, a Foucauldian critique of the modern "regime of truth" that overlooks its deep inscription by the circular/specular discourse of metaphysics *and* the planetary scope of its "colonizing" project, is a critique blinded by its (partial/disciplinary) insight. Indeed, to think this as yet unthought project should be, I submit, the essential task of the posthumanist or postanthropological countermemory, especially of its interrogation of the deceptively "heterogeneous" discourses and practices of the institutions of knowledge production (not the least the university).[56]

Only a rethinking of the post-Enlightenment in terms of the decentering of the perennially privileged centered circle and its specular metaphysics, I am suggesting, can be adequate to the genealogy and critique of a modernity whose specular instruments of discreet domination are both lyrical and scientific and whose hegemonic reach is not restricted to the boundaries of the Occident but, as the rhetoric that represents the immediate contemporary occasion as the "new world order" suggests, extends throughout the planet and beyond. To put this initiative in terms of the positive phase of the destructive genealogical project: only such a rethinking can be adequate to the emancipatory implications of the epochal refusal, during and immediately after the Vietnam War, of spontaneous consent to the discourse and practice of truth by a multiplicity of *distinct but affiliated* voices hitherto spoken for by the hegemonic discourse of truth. These were voices of constituencies of the human community marginalized, repressed, or increasingly accommodated by the ruse of the "repressive hypothesis" or, alternatively, the deceptions of the *hintergehendens Umgehung*. For only a critical theory that recognizes the Being represented by the Occident as a totalized construction—an indissoluble, however asymmetrically distributed, relay of discreet repressions that is not simply Western but planetary, even galactic, in scope— is capable of overcoming the limitations of the emancipatory discourses presently in circulation. Only such a critical theory, to be more specific, can get beyond the disabling vestigial essentialism of even the most progressive Marxist discourses, on the one hand, and the disabling vestigial disciplinarity of the various poststructuralist discourses (including Heidegger's and Foucault's) on the other.[57] The impasse of the discourses of the left in the face of the massive Western representation of the recent epochal events in the "East"—the sociopolitical revolutions from below—as the definitive global triumph of "liberal democracy" bears dramatic testimony to this historically precipitated imperative to rethink the genealogy of Occidental modernity.

Chapter 6
Heidegger, Nazism, and the "Repressive Hypothesis": The American Appropriation of the Question

In the next land we found were Kyklopês,
giants, louts, without a law to bless them.
In ignorance leaving the fruitage of the earth in mystery
to the immortal gods, they neither plow
nor sow by hand, nor till the ground, though grain—
wild wheat and barley—grows untended, and
wine-grapes, in clusters, ripen in heaven's rain. . . .
The isle, unplanted and untilled, a wilderness,
pastures goats alone. And this is why:
good ships like ours with cheekpaint at the bows
are far beyond the Kyklopês. No shipwright
toils among them, shaping and building up
symmetrical trim hulls to cross the sea
and visit all the seaboard towns, as men do
who go and come in commerce over water.
This isle—seagoing folk would have annexed it
and built their homesteads on it: all good land,
fertile for every crop in season. . . .

Homer, *The Odyssey*, Book 9

That before living agent [his "great natural intellect"], now became the
living instrument. If such a furious trope may stand, his special lunacy

stormed his general sanity, and carried it, and turned all its concentered cannon upon its own mad mark; so that far from having lost his strength, Ahab, to that one end, did now possess a thousandfold more potency than ever he had sanely brought to bear upon any one reasonable object.

Herman Melville, *Moby-Dick*

Our worst dread of yellow peril became realized: we saw them dying by the thousands all over the country, yet they didn't seem depleted, let alone exhausted, as the Mission was claiming. . . . We took space back quickly, expensively, with total panic and close to maximum brutality. Our machine was devastating. And versatile. It could do anything but stop. As one American major said, in a successful attempt at attaining history, "We had to destroy Ben Tre in order to save it." That's how most of the country came back under what we called control, and how it remained essentially occupied by the Viet Cong and the North until the day years later when there were none of us left there.

Michael Herr, *Dispatches*

I

The publication in French of Victor Farías's book *Heidegger et le nazisme* in 1987 kindled a fierce debate in Europe, especially in France, over the question of Martin Heidegger's politics. With the publication of "A Symposium on Heidegger and Nazism" in the Winter 1989 issue of *Critical Inquiry*, the editors of this prestigious journal devoted to "theory" translated this European debate to the North American intellectual milieu. This issue, edited by Arnold I. Davidson, a coeditor of *Critical Inquiry* and member of the Committee on General Studies in the Humanities and on Conceptual Foundations of Science at the University of Chicago, contains Davidson's lengthy introduction, which, as I will show, is misleadingly entitled "Questions Concerning Heidegger: Opening the Debate"; brief interventions by Hans-Georg Gadamer, Maurice Blanchot, Emmanuel Lévinas (originally published in *La Nouvelle Observateur* between January 22 and January 28, 1988); a brief excerpt from Philippe Lacoue-Labarthe's *La fiction du politique* and a somewhat longer one from Jacques Derrida's *De l'esprit: Heidegger et la question* (both written before the publication of Farías's book); and an extended essay by Jürgen Habermas (originally written as the foreword to the German edition of Farías's *Heidegger et le nazisme*).[1] As the editor himself observes (echoing Gadamer), Farías contributes only minimally to what has been known for a long time about Heidegger's affiliation with National Socialism and nothing to the understanding of Heidegger's thought.[2] What, then, has incited this resurgence of interest in Europe in the question of Heidegger's politics? And, more important for my purposes, what has prompted the editors of *Critical Inquiry* to displace this European debate to North America at this particular historical juncture?

For Davidson and (it is reasonable to presume) the other editors of *Critical Inquiry*, "Perhaps the major benefit of Farías' book [for American intellectuals] has been the intervention, into the debate concerning Heidegger and Nazism, of some of the most significant European philosophers writing today" (QCH, 408). This, of course, is not an answer to the latter question I am posing. But in bypassing the first question in favor of orienting the "main benefit" of a book the credibility of which (both its facts and its motive) is in question[3] to the American intellectual context, Davidson's rhetoric betrays, if not an answer to the second, at least a by now familiar gesture the ideological resonances of which need to be examined. I mean the slide from the question of Heidegger's personal politics (the anecdotal) to the question of Heidegger's philosophy (his philosophical writing). It is a slide mirrored in the selection and excerpting of the materials of this symposium. My intention in the following intervention, then, is neither to exculpate Heidegger's practice during the Third Reich, nor even to extricate his philosophical thought from a certain reactionary politics. My primary purpose, rather, is to interrogate the curious yet familiar slippage that marks Davidson's text. For it suggests that the alleged "opening of the [American] debate" sponsored by the editors of *Critical Inquiry* is ultimately, if not strategically or conspiratorially, intended, with the (unwitting) collusion of at least "some of the most significant European philosophers writing today" (all of whom were or have been profoundly influenced by Heidegger's thought) to close it: not at the expense of Heidegger's thought only, but also, and more important, at the expense of the contemporary theoretical discourses at large that Heidegger's enabled. I mean those discourses that have called into question the dominant humanistic discourse and now threaten its hegemony in North America. In taking my point of departure from Davidson's introduction, I do not want to imply that my intervention in the debate is intended to engage his discourse or the *Critical Inquiry* project as such. As my reference to the *familiarity* of Davidson's discursive slippage suggests, it is intended rather to engage the ideological frame of reference—the problematic, in Althusser's term—that his critique of Heidegger's thought synecdochically represents: humanism, or, alternatively, anthropology.[4]

The "reopening" of the question of Heidegger's politics undertaken by the editors of *Critical Inquiry* in the wake of the publication of Farías's book takes the form of a symposium that includes essays by prominent

European philosophers who have been influenced by Heidegger's thought, but who (with the exception of Gadamer) have in some degree or other either turned against it or become defensive about the Heideggerian origins of their deconstructive discourse in the face of the mounting implication by humanists of Heidegger's "antihumanism" with the politics of fascism. Further, these essays are framed by an introduction that rhetorically shifts the focus of the question from Heidegger's National Socialist practices to Heidegger's philosophy. Despite the protestations of objectivity, this "recollection" of what has been known about Heidegger's affiliations with German National Socialism for a long time, betrays at some level an effort to identify Heidegger's writing with National Socialist practice: its complicity, that is, with the "Final Solution." This is not to say that its project is limited to discrediting Heidegger's anti-anthropological discourse as such. As is well known, Heidegger's interrogation of metaphysics, of the *anthropo-logos* of modern Occidental Man, especially in *Being and Time* but also in all that follows the so-called turn (*Kehre*), has served as the catalyst, if not precisely the origin, of the oppositional discourse that has come to be called (pejoratively) "theory." Given this inextricable affiliation between Heidegger's thought and contemporary theory, the ideological agenda informing the "opening" of the debate by the editors of *Critical Inquiry* must also be seen as a significant instance of the mounting initiative of an embattled humanist establishment (ironically unthought, it would seem, by the European contributors to the symposium)[5] to discredit what has variously (and misleadingly) been referred to as the discourse of "postmodernism" or "poststructuralism," but which I prefer to call "posthumanism."[6] I mean the discourse that at this historically specific conjuncture (since the 1960s) threatens not only the hegemony of the discourse of humanism, but also of the disciplinary and neoimperial society at large: the "liberal" or bourgeois / late capitalist democracies this discourse was invented to legitimate and reproduce. In France, not incidentally, it has been the *nouveaux philosophes* and their humanist progeny who have welcomed Farías's book most enthusiastically, because it has given them the opportunity not simply to discredit Heidegger's discourse as such, but, above all, the *anti-humaniste* discourses of the "new left" (those "critical intellectuals" who would "foist . . . a 1960s attitude" on the 1980s): oppositional theorists such as Jacques Derrida, Philippe Lacoue-Labarthe, Jacques Lacan, Louis Althusser, Pierre Bourdieu, and Michel Foucault, who have called the humanist subject into question:

> Against the critics of criticism, against those who attacked Marxism and Heideggerianism as two contemporary strains of antihumanism, and thus "risked" a calculated reconciliation with the democratic world—in short, against the thought of the 1980s—it became

possible, thanks to a purified Heidegger, to reinstate the figure of the critical intellectual and to foist onto the contemporary world a 1960s attitude about the consumer society or mass culture.

For all its irritating flatness, Farías's book suddenly prevented thinking in circles and struck a discordant note in the new *consensus* of critical intellectuals. . . .

The virtue of Farías's book . . . is to make us rethink a question that surely would have been once again swept under the rug by a consensus of intellectuals: under what circumstances can the contemporary world be subjected to criticism that is not inexorably attended by a sweeping negation of the principles of democratic humanism? We need to spell this out: the neo-Heideggerianism of the 1980s played a game in which all the moves are familiar. Why can't we see that the main drift of Heidegger's thinking was that, from the birth of subjectivity to the world of technology, the sequence is inevitable? Why can't we realize that under these circumstances criticism of the contemporary world is basically— *Heidegger himself knew this and said it plainly*—radically incompatible with the minimum of *subjectivity* needed for *democratic* thinking, in whatever form we conceive it? Mustn't we give the idea of democracy a meaning—if only, once again, a minimum one—and assume not only pluralism (which, if necessary, Heideggerianism could conceive of), but also the possibility for human beings to be somehow the authors of the choices they make, or should make, in common? In short, how can we think of democracy without imputing to man the minimal will and mastery that Heidegger denies him because will and mastery in some sense already contain the seeds of the world of technology conceived of as the "will to will"?[7]

Against my implication of *Critical Inquiry*'s "Symposium" into a larger humanist project to delegitimate the antihumanist discourses of contemporary theory at large, the editor would, of course, cite the extended passage in his introduction, where, *apparently* in opposition to Habermas's claim that *Being and Time* is continuous with the "Rectorship Address" and the "reactionary" discourse that follows,[8] he locates the origins of Heidegger's continuing adherence to the *Führerprinzip* after *Being and Time* in the "Rectorship Address." It is with his assumption of the rectorate of Freiburg University in 1933 that, according to Davidson, Heidegger not only abandoned the Kantian principle of the "autonomy" of "public reason," but also the voluntarist structure of individual "resoluteness," which, "by way of anxiety, guilt, and conscience, brings Dasein to the authenticity of Being-one's-Self," which, that is, always already resists the "dictatorship of the 'they' [*das Man*]." (QCH, 418). Henceforth, Heidegger will privilege "following": "obedience," first to "the people, state, and German fate" (QCH, 419) and then, after

Heidegger found that German National Socialism itself " 'was caught up in the consummation of nihilism' " (QCH, 420),[9] to "Being." "From the 'Rectorship Address' to Heidegger's late writing," the editor observes, "the human is always being led, and what leads humanity seems to so envelop or override it that its disappearance is constantly threatened. Heidegger will never again appeal to a Führer to lead. The appeal now comes from Being and requires a response that 'is a giving way before the appeal' " (QCH, 422).[10]

But this all too familiar dissociation of *Being and Time* from the writings of the rectorate and after is, in fact, a characteristic, or an inscribed, strategy of the humanistic problematic; namely, its intrinsic capability of accommodating difference to an ontologically prior identity. In representing Heidegger's "authentic self" (*Eigentlichkeit*) as essentially self-present, it also (mis)represents *Being and Time* as a discourse ultimately affiliated with the autonomous self of Kant's "public reason"—with the "disinterested" anthropological discourse of liberal humanism: "the public [as opposed to the private] uses of reason, 'the uses which a person makes of it as a scholar before the reading public,' must, Kant claims, 'always be free, and it alone can bring about enlightenment among men.' " (QCH, 414).[11] This misleading representation of *Being and Time*, which strains to affiliate (if not identify) the Heideggerian "self" with the reason of the Enlightenment, disarms by co-opting a substantially different reading of the continuity between the antisubjectivist (and finally anti-Kantian) discourse of *Being and Time* and the later antihumanist postwar texts (and even perhaps those of the rectorate, for all their political naïveté): one less damning than Habermas's surprisingly crude version of this continuity.

Such a humanist representation of *Being and Time*, to be more specific, puts out of play a reading of the continuity of Heidegger's philosophical itinerary that would thematize the emancipatory possibilities of Heidegger's sustained critique of the repressiveness of reason: of the humanist problematic. I do not mean only the emancipatory possibilities disclosed by Heidegger's decolonization of the temporality of being colonized by the philosophical discourses of the ontotheological tradition. I also mean the more practical emancipatory possibilities opened up by his disclosure of the leveling ontic operation of the anthropological problematic, which, in the process of fulfilling its accommodational imperatives, legitimates and reproduces a relay of repressions extending from the subject through language and culture to the organization of the earth (technology) and the sociopolitical order. I mean the emancipatory possibilities that, however underdeveloped or even unthought because of Heidegger's emphasis on the ontological question (*die Seinsfrage*), it has been the collective Heideggerian project of contemporary theory to think.

II

It is not my intention here to intervene in the "debate" over Heidegger's politics at the site chosen by Farías, established by the European participants, both French and German, and transported to and imposed on the intellectual milieu of North America by the editors of *Critical Inquiry*. I mean Heidegger's rectorate at Freiburg University: the site of his practice as a member of the National Socialist Party. For the overdetermination of this site makes it all too easy to fix it as the center, the presence, the end, that despite variations informs his discourse from at least this beginning, if not from *Being and Time* itself, to the end; and thus to demonstrate retrospectively its unpardonable complicity with the horrors perpetrated by German fascism. To enter the debate at this site—to undertake a defense of Heidegger's discursive practice at large against the charge of complicity with the Nazis' "Final Solution" or, at best, of insensitivity to the horrors it perpetrated—would be to take the (disabling) lure set by Farías and the liberal humanists who have appropriated Farías's anecdotal problematic (if not his specific reading). I am referring to what Foucault has called the ruse of the repressive hypothesis, the presupposition that truth and power are binary opposites: that power, on the one hand, is always visible/repressive, a matter of negativity, of constraint, of direct coercion, i.e., of overt violence; and that truth, on the other, is in essence external to and thus the fundamental adversary of power. This critique of the "truth" of modernity, not incidentally, has its immediate origins in Gramsci's and Althusser's notion of "hegemony." But, significantly, its ultimate source resides in Nietzsche's genealogy of humanistic morality and of disinterested (Kantian) inquiry at large (his exposure of their source in the violence of *ressentiment*), and, especially, in Heidegger's genealogy of humanistic "common sense" (his disclosure of its origins in the repression of originary thinking) and of humanistic pedagogy (his disclosure of its origins in the Roman republic/empire: the transformation and reduction of a *paideia* [un]grounded in truth as *aletheia* into *eruditio et institutio in bonas artes* [scholarship and training in good conduct]).

I will return later to the Foucauldian critique of this essential assumption of the discursive practices of liberal humanism, of what Foucault calls "the regime of truth." It will suffice here to say provisionally that to situate the debate (as the *Critical Inquiry* supplement implicitly, i.e., enticingly, demands) over the relationship between Heidegger's philosophy and political practice *exclusively* at the site where the power with which it is alleged to be complicitous is most visible, direct, and violent is to privilege a context that lends itself to a distortion of Heidegger's de-structive philosophy: the reduction of an essentially "projective"/ emancipatory discourse into a reactionary/totalitarian—and dehumanizing—one. It also, more importantly, deflects attention away from the question of the complicity of the discursive practices of humanism with repressive violence: from the powerful testimony of all those contemporary thinkers influenced by Heidegger—Derrida, Lacan, Foucault, Irigaray, Lyotard, Althusser, and so many others—who have called into question the anthropological discourse of Man.

In resisting the lure to intervene in this debate at the time and place overdetermined by Farías, the French, the Germans, and most recently— and questionably—the editors of *Critical Inquiry*, my intention is not to circumvent the question of Heidegger's culpability: I do not wish to imply that his discourse and practice during the period of the rectorate were not guilty of a certain essential complicity with the Nazis' crude geopolitical project, or, for that matter, that his refusal to dissociate himself from the Nazi Party after his resignation in 1934 and his silence in the face of the accomplished grotesque reality of Auschwitz was innocent of a fundamental failure of sensitivity to the human suffering perpetrated by the Nazis. My intention, in other words, is not to take up the cause either of those "orthodox Heideggerians" in France who have misrepresented Heidegger's Nazi affiliations in behalf of legitimating a philosophically and politically reactionary French "Heideggerianism," or of those conservative German historians in what has come to be called the *Historikerstreit*, who have invoked Heidegger's thought in some degree or other (against Habermas and the contemporary German left he represents) to recuperate the German national identity shattered by the barbarous politics of the Third Reich in behalf of the relegitimation of a right-wing—and Cold War—ideology.

Let it be conceded to Heidegger's humanist critics at once and in no uncertain terms: Heidegger indeed was guilty of a remarkable lapse in human sensitivity, and further, that the particular bias of his antihumanism had as one of its deplorable consequences his inability to acknowledge the Nazi persecution of the Jews. But was his culpability purely and simply that finally unpardonable crime represented by these humanist prosecutors of the "case" against Heidegger? Is Heidegger's discourse, even after *Being and Time*, one in which "the suppression of the other, the human," in the name of the imperative of "following" Being, "accounts . . . for the absence . . . of the experience of horror," for "a silence about the gas chambers and death camps," which constitutes " 'a kind of consent to the horror' " (QCH, 425)?[12] Let me put these questions in another way: Doesn't this representative judgment essentialize Heidegger's philosophical discourse? Doesn't it overlook and repress the contradictions inhering in its errant measure—the enabling aporias that Heideggerians such as Derrida have shown to be fundamental to Heidegger's texts? Dosn't it, that is, preclude a certain reading of Heidegger's antihumanism that, like Derrida's, de Man's, Lacoue-Labarthe's, Lyotard's and, in a different way, Althusser's and Foucault's, exposes the disabling limits of precisely this critical perspective? Isn't this humanist condemnation of Heidegger enabled by the publication of Farías's *Heidegger et le nazisme* at bottom an effort at censoring the reading of his texts in behalf of recuperating the hegemonic discourse of humanism that the (dissident) Heideggerians, not to say the events of the Vietnam decade, have radically called into question? If the main thrust of Heidegger's antihumanist project prevented him from "pronouncing the name of the Jews," (QCH, 424) doesn't this anti-antihumanism that liberal humanists bring to their reading of Heidegger's essentially aporetic text preclude pronouncing the name of all those "others"—not least, given the American context of his discourse, the Vietnamese—that, however less in scale, have suffered the violence inhering in the Western anthropologos?

It is precisely at the site of this question of the contested term "human" in Heidegger's philosophy that I want to intervene. This is because it is clear that, despite the "beginning" alleged by the editor of the *Critical Inquiry* symposium—the "Rectorship Address"—it is not so much Heidegger's literal membership in the Nazi Party nor even his practice during the rectorate that is the real target of his critique: "I do not intend, in making clear Heidegger's invocation of the *Führerprinzip*, simply to associate Heidegger with Hitler, since that association by itself ought to carry no force" (QCH, 415). Davidson's ultimate purpose, rather, is "to disassociate Heidegger from Kant, relating Heidegger's conception of the mission of the university to his critique of the Kantian idea of reason" (QCH, 415). His target, that is to say, is Heidegger's "betrayal" of the Kantian understanding of *philosophy*: "As for Kant, if philosophy is *led* by anything other than reason, it can no longer fulfill its proper role; indeed, it is no longer philosophy. What follows is the abdication of philosophy in favor of something else, whether it be revelation, the state or some other unyielding spiritual mission. When *philosophy thus ceases to be autonomous* this must look to us as if reason is not being rethought, but overthrown or, say, 'overcome' " (QCH, 416, my emphasis).

But to thematize Davidson's ultimate purpose as an effort to defend Kantian philosophy against Heidegger's project to "overthrow" it is to put it too abstractly. As the slide in Davidson's rhetoric from Kant's "idea of reason" to philosophy as autonomous and disinterested inquiry to "philosophy" as such suggests—not to say his putting "philosophy" and its "proper role" into opposition with "revelation, the state or some other unyielding spiritual mission" (as if that was the only alternative to "disinterested" inquiry)—his agenda can be stated in more specific terms. Like that of the more forthright French *nouveaux philosophes*, it is to discredit Heidegger's project to "overcome" humanism in behalf of recuperating the hegemonic authority it lost in the last decades of this century: in the wake, that is, of Heidegger's enabling critique of modernity (what he appropriately calls *"die Zeit des Weltbildes,"* the age of the world picture) or, to retrieve the historically specific context of this delegitimation, in the wake of the intervention of the United States in Vietnam. I am referring to the epochal historical occasion that this humanist critique "forgets": the massive international student protest movement (its refusal of spontaneous consent to the hegemonic discourse of the institutions of higher learning), and the simultaneous emergence of poststructuralist theory (its exposure of the center elsewhere—the logocentrism—informing philosophy; that is, the will to power informing "autonomous and disinterested" inquiry). I am referring to the related practical and theoretical initiatives that disclosed the complicity of the discourse of humanism with the state apparatuses conducting or supporting the imperialist/racist war in Vietnam.

In representing Heidegger's project to "overcome" philosophy as an effort to "overthrow" it, to annul its "proper role," Davidson's ultimate purpose is not simply to undermine Heidegger's argument against humanism as such—his displacement of Man from the center—but also to recuperate the lost authority of humanism. This double agenda becomes clear in the final pages of the introduction of the *Critical Inquiry* "Symposium" that allegedly "opens the debate":

> This introduction is not the place to attempt a full assessment of Heidegger's thinking concerning humanism. But the topic of humanism cannot be avoided when confronting Heidegger's involvement with Nazism. Heidegger, as is well known, wanted to overcome metaphysical humanism by thinking about the essence of the human in terms of our claim by Being. So that "in the determination of the humanity of man . . . what is essential is not man but Being." All of the traditional representations of philosophy are to be reoriented, and thus overthrown, in thinking them through by reference to Being and its history. Yet however much Heidegger may wish to recover the human by way of Being, one is struck, almost uncannily, by the abstractness of the human voice, the human face and body, in his late thought. (QCH, 422)[13]

It is no small irony that Davidson should (insistently) interpret the "Being" (as well as the "subject") of Heidegger's thought to be precisely that reified understanding of being it was the project of Heidegger's de-struction of the ontotheological tradition to interrogate, not only in *Being and Time* but also in *Kant and the Problem of Metaphysics*, "What is Metaphysics?," "On the Essence of Truth," (before the war), the Nietzsche lectures, the lectures on *The Parmenides* (during the war), and "Letter on Humanism" and other texts (after the war). I will return to this question later. At this point it will suffice to recall that Heidegger's de-structive hermeneutics constitutes a sustained, however imperfectly realized, effort to de-structure the *concept* (*con* + *capere*: "to grasp") of Being—the reification or spatialization of the unconceptualizable *temporality of being*—precisely in order to retrieve (*Wiederholen*) the differences it always already disseminates from the closure of structure. Here I want to focus on what immediately follows from Davidson's claim that, in displacing Man as determinant of his or her humanity in favor of "Being," Heidegger's philosophy abstracts the "human voice, the human face and body." For it is what follows from Heidegger's philosophical discourse, or rather, from his "abdication" of philosophy—far more than Heidegger's "merely historical" affiliation with the National Socialist Party as such—that is "beyond pardon" (QCH, 424) for Davidson and the humanist project his discourse represents.

Indeed, nothing could be more damning for Heidegger's project, according to this representation, because what follows is so utterly and self-evidently damning. It is "a philosophical pronouncement from Heidegger (is it also political?) uttered in a 1949 lecture" (QCH, 423), long after the horrors of Auschwitz, of Belsen, of Buchenwald, of Mauthausen, of Treblinka, of Chelmno had been fully exposed, which represents Heidegger's postwar attitude towards the Nazis' "Final Solution":

> Agriculture is now a mechanized food industry. As for its essence, it is the same thing as the manufacture of corpses in the gas chambers or the death camps, the same thing as blockades and reduction of countries to famine [Heidegger is referring, no doubt, to the Berlin blockade], the same as the manufacture of hydrogen bombs. (QCH, 423)[14]

What I want to call attention to before addressing the specific use to which Davidson puts it is that this "damning" passage (from an unknown textual context) is not only the determining point of departure of his (and, predictably, many other humanists') analysis of the question of the complicity of Heidegger's thought with Nazi fascism. It is also central to the interrogations of Heidegger's discourse and practice by the European contributors to the *Critical Inquiry* "Symposium." It is invoked directly by Lacoue-Labarthe, whose lead Davidson is immediately following, by Maurice Blanchot in "Thinking the Apocalypse" (pp. 478–

79), and by Emmanuel Lévinas in "As If Consenting to the Horror" (p. 487). In the case of Habermas's contribution to the "Symposium," he cites a letter written by Herbert Marcuse to Heidegger on May 13, 1948, in response to a similar self-damning identification by Heidegger, in this case between the extermination of the Jews and the fate suffered by the East Germans at the hand of the Allies during and after the war. (Although I have no way of specifying the reference, I suspect it has to do with the Dresden firebombing and the forced relocation of civilians in East Germany as a consequence of the Allies' partition of Germany.):

> You write that everything I say about the extermination of the Jews holds equally for the Allies, if instead of "Jew" we write "Eastern German." With this sentence, do you not place yourself outside the realm in which a conversation among humans is possible at all—outside the logos? For only from fully beyond this "logical" dimension is it possible to explain, adjust, "comprehend" a crime by saying that others did the same thing too. More: how is it possible to place the torture, mutilation, annihilation of millions of people on the same level as the forcible resettlement of groups in which none of these misdeeds has occurred (save perhaps in a few exceptional cases)?[15]

Needless to say, Habermas's reaction to Heidegger's identification is akin (though not identical) to that of the French contributors, Lacoue-Labarthe, Blanchot, and Lévinas. But insofar as he understands Heidegger's insensitivity to the gas chambers as a necessary extension of his philosophical writing, his reaction is precisely that of Davidson: "In the shadow of the 'universal rule of the will to power within history, now understood to embrace the planet,' everything," Habermas observes,

> becomes one and the same: "today everything stands in this historical reality, no matter whether it is called communism, or fascism, or world democracy." [R, 485] That is how it was in 1945, and that is how Heidegger always repeated it: abstraction by essentialization. Under the levelling gaze of the philosopher of Being even the extermination of the Jews seems merely an event equivalent to many others. Annihilation of Jews, expulsion of Germans—they amount to the same.[16]

Davidson's commentary on this by now synecdochical passage needs to be quoted at length. This is not only because its "callousness" justifies the outrage informing his conclusion that Heidegger's philosophical discourse after the rectorate is dehumanized and dehumanizing. It is also because, in invoking it in a determining way, he selectively marshals against Heidegger's post-1934 philosophical writing—and in behalf of his humanist outrage—the moral force of the reiterated testimony of the

European philosophers, all profoundly influenced by Heidegger, who have in some degree or other expressed dismay at his sustained silence concerning the Holocaust:

> Philippe Lacoue-Labarthe, who brought this statement to prominence and discusses it at length in *La Fiction du politique*, admits that insofar as Heidegger intended to refer the gas chambers and death camps to the essence of technology his thought is "absolutely just." But the justice of this condemnation, by way of the relation between technology and nihilism, is by itself "scandalously insufficient." According to Lacoue-Labarthe, this scandalous insufficiency results from the fact that Heidegger never acknowledged that this mass extermination was essentially [*pour l'essentiel*] the extermination of the Jews, and that this fact makes for an incommensurable difference from the economic and military practice of blockades, or even the production of nuclear weapons, not to mention the mechanization of the food industry. For Lacoue-Labarthe, as for Blanchot and Lévinas, Heidegger's silence concerning the Final Solution, his failure to pronounce the name of the Jews, is what remains beyond pardon. And I think that behind this silence, when one encounters Heidegger's 1949 pronouncement, one cannot but be staggered by his inability—call it metaphysical inability—to acknowledge the everyday fate of bodies and souls, as if the bureaucratized burning of selected human beings were not all that different from the threat to humanity posed in the organization of the food industry by the forces of technology. The mechanization of agriculture may be a cause for worry; the production of hydrogen bombs is a reason for terror; the economic blockades of countries may be evil; but the production of corpses in the gas chambers and death camps brings us face to face with the experience of horror. Where have these distinctions gone? Humanism aside, what has become of the human? At Auschwitz, says Lacoue-Labarthe, the Jews were treated as industrial waste. Do we have no criteria of evaluation to distinguish between waste products of technology and the production of human corpses in the gas chambers? Are the advances of Heidegger's thought inseparable from the indifference to the specifically human? (QCH, 423–24)

One cannot but concede the charge that Heidegger betrays a remarkable insensitivity to the differences in the degree of human suffering incumbent on the violent practices he enumerates in this passage (even though there is something suspect about invoking it centrally without reference to the textual context from which it has been taken). But let us be as clear as possible about what is being said in this culminating judgment of Heidegger's philosophy/politics. Putting aside for the moment Davidson's selective reduction of Lacoue-Labarthe's much more nuanced overall response to this passage in *La fiction du politique* (as well as his appropriation of the specifically European context Lacoue-Labarthe's text addresses for an American milieu), it should be noted that Davidson's judgment against Heidegger's philosophical, indeed, moral insensitivity is, like Lacoue-Labarthe's (and Habermas's), won all too easily. He virtually disregards what is, according to its rhetoric, fundamental to the antihumanism of this passage—indeed, to Heidegger's antihumanist thought at large, from *Being and Time* to "The Question Concerning Technology" and beyond: that the constructed *essence*, if not the worldly manifestations, of this relay of violent practices is the same. However unevenly materialized and distributed its worldly manifestations at any historically specific time and place in modernity, they are the manifest practical consequences of a *logic of construction*—a process of *technologization* or *reification*—that has come to its fulfillment and "end" in the anthropological "age of the world picture": the age that has borne witness to the reduction by enframing (*Ge-stell*) of the temporality of being and the differences it disseminates to "standing reserve" (*Bestand*), a condition in which even the dying of death cannot be lived.

Against the disciplinary compartmentalization of being, Heidegger insists everywhere in his writing—even if he did not adequately practice its imperatives—that to think the humanist tradition is to think *simultaneously* all its manifestations, from the subject through language to the scientific, economic, and sociopolitical domains.[17] Despite this insistence, Davidson refuses to think the phrase "its essence," and this refusal facilitates an easy and misleading slide in his rhetoric that obscures and minimizes Lacoue-Labarthe's gesture acknowledging the justness of Heidegger's equation. It is a slide that focuses exclusively on Heidegger's insensitivity to the differences in order to advance an all too obvious perspective against Heidegger that for all practical purposes *absolutizes* the difference between the technologization of the material world, on the one hand, and the violent outrages against the human, on the other. Despite its justified thematization of Heidegger's insensitivity to the differences in the degree of suffering occasioned by these violent practices, in other words, Davidson's criticism is determined by a disciplinary/moral perspective that tacitly reaffirms the privileged centrality of Man and his dominion over the earth. For Davidson (as in some degree his European authority) "the mechanization of agriculture may be cause for worry; the production of hydrogen bombs is a reason for terror; the economic blockades of countries may be evil; *but* the production of corpses in the gas chambers and death camps brings *us* face to face with the experience of horror" (my emphasis). The threat to humanity of the first three practices in this familiar rearrangement of the terms of Heidegger's statement, it should be noted, is put in the future. The horror latent in these practices is merely potential and thus presumably avoidable. Only the third is put in terms of the specific present, since "the production of corpses in the gas chambers and death camps brings us face to face with the experience of horror." Which is to say that Davidson's teleologically determined—and morally outraged—argument against Heidegger's dehumanized and dehumanizing philosophy compels him to misrepresent the historically specific reality of the manufacture of bombs, hydrogen or otherwise. In the name of a correctable possibility, it not only forgets that the so-called Western Allies ("so-called," because the alliance with the Soviet Union was a matter of convenience) perpetrated the unspeakable incendiary bombing of Dresden (an open city) on February 13 and 14 (in the last days of the war when nothing—except the fear of Soviet dominance—was strategically at stake), which in 24 hours extinguished by fire the lives of 135,000 women, children, and men.[18] It also forgets that the government of the United States, with the backing of most of its scientist and humanist advisors (I think, for example, of the role played by James Bryant Conant, president of Harvard University, in the making of this decision), exploded the atomic bomb on Hiroshima and Nagasaki in August 1945, which immediately incinerated 100,000 human beings in Hiroshima, and 75,000 in Nagasaki, in two cataclysmic moments, and rendered the daily lives of those who survived and the future generation they carried in their bodies at the same time an experience of horror. What *is* the difference, except in degree, that is, *as such*, one is compelled to ask when we retrieve the reality of hydrogen bomb production that Davidson (and Lacoue-Labarthe) projects simply as an avoidable possibility of the future? Is it that perpetrating the firebombing of Dresden and the atomic bombing of Hiroshima and Nagasaki from the distance of the sky is *essentially* different from perpetrating the incineration of the Jews at Auschwitz immediately? Is it that dying by fire is *essentially* different from dying in gas chambers? Is it that the women, children, and men who died in Dresden and Hiroshima and Nagasaki were German and Japanese, that is, "political" civilians and thus *essentially* different from and less innocent than the Jewish women, children, and men who died in Germany?[19] In privileging the Holocaust, to put it provisionally, is not the judgmental discourse represented by Davidson (and even Lacoue-Labarthes) an instance of that Eurocentrism which it has been the purpose of the posthumanist project to expose?

But Davidson's condemnation of Heidegger cannot rest on Heidegger's "equation" of hydrogen bomb production and economic blockades that produce famines with the Nazi gas chambers and death camps. For the radical difference he is asserting, it seems, is unfortunately not quite obvious enough in these two instances. What *is* obvious and *will unquestionably* justify his universalized moral outrage—what "one cannot but be staggered by"—is Heidegger's appallingly callous identification of the technologization of agriculture with the Nazi's "Final Solution." This strategic elision is clearly suggested, despite his effort to conceal it, by the inordinate—and misleading—emphasis he gives it in his shared summary of Lacoue-Labarthe's moral judgment of Heidegger's text, in which he convicts Heidegger of being *incapable* of perceiving the "incommensurable difference" between "the extermination of the Jews" and "the economic and military practice of blockades, or even the production of nuclear weapons, *not to mention the mechanization of the food industry*" (my emphasis).[20] And it is given a determinative judgmental force two sentences later, when, in his "own" voice,[21] he reduces the multisituated equation to that between the gas chambers and the mechanization of agriculture: "one cannot but be staggered by [Heidegger's] inability—call it metaphysical inability—to acknowledge the everyday fate of bodies and souls, as if the bureaucratized burning of selected human beings were not all that different from the threat to humanity posed in the organization of the food industry by the forces of technology."

From Davidson's humanist perspective, then, what is so self-evidently "beyond pardon," what *all* men and women in America as well as Europe and, presumably, the people of the Third World, will or ought to be staggered by, is Heidegger's incredibly dehumanized identification, induced by his dehumanizing philosophical discourse, of such a trivially threatening (because endemically Western, above all, American) practice as the mechanization of agriculture with the incommensurably different because visibly violent nihilism that apparently constitutes an absolute break from the essential rationality of the civilized tradition of the Occident. And, of course, from the perspective that represents the mechanization of agriculture as essentially and world-historically benign, such a representation of Heidegger's "pronouncement" and the moral judgment against him appear to be unchallengeable. For, as the perennially privileged status of the resonant passage from Homer's *Odyssey* quoted as one of my epigraphs suggests, this technological humanist perspective exists essentially to cultivate and bring to fruition (to "colonize," in the Roman sense of the word) that which is "unplanted" and "uncultivated," a wilderness. Though this "technological" perspective is admittedly subject to abuse, the abuse is, of course, correctable. It is, after all, the perspective that marks off the greatness of Occidental humanist culture. (This perspective is *not*, finally, that of Lacoue-Labarthe, but insofar as he fails to dissociate his critique from it by inordinately emphasizing the *incommensurable* difference, he lends his discourse to humanist appropriation.)

But what if, instead of isolating our focus on the "unique" fate of the Jews at the hands of the Nazis, we read Heidegger's grotesque and self-convicting "pronouncement" from the point of view of the peoples of non-Western cultures who have experienced the practices of Western mechanized agriculture, above all after the Kantian Enlightenment? That we owe it to Heidegger, or to Heidegger's discourse, to make such an effort should be evident from his unrelenting, however theoretical, reminders, especially in his later writings, that the "enlightened" (representational) discursive economy of the West has been insistently blind or indifferent to this "other" in its arrogantly monomaniacal and careless pursuit of planetary hegemony. I think, for example, of "A Dialogue on Language, between a Japanese and an Inquirer," although one could refer to any number of texts, since in these the fulfillment in modernity of the aspirations to global domination of the representational discursive practices of "Europe" is a fundamental symptom of the "end of philosophy":

J: . . . as I indicated, the temptation is great [in the East] to rely on European ways of representation and their concepts.

I: That temptation is reinforced by a process which I would call the complete Europeanization of the earth and man.

J: Many people consider this process the triumphal march of reason. At the end of the eighteenth century, in the French Revolution, was not reason proclaimed a goddess?

I: Indeed, the idolization of that divinity is in fact carried so far that any thinking which rejects the claim of reason as not originary, simply has to be maligned as unreason.

J: The incontestable dominance of your European reason is thought to be confirmed by the successes of that rationality which technical advances set before us at every turn.

I: The delusion is growing, so that we are no longer able to see how the Europeanization of man and of the earth attacks at the source everything that is of an essential nature. It seems that these sources are to dry up.[22]

What if, to be more historically specific, we read Heidegger's statement not simply in terms of a "European" problematic—in the context of the Third Reich, the Holocaust, and the question of German national identity (the context which has come to be called the *Historikerstreit*)—but also, as the American appropriation of the debate surely demands, from the immediate perspective of the Vietnamese "other": those people who suffered face to face (and continue to suffer) the dreadful consequences of the American intervention in Vietnam undertaken in the name of the "free world," which is to say, of the liberal discourse and practices of the West? In referring to the "American intervention" in Vietnam, I do not mean to suggest a purely military act of violence (an "atrocity") which was radically different from the cultural discourse and the political, social, and economic (including agricultural) practices accompanying this intervention, a violence which, therefore, was essentially and solely responsible not only for the massive and gratuitous destruction of human (civilian) life, but also for the devastation of a culture—more specifically, of a "rice culture," a traditional way of life utterly and resonantly integral with the Vietnamese *earth*, in this case, the rice paddies. Such a dissociation of American military violence from American cultural discourse would be the reading demanded by the binary logic of Davidson's interpretation of and judgment against Heidegger's synecdochical text, if this last were applied to the American intervention in Vietnam, *as significantly it has not been nor even thought*. What I mean, rather, is that the American intervention constituted a *relay* of interventions, which were *in essence* the same. However uneven the distribution of destruction, they were informed through and through by a hyperinstrumentalized reason—the advanced, end-oriented technology that, according to Heidegger, in extending its dominion over the planet, promises the fulfillment and "end of philosophy." As I will show, they were also the same in the sense that the culpability for the horrible human consequences of this relay of interventions defies moral discrimination.

This distinction I am drawing between an intervention that radically discriminates between broadly cultural practices and military atrocities and one that insists on the continuity—the seamless, however differential, relationship—between them is a crucially important one. For to think through the continuity between official representations of the war and the political and economic practices based on it, on the one hand, and the use of Agent Orange for purposes of defoliation, the napalm bombing of the Vietnam landscape, the torching of villages, the apparently gratuitous mass execution of women, children, and men (as in the much publicized but not isolated case of My Lai), on the other, will not only shed a different, more positive and sympathetic light on Heidegger's postwar synecdochical statement (and his virtual silence on the "Final Solution"). More significantly, it will tell us much about the ideological motives ultimately informing Davidson's scandalized and indignant judgment against Heidegger's silence, and about the ideological subtext informing his (and by extension, *Critical Inquiry's*) representative invocation and deployment of the Kantian principle of "public reason"—of the "autonomy of philosophy"—against Heidegger's philosophical effort to "overcome philosophy." It will show that the humanist problematic determining Davidson's judgment (the frame of reference that sets the limits of the questions that can be posed—and answers attained) and renders it seemingly unchallengeable is ultimately a manipulative strategy intended to demonize opposition (the kind of question I am posing concerning the Vietnamese people). It will show, in short, that it is intended to censor any critique of his judgment.

III

Let me therefore be more specific about the American intervention in Vietnam as it seems to have been understood by the Vietnamese people, particularly those who participated in resisting it. I am aware of the possibility that such a specific analysis may seem on the surface to be simply a digression from or even a circumvention of the issue at stake. But it is a risk worth taking for the light I hope it will shed on what Davidson and all those other humanists (as well as their European authorities) who have invoked it to discredit Heidegger's thought take to be the weakest link in Heidegger's multiple equation. I mean his especially "self-damning" identification of the mechanization of agriculture and the Nazi gas chambers and death camps, to which they reduce Heidegger's more complex statement by inflating it into a "pronouncement"; by disregarding the ghastly resonance of Heidegger's reference to the "Final Solution" as "the manufacture of corpses in the gas chambers and the death camps"; and, above all, by minimizing the violence of the other practices in the series.

It is by this time well known, if not determinative in present foreign policy deliberations, that the American intervention after the defeat of the French colonial army it was supporting morally and financially, and the Geneva Accords of 1954, took the form of a covert and later overt military operation intended to "save" Vietnam (and the other Southeast Asian nations) from Communist domination and, simultaneously, of a cultural project intended to "win the hearts and minds" of the Vietnamese people. As President Lyndon Johnson summarily (and cynically) put it before the Honolulu Conference (February 1966), ten months after overtly committing the first combat troops to battle, "We are here to talk especially of peace. We will leave here determined not only to achieve victory over aggression but to win victory over hunger, disease, and despair. We are making a reality out of the hopes of the common people."[23] This cultural/military strategy which (it should not be overlooked) represented the Vietnamese people in the image of Johnson's "Great [American] Society," met with severely disabling obstacles for a variety of reasons. But the most important was the counterstrategy of the National Liberation Front (NLF) and, later, of the North Vietnamese Army (NVA): a strategy of resistance, namely, that exploited the knowledge of the Western structure of consciousness gained from the practices of French colonialism—its *mission civilatrice*—over several generations, but especially in the struggle for national independence against the French colonial army.

It is impossible here to convey the full scope and depth of this counterstrategy of the (non-European) "other." But perhaps the essence of its otherness can be suggested by invoking one of the most persistent reactions to it by those American soldiers actually fighting the war in Vietnam. As opposed to the ideologically compelled confidence of the government bureaucracy in Washington and the Military Command in Saigon (MACV) which were conducting it from an enormous topological and mental—one might say "panoptic"—distance from the human carnage, the immediately engaged American soldier was confused, ("spooked") and frustrated by the *uncanny invisibility* of the "enemy":

> I saw cruelty and brutality that I didn't expect to see from our
> people against the villagers. It took me a while in country to realize
> why it was happening. In this type of fighting it was impossible to
> know who the enemy was at any one time. Children were suspect,
> women were suspect. Frequently the ARVNs [soldiers of the Army
> of the Republic of Vietnam] themselves were on two payrolls. Their
> army was heavily infiltrated with Viet Cong or people who were
> politically ambivalent, who could change sides as easily as changing
> clothes.
>   When, for example, we would patrol an area of villages for a
> number of weeks and continue to lose men to booby traps, and the
> people in the villages who pretended not to know anything about
> these booby traps walked the same trails that we did day after day
> without stepping on them, it became obvious that these people were
> well informed by the VC where the booby traps were.[24]

To invoke the terms of posthumanist theory, which in large part was precipitated by the contradictory spectacle of a brutal intervention in the affairs of a non-European people in the name of (European) freedom, the counterstrategy of the NLF and the NVA could be said to constitute a deliberate refusal to accommodate the imperative of *presence* informing the cultural, political, and military practices of the United States. American military tactics and practice were determined by a "technological"— an end-oriented (and ethnocentric)—mindset that perceived the differential complexities of Vietnamese life and the actual conditions of the war (the "problem") in spatial or panoptic terms. It was a perspective that represented the dislocating otherness as a microcosmic "world picture" or (tactical) map in which every resistant (differential) thing/event could be, in the term Heidegger employs to characterize the essence of technology, "enframed" (*Gestell*) or, in Foucault's term "disciplined"— compelled into its proper place in the gridded whole and pacified—and reduced to "standing reserve" (*Bestand*) or "useful and docile body" (the "solution"). In opposition the NLF and NVA simply *obscured* this representational map, blurred the categorical distinctions necessary to the restrictive narrative economy of the panoptic gaze. In the recurrent metaphorics precipitated by the American soldier's existential experience in Vietnam—his experience of uncanniness—this counterstrategy of the other transformed the illuminating map into an obscuring maze:

> Guarding, but mostly concealing, the hedgerows in Quang Ngai sometimes seemed like a kind of smoked glass forever hiding whatever it was that was not meant to be seen. Like curtains, or like walls. Like camouflage, so where the paddies represented ripeness and age and depth, the hedgerows expressed the land's secret qualities: cut up, twisting, covert, chopped and mangled, blind corners leading to dead ends, short horizons always changing. It was only a feeling. A feeling of marching through a great maze, a sense of entrapment mixed with mystery. The hedgerows were like walls in old mansions: secret panels and trapdoors and portraits with moving eyes. That was the feeling the hedges always gave him, just a feeling.[25]

To put this strategy of dislocation in terms of a related metaphorics that pervades the discourse of the war, the NLF and NVA disrupted and fragmented the American command's idea of structure by refusing to accommodate its expectations of closure; the closure carried out by a military practice informed by a representation of the people of Vietnam and the unfolding process of their history in terms of a narrative structure (often perceived as a John Wayne Western) with a beginning, middle, and (promised) end. In terms of the specific context of the war, the NLF and NVA refused to provide the center-oriented, time-conscious, and obdurate American military strategists the possibility of achieving a quick, economical, and climactic conclusion. For the NLF, according to Herman Rapaport in a Deleuzian analysis of the Vietnam War, "the art of war [was] anticlimactic"; it involved a deliberate effort to frustrate the U.S. Army's expectation of the "decisive battle":

> Truong Son of the N.L.F. reports that the North Vietnamese took very much into account the American expectation that one ought to win "decisive battles" in Vietnam. "Though somewhat disheartened, the Americans, obdurate by nature and possessed of substantial forces, still clung to the hope for a military solution, for decisive victories on the battlefield." Truong Son's comments are based on the perception that an American view of an all-or-nothing victory can easily be converted to a tactic by which the "superior forces," anxious for quick victory, are by way of a certain fracturing, reduced to something less than victory. That is, the North Vietnamese

immediately realized that a molecularization of its forces among those of the Southern resisters would force the United States to spread its resources thin. Son's assessment of the American strategy is that "it did not specifically center on anything" and that "the Americans and their puppets had no definite way of utilizing their mobile and occupation forces. . . ." For this reason, even when conflict was "head on," that conflict would be articulated in terms of a certain passivity, since action did not necessarily lead to anything more than action itself. Moreover, the communists saw to it that the "corps" would be disarticulated along various mobile "fronts" all at the same time. In doing so they insured that "action" would be reduced to random or marginalized events which even if successfully won by the Americans would not mean victory. As so many soldiers said to themselves over and over again, "What a waste. . . ."[26]

What was the American response to this tactical refusal by the NLF and NVA to accommodate its military practice to the metaphysical/ethnocentric narrative expectations inscribed in what Andrew Krepinevich, in his in-house critical analysis of the U.S. Army's defeat, calls the "Army Concept" (the "European" military frame of reference developed during World War II which, despite token gestures toward "low intensity" warfare, determined the American command's conduct of the war)?[27] We know all too well that the military answer was to unleash unprecedented technological firepower in a war of attrition that did not discriminate between enemy and peasant civilian. This was the testimony of the media coverage of the war, after the escalation of American violence could no longer be concealed by official representations that emphasized the Army's mission to win the "hearts and minds" of the Vietnamese people. It was also the testimony of those responsible intellectuals such as Noam Chomsky, Susan Sontag, Tom Hayden, I. F. Stone, Bernard Fall, Jean-Paul Sartre, and Bertrand Russell, among others, who to some degree penetrated the benign discourse of Western hegemony to its violent essence. Since the early 1980s, however, especially in the aftermath of the dedication of the Vietnam Veterans War Memorial in Washington, a massive and multisituated recuperative discursive campaign on the part of the custodians of the American cultural memory has gone far to "heal the wound" suffered by the American psyche when the awful contradictions inhering in its "benign" (Western) narrative of technological progress were (self-)exposed.[28] (This recuperative momentum has been greatly abetted by the events of 1989 in Eastern Europe, which are being represented as the triumph of liberal democratic principles or, conversely, the fall of Communism, and by the decisive American victory against Saddam Hussein in the Gulf War, which is being represented not simply as the vindication of the American military but also, in the words of President George Bush, as "kicking the Vietnam Syndrome"—as the curing of a national neurosis precipitated by an "un-American" minority that prevented the American command from winning the war in Vietnam.)

To decode this by now naturalized cultural metaphorics, the massive discursive campaign to recuperate the American Identity (and consensus) shattered by the war has all but obliterated the knowledge of the excesses of violence—the atrocities—perpetrated by the American intervention against the Vietnamese people and their earth in the name of a superior liberal Western democracy. To put it positively, it has, as the renewed interventions in the Third World in the name of the "new world order" suggest, all but reestablished the hegemony of the American cultural memory. It is therefore necessary to retrieve this historical knowledge from the amnesiac cultural memory, however summarily, in all its multidimensional horror. What I mean by this imperative is not simply the retrieval of the knowledge of American military violence—the disciplinary knowledge all too disablingly foregrounded by the oppositional discourse of liberal intellectuals in the 1960s. I also mean the retrieval of the historical role played by cultural production in the wasting of Vietnam. For what we have learned since then by way of the failure of this oppositional discourse to effect lasting changes in our cultural and political institutions, and by way of the contemporary discourses that have theorized this failure, is that the discourse of knowledge and the practice of power in the Occident, especially since the Enlightenment, constitutes not an opposition but an indissoluble relay. To put this disclosure in terms of the practices at issue in Heidegger's "pronouncement," we have learned that the production of agricultural knowledge and the political practice of domination are *essentially* complicitous, however *differential* their historically specific antihuman consequences.

To repeat this all but forgotten history, then, the tactical refusal of the NLF and NVA to engage the American army in "decisive battles"—to participate in the restrictive terms of the narrative of presence or closure[29]—did not occasion a rethinking by the American command of its ethnocentric representation of the Southeast Asian mind and culture and thus of the American intervention. Rather—and predictably—this refusal triggered an *intensification* of the binarist misrepresentation of this "Orientalist" representation. It compelled the American command to see the humanity it encountered—not only the Communist "Viet Cong" and the North Vietnamese, but *all the Vietnamese people*, indeed, the very Vietnamese earth—as an absolutely dedifferentiated and reified negative entity, a differential obstacle called "the gook" or "slope" in the path of the American command's positive narrative journey.[30] Despite the effort on the part of the state apparatuses—the United States government and the military command—to exculpate themselves by the court-martial of Lieutenant William Calley for the massacre at My Lai, the lieutenant's representation of the Vietnamese in his justification of the massacre applies as well to the logic of the institutional agents who judged his behavior a war crime, as Frances FitzGerald has observed:

> To say that one "gook" was a Communist whereas another was not [as the official representation of the American soldier's mission in Vietnam would have it] was to make what seemed to be a purely metaphysical distinction which, if wrongly made, might cost you your life. As Calley said after his trial, "When my troops were getting massacred and mauled by an enemy I couldn't see, I couldn't feel and I couldn't touch—that nobody in the military system ever described them as anything other than Communism. They didn't give it a race, they didn't give it a sex, they didn't give it an age. They never let me believe it was just a philosophy in a man's mind. That was my enemy out there." Thus in the My Lai massacre the soldiers abandoned the unrealistic war aims of Dean Rusk and drew their mistaken but nonetheless understandable conclusion: since all Communists in Vietnam are Vietnamese, and since the only good Communist is a dead one, then all Vietnamese had to be killed.
>
> Of course, the syllogism was faulty, and the defenders of Calley were being disingenuous in describing the cold-blooded murder of babies and old women as necessary to the safety of his troops. . . . But there were many other cases in which the moral issue was much less clear. When, as happened frequently, a unit received enemy fire from a village, the officer in charge would have the choice of flattening the village with artillery or ordering his troops to go in and search it. If he chose the first alternative, he might discover that the village contained only one or two snipers and a large number of civilians—many of them now dead. If he chose the second, he might find it contained an enemy company, and that he had (unnecessarily?) forfeited the lives of his own men. . . . The basic problem was, of course, that the U.S. official picture of "the Viet Cong" as an army and a coercive administration fighting over an apolitical peasantry was simply a misrepresentation of the facts. . . . Where . . . was the distinction between "soldiers" and "civilians"? In many regions "the Viet Cong" were simply the villagers themselves; to "eliminate the Viet Cong" meant to eliminate the villages, if not the villagers themselves, an entire social structure and way of life. It is in this context that charges of war crimes against the American civilian and military authorities who directed the war have a certain validity. In the first place, by the very act of sending American soldiers to Vietnam the U.S. command was denying many of its soldiers and field officers the very power of choice over killing civilians. It was making some civilian deaths inevitable. In the second place the U.S. command's decision to use certain weapons

and certain strategies insured that the number of civilian deaths would be sizable.[31]

Mystified and utterly frustrated by the enemy's decentered "invisibility," the agencies conducting the war eventually reacted to the uncanny impasse in the same, if deviously rationalized, way that Lieutenant Calley did: they unleashed overtly and massively the latent (racist) violence inhering in the liberal democratic ("can do")[32] representation of the American intervention in Vietnam. It was, to be specific, the subversion of their inscribed assumption of presence and desire for and expectation of *closure*—the resolution of the narrative that promised decisive victory—that, after 1965, provoked the full fury of American technology against *all* the Vietnamese: the saturation B-52 bombings that decimated the Vietnamese landscape and contributed to making the agrarian people of Vietnam a population of urban refugees;[33] the indiscriminate use of herbicides like Agent Orange that defoliated and contaminated vast areas of the earth of Vietnam; the mechanized "search and destroy" (later recoded as "search and clear") missions and the bracketing of "free-fire zones" that resulted in the undifferentiated destruction of entire villages and untold numbers of villagers; the systematic, concealed brutalization and torture of prisoners of war, and of those villagers suspected of being "Viet Cong," that spread terror throughout the Vietnamese populace; and the various "pacification" projects: the relocation of the peasantry in what were euphemistically called "New Life Hamlets," but which, like their predecessors, the "Strategic Hamlets" of the Diem regime, were in fact more like concentration camps.[34] One catches a glimpse of the awful violence of the American command's policy of "attrition"—the concentrated American impulse to force a rational/technological solution on the recalcitrantly de-centered context generated by the anticlimactic strategy of the NLF and NVA—in the following grotesquely self-parodic instance (one of many) recorded by Michael Herr in his brilliant deconstruction of the official history of the war in Vietnam:

> At the end of my first week in-country I met an information officer in the headquarters of the 25th Division at Cu Chi who showed me on his map and then from his chopper what they'd done to Ho Bo Woods, the vanished Ho Bo Woods, taken off by giant Rome plows and chemicals and long, slow fire, wasting hundreds of acres of cultivated plantation and wild forest alike, "denying the enemy valuable resources and cover."
>
>   It had been part of his job for nearly a year now to tell people about that operation; correspondents, touring congressmen, movie stars, corporation presidents, staff officers from half the armies in the world, and he still couldn't get over it . . . it really showed what you could do if you had the know-how and the hardware. And if in

206 □ Heidegger, Nazism, and the "Repressive Hypothesis"

the months following that operation incidences of enemy activity in the larger area of War Zone C had increased "significantly," and American losses had doubled and doubled again, none of it was happening in any damn Ho Bo Woods, you'd better believe it.[35]

In thus retrieving this all but forgotten (or rewritten) history, I want to emphasize two related points that pertain to the humanist effort to discredit Heidegger's thought for its inhumanity. The military response to the differential nomadic counterstrategy of the NLA and NVA took the form of an advanced technological bludgeoning (*Nievellierung*, "leveling," to appropriate the term Heidegger uses to characterize the representational and dedifferentiating discursive practices of the modern "age of the world picture") that resulted in the apparently gratuitous but in fact systematic (in the sense that it was essential to "the Army Concept") mass killing and maiming of an untold number of Vietnamese peasants. Simultaneously—and equally significant in the context of the outpouring of moral outrage precipitated by the reinvocation of Heidegger's "identification" of the mechanization of agriculture and the "manufacture of corpses in the gas chambers and the death camps"—it involved the systematic technological laying waste (leveling) of vast amounts of the Vietnamese *earth*. (I stress this word, despite the problems it poses, to alienate the predictably derisive representation by contemporary liberal humanists of Heidegger's invocation of *die Erde* and/or *die Volk* as an unqualified and dangerous form of nostalgic idolatry.)

It must not be overlooked, as it callously was by those who directed the American intervention in Vietnam (and even those liberal humanists who protested against the intervention as immoral), that for the Vietnamese peasantry the earth they cultivated was not, as it has become in the "developed" Occident, simply a technologically exploitable space. As the NLF officer envisaged by the baffled American soldier protagonist of Tim O'Brien's novel *Going After Cacciato* says in his laconic account of the Party's finally impenetrable strategy of invisibility, for the peasant the Vietnamese earth was "*Xa*":

> "The land," Li Van Hgoc murmured. . . .
> "The soldier is but the representative of the land. The land is your true enemy." He paused, "There is an ancient ideograph—the word *Xa*. It means—" He looked to Sarkin Aung Wan for help.
> "Community," she said. "It means community, and soil, and home."
> "Yes," nodded Li Van Hgoc, "Yes, but it also has other meanings: earth and sky and even sacredness. *Xa*, it has many implications. But at heart it means that a man's spirit is in the land, where his ancestors rest and where the rice grows. The land is your enemy."[36]

The name O'Brien gives to the NLF officer is an ironic allusion to Vincent Van Gogh: the modern Occidental artist whose paintings, perhaps more than anyone else's, depict the earth and those who dwell on it in a way that resonates with a meaning similar to that inhering in the Vietnamese *Xa*. What may be worth recalling, in the context of the question I am addressing, (and in the face of a criticism that now represents Heidegger's notion of the *Volk* as a dimension of an essentialist understanding of being), is Heidegger's celebration of Van Gogh's art (the pair of peasant shoes) as exemplary of that "strife between world and earth" that the technologization, the "enframing" and reduction of being as temporality to "standing reserve" has all but annulled.[37] More specifically, the cultivation of the rice paddies by the Vietnamese peasants was not simply a matter of the production of food for consumption. As the relation between the circumscribing rice fields and the village nucleus suggests, it was integral with the perennial rhythms of the peasants' communal lives—their *culture*:

> With a stable technology and a limited amount of land the traditional Vietnamese lived by constant repetition, by the sowing and reaping of rice and by the perpetuation of customary law. The Vietnamese worshiped their ancestors as the source of their lives, their fortunes, and their civilization. In the rites of ancestor worship the child imitated the gestures of his grandfather so that when he became the grandfather, he could repeat them exactly to his grandchildren. In this passage of time that had no history the death of the man marked no final end. Buried in the rice fields that sustained his family, the father would live on in the bodies of his children and grandchildren. As time wrapped around itself, the generations to come would regard him as the source of their present lives and the arbiter of their fate. In this continuum of the family "private property" did not really exist, for the father was less the owner than a trustee of the land to be passed on to his children. To the Vietnamese the land was the sacred, constant element: the people flowed over the land like water, maintaining and fructifying it for the generations to come.[38]

In its monolithic will to accomplish the imperatives of an imperial economy (which it represented as a benign "mission to save a free Vietnam" from the "savagery" of Chinese Communist domination), in the face of a bafflingly elusive "other," the American command visited death and mutilation on the peasant population of Vietnam at large; in devastating the Vietnamese earth in the process, it violently uprooted a traditional, stable, agricultural, and family-oriented people (those who survived), transforming them into a population of spiritually as well as physically mutilated refugees.[39] In short, the American military command's massive and indiscriminate use of high-technology fire power against an enemy who refused to distinguish his or her person from the land on which he or she dwelled, also destroyed the culture of the Vietnamese people. This terrible experience of cultural death, even more than the violence of the "face-to-face experience of horror," of mass death and mutilation, according to Frances FitzGerald, was, from the point of view of the Vietnamese people at large, the dreadful legacy of the American intervention in Vietnam:

> The physical destruction is not, perhaps, the worst of it. The destruction of an entire society—"That is, above all, what the Vietnamese blame Americans for," said one Vietnamese scholar. "Willfully or not, they have tended to destroy what is most precious in us: family, friendship, our manner of expressing ourselves." For all these years, the columns in the Saigon newspapers denouncing Americans for destroying "Vietnamese culture" have sounded somehow fatuous and inadequate to those Americans who witnessed the U.S. bombing raids. But it is the social death caused by the destruction of the family that is of overriding importance. . . . The land and the family were the two sources of national as well as personal identity. The Americans have destroyed these sources for many Vietnamese, not merely by killing people but by forcibly separating them, by removing the people from the land and depositing them in the vast swamp-cities.[40]

But to restrict this violence against an absolutely demonized "other" simply to the context of military operations—the direct and visible use of force by the state—is misleading in a way that disables criticism. For, like the representations of American violence by the liberal humanist opponents of the war—even those who raised the question of war crimes and genocide—to isolate critique to the site of the overt manifestation of power is to lend such critique to the radical discrimination between the military intervention and the cultural discourse and practice accompanying it: to the rationalized conclusion that the American destruction of Vietnam and its culture was the result, not of the fulfillment of the American ideological narrative, but of the betrayal of its liberal humanist (disinterested) value system. What the actual events of this shameful period in American history disclosed more dramatically and forcefully than any other historically specific moment—even that extended period in the nineteenth century bearing witness to the brutalities of slavery and the genocidal practices of Manifest Destiny—is, to use an Althusserian terminology, that the cultural apparatuses, the agencies of knowledge production, were absolutely continuous with the (repressive) state apparatuses: that the American command that wasted Vietnam in trying to fulfill its restricted narrative economy was not purely a military/political command. It was, rather, a *relay* of commands extending from the government through the military/industrial complex to the network of technical advisory agencies (military, political, cultural, social, informational, economic, etc.), and, as the protest movement made clear in exposing the complicity of the university with these commands, especially the institutions of knowledge production.[41]

One has only to read the secret memoranda recorded in *The Pentagon Papers*, as Richard Ohmann did in 1975, to perceive this otherwise invisible relay. I am referring to the "rational" discourse (and the problem-solving model)[42] that those liberal humanist intellectuals responsible for American foreign policy—Robert MacNamara, McGeorge Bundy, William Bundy, Walt Rostow, John McNaughton, to name only the most prominent—used in planning the conduct of the war. Such a reading discloses that these systematic "can do" memoranda constituted a technological discursive practice that, in its unerring obliteration of potentially disruptive differences in the name of identity, was *in essence* the same as the military technological practices that unerringly and indiscriminately destroyed Vietnam in order to achieve a decisive victory (for the principles of "freedom"), a "final solution," as it were, to the Vietnam "problem":

> Of course it is the job of generals to win, and political impact be damned. The more surprising and dismaying revelation of *The Pentagon Papers* is how much the *civilians* running America came to share this perspective. Perhaps the neatly symmetrical form . . . and the mechanical quality of the whole paradigm, helped dull their senses and made the unspeakable a daily routine.
>
> An all-pervasive metaphor accompanies the argumentative strategy [of the problem-solving model]: that of cost and benefit. . . . They must solve the problems, even if it means subtracting cabbages from kings. Thus, McGeorge Bundy in February, 1965, advocating a course of "sustained reprisal" against North Vietnam for "offenses" in the south: "While we believe that the risks of such a policy are acceptable, we emphasize that its costs are real." These costs include "significant air losses," "an extensive and costly effort against the whole air defense system of North Vietnam," high U.S. casualties, and arousal of American "feelings." "Yet measured against the costs of defeat in Vietnam, this program seems cheap. And even if it fails to turn the tide—as it may—the value of the effort seems to us to exceed its cost." . . .
>
> What arguments like these have in common is a lunatic incommensurability. Even now, reading these documents, I want to shout, "You destroyed the South Vietnamese people, and talked of piaster spending. You held off from still greater killing only because

open debate in America about doing so might encourage the North Vietnamese." The main point to make, in this context, is that since the suffering of the Vietnamese didn't impinge on the consciousness of the policy-makers as a cost, it had virtually no existence for them—at least not in these memoranda.[43]

Ohmann limits his analysis of *The Pentagon Papers* to the general complicity of the "civilians running America" with the generals' "will to win and political impact be damned." What I want to contribute to his chilling disclosure is a specificity that bears centrally on the question of Heidegger's "pronouncement." The routinized indifference to the Vietnameses' "face-to-face experience of the horror" inscribed in the technicist discursive practices of this relay of American commands applies with exceptional force to the agencies responsible for the dissemination of agricultural knowledge and practice—especially that of the cultivation of rice—to the Vietnamese people. Like the overdetermined military and political practices, these "benign" agencies dispensing agricultural aid were, in fact, acts of systematic violence determined by the technological American end.

For the Vietnamese peasants, we recall, the cultivation of rice was not simply a matter of the production of another food commodity. It was a traditional way of life, bearing little resemblance to Lyndon Johnson's (ideological) representation of Vietnamese society as one of "hunger, disease, and despair." As the English combat photographer Philip Jones Griffiths says in his great photographic history of the American destruction of the culture of Vietnam:

> The Vietnamese are a rice-growing people. For two thousand years their adeptness at pursuing this perennial task has been sustained by their belief in a harmony between man and nature. This belief, born of Buddhism, structured by Confucianism, and mystified by Taoism, sees every man, every thought, every action as significant and interrelated within a universal order. It transcends Western religious dogmas: it is a collective acceptance of the values recognized by all for their self-evident virtue.
>
> The environment, their world, is the paddy field, and their horizons are delineated by the borders of these flat rice lands. . . .
>
> The secret of their strength lies in the nature of their society. The foundation of their society is the village. Set amid the sea of rice fields, villages rise like identical islands, surrounded by sheer cliffs of bamboo. Inside live those who tend the rice, in great proximity to one another (every precious bit of land is needed for rice-growing), but within a well-organized whole. . . . While each village was a self-contained unit, independent, self-sufficient, and relying on no one, it was bound to each and every other village as a partner in the

common task of growing rice. Harmony as the supreme virtue—
and being part of that harmony—was the motivating force, enabling
the villagers to accept toil in the fields. Rites and rituals gave
meaning to the work far beyond simply providing food to eat. In
the fields were buried one's ancestors whose spirit passed through
the soil into the rice, so that eating it became the ritual by which one
inherited one's ancestors' souls.[44]

As I have taken some pains to emphasize, the callously indiscriminate
bombing of the countryside, the use of herbicides, the designation of
"free-fire zones," and the forced relocation of the peasants in "New Life
Hamlets" constituted a technological relay we can call, on the authority
of the American command's own rhetoric, the "pacification" of the radical (and disruptive) difference that was Vietnam. These violent leveling
practices *all* contributed to the destruction of this "alien" rice culture.
What did the United States—specifically, the agricultural knowledge industry and the technical agencies whose responsibility it was to "win the
hearts and minds" of the Vietnamese—offer the peasants in compensation for the systematic destruction of their rice fields and the burning of
their nuclear villages undertaken in the name of " 'denying the enemy
valuable resources and cover' "?[45] It was not simply American rice,
which, according to Griffiths, "the people hate" and so "try to sell for
pig food to get money to buy what Vietnamese rice is available." It was
also—and here, at last, we rejoin Heidegger's "unpardonable pronouncement"—the introduction of IR 8, the faster-growing and higher-yielding—
"miracle"—rice strain developed in "international" experimental stations
controlled and ideologically manipulated by American capital.[46] (The
"miracle rice" Griffiths refers to had its origin in the experimentation of
the International Rice Research Institute (IRRI) founded by J. George
Harras and Forrest F. Hill of the Ford Foundation in the late 1950s—at
the height of the Cold War. This Western, but basically American, initiative in the Third World went characteristically by the benign name
"the Green Revolution." But it soon became clear that its essential purpose was ideological, a weapon in the Cold War: the exportation of
capitalism/technology into peripheral areas where national liberation
movements were emerging to counter Western colonialism. When, in
the 1970s, the ecological and political contradictions of "the Green Revolution" began to manifest themselves in the form of decreasing yield
and, above all, peasant resistance to the radically unequal distribution of
benefits, the response of the disillusioned liberal humanists who had
committed their energies to the program was to dramatize the unrest and
to call for an administrative revision that would accommodate the peasants' demands to the "aid system in place."[47]

This appallingly insensitive compensatory gesture was well known at the time, but with the exception of Griffiths and FitzGerald, as far as I know, it was not understood by the liberal opponents of American intervention as the grotesquely violent practice it actually was. This was because the discourses and practices of agricultural aid to this "poor" and "underdeveloped" country was an extension of a general liberal discourse and practice that was represented as essentially *different* from and in opposition to that of the violent military intervention in Vietnam: as a discourse and practice the essential benignity—the "truthfulness"—of which was betrayed by a (historically accidental) American imperial will to power. Understood in the light of the above retrieval of the historical specificity of the American involvement in Vietnam, we recognize, on the contrary, the essential continuity between the two practices. We see that the massive introduction of the technologically produced "miracle" rice strains was *in essence* the same as the massive introduction of the technological war machine; that the indifference to human suffering betrayed by the "liberal" discursive practices of American agricultural aid agencies was, like all the other "humane" cultural programs, complicitous with the indifference to the suffering of the "other" betrayed by the dehumanized discursive practices of the political and military commands.[48] Above all, we see all too clearly the essential *commensurability* between the "horrors" perpetrated by both. One should not be misled by the carnivalesque Nietzschean rhetoric with which the war correspondent Michael Herr puts this commensurability between the saturating practices of the military, the diplomatic, and the technical advisory machines—synecdochically, between General Westmoreland, Ambassador Averell Harriman, and Robert Komer—in the following passage. Pushing the perennial American cultural logic that represents the polyvalent "can do" technics as massively benign to its self-parodic limits (where it becomes masquerade) is for Herr the only way of saying what was unsayable:

> The mission and the motion: military arms and civilian arms . . .
> Gun arms, knife arms, pencil arms, head-and-stomach arms,
> creeping-peeping arms, information arms as tricky as the arms of
> Plastic Man. At the bottom was the shitface grunt, at the top a
> Command trinity: a blue-eyed, hero-faced general, a geriatrics-
> emergency ambassador and a hale, heartless CIA performer (Robert
> "Blowtorch" Komer, chief of COORDS, spook anagram for Other
> War, pacification, another word for war. If William Blake had
> "reported" to him that he'd seen angels in the trees, Komer would
> have tried to talk him out of it. Failing there, he'd have ordered
> defoliation.) All through the middle were the Vietnam War and the
> Vietnamese. . . . If milk snakes could kill, you might compare the
> Mission and its arms to a big intertwined ball of baby milk snakes.

Mostly they were that innocent, and about that conscious. And a lot, one way or the other, had some satisfaction. They believed that God was going to thank them for it.[49]

But it is simply not enough to point to the *essential* relationship between a technological discursive practice that reduced human beings to counters in an ideologically articulated tactical map and the technological military practice that wasted large numbers of Vietnamese people—women, children, and men—and destroyed their culture in the single-minded pursuit of its self-privileged end. However true, such a conclusion remains determined by an interpretive strategy that restricts evidence to what the text says. We have learned from "theory," not least from Heidegger's disclosure that the meaning of a text is not, as it is in the ontotheological tradition, exclusively a matter of what is said about the object of inquiry, but also of what it does not say about it: what, in Althusser's term, its visual "problematic"—its oversight—precludes seeing and invisibly defers, as it were.[50] We therefore have to consider that aspect of the specific context necessarily left out of account by the restricted and restrictive narrative economy of American policy planners' liberal discourse. Those who were killed and maimed by the American war machine were not simply "human beings" in general; they were human beings who were also Vietnamese or, more broadly, Oriental. And the culture it destroyed was not any culture; it was the Vietnamese rice culture or, more broadly, an "Oriental" culture. They were, that is, a people and a culture represented by the dominant West as (technologically) "underdeveloped" and therefore inferior: "non-European." If we recall Heidegger's identification of technology with the Occident and its end with the triumphant imposition "of the social order proper to [it]" on the planet at large, we must extend Ohmann's analysis of the discourse of *The Pentagon Papers* to include the category of racial discrimination. We must, that is, add that the technological discursive practices of the liberal intellectuals planning and directing the Vietnam War from the distance of the imperial metropolis were complicitous with the racism informing the callous indifference to the human carnage manifested in the military command's indiscriminate use of high technology in its effort to achieve a decisive victory in Vietnam.

How fundamental and pervasive racism was can be measured by the fact that it was not limited to the discourse of those "hawks" who participated in or supported the American war against the "gooks" (a name no less obscene than those applied to Jews by the Nazis). As Noam Chomsky insistently observed, racism informed the discourse of all too many of those liberal intellectual "doves" who opposed or came to oppose it. In an essay written in the aftermath of the publication of the

214 □ Heidegger, Nazism, and the "Repressive Hypothesis"

proceedings of the Russell International War Crimes Tribunal in 1968 to encourage the publicizing of its findings, Chomsky cites the example of undersecretary of the Air Force, Tounsend Hoopes, who became a leading dove after the Tet Offensive:

> We [Americans] believe the enemy can be forced to be "reasonable," i.e. to compromise or even capitulate, because we assume he wants to avoid pain, death, and material destruction. We assume that if these are inflicted on him with increasing severity, then at some point in the process he will want to stop this suffering. Ours is a plausible strategy—for those who are rich, who love life and fear pain. But happiness, wealth, and power are expectations that constitute a dimension far beyond the experience, and probably beyond the emotional comprehension, of the Asian poor.

To this familiar rationale for the withdrawal of the United States from Vietnam, Chomsky responds:

> Hoopes does not tell us how he knows that the Asian poor do not love life or fear pain, or that happiness is probably beyond their emotional comprehension. But he does go on to explain how "ideologues in Asia" make use of these characteristics of the Asian hordes. Their strategy is to convert "Asia's capacity for endurance in suffering into an instrument for exploiting a basic vulnerability of the Christian West." They do this by inviting the West "to carry its strategic logic to the final conclusion, which is genocide. . . ." At that point we hesitate, for, remembering Hitler and Hiroshima and Nagasaki, we realize anew that genocide is a terrible burden to bear.
>
> Thus by their willingness to die, the Asian hordes, who do not love life, who fear no pain and cannot conceive of happiness, exploit our basic weakness—our Christian [and, I would add, humanist] values which make us reluctant to bear the burden of genocide, the final conclusion of our strategic logic. Is it really possible to read these passages without being stunned by their crudity and callousness?[51]

Given this racist crudity and callousness, it is no accident that intellectuals such as Chomsky, Bertrand Russell, and Jean-Paul Sartre, among many others both in the United States and abroad, were compelled at a certain point in the escalation of death and destruction to draw comparisons between the American conduct of the war and Nazi atrocities; indeed, between the inclusive and indiscriminate logical violence of the American effort to gain a decisive victory in the face of the "Asian hordes"—the "invisible" and "unnameable" "other"—and Nazi genocide, the "Final Solution":

At the outset, they [the American soldiers] were probably disappointed: they came to save Vietnam from "communist aggressors." But they soon had to realize that the Vietnamese did not want them. Their attractive role as liberators changed to that of occupation troops. For the soldiers it was the first glimmering of consciousness. "We are unwanted, we have no business here." But they go no further. They simply tell themselves that a Vietnamese is by definition suspect. And from the neo-colonialists' point of view, this is true. They vaguely understand that in a people's war, civilians are the only visible enemies. Their frustration turns to hatred of the Vietnamese; racism takes it from there. The soldiers discover with a savage joy that they are there to kill Vietnamese they had been pretending to save. All of them are potential communists, as proved by the fact that they hate Americans. Now we can recognize in those dark and misled souls the truth of the Vietnam war: it meets all of Hitler's specifications. Hitler killed the Jews because they were Jews. The armed forces of the United States torture and kill men, women and children in Vietnam merely because they are Vietnamese. Whatever lies or euphemisms the government may think up, the spirit of genocide is in the minds of the soldiers. This is their way of living out the genocidal situation into which their government has thrown them. As Peter Martinsen, a twenty-three-year-old student who had "interrogated" prisoners for ten months and could scarcely live with his memories, said: "I am a middle-class American. I look like any other student, yet somehow I am a 'war criminal.' " And he was right when he added: "Anyone in my place would have acted as I did." His only mistake was to attribute his degrading crimes to the influence of war in general. No, it is not war in the abstract; it is the greatest power on earth against a poor peasant people. Those who fight it are living out the only possible relationship between an over-industrialized country and an underdeveloped country, that is to say, a genocidal relationship implemented through racism—the only relationship, short of picking up and pulling out.[52]

Sartre's early indictment, like that of other oppositional participants in the struggle who invoked the specter of American genocide, betrays analytic limitations induced perhaps by his immediate engagement in a profoundly felt cause that, however just, was, given the uneven balance of power, finally unwinnable. Nevertheless, his insight into the complicity of the psychological, neocolonialist, and racist elements with a genocidal military momentum analogous, if not equivalent, to that of the Nazis continues to resonate with the force of a truth. This polyvalent dynamics of American violence needs therefore to be recalled by oppositional American intellectuals, in the face of the strategic amnesia of the American cultural memory, which has all but obliterated the memory of the appalling reality of the American intervention in Vietnam, *both the practice and the logic determining it.* This amnesia is especially characteristic of those American anti-antihumanists who, in their enthusiastic appropriation of the European occasion to "expose" the inhumanity of Heidegger's anti-humanist thought, do not or, given their problematic, cannot pronounce the name of Vietnam.

Let me be as explicit as I can about this point. I am *not,* as the above qualification suggests, *equating* the American devastation of Vietnam with Nazi genocide, since, of course, the fulfillment of the genocidal logic of the American intervention was finally blocked. Nor, therefore, am I implying that Heidegger's "silence" about the extermination of the Jews can be justified by the failure of his critics to remember the genocidal momentum of the American intervention on which Sartre insists. What I am saying is that the *logic,* however disproportionate its manifestations, was essentially the same. (As General Westmoreland's—and the culture industry's—postwar narrative symbolically suggests, this reading is enforced by that most recent aspect of the amnesiac project which represents the defeat of the United States in terms of "the Vietnam Syndrome": the consequence of a misguided resistance—indeed, a national neurosis—that prevented the military from employing all the means at its disposal to win the war.) If, therefore, it is recalled that Heidegger's thought enabled a theoretical discourse that has put the humanist problematic into crisis by thematizing the essential violence inhering in its (anthropo)logic, one cannot but conclude that a humanist attack on Heidegger's "silence" which continues, in the face of this disclosure, to assume the validity of its problematic, is suspect.

"We had to destroy Ben Tre in order to save it." This synecdochical justification by an American major, who was successful in his "attempt at attaining history," synecdochically betrays the terrible contradictions informing the American command's "benign" mission in Vietnam. But it does much more than that. As suggested by the chillingly resonant parallel with *Moby-Dick,* Herman Melville's uncannily genealogical and proleptic representation of the Puritan/frontier psyche, it also betrays the "end" of America's cultural self-representation: the will to planetary domination. The furious and single-minded American obsession to "save" this Third World country from a Communism which was also a "yellow peril," in the face of the uncanny enemy—an enemy who would not be *contained within* the expanding (neo)imperial perimeter and objectified or reduced to "standing reserve"—exposed its rational, humane, and liberal discourse and practice to be a monomaniacal obsession to bring its American version of the centered Occidental narrative of presence—its "errand in the wilderness"—to a "final (re-)solution." To "build its City on the Hill" in a recalcitrant Southeast Asia, the United States had to destroy (all of) Vietnam:

> No turbaned Turk, no hired Venetian or Malay, could have smote him with more seeming malice. Small reason was there to doubt, then, that ever since that almost fatal encounter, Ahab had cherished a wild vindictiveness against the whale, all the more fell for that in his frantic morbidness he at last came to identify with him, not only *all* his bodily woes, but *all* his intellectual and spiritual exasperations. The White Whale swam before him as the monomaniac incarnation of *all* those malicious agencies which some deep men feel eating in them; till they are left living on with half a heart and half a lung. The intangible malignity which has been from the beginning; to whose dominion even the modern Christians ascribe one-half of the worlds; which the ancient Ophites of the east reverenced in their statue devil;—Ahab did not fall down and worship it like them; but deliriously transferring its idea to the abhorred white whale, he pitted himself, all mutilated, against it; *all* that cracks the sinews and cakes the brain; *all* the subtle demonisms of life and thought; *all* evil, to crazy Ahab, *were visibly personified, and made practically assailable in Moby Dick.* He piled upon the Whale's white hump the *sum of all* the general rage and hate felt by his whole race from Adam down; and then, as if his chest had been a mortar, he burst his hot heart's shell upon it.[53]

But there is a significant difference that should not be overlooked between Melville's representation of the American cosmic mission and that implicit in Michael Herr's portrait of the American major who makes this grotesque boast. Melville's is imaginatively proleptic: it points to the latent violence inhering in a yet historically unfulfilled totalizing cultural discourse, and thus assumes a vestigially tragic form. Herr's, on the other hand, is documentary: it reports the terrible contradictions of the American cosmic mission in the context of the historical fulfillment of the ("practical") violence inhering in its totalizing narrative economy and thus shows it to be self-parodic. The historical occasion of Melville's text allows for the vestigial compensation of the tragic emotion. The historical occasion of Herr's precludes the tragic and thus the possibility of rationalizing catastrophe. The major's synecdochical boast grotesquely absolutizes the dreadful contradictions inscribed in America's self-representation of its cosmic mission, renders the narrative so utterly incommensurable with the horror of the reality it represents as to precipitate the demystifying laughter of carnival. Unlike Melville's, that is, Herr's historical occasion—which includes his awareness of the NLF's strategy of invisible resistance—facilitates, indeed compels, an "irrealizing genealogy," an understanding and representation of the totalizing narrative of the American cosmic mission precisely in the postmodern or posthumanist terms Foucault bears witness to, calls for, and practices. I am referring to his commentary on Nietzsche's parodic account of the "monumental"—humanist—historian's representation of European history; his reduction of everything ("all") that is disruptively different ("the actual intensities and creations of life") to the (self-parodic and self-disclosing) "masquerade" demanded by adherence to an absolute origin, a logos, an eternal presence:

> Historians supplied the Revolution with Roman prototypes, romanticism with knight's armor, and the Wagnerian era was given the sword of a German hero—ephemeral props that point to our own unreality. No one kept them from venerating these religions, from going to Bayreuth to commemorate a new afterlife; they were free, as well, to be transformed into street-vendors of empty identities. The new historian, the genealogist, will know what to make of this masquerade. He will not be too serious to enjoy it; on the contrary, he will push the masquerade to its limit and prepare the great carnival of time where masks are constantly reappearing. No longer the identification of our faint individuality with the solid identities of the past, but our "unrealization" through the excessive choice of identities. . . . In this, we recognize the parodic double of what the second of the *Untimely Meditations* called "monumental history": a history given to reestablishing the high points of historical development and their maintenance in a perpetual presence. . . . But in 1874, Nietzsche accused this history, one totally devoted to veneration, of barring access to the actual intensities and creations of life. The parody of his last texts serves to emphasize that "monumental history" is itself a parody. Genealogy is history in the form of a concerted carnival."[54]

IV

Let me circle back, after this extended digression from Europe to America in Vietnam, to Heidegger's notorious "pronouncement":

> Agriculture is now a mechanized food industry. As for its essence, it is the same thing as the manufacture of corpses in the gas chambers and the death camps, the same thing as the blockades and reduction of countries to famine, the same thing as the manufacture of hydrogen bombs.

And to Arnold Davidson's astonishment at Heidegger's unpardonable callousness: the astonishment, according to a certain interpretation of his rhetoric, which *all* mankind, including presumably the Vietnamese people, must also feel:

> When one encounters Heidegger's 1949 pronouncement, one cannot but be staggered by his inability—call it metaphysical inability—to acknowledge the everyday fate of bodies and souls, as if the bureaucratized burning of selected human beings were not all that different from the threat to humanity posed in the organization of the food industry by the forces of technology.

I want to reiterate that my purpose in invoking the American intervention in Vietnam has been neither to annul the significant differences between the American violence against the people of Vietnam and the Nazi violence against the Jews, nor to defend Heidegger against the charge of insensitivity to the distinction between the manufacturing of food (and of blockade-induced famines and nuclear bombs) and the manufacture of corpses in the gas chambers. Quite obviously there is, in the first instance, a significant difference and, in the second, an insensitivity that demands severe criticism. My purpose in retrieving the event of Vietnam—in putting its force back into play—has been, rather, to show that this difference is not an incommensurable one, but a difference of degree—that *in essence* they are the same—and thus, without exculpating Heidegger, to show that in some fundamental sense Heidegger's statement, whatever its occasion and whatever he meant by it, resonates with the compelling force of a truth that should not be overlooked. Indeed, to overlook or repress this essence in favor of overdetermining the difference, as the humanists who have pounced on this statement to demonstrate the complicity of Heidegger's philosophy with Nazi practice have done, is to betray an ideological motive: in the case of the "autonomous" discourse represented by Davidson's attack, the *anthropologism* that the *event* of Vietnam, as well as Heidegger's discourse and the discourses it enabled, have called radically into question.

When Davidson's universalized moral outrage (as well as that expressed by Lacoue-Labarthe and the other European philosophers who have focused their condemnation of Heidegger on this equation and whose authority Davidson has invoked) is seen in the retrieved context of the complicity of American agricultural technology with American military technology in the United States' neoimperialist/genocidal intervention in Vietnam, it sounds remarkably hollow and self-righteous. Indeed, it takes on the implications of something like a metaphysical policing action as callous of human suffering as Heidegger's is alleged to be. To repeat my question: would, I wonder, the Vietnamese people, who underwent the "face-to-face experience of the horror" of the American strategy of pacification by attrition, subscribe to Davidson's representative minimization of the human consequences of the mechanization of agriculture to "a cause for worry" and his projection of these to some hypothetical future in favor of privileging the "incommensurability" of the horror of the Nazi gas chamber and death camps in the name of humanism?

The historically specific context I have retrieved can hardly be escaped by any responsible Western—especially American—intellectual addressing the philosophical and moral issues Heidegger's "pronouncement" raises. One is thus compelled to ask: Why do the American humanists who condemn Heidegger's "failure to pronounce the name of the Jews" as "beyond pardon," fail, in turn, to pronounce the name of the Vietnamese? Why, that is, do they resist the imperative to examine the political implications of their own Kantian discourse of "public reason" in condemning Heidegger's for its blindness to or complicity with the Nazis' "Final Solution"? One can understand, if not entirely endorse, the moral judgment against Heidegger's refusal to confront the issue of the Nazis' "Final Solution" made by German critics such as Jürgen Habermas and Otto Pöggeler and even French critics such as Lacoue-Labarthe, Blanchot, Lévinas, and Lyotard. After all, for these European intellectuals, the horror of the death camps and gas chambers was and continues to be an immediate presence not simply in a topological sense, but also, and more important, in the sense of the German and French peoples' massive complicity with and guilt over the virulent anti-Semitism that precipitated the "Final Solution."[55] Furthermore, the European interrogation of Heidegger's "silence" concerning the Nazis' "Final Solution" has been precipitated by more than Farías's book; another catalyst has been the recent emergence of a conservative historical/political discourse in Germany (and France) intended to rationalize (and in some cases to obliterate the historical reality of) the gas chambers and the death camps in behalf of recuperating the authority the right lost as a consequence of the democratic "revolt of '68." (It is the measure of the sociopolitical viability of Jean-Paul Sartre's engaged discourse that he transcended the narrow limits in which Lacoue-Labarthe, Blanchot, Lévinas, Lyotard, Habermas, and even Derrida now frame the question of Heidegger's complicity precisely by emphasizing the analogy between Nazi genocide in the period of World War II and American genocide in the decade of the Vietnam War.) In the case of the American intellectuals who have taken up the European debate, on the other hand, we are faced with the recalcitrant immediacy of the systematic violence unleashed by the United States in Vietnam in the name of the "free world": a violence that was also racist and genocidal and thus in some fundamental sense commensurate in its horrible consequences for the Vietnamese people with the horror of the Nazi project to exterminate the Jews. It is thus much more difficult to assent to their narrowly self-righteous and reductive judgment against Heidegger and especially Heidegger's philosophical discourse, though not, of course, to their condemnation of the Nazis, and even of Heidegger's insensitivity.

To put this objection more specifically, it is difficult not to suspect that Davidson's synecdochical humanist condemnation of Heidegger's thought—Heidegger's philosophical effort to "overcome philosophy"—as a dehumanizing instrument has another, more historically specific and institutionally political agenda. One is compelled by the glaring invisible in Davidson's text to suspect that his (and *Critical Inquiry*'s) appropriation of the European *question* has more to do with the renewed opportunity afforded by the publication of Farías's *Heidegger et le nazisme* to recuperate Kantian "public reason" or "the autonomy of philosophy" (understood as "disinterested" inquiry) in the face of Heidegger's extraordinarily influential project to "overcome philosophy." As his focus on Heidegger's "thinking concerning humanism" (QCH, 422)—his ellision of Heidegger's interrogation of "philosophy" and "humanism"—suggests, one is led to suspect that, like the more overtly recuperative ideological project of the "anti-antihumanist" *nouveaux philosophes* and their followers in France, it also has to do with the opportunity afforded by the recent critique of Heidegger's thought by "some of the most significant European philosophers writing today" to relegitimate the institutional authority of the dominant discourse in the face of the recent intellectual ferment in the American academy which threatens to displace it. I am referring, of course, to the crisis in the *litterae humaniores* and its discourse of "deliverance" (as one of its most influential modern celebrants called it over a century ago)[56] precipitated, if not by Heidegger's interrogation of the humanist subject as such, then by the relay of theoretical discourses against anthropology enabled in some degree or other by Heidegger's interrogation: that of Derrida, Lacan, Althusser, Foucault, Bourdieu, Lyotard, Irigaray, and so on. These, it should be recalled, are the discourses that got their historically specific impetus in the period of the Vietnam War when the "public reason" Davidson and other American humanists espouses against Heidegger revealed itself, by way of its complicity with the state, to be an ethnocentric—an Ahabian—madness.[57]

In 1949—at the outset of the Cold War, when the United States and the Soviet Union (with a defeated Germany in between) were threatening nuclear war in pursuing their hegemonic imperial projects—Heidegger claimed that the technologization of agriculture, the inducement of famine through blockading, the production of atomic bombs, and the manufacture of corpses in the gas chambers and the death camps were *in essence* the same. In so doing, he was, indeed, being consistent not only with the philosophical discourse of the period of the rectorate and after but also (contrary to Davidson's representation) with that of *Being and Time*. But not essentially in the way it is now being represented: as a (dehumanizing) fascism. *Being and Time* exposes the philosophy of modernity (the anthropological philosophy that has brought the ontotheological tradition to its end in what Heidegger will later call the "age of the world picture") to be, despite its claims to autonomy, ontic—and ideological—through and through: a secondary and derivative discourse informed by the will to power over the temporality of being. The lectures on the *Parmenides* and the "Letter on Humanism," trace the genealogy of the "disinterested" discourse of modern humanism back to the Roman translation of the Greek *aletheia* to *veritas* and, through this translation, to Roman imperialism. And the notorious "pronouncement" of the Bremen lecture posits technology and its planetary hegemony as the essence of the mechanization of agriculture, blockades, and the manufacture of atomic bombs *and* the Nazis' "Final Solution." From beginning to end, as this itinerary suggests, Heidegger's project was to make explicit the violence latent in the traditional (re-presentational) understanding of truth.

Heidegger's abiding project was to suggest that the pursuit of knowledge is necessarily interested, and to discriminate between two kinds of interested inquiry: that which knows itself to be interested and thus always already remains open to (self-)criticism (thinking) and that dominant mode, which, like Kant's (or Descartes's or Hegel's, not to say his American humanist critics') does not know itself to be interested (takes itself to be self-evidently original and natural) and thus is incapable of self-criticism (philosophy). In attempting to extricate thinking from (modern) philosophy (*aletheia* from *adequaetio intellectus et rei*, or alternatively, the ontic/ontological hermeneutic circle from the ontic/metaphysical circle), Heidegger's project in its critical phase was in essence to demonstrate the complicity of the humanist discourse of truth with the overt practices of power.

Indeed, as I suggested in chapter 5 by invoking Heidegger's ontologico-political analysis of the true/false opposition (*veritas/falsum*) of this discourse in the *Parmenides* lectures, the critical phase of Heidegger's destructive thinking was to disclose the complicity of the circular/panoptic truth of humanism with the (Roman) imperialist project. The relevant part of this passage bears repetition at this juncture not only for the estranging light it throws on Heidegger's antihumanism in general, but also on the question of the commensurability of the three terms in his "pronouncement"—and, perhaps, on his "silence" in the face of the humanist prosecutors of the "case" against Heidegger, who would demand an apology from the defendant:

The commanding overseeing [*Übersehen-können*], is the dominating vision which is expressed in the often cited phrase of Caesar's: "*Veni, vedi, vici*"—I came, I *oversaw*, I conquered. Victory is already nothing but the consequence of the Caesarian gaze that dominates [*Übersehens*] and the seeing [*Sehens*] which has the character of *actio*. . . . The imperial *actio* of the constant surmounting over others implies that the others . . . are fallen [*gefällt werden*]—in Roman: *Fallere* (participle: *falsum*). The "bringing-to-fall" [*das Zu-Fall-bringen*] belongs necessarily to the domain of the imperial. The "bringing-to-fall" can be accomplished in a "direct" assault [*Ansturm*] and an overthrowing [*Niederwerfen*: literally, "throwing down"]. But the other can also be brought to fall by being outflanked [*Um-gehung*] and tripped up from behind. The "bringing-to-fall" is now the way of deceptive circumvention. . . . Considered from the outside, going behind the back is a complicated, circumstantial and thus mediate "bringing-to-fall" as opposed to an immediate overthrowing [*Niederwerfen*]. In this way, what is brought to fall does not thereby become annihilated, but in a certain manner redressed within the boundaries [*in den Grenzen*] which are staked out by the dominators. This "staking out" is called in Roman *pango*, whence the word *pax*, peace. This, thought imperially, is the firmly established condition of what has been brought to fall. In truth, the bringing-to-fall in the sense of deception and outflanking is not the mediate and derived imperial *actio* but the imperial *actio* proper. It is not in war, but in the *fallere* of deceptive outflanking [*hintergehenden Umgehens*] and its appropriation to the service of dominion that the proper and "great" trait of the imperial reveals itself.[58]

Heidegger failed to adhere to the radically dialogical imperatives of his de-structive project, and the consequences were disastrous. But this failure, however rightly open to severe criticism, should not be cause for the delegitimation of his philosophical project as such. For in thus disclosing the imperial will to power and the latent violence inhering in the "disinterested" inquiry of humanism, Heidegger established a theoretical context that enabled oppositional intellectuals faced with the problem of justifying a Marxist discourse that had become Stalinist. More specifically, Heidegger's exposure of the "autonomous" discourse of "public reason" as a ruse of power went far to enable those coming after him to revise the essentially humanist representation of the relation between truth and power that has dominated the production of knowledge in the West, especially since the (Roman-inspired) Enlightenment. I mean the principle that truth ("philosophy" in Davidson's Kantian term) and power are opposite and external to each other; that, unlike power, which is always a matter of overt and direct repression (visible violence), truth is not simply disinterested as such but also the agency of liberation from power. To put it positively, Heidegger's disclosure of the complicity between philosophy and the sociopolitical practices of domination in the West—especially since the rise to privileged status of representational thought and the advent of the technologized and detemporalized (spatialized) modern "age of the world picture"—enabled, if it did not itself (in its relationship to German National Socialism) carry out, an understanding of power relations in which the discourse of "truth," far from being autonomous, serves, by way of the production of knowledge, to extend and deepen the hegemony of the dominant and dominating sociopolitical order.

It is this revision of the humanist representation of the relations between truth and power—a process, it must not be forgotten, precipitated by the self-exposure of the contradictions inhering in the (Cold War) discursive practices of liberal humanism during the Vietnam decade—that distinguishes postmodern, poststructuralist, or, as I prefer, posthumanist critical theory from an earlier and largely delegitimated oppositional discourse. The recent massive shift of oppositional criticism's focus away from traditionally visible centers of power (economic production and the state) to the sites of culture and knowledge production (a momentum intensified in the wake of the events of 1989 in Central and Eastern Europe) is testimony to this revision. It underlies Derrida's exposure of the complicity of Western philosophy with logocentrism, Lacan's exposure of the complicity of the discourse of traditional psychoanalysis with the repressive bourgeois family, Kristeva's exposure of the complicity of the traditional discourse of the public sphere (the "symbolic order") with the repression of women, Althusser's (Gramscian) exposure of the complicity of the schools with the capitalist order (the ideological state apparatuses with the repressive state apparatuses), Said's exposure of the complicity of the discourse of Orientalism with Occidental colonialism. But this revision of knowledge/power relations is most clearly and forcefully articulated by Michel Foucault in his analysis of the complicity with power of the "repressive hypothesis": that humanist economy of power invented by the postmonarchical (and "Roman") culture of the Enlightenment,[59] which effaced the essential continuity between knowledge production and what he calls "the disciplinary society" or the "regime of truth" by proclaiming the *incommensurability* of the pursuit of truth and the violent practices of power:

> The important thing here, I believe, is that truth isn't outside power, or lacking in power: contrary to a myth whose history and functions would repay further study [this is the myth that conjoins the "universal intellectual" and "the repressive hypothesis"], truth isn't the reward of free spirits, the child of protracted solitude, nor the

privilege of those who have succeeded in liberating themselves. Truth is a thing of this world: it is produced only by virtue of multiple forms of constraint. And it induces regular effects of power. Each society has its regime of truth, its "general politics" of truth: that is, the types of discourse which it accepts and makes function as true; the mechanisms and instances which enable one to distinguish true and false statements, the means by which each is sanctioned; the techniques and procedures accorded value in the acquisition of truth; the status of those who are charged with saying what counts as true.

In societies like ours, the "political economy" of truth is characterized by five important traits. "Truth" is centered on the form of scientific discourse and the institutions which produce it; it is subject to constant economic and political incitement (the demand for truth, as much for economic production as for political power); it is the object, under diverse forms, of immense diffusion and consumption (circulating through apparatuses of education and information whose extent is relatively broad in the social body, notwithstanding certain strict limitations); it is produced and transmitted under the control, dominant if not exclusive, of a few great political and economic apparatuses (university, army, writing, media); lastly, it is the issue of a whole political debate and social confrontation ("ideological" struggles).

It seems to me that what must now be taken into account in the intellectual is not the "bearer of universal values." Rather, it's the person occupying a specific position—but whose specificity is linked, in a society like ours, to the general functioning of an apparatus of truth.[60]

The repressive hypothesis normally functions below the threshold of visibility, since it is a ruse, a disarming strategy of the disciplinary discourse of hegemony. But it surfaces at times of sociopolitical crisis, when the contradictions inhering in the discourse of disinterested truth—its complicity with the structures of visible and direct power—activate critical consciousness in the hitherto acquiescent mass. What Foucault says only indirectly about the historical dynamics of the relationship between the discourse of "truth" and the use of overt force is explicitly theorized by Antonio Gramsci (clearly one of Foucault's sources), who points both to the hidden complicity of the discourse of hegemony with the state and to its vulnerability at moments of sociopolitical discontent:

The intellectuals are the dominant group's "deputies" exercising the subaltern functions of social hegemony and political government. These comprise: (1) The "spontaneous" consent given by the great masses of the population to the general direction imposed on social life by the dominant fundamental group; this consent is "historically" caused by the prestige (and consequent confidence) which the dominant group enjoys because of its position and function in the world of production. (2) The apparatus of state coercive power which "legally" enforces discipline on those groups who do not "consent" either actively or passively. *This apparatus is, however, constituted for the whole of society in anticipation of moments of crisis of command and direction when spontaneous consent has failed.*[61]

As I have suggested, the period of the Vietnam War was such a moment of crisis. The refusal of spontaneous consent by "the great masses of the population" to the discourse and practice of hegemony provoked the direct use of force by the otherwise invisible apparatuses of state power; which is to say, the self-exposure of the complicity of knowledge production with power. It thus bore dramatic witness to the way the humanist ruse of the repressive hypothesis functions in so-called liberal democratic societies to displace critical attention away from the microphysics of power. But in the present historical occasion—by which I mean the cultural context into which American humanists have imported the renewed European "debate" over the complicity of Heidegger's philosophy and the Nazi "Final Solution"—this break in the logical economy of the discourse of humanism has been all but forgotten by the massive renarrativization of the crucial demystifying testimony of the Vietnam decade: an amnesia aided and abetted by the events in Eastern Europe and the Middle East, which the late capitalist world represents as the triumph of the "new world order" under the aegis of the principles of humanist democracy. Further, this forgetful recollection of the history of the American intervention in Vietnam has also obscured the historically specific origins of the posthumanist critique of the repressive hypothesis. It is important for these reasons to repeat this history, however briefly, at the site of knowledge production: where, that is, the protest against the American intervention in Vietnam was enacted. More specifically, the rewriting of the relationship between knowledge and power in the present historical conjuncture compels us to retrieve the response of the majority of American liberal humanist intellectuals to the student activists' indictment of and action against the university.

In refusing their spontaneous consent to the received representation of the university as a value-free space—the Kantian representation that humanists invoke against Heidegger's—the students were in an intuitive if not adequately theorized way focalizing the complicity of the American institutions of knowledge production with the state's genocidal war against the Vietnamese people. More specifically, their resistance foregrounded the complicity of university research with the military/industrial/political complex (mostly, but not exclusively, with the use of high-tech weaponry: napalm, chemical defoliants, herbicides, etc.) and the affiliated technocratic and strategic planning systems (those devised and practiced, for example, by the Institute for Defense Analysis, the Rand Corporation, and the Central Intelligence Agency). In response to the students' indictment, these leading humanist intellectuals attempted to justify the university by separating the *idea* of the university from what they represented as its *historically accidental practices*: by localizing its culpability in those specific areas where the "abuse" of its essential neutrality was most visible, direct, and re-formable. They interpreted these historically specific complicities of the university with the violent worldly practices of the state apparatuses as local violations of the ideal Kantian model of the university: that which, in following Kant's *The Conflict of Faculties*, represents the university as a value-free, which is to say an essentially ahistorical, space devoted to the principle of "autonomous" or "public" reason and the pursuit of its "truth."

I cannot here demonstrate the centrality of the argument that *differentiated* between the "true mission" of the university (its disinterested pursuit of truth) and the violent practices of power[62] in the rationale of the liberal humanists throughout this period of sociopolitical crisis precipitated by the protest movement against the war. It will suffice to cite one of many possible instances: Charles Frankel's *Education and the Barricades*, a widely read and discussed book by an eminent humanist scholar published in the immediate aftermath of the turbulent events at Columbia University in the spring of 1968. These events, we should recall, culminated in the bloodbath instigated by the administration's "reasonable" appeal to the New York City police to forcibly evict the students occupying Hamilton Hall. It should come as no surprise that this liberal humanist—or "universal"—intellectual attempts to exculpate the university by distinguishing the *idea* of the university from its historically specific practices. He does this by representing it as an ideal space devoted to the autonomous pursuit of reasonable truth (and criticizing the excesses—the interested "violence"—of the student militants), while at the same time questioning the wisdom of, if not criticizing, Columbia University, the *specific* institution: its ill-conceived Morningside gymnasium project (which would callously deprive the residents of Harlem of its park) and its sponsorship of the Institute for Defense Analysis and other specific manifestations of the betrayal of its ideal function. I quote at some length not only to suggest the Kantian essence of Frankel's justification of the university, but also the remarkable susceptibility of his humanist representation of power relations in the liberal democratic society to the Foucauldian critique of the repressive hypothesis:

These gradations in the nature of force [between socially necessary constraints and culpable violence] are . . . the decisive consideration with regard to the argument [of the militant students at Columbia University and the intellectuals who supported them] that our existing society relies on force and violence, and that everyone employs these methods or acquiesces in them, and that no one, therefore, is in a position to point the finger of blame at anyone else. It is true that in American society, as in all societies, democratic or not, almost everyone is coerced in some respects. People pay bills or obey traffic laws at least sometimes because they fear the application of force against them. It is true, too, that in American society many gross injustices are maintained through unfair laws that are backed by force, or through the connivance of the authorities with illegality, and, sometimes, as in the case of the murdered civil rights workers in Mississippi, through outright violence. But to say that this society, taken as a whole, relies on force and violence, and that all decent, law-abiding citizens share the guilt of this state of affairs, is to ignore distinctions that have fundamental import for everyday human experience, and for the quality of human relations, human feelings, and human conduct.

Force that is merely latent has a different social and psychological significance from force that is actively employed. Force that is employed subject to strict legal restrictions is not the same genre with force that does not recognize such bounds. To utter broadside denunciations of the force and violence on which society depends while ignoring such facts is to imply that there is no significant difference between the conditions of a man who pays his taxes because he does not want to go to jail and that of a man who is afraid to vote because his house may be bombed. It overlooks the difference—and it is not an abstract difference but something as palpable as a knife in one's side—between living under the law and living in terror. . . .

So we return to the four propositions on which the rationale for the methods used by the student activists depends. . . .

Begin with the first proposition: that exceptional methods were in order because the evils being combatted—Vietnam and race-cum-poverty . . .—were extreme. *But there are places closer than a university campus to these evils, where they can be combatted more directly.* The university campus is merely convenient, safer, and more vulnerable because force is so alien to its habits and so lethal to it. Would anyone accept the contamination of public beaches or the invasion of hospitals as a legitimate means of protest against the war? Why, then, the university?

The answer that is given, of course, is that universities are in the service of the war machine and racism. But this is not a proposition that can be defended without significant qualifications. If it is true at all, it is true only in part. The universities of the United States have been principle centers of protest against the war in Vietnam and against racist practices. *Only in certain of their activities can a connection be drawn between them and these wrongs. If complaint is justified, therefore, it has to be a specific complaint.* If there is to be an issue, a concrete issue has to be found, based on a definite and particular connection between the university and the wrongs under attack. And the fact is that, at Columbia, this is what was attempted. Some sort of ostensible connection had to be established between the university and the great evils, which, in theory, justified disruptive action. The *specific* issues being fought on the Columbia campus were not Vietnam and race-cum-poverty; they were a relationship to the Institute for Defense Analysis, a gymnasium project, and a maldistribution, real or alleged, of power in the university. . . .

If we accept the description of events at Columbia and other institutions that has been offered by the most ardent defenders of the student activists, *there has been no issue of fundamental student rights (e.g. the right to dissent), no issue of academic freedom, no issue of forced collaboration with either racism or the Vietnam War.* These, conceivably, might qualify as issues justifying a forceful defense of basic principles.[63]

The symmetry between Frankel's synecdochical humanist justification of the American university in the face of its flagrant participation in the violent conduct of the war in Vietnam and Foucault's critical analysis of the repressive hypothesis is obvious. It assumes uncritically that *in essence* the university is not simply a value-free zone, but one in which the discourse of truth and the practices of power ("force that is actively employed") are external to each other: in which power, that is, is represented as overtly repressive ("evil") and truth is seen as the only agency of deliverance from the violence of power. In so doing, Frankel's humanist "juridico-discursive" view of power[64] betrays its own complicity not only with the violence perpetrated by Columbia University against the black community and the students, but also, however invisibly, with the violence being perpetrated in 1968—at the height of its techno-military aggression—by the United States against the people of Vietnam.

What does need to be thematized, however, is the remarkable symmetry between Frankel's and Arnold Davidson's representations of the truth/power nexus. Frankel's liberal humanist discourse justifies the university in the context of the American intervention in Vietnam in *precisely* the Kantian terms invoked by Davidson to discredit Heidegger's project to "overcome philosophy": "Specific" practices at Columbia University may have contributed to the "evils" the students were combatting; but if these specific practices were at all culpable—and it is not certain to Frankel that this was the case—they were the consequence of the betrayal of its unworldly principle of autonomous reason, of its "Kantian" essence, and thus correctable. For "force," according to Frankel, is *in essence* "alien to [the American university's] habits and . . . lethal to it." In thus defending the idea of the university as a value-free space, Frankel also assumes a view of the relationship between the pursuit of truth and the practices of power which Davidson invokes centrally in order to condemn as "unpardonable" Heidegger's "staggering" identification of a technologized agriculture and the Nazi gas chambers and death camps: the "incommensurability"—the radical difference—between knowledge production and the violent practices of power. "Force that is merely latent [i.e., the beneficial constraints of laws produced by autonomous reason]," he declares, "has a different social and psychological significance from force that is actively employed. Force that is employed subject to strict legal restrictions *is not the same genre* with force that does not recognize such limits."

What I am suggesting in thus invoking Foucault's analysis of the repressive hypothesis in the context of the American liberal humanists' radical differentiation of knowledge production (the university) from the relay of technological instruments (weapons) that devastated Vietnam and its people's culture is the following: Davidson's typically humanist condemnation of Heidegger's project to "overcome" philosophy and his consequent equation of the technologization of agriculture and the production of corpses in the gas chambers and the death camps is a remarkably parochial (ethnocentric), if not calculatedly duplicitous, strategy. Understood in this American context, to put it alternatively, Heidegger's project and his "pronouncement," whatever its limitations vis-à-vis specificity, takes on a quite different—a far more justifiable—significance from that attributed to it by his humanist prosecutors. For the humanist representation of these leaves unsaid Heidegger's thematization of the modern Occident's reduction of truth as *aletheia* to truth as *adequaetio intellectus et rei* (an originary or dialogic thinking to derivative or monologic "philosophy"), and its reduction of being (the indissoluble lateral continuum from the subject through language and culture to the economy and the political state) to a universally technologized "standing reserve." This humanist representation also overlooks the critique of Occidental discursive practices, especially since the Enlightenment, enabled by Foucault and by poststructuralism or posthumanism at large: the critique, I want to reiterate, that Heidegger's interrogation of the discourse of humanism catalyzed.[65]

Putting this obliterated occasion back into play, it simply will not suffice to admit, as Davidson does (appropriating Lacoue-Labarthe and the European context), that "insofar as Heidegger intends to refer the gas chambers and the death camps to the essence of technology his thought is 'absolutely just' " and then to utterly dismiss (as Lacoue-Labarthe does not quite) its resonant justice as " 'scandalously insufficient' " in favor of an interpretation of Heidegger's representative "pronouncement" that insists on the "incommensurable difference" between the extermination of the Jews and "the economic military practice of blockades, or even the production of nuclear weapons, not to mention the mechanization of the food industry." Given his membership in the Nazi Party, Heidegger's minimal reference after the war to the "Final Solution" and his failure to differentiate the various violent practices he identifies with technology, when he did refer to it, betray an indefensible insensitivity to the enormity of both the calculated barbarism of the Nazis' program to exterminate the Jews and the unspeakable human suffering that was its consequence. It was, furthermore, a personal and sociopolitical callousness that in some fundamental way was the result of a certain restricted understanding of disclosures vis-à-vis "the other" enabled by his interrogation of the discourses of the ontotheological tradition, especially that of the *anthropologos* (humanism). Heidegger was perhaps obliged by the infamous history of the Third Reich to denounce the appalling systematic effort to exterminate the Jews undertaken by the Nazis, with whom he had earlier been unequivocally affiliated, and to differentiate between the violence and human suffering caused by the practices he identified in his 1949 statement. But the very fact that his silence on the "Final Solution" and his dedifferentiation of these practices in favor of insistently reiterating their common essence is *so obvious* should give pause to those conversant with his thought who would pounce on this silence and this statement as definitive evidence of his anti-Semitism or the utterly dehumanizing consequence of his philosophical discourse at large. Since it has not provoked such a doubt, one is compelled to conclude that this telling slide, whatever the motive, finally rests not on thinking but on a reactive (and by now, unfortunately, all too familiar) understanding of the Nazis' "Final Solution" that represents this horrible event as a rupture, indeed, as a negatively mystical—an "apocalyptic"—event, in the history of the Occident; an event, that is, incommensurable in its uniqueness with all the other instances of Western (i.e., technological/racist)[66] violence against the "other": for example, the violence of American westward expansion that decimated the native American population and the violence of American slavery whose barbarous civilized machinery was inflicted on an untold number of native Africans and their American descendants for over a century—and presumably the violence inflicted by the Allies on the German civilians in Dresden and Japanese civilians in Hiroshima and Nagasaki in 1945, and, not least, on the Vietnamese civilians by the United States during the decade of the undeclared Vietnam War.

Even Lacoue-Labarthe succumbs in some degree to the temptation (or the pressure of the discourse of hegemony) to read the Holocaust in this way, thus inadvertently allowing the humanist Davidson to selectively appropriate his analysis of Auschwitz for his anti-antihumanist attack on Heidegger's thought. But it is important for the purpose of making Davidson's ideological (humanist) agenda explicit to differentiate between Lacoue-Labarthe's more complex, if equivocal, understanding of the event called "Auschwitz" from Davidson's, which, like that of virtually all the humanist critics of Heidegger's statement, simply assumes the prevailing discourse of the Holocaust: the view that it constitutes an absolute rupture with the Occidental tradition. Appropriating the term *césure* from Hölderlin's account of the law of tragedy (and historicity) to characterize the event of Auschwitz, Lacoue-Labarthe writes:

> Caesura would be what, in history, interrupts and opens up another possibility of history, or else closes all possibility of history. But two precisions are rigorously necessary.
> 1. One can speak of a caesura only as a pure event, that is, empty or nul, in which is revealed—without revealing itself—a withdrawal or the nothing-ness (*né-ant*)
> 2. There is a caesura only when an attempt at immediacy (an excessiveness) is interrupted or cut off, that is, a crime against the—historial—Law of finitude.
> In the case of Auschwitz—which Blanchot calls the "event without response"—these two conditions are, as the sinister resonance of the phrase has it—"satisfied." And for the first time, I believe, in modern history (this is why Auschwitz opens up, or closes, an entirely other history than the one we have known until now).[67]

Read out of context, Lacoue-Labarthe's reference to Auschwitz as a "pure event" in history that "interrupts history and opens up a [totally] other possibility of history or even closes off all possibility to history" might be interpreted to mean that Auschwitz is finally and absolutely unspeakable, as it often does for contemporary Western intellectuals. A contextual reading, however, problematizes, if unfortunately it does not altogether preclude, such an interpretation. As his invocation of Blanchot's reference to Auschwitz as "this event without response" suggests, Lacoue-Labarthe could also mean that the humanist exponents of the Occidental tradition no longer have recourse to speculation about—to a *rationalization* of—Auschwitz. For the event of Auschwitz exposes the essence of this tradition to be an absolute contradiction of its historical self-representation. This possibility is further supported by Lacoue-Labarthe's insistent reference to two related motifs: (1) "Dans l'apocalypse d'Auschwitz ce n'est ni plus ni moins que l'Occident, en son essence, qui c'est révélé—et ne cesse, depuis, se révéler [In the apocalypse of Auschwitz it is nothing more nor less than the Occident, in its essence, which was revealed—and which since then does not cease to reveal itself]" (F 59); (2) "Le nazisme est une humanisme. . . . [Nazism is a humanism. . . .]," (F 138).

Whatever Lacoue-Labarthe means by the *césure* which was Auschwitz (and it is not at all clear that he finally means the first), it is quite certain in Davidson's text (as well as those of the French *nouveaux philosophes* and the liberal humanists who have appropriated the prevailing discourse of the Holocaust in behalf of their anti-antihumanist ideology) that it is the first interpretation that determines both his reading of Lacoue-Labarthe and his critique of Heidegger's equation. And the reason for this, as I have suggested, is that such an interpretation is inscribed in a logic that makes the Nazis the absolutized scapegoat of Occidental humanism and thus exonerates the latter—especially the English, the French, and the Poles—of its complicity in this event and with racism in general.[68] I "repeat" my question to the American humanist critics of Heidegger who have appropriated the European debate: How would the Vietnamese respond to this minimization of their face-to-face experience of the horror perpetrated by the unsolicited American intervention in its people's war? In the light of the self-destruction of the problematic that determined the United States' intervention in Vietnam and its conduct of the war, could not one say, in turn, that this failure of self-criticism—this failure to pronounce the name of Vietnam, as it were—that Davidson's discourse (and the discourse of all those American humanists who have invoked Heidegger's "scandalously inadequate pronouncement" against him) is no less guilty of "the suppression of the human" and of "the horror"?

In putting the question in this way, my intention is not at all to minimize the appalling horror that is concentrated in the name of Auschwitz. Nor is it to lend my argument to the recent project of those historians, such as Ernst Nolte and Andreas Hillgruber, among other conservative ideologues in contemporary Germany, who would renarrativize the terrible history of the Third Reich by reading the Holocaust as a radical aberration of the national identity in order to recuperate a German right wing (and the Cold War context) in the face of the democratic gains achieved since the "revolt of 1968." The Nazi project to exterminate the Jews in the gas chambers and the death camps was appallingly horrible, and this grotesque event must not be forgotten. Rather, my purpose is to interrogate the ideological uses to which the discourse of the Holocaust has been put. For in proclaiming "Auschwitz" to be "unspeakable," it has virtually prohibited analysis and debate about the ideological origins and the scope of these appalling Nazi practices: Why, for example, given the insistent reference in the planning discourse of official Nazism to "judeobolshevism" as the essential enemy of Germany, isn't the Nazis' extermination of an untold number of civilian Slavs, not to say other "inferior" peoples, a part of the discourse of the Holocaust?[69] As the (ab)use of the discourse of the Holocaust by the state of Israel in its effort to repress the legitimate claims of the Palestinian people makes clear, it has also lent itself to onerous political purposes.

As the historian Charles Maier observes in the conclusion of his remarkably judicious analysis of the *Historikerstreit*:

> If it behooves Germans to stress the anti-Jewish specificity of the Holocaust, it is sometimes important for Jews to do the opposite. In Israel, of course, the Holocaust can be a public as well as a private sorrow. It certainly helps legitimate the state, even if it cannot legitimate any particular frontiers or policies. There are reportedly ten public institutions in Israel, such as museums and research centers, devoted to the Holocaust—what a liberal American Jewish magazine has called a "memory industry." This "industry" has produced what one Israeli theologian has condemned as a new Holocaust religion that refuses to credit other genocides as equally authentic: "Biafra was only hunger, Cambodia was only a civil war; the destruction of the Kurds was not systematic; death in the Gulag lacked national identification marks . . . The Holocaust is a collection of human acts which has turned into a transcendent event." But in fact, . . . "The Jewishness of the Holocaust (like its Germanness) is only one aspect of its horror, the most crucial aspect from our point of view but by no means exclusive." The only response must be to understand the Holocaust as a human possibility that arises from the discourse of exclusion, and not just as the basis for a new Jewish national religion. The difference between this perverted Holocaust myth and the appropriate one "is essentially political: It is the difference in the use which the living make of the memory of the dead, the present of its history." It is the perverted myth that exploits the memory of an infinite horror to justify even a far less repressive behavior.[70]

My purpose, to put it positively, is to specify and maximize the horrors perpetrated in the name of "civilization" not simply by Nazi Germany, but by the modern West at large: the West which is, according to Heidegger, coming to its humanist end in "Europeanizing the earth" and imposing the "social order proper to" its technological/calculative essence. My purpose is to retrieve Heidegger's testimony vis-à-vis humanist modernity in the face of those such as Lacoue-Labarthe and Lyotard, whose critique of Heidegger's "silence" or "forgetfulness of the 'forgotten' (*L'Oubli*),"[71] is, however justified, won at the expense of discounting these dreadful instances of "civilized" barbarism; or, as in the case of the coeditor of *Critical Inquiry*, is appropriated for the purpose of repressing the larger, essentially Heideggerian posthumanist projects of Lacoue-Labarthe and Lyotard, and for obliterating the memory of the complicity of the discourse of humanism with the American genocidal assault on Vietnam. For in thus "privileging" the Nazis' project to exterminate the Jews in their critique of Heidegger's "pronouncement," these critics in effect would paralyze criticism (in and of the West): criticism of the illicit political uses to which the mystified discourse of the Holocaust has been put (especially by the state of Israel), and also, and more fundamentally, criticism of the hegemonic discourse of humanism (epitomized, according to Davidson, in Kant) enabled by Heidegger's interrogation of the *anthropologos*. To be more specific, these critics would annul Heidegger's demystification of the binary opposition between philosophy and the will to power that determines modern Western discursive practices and his disclosure of the complicity between them: not simply the relay of power that Heidegger points to in his identification of mechanized agriculture, the manufacture of corpses at Auschwitz, the blockades that reduce countries to famine, and the manufacture of hydrogen bombs, but also, if tacitly, that relay that informed the various discourses and practices, from cultural to military, of the American intervention in Vietnam. In so doing, they would also discredit by falsification or by "oversight" the critical gains of poststructuralism largely enabled by Heidegger's discourse: the demystification of the binary opposition between truth and power, cultural production grounded in "autonomous" inquiry (philosophy) and the (repressive) state apparatuses. I mean the recognition (1) that the technological / industrial / late capitalist societies of the West exist essentially, not to interrogate but to reproduce the structure of power; (2) that the direct and visible use of force in such societies ("regimes of truth," in Foucault's formulation) is no longer the norm (as it was, according to Foucault, in the *ancien régime*), but an anomaly precipitated by a "crisis of command and direction when spontaneous consent [to the humanist/democratic/capitalist discourse of hegemony] has failed;" and (3) that to understand the direct use of force in modernity as normative is to be disablingly misled about its fundamental causes: to succumb to the ruse of the repressive hypothesis.

What I am suggesting, finally, is that Davidson's representation to an American audience of Heidegger's synecdochical "pronouncement" as symptomatic of an unpardonable failure of moral integrity is a strategic misreading intended not simply to discredit Heidegger's philosophical discourse at large. As the omission of interventions by or reference to such French humanist heirs of the *nouveaux philosophes* as Luc Ferry and Alain Renaut, whose advocacy of Farías's book is overtly intended to discredit *"les gauchistes"* (the poststructuralist *"heideggériens dissidents, Der-*

rida et les siens"), suggests,[72] Davidson's anti-antihumanist representation like that of Tom Rockmore, Richard Wolin, and David Hirsch, is also intended, whatever the degree of calculatedness, as a policing action to delegitimate the discourse of resistance Heidegger's thought has enabled—particularly the discourse of contemporary American posthumanism and its essential insight into the representation of power relations inscribed in the official discourse of humanism. Put positively, the ultimate purpose of Davidson's representative misreading of Heidegger's postwar statement (and of *Critical Inquiry*'s tendentiously selective appropriation of the European debate) is to recuperate the authority that the anthropological discourse of humanism lost in the self-exposure of its complicity with the American industrial/political/military devastation of Vietnam.

In this recuperative effort, Davidson's project, like that of the other humanists who have been encouraged to enter the lists by the publication of Farías's book and by the rendering of Heidegger's scandalous "pronouncement" a media event, thus joins, however indirectly, the massive current recuperative project of the American cultural memory, not so much to "trash the 60s," as some cultural critics maintain,[73] as to rewrite—to renarrativize—the history of that disruptive and revealing decade in terms of the restrictive economy of the humanist problematic. To be specific, the *Critical Inquiry* "Symposium on Heidegger and Nazism" joins the present massive reactionary movement in the United States characterized by the essential, however differentially articulated, solidarity of humanist intellectuals, conservatives and liberals alike (E. D. Hirsch and Wayne Booth, for example, as well as William Bennett, Walter Jackson Bate, Allan Bloom, Roger Kimball, Hilton Kramer, David Lehman, Dinesh D'Souza, etc.), the university (the reinstitutionalization of the "core curriculum" initiated by Harvard, for example), the culture industry (the inordinate quantity of revisionary representations of the Vietnam War in film, video, fiction, and autobiographical and journalistic writing), the late capitalist economy, and the state. I am referring to the post-Vietnam cultural initiative, the purpose of which is, in the current formula, to "heal the wound" suffered by the American psyche (the "Vietnam syndrome")—which is to say, to *recuperate* the humanist representation of the American cultural identity—when the United States' intervention in Vietnam exposed the imperialist and racist violence latent in its perennial self-representation as a disinterested, humane, gentle, and solicitous society: a society not dedicated to conquest but to "winning the hearts and minds" of the unfortunate others. In thus joining this recuperative initiative, Davidson's cultural project also, however indirectly, joins the state's post-Cold War neocolonial initiative in the Third World, especially in Latin America and the Middle East, which threatens increasingly to repeat the pattern of American involvement in Vietnam.

It is this contemporary recuperative project of the American cultural memory with which I am concerned in this essay. But it would be an omission of no small consequence if I were to overlook the paradoxical role played in this project by the European poststructuralist contributors to the *Critical Inquiry* supplement. Given the obviousness of its editors' commitment to humanist "pluralism," not to say Davidson's overt and virtually total (and ideologically selective) reliance on the authority of one of them in his introductory effort to rehabilitate the discourse of humanism, it is with some dismay that one finds radical Heideggerians contributing to it, such thinkers as Lacoue-Labarthe, Jacques Derrida, and Maurice Blanchot, all of whom, like Heidegger, have in one way or another called the Kantian principle of public reason and the university it has produced and legitimated into question.

It is quite appropriate—indeed, imperative—for poststructuralist critics to read Heidegger against himself: to interrogate his discourse of the rectorate period and the vestigial metaphysics in his thought at large. Such an interrogation is precisely what Heidegger's originary thinking (the ontic/ontological hermeneutic circle) insists on in opposition to "philosophy," which, because it assumes its mode of inquiry to be autonomous, original, and natural, finally precludes self-questioning. Rigorous self-criticism of its problematic is one of the legacies of the poststructuralist exposure of the "center elsewhere" or "Transcendental Signified" informing and standing outside of the discourse of "philosophy," or of its commitment to undecideability. Indeed, this imperative is what fundamentally distinguishes poststructuralism from the logocentric humanist discourse of "deliverance" (as the predictability of the humanists' response to Heidegger's "pronouncement" suggests). But it is quite something else for a poststructuralist to undertake such an interrogation of Heidegger's discourse and practice in the pages of a journal that, given its ideological commitments and its authority in North America, is likely to use it, as Davidson does Lacoue-Labarthe's nuanced interrogation of Heidegger's thought, to discredit the very cultural project of the poststructuralist contributors.

One could argue, of course, that the publication of such ultimately antianthropological texts in a journal such as *Critical Inquiry*, the editorial policy of which is informed by the humanist ideology, is intended to deconstruct the oversimplified (reduced) representation of Heidegger's discourse demanded by the humanist problematic, to preserve the differential elements in his texts that confound the desire for a (purely negative) decisive meaning. But such an argument, often advanced by so-called adversary intellectuals who publish in establishment journals and presses, is at best self-defeating. This is because it self-contradictorally assumes that the "debate" takes place in a realm where the political authority of the oppositional discourse is as viable as that of the institutional medium it is challenging, where all things are equal, which is to say, in a realm that is no place and no time, whereas in fact it takes place at a historically specific site where the balance of power is obviously quite unequally distributed. To what degree, one is thus driven to ask by this curious spectacle, are these critics still captivated by the institutional discourse they would ostensibly repudiate? To what degree does their discourse, despite the force of their engaging disclosures, continue to remain "philosophical"—and academic? These are questions that I am not the first one to ask.

V

In thematizing the ideological agenda concealed within Davidson's Kantian critique of Heidegger's postwar statement, it has not been my intention, I want to insist, to join those French orthodox Heideggerians like Jean Beaufret and François Fedier[74] in a flagrantly reductive project of exonerating Heidegger's discourse and practice in the period of the rectorate and after. My purpose has been to provide a context for addressing *the question* in a way that puts back into play the wider context that Davidson (and, in some degree, his European authorities) and the *Critical Inquiry* supplement suppress: the historically specific part Heidegger's philosophical texts at large have played in enabling the interrogation of the discursive economy of the subject and in precipitating the crisis of humanism in the West, especially in North America where its institutional authority has been visibly shaken by the self-exposure of its contradictions in the 1960s. Besides calling attention to the inadequacy—the ideologically determined narrow self-righteousness—of Davidson's moral condemnation of Heidegger and his thought and *Critical Inquiry*'s ideologically selective appropriation of the European debate, my purpose has also been to provide the occasion for a different—a more complex—reading of Heidegger's discourse and practice in the period of the rectorate and after. Such a reading would render the former less offensive than his American humanist critics make it out to be, in some sense understandable, if not free of a significantly deplorable willfulness and historically specific blindness. More important, since the humanists' target is not the historically specific Martin Heidegger, but Heidegger's living postwar thought, it would demonstrate that Heidegger's interrogation of the global imperial project of modern technology in such post-rectorate texts as *An Introduction to Metaphysics*, "On the Essence of Truth," "Plato's Doctrine of Truth," the Nietzsche and the Parmenides lectures, the *Beiträge*, "Letter on Humanism," "The Age of the World Picture," "*Gelassenheit*," "The Question Concerning Technology," "The

End of Philosophy and the Task of Thinking," and "The Rectorate 1933–34," to name but a few of those that are now being vilified, constitutes and remains a positive contribution, however theoretical Heidegger's emphasis and unthought his theory, to an oppositional criticism that contemporary history has compelled to shift its focus from the overt practice of power to the discourse of truth. Such a reading, that is, would demonstrate that Heidegger's unrelenting identification of this planetary technology with a concept of truth informed by the commanding will to "enframe" temporality and thus reduce the differences it disseminates to "standing reserve"—in short, with the "Europeanization of the earth"—is indispensable to a cultural criticism that would resist the "regime of truth": the dominant discursive practice that, founded as it is on the Roman *veritas*, either does not know itself to be complicitous with sociopolitical power (including the power that had its end in Auschwitz) or strategically refuses to acknowledge this complicity in the name of a truth understood as the essential adversary of power.

Given the constraints of space, however, I cannot undertake this reading here. Such a project, which would not only have to thematize the historically specific causes of Heidegger's embrace of the National Socialist Party for a ten-month period of his rectorate (April 1933-February 1934) and his continued adherence to "the inner truth and greatness of [the National Socialist] movement"[75] after his resignation until around 1945 (causes, I would suggest, substantially different from the odious ones attributed to him by Farías and other humanist critics). It would also have to make explicit the resonant positive critical possibilities implicit in his postwar discourse on *Technik*. It will thus have to wait for another occasion. But the contours of this reading have already been suggested by my refusal to succumb, like Lacoue-Labarthe, Blanchot, Lévinas, Lyotard, and Habermas, to the temptation (or invisible pressure) to react to the *Shoah* as if it were an unprecedented and singular event—an apocalyptic rupture or irruption in Western history—and to the lure of the liberal humanist repressive hypothesis held out enticingly to the readers of *Critical Inquiry*.[76]

For to *think* Heidegger's synecdochical "failure" to differentiate between the technologization of agriculture, the manufacture of corpses in the gas chambers and death camps, the blockading and reduction of countries to famine, and the production of hydrogen bombs in the historically specific global context of the American genocidal annihilation of the Vietnamese earth (*Xa*) and its people's culture—one is entitled by the problem-solving (technological) essence of the memoranda of the *Pentagon Papers* to say its culturally inscribed determination to achieve a "Final Solution" in Southeast Asia—is to discover (at least the possibility) that Heidegger's "failure," however ill-advised, was not, as Lacoue-

Labarthe portentously announces, a radical *"faute"*: "Ce n'est pas une erreur mais une conséquence. Et si cette conséquence a pu avoir pour conséquence, ne serait-ce que dix mois, d'*admettre* le nazisme, c'est-à-dire quelque chose de tel, alors c'est de *faute* qu'on doit parler [It is not an error, but a consequence. And if that consequence had as its consequence, even if for only a period of ten months, *consenting to* Nazism—to something like that—then we must speak of a crime].⁷⁷ Put positively, to think Heidegger's admittedly problematic equation in this larger context is, I submit, to discover that his "failure" was a failure to think *adequately* his destructive philosophical project's materiality—the worldly implications of his retrieval of the forgotten "other." It is to realize that his philosophizing remained vestigially inscribed by the ontotheological philosophical tradition's separation of the ontological and the ontic: of theory and practice. For all Heidegger's theoretical insistence that thinking is historical—is a revolutionary emancipatory *praxis* of e-mergence— it continued in large part, and with dire consequences, to be *theoria*: a *looking at* material history (the domain of the ontic) from a disablingly speculative and totalizing distance.

More specifically, to think Heidegger's notorious equation in this larger context compels us to put the question of Heidegger's complicity with the National Socialist Party not from the historically accomplished vantage point of the gas chambers and death camps (as Heidegger's humanist critics invariably tend to do), but in terms of its historically specific occasion. I am referring to the period immediately preceding Heidegger's rectorate (the period of Weimar Republic), which, as he put it later in "The Rectorate 1933–34," was a time of profound, of "essential distress"⁷⁸ (This phrase recalls the "rift" [*der Riss*] between *Welt* and *Erde* and alludes, not only to the radical disclosure of the disabling contradictions of the "World" of that unprecedented time in the history of modern "Europe," but to the potentialities of a retrieval or repetition [*Wiederholen*] of a *polis* [un]grounded in originative thinking.) It was the period of world depression induced by the imperial excesses of Western capitalism driven by *Technik*. In Germany this distress was radically exacerbated by the inordinate reparation demands inflicted on the defeated nation by the victorious allies in the Treaty of Versailles and the French occupation of the industrial Ruhr, both of which contributed fundamentally to the destruction, despite a brief respite in the mid-twenties, of the German economy. (At the time of Hitler's assumption to power there were six million unemployed people in Germany.)⁷⁹ There was also from the German perspective the threat of an emergent Stalinist Communism, the collectivity of which was not the true legacy of Marx, as Heidegger seems to have understood it in "Letter on Humanism,"⁸⁰ but simply the obverse face of American-style capitalism. "This Europe," he says, with prophetic justification (if we can extricate ourselves from the binarist inscriptions of Cold War discourse) "in its ruinous blindness forever on the point of cutting its own throat, lies today in a great pincer, squeezed between Russia on the one side and America on the other. From a metaphysical point of view, Russia and America are the same; the same dreary technologized frenzy, the same unrestrained organization of the average man."[81] In the following neglected but representative passage from a now highly publicized address to an election meeting of German scholars in Leipzig on November 11, 1933, for example, Heidegger envisions a world community based on the principle that difference is the condition for the possibility of identity and not the other way around. Read in the larger historically specific context I have retrieved, it does not categorically imply *une faute*, however equivocal its representation of the collective self, reductive of the complex realities of that historical moment, and blind to or tolerant of the actual violent—and racist—political practices of the *Führer* it indeed is:

> It is not ambition, not desire for glory, not blind obstinacy, and not hunger for power that demands from the *Führer* that Germany withdraw from the League of Nations. It is only the clear will to unconditional self-responsibility in suffering and mastering the fate of our people. That is *not* a turning away from the community of peoples. On the contrary: with this step, our people is submitting to that essential law of human Being to which every people must give allegiance if it is still to be a people.
> It is only out of that parallel observance by all peoples of this unconditional demand of self-responsibility that there emerges the possibility of taking each other seriously so that a community can also be affirmed. The will to a true national community [*Volksgemeinschaft*] is equally far removed both from an unrestrained, vague desire for world brotherhood and from blind tyranny. Existing beyond this opposition, this will allows peoples and states to stand by one another in an open and manly fashion as self-reliant entities [*das offene und mannhafte Aufsich und Zueinanderers stehen den Völken und Staaten*].[82]

Retrospectively—from the "future anterior" vantage point of Auschwitz—Heidegger's decision to join the National Socialist Party and to participate in its "nationalist" project as rector of Freiburg University seems unpardonably reactionary: *une faute* of disablingly major proportions. But at that time of crisis—when the technological capitalism informing the democracies had exploded into a period of universal imperial violence extending from World War I through the period of the Great Depression—Heidegger's political preference for a revolutionary *national socialism* is quite understandable if not very wise. This is especially the case if, as the passage quoted above demands, we understand Heidegger's politics during the rectorate as a national socialism dedicated to the retrieval *not simply* of the German difference (its "self-affirmation") *but also and simultaneously* of the originary ("Greek") thinking that characterized the origins of "Europe" from a contemporary technological/capitalist democracy and a technological/Stalinist totalitarianism, both grounded in derivative thought and both attempting to recuperate or extend their imperial hegemony at the expense of the identity of the defeated German people (as well as other ethnic groups). And this applies, I submit, to Heidegger's much maligned presumption—articulated after his resignation of the rectorate—that it was Germany's chosen or destined role to inaugurate the renewal of "Europe":

> We are caught in a pincer. Situated in the center, our nation incurs the severest pressure. It is the nation with the most neighbors hence the most endangered. With all this, it is the most metaphysical of nations. We are certain of this vocation, but our people will only be able to wrest a destiny from it if *within itself* it creates a resonance, a possibility of resonance for this vocation, and takes a creative view of its tradition. All this implies that this nation, as a historical nation, must move itself and thereby the history of the West beyond the center of their future "happening" and into the primordial realm of the power of being. If the great decision regarding Europe is not to be annihilation, that decision must be made in terms of new spiritual energies unfolding historically from out of the center.
>
> To ask "How does it stand with being?" means nothing less than to recapture, to repeat (*wiederholen*), the beginning of our historical-spiritual existence, in order to transform it into a new beginning. This is possible. It is indeed the crucial form of history, because it begins in the fundamental event. [Heidegger is referring here to the advent of (originary) Greek thinking.] But we do not repeat a beginning by reducing it to something past and now known, which need merely be imitated; no, the beginning must be begun again, more radically, with all the strangeness, darkness, insecurity that attend a true beginning. Repetition as we understand it is anything but an improved continuation with the old methods of what has been up to now.[83]

According to Lacoue-Labarthe, Heidegger's project to retrieve (*wiederholen*) Greek thinking derives from and was consonant, at least until 1955, with the Greek model articulated by the German philosophical/poetic tradition of classical studies initiated by Winckelmann and ultimately devoted to the achievement of a *national-ésthetisme*, which, in turn, was appropriated by the Nazi regime:

Derrière . . . les déclarations de Goebbels et quelques autres [which represented their Germany as a *Gesamtkunstwerk*] . . . se profile toute une tradition, bimillénaire en effet, ou tout au moins le rêve que cette tradition aura engendré dans la pensée allemande depuis la fin de l'*Aufklärung*. Et ce rêve est bien, de fait, celui de la Cité comme oeuvre d'art.

Il faudrait différencier: Schlegel, c'est certain, ne "rêve" pas comme Hölderlin ou Hegel, lesquels à leur tour ne "rêvent" pas comme Nietzsche—par example. Néanmoins des traits communs existent, parfaitement repérables (probablement parce que tous ces "rêves," tres divers, sont commandés par un "reste diurne" unique: la lecture de Winckelmann).

[Behind the emphatic declaration of Goebbels and certain others (who represented their Germany as a *Gesamtkunstwerk*) . . . is outlined a whole tradition that in fact is two thousand years old, or at least the dream that the tradition has engendered in German thought since the end of the *Aufklärung*. And this dream is, in fact, that of the City as work of art.

It is necessary to differentiate: Schlegel, it is certain, does not dream like Hölderlin or Hegel, who, in turn, do not dream like Nietzsche, for example. Nevertheless, there are common traits which are perfectly identifiable (probably because all these very diverse "dreams" are determined by a single "diurnal residue": their reading of Winckelmann).][84]

Thus, according to Lacoue-Labarthe, Heidegger's call for the retrieval of a Greek *poiesis* in the period extending from the rectorate until after the fall of Nazism was in some fundamental way affiliated with and supportive of the Nazis' (humanist) aesthetic/political brand of fascism.

To be sure, Lacoue-Labarthe is intent on showing that Heidegger saw the danger of the sociopolitical dynamics of national estheticism— its "ontotypology"—from the beginning ("des la 'rupture' avec le nazisme"). And he attempted to derail the ominous momentum of this identification of the (artistic) "genius" of a people with the organization of the *polis* by calling the collective (mythic) subject into question: "It is what orients his thought right up to the meditation on the essence of technique and language, in his final years."[85] Indeed, it is this insight that renders Heidegger's discourse "sur l'art, dans son project historial (politique)" indispensable to the project of thinking the essence of Nazism: "[il] jette une lumière précise sur l'essence, plus ou moins demeurée voilée dans les discours dominans à ce sujet, du national-socialisme. [It throws a precise light on the essence of National Socialism, which has remained more or less veiled in the dominant discourses on the subject.]"[86] Nevertheless Lacoue-Labarthe also declares that "en même temps quelque chose lui en est resté occulté, comme si son exclusion brutale de la *mimèsis* l'avait laissé à son insu prisonnier d'une mimétologie au fond traditionnelle, c'est-à-dire platonicienne: celle qui rapporte la *techné* à la fiction [At the same time something in all this remained invisible to him, as if his brutal exclusion of *mimesis* had left him unknowingly the prisoner of a basically traditional, that is, Platonic, mimetology: that which identifies *techne* with fiction]."[87]

Lacoue-Labarthe's genealogy of the Nazi's *national-ésthetisme*—its self-fashioning on the "Greek" model prepared by the German classical tradition—is compelling. But his representation of Heidegger's project of retrieval is misleading and damaging insofar as it identifies the latter's "Greece" with the Greece represented by the German *humanist* tradition, which, as Lacoue-Labarthe persuasively claims, lends itself to the triumph of Nazism. For, as I suggested in chapter 5, it was precisely Heidegger's recognition of the disciplinary and imperial Romanism informing the German humanist tradition inaugurated by Winckelmann and the "Greek" cultural trappings of the Third Reich that precipitated not only his "reciprocal rejoinder" to European humanism but also to official German National Socialism.[88] In the passage quoted in chapter 5 from "Letter on Humanism" (1946) tracing the genealogy of humanism back to the Roman translation of *aletheia* to *veritas*, Heidegger, in fact, *explicitly* rejects the traditional (humanist) German representation of classical Greek art in favor of thinking the antihumanist *élan* of Hölderlin's more originary interpretation. Far from retrieving the Greeks' originary (ontic/ontological) thinking and *poiesis* (which, according to Heidegger, is always already on the way), the German tradition inaugurated by Winckelmann (*Thoughts on the Imitation of Greek Art in Painting and Sculpture* [1755] and *History of Ancient Art* [1764])[89] recuperates the *Roman* appropriation of them: a secondary or derivative (technological) thinking and *poiesis*, the meta-physical (panoptic) (retro-)perspective of which is congenial to the production of *homo romanus*: a self-identical community of "good," (disciplined and reliable) citizens; which is to say, to the Roman (and Nazi?) imperial project as that project is articulated in the *Parmenides* lectures of 1942. Because Lacoue-Labarthe strangely overlooks this crucial passage, which epitomizes Heidegger's writing on this subject, it deserves repeating at this juncture for the light it throws on Heidegger's quite different "national socialism" during this period:

> *Humanitas*, explicitly so called, was first considered and striven for in the age of the Roman Republic. *Homo humanus* was opposed to *homo barbarus*. *Homo humanus* here means the Romans, who exalted and honored Roman *virtus* [manliness, power] through the "embodiment" of the *paideia* [education] taken over from the Greeks. These were the Greeks of the Hellenistic age, whose culture

was acquired in the schools of philosophy. It was concerned with *eruditio et institutio in bonas artes* [scholarship and training in good conduct]. *Paideia* thus understood was translated as *humanitas*. The genuine *romanitas* of *homo romanus* consisted in such *humanitas*. We encounter the first humanism in Rome: it therefore remains in essence a specifically Roman phenomenon which emerges from the encounter of Roman civilization with the culture of late Greek civilization. The so-called Renaissance of the fourteenth and fifteenth centuries in Italy is a *renascentia romanitatis*. Because *romanitatis* is what matters, it is concerned with *humanitas* and therefore with Greek *paideia*. But Greek civilization is always seen in its later form and this itself is seen from a Roman point of view. The *Homo romanus* of the Renaissance also stands in opposition to *Homo barbarus*. But now the in-humane is the supposed barbarism of gothic Scholasticism in the Middle Ages. Therefore a *studium humanitatis*, which in a certain way reaches back to the ancients and thus also becomes a revival of Greek civilization, always adheres to historically understood humanism. For Germans this is apparent in the humanism of the eighteenth century supported by Winckelmann, Goethe, and Schiller. On the other hand, Hölderlin does not belong to "humanism" precisely because he thought the destiny of man's essence in a more original way than "humanism" could.[90]

Given the historically specific conditions of this period of "distress"—the degree, that is, to which the events of European history from 1914 to 1933 had disclosed the contradictions inhering in the self-representation of the liberal democracies, it should not be surprising that many other leading European intellectuals besides Heidegger, both of the right and the left, either succumbed to the lure of a national socialism or found little in National Socialism to resist, thus blinding themselves in some degree or other to the ominous rhetoric and practice of Hitler and the Nazi Party or dismissing them in terms of profit and loss. As Lacoue-Labarthe admits in locating Heidegger's "*faute*" elsewhere, Heidegger

à surestimé le nazisme, et probablement passé au compte des profits et pertes ce qui s'annonçait dés avant 33 et contre quoi, pourtant, il etait résolument opposé: l'antisémitisme, l'idéologie (la "science politisée"), la brutalité expéditive. Mais j'ajouterai: qui, dans ce siècle, devant la mutation historico-mondiale sans précédent dont il a été le théatre et l'apparante radicalité des propositions révolutionaires, qu'il fût "de droite" ou "de gauche," n'a pas été floué? Et au nom de quoi ne l'aurait-il pas été? "De la démocratie"? Laissons cela à Raymond Aron, c'est-à-dire à la pensée officielle du Capital (du nihilisme accompli, pour lequelle en effet tout *vaut*). Mais ceux qui furent grands dans leur ordre? Au hasard: Hamsum, Benn, Pound, Blanchot, Drieu et Brasillach. . . . Ou bien, de l'autre côté: Benjamin, Brecht, Bataille, Malraux (je n'excepte pas Sartre, dont l'authenticité morale ne fait aucun doute.) Que leur offrait le vieux monde pour résister à l'irruption du soi-disant "nouveau monde"? Sous cet angle et tout bien considéré, le mérite de Heidegger, incalculable *aujourd'hui*, aura été de ne céder que dix mois a cette illusion *bifrons* des "temps nouveau."

[Heidegger overestimated Nazism and probably wrote off as incidental expense what had already announced itself before 1933, and against which he was, in fact, resolutely opposed: anti-Semitism, ideology ("politicized science") peremptory brutality. But I should add: Who in this century, in the face of the unprecedented world-historical transformations and of the apparent radicality of its revolutionary propositions, whether of "the right" or of "the left," has not been duped? And in the name of what? Of "democracy?" Let us leave such things to Raymond Aron, that is, to the official philosophy of Capital (of the achieved nihilism for which in effect *anything goes*). But what of those who were great figures in their own ways? At random: Hamsun, Benn, Pound, Blanchot, Drieu, and Brasillach. . . . Or, in the other camp, Benjamin, Brecht, Bataille, Malraux (I do not except Sartre, whose moral authority is quite beyond doubt). What did the old world have to offer them in order to resist the irruption of the so-called "new world"? From this angle, and all things considered, the merit of Heidegger, incalculable today, will have been to have succumbed for only ten months to this double-faced illusion of "new times."][91]

What should be surprising and cause for pause to anyone not caught up in "the official thought of Capitalism" is that the Heidegger of the rectorate and of his discourse should be singled out for censure at this late date—which has since borne witness to the recurrence of the "pincer" situation, this time in Southeast Asia (the "domino theory" of the Cold War).

What *is* unacceptable in Heidegger's decision to commit himself and the German university to the Nazi project in 1933 is his failure, despite the worldly and material dialogic imperatives (*Auseinandersetzung*) of his de-structive/projective hermeneutics, to perceive the difference between his *theoretical* national (not racist/nationalist) socialism and the *real* National Socialism of Hitler and the thugs who controlled its political machinery. It is one thing to recognize, as Heidegger says he did (and there is no reason, even in the "Rectorate Address," not to believe him), the threat to his understanding of the university implicit in Minister Wacker's "opinion" of the "Rectorate Address":

1. that this was a kind of "private" National Socialism, which circumvented the perspective of the party program.

2. Most importantly, that the whole had not been based on the concept of race.

3. That he could not accept the rejection of the idea of "political science," even if he would be willing to admit that as yet this idea had not been given a sufficient foundation (R 490)[92]

It is quite something else not to recognize that these ideological objectives of the Nazi Party which Heidegger theoretically resisted—its political/aesthetic program, its biological racism, its commitment to "political science" (the politico-technologization of knowledge production)—were being realized all around him in the real world of Hitler's Germany, or to minimize these real violent practices in behalf of a larger theoretical vision of a renewed, differentially animated "Europe." Given his theoretical retrieval of the forgotten "other" from the discourse of anthropology, it is especially unacceptable that he should have blinded himself to the Nazis' persecution of the Jews undertaken in the name of the "German/European" identity.

But it is not Heidegger's historical affiliation with the National Socialist Party as such which is at stake in the renewed debate; it is rather his philosophical discourse and its impact on the contemporary interrogation of "Man." More important than Heidegger's personal involvement with Nazism, therefore, to think Heidegger's notorious equation in the context I have retrieved—above all, the dreadful fate of the people of Vietnam and its culture at the hands of American technology—is also to realize that, *in theory*, Heidegger's pursuit of the question of being (*die Seinsfrage*) after the so-called *Kehre* was not, as Davidson and other humanist critics of Heidegger too easily assume, finally to recuperate *Being*—the principle of presence (or the center) that circumscribes and *comprehends* difference within the totalizing structure of a guiding identity demanding passive obedience. It was not, that is, to recuperate fascism in another form, whether as "Art" or as "Spirit." However vestigially metaphysical it remained (and this, after Derrida, cannot be denied), Heidegger's purpose following his resignation of the rectorate was, rather—as his disclosure of the complicity between European modernity at large with the commanding gaze, the *imperium*, and the imperial *pax* of the Roman *veritas* in the *Parmenides* lectures make clear—to continue, *henceforth indirectly*, his original project to retrieve (*wiederholen*) the temporality of being (the differences that temporality disseminates), which the representational (metaphysical/aesthetic) discourse and practice of the Occident, especially in the wake of the (Romanized) Enlightenment, had virtually spatialized/reified. If we recall the ideologically strategic prominence of the metaphorics of mapping in the American command's conduct of its imperial war against Vietnam, it will perhaps be seen that this project of retrieval underlies Heidegger's naming of the modern age "the age of the world picture" (*Die Zeit des Weltbildes*) in 1938: after he had come to realize that the essence of "science" and its totalizing representational objective could "no longer be influenced by attempts at its renewal, nor delayed in its essential transformation into pure technology [*Technik*]" (R 497); after, that is, he had come to see that Nazism, no less than "communism" or "world democracy," was itself caught up in the nihilistic planetary project of Western technology (R 485).[93]

Put in terms of Heidegger's postwar discourse, whether on the question of being or that of *poiesis* (*Denken* and *Dichtung*), to think his notorious equation in the light of the contemporary occasion is also to realize that Heidegger's abiding and "conservative" concern for (*Sorge*) the earth (*die Erde*)—what Davidson (among others, most notably Richard Wolin and Tom Rockmore) reduces to and contemptuously calls Heidegger's "idolatry of the village life of the [German] peasant" (QCH, 425)— against the imperial claims of a *techné* become *Technik* was, in essence, however incompletely realized, a concern dedicated to the preservation of the rift between world (inscription) and earth (temporality as *aletheia*). It was, to put it alternatively, an *"ecological"* commitment to the integrity of the ontological difference—to the principle that difference is the condition for the possibility of identity—in the face of the totalitarian Occidental effort to annul the rift and to reduce difference to the same: in the face, that is, of the "West's" (including the Soviet Union's) multisituated imperial project—its planetary "will to power" (R 499)—to colonize and *pacify* (I stress the analogy with the American command's essential strategy in Vietnam) all those "others" constituting the indissoluble relay he calls "being" (*Sein*) by transforming and reducing them to properly located present-at-hand objects in the inclusive and panoptically supervised "world picture."

In thus retrieving a strain in Heidegger's thought—his insistence on the *finitude* of *Dasein* (its being-in-the-world) and the ontological difference—that his anti-antihumanist critics too easily forget or willfully discount in their selective reading of the "'Rectorate Address' to Heidegger's last writings" as a monolithic and uniform body of discourse in which "the human is always being led, and what leads humanity seems to so envelop or overwhelm it that its disappearance is constantly threatened" (QCH, 422) I am suggesting its appropriatability for emancipatory practice. This has been no more acutely and precisely put than by the Marxist Fredric Jameson in an interview with the editors of *Diacritics*:

> Heidegger . . . describes the effect and function of the "authentic" work of art as the inauguration of a "rift" between what he calls World and Earth—what we can rewrite in other language as the dimensions of History and the social project on the one hand, and

Nature or matter on the other, ranging from geographical or ecological constraint all the way to the individual body. The force of Heidegger's description lies in the way in which the gap between these two dimensions is maintained; the implication is that we all live in both dimensions at once, in some irreconcilable simultaneity (and I would think that this distinction both includes and largely transcends more traditional categories like those of the "public" and the "private"). We are at all moments in history and in matter; we are at one and the same time historical beings and "natural" ones, living in the meaning-endowment of the historical project and the meaninglessness of organic life, without any ultimate "synthesis" between these two dimensions ever being possible or conceivable. The Heideggerian formula thus repudiates any such conception of a possible synthesis between History and Nature (such syntheses are called "metaphysics"), and at one and the same time repudiates any such conception of the work of art which would aim at reuniting both symbolically, under some repression of History and Nature, or the reverse. The work of art can therefore never heal this fundamental "distance"; but it can do something else, and better—it can stage the very tension between the two dimensions in such a way that we are made to live *within* that tension and to affirm its reality. This has always seemed to me an extraordinarily suggestive conception of the inaugural "poetic" act, which Heidegger goes on to assimilate to the comparable philosophical act (the deconcealment of Being) and to the act of political revolution (the inauguration of a new society, the production or invention of radically new social relations).[94]

One need only add that Jameson no doubt is taking up Heidegger's invitation in "Letter on Humanism"—totally overlooked by those critics, liberal and Marxist humanists and deconstructionists, who would either identify his post-rectorate discourse with Nazi fascism or salvage it by textualizing it—to think productively the relationship between his and Marx's diagnosis of modernity as "homelessness" and "estrangement," respectively:

Homelessness is coming to be the destiny of the world. Hence it is necessary to think that destiny in terms of the history of Being. What Marx recognized in an essential and significant sense, though derived from Hegel, as the estrangement of man has its roots in the homelessness of modern man. This homelessness is specifically evoked from the destiny of Being in the form of metaphysics and through metaphysics is simultaneously entrenched and covered up as such. Because Marx by experiencing estrangement attains an essential dimension of history, the Marxist view of history is superior to that of other historical accounts. But since neither Husserl nor—so far as I have seen till now—Sartre recognizes the

essential importance of the historical in Being, neither
phenomenology nor existentialism enters that dimension within
which a productive dialogue with Marxism first becomes possible.[95]

Lest this passage be read, as it is now likely to be, as an indirect accommodation of Marx's accounts of history and alienation to the German
homeland (understood as *Vaterland*), let me recall Heidegger's witness in
Being and Time: that the primordial condition of finite *Dasein* is its *Unheimlichkeit*, its not-at-homeness. This means that homelessness is what
metaphysical at-homing precipitates, and conversely, to be authentically
at-home—"to dwell"—in the world is to "be-in-the-not-at-home," or,
as he puts it later, in the "rift."

Perhaps we will never know Heidegger's motive for his "failure" to
"pronounce the name of the Jews" in the postwar period. (If we put him
on trial we must—and I am not at all convinced that the empirical project
is adequate to such a task; whether it does not itself harbor a violence
analogous to that which it condemns—it seems to me reasonable and
just, given the acknowledged inadequacies of Farías's history of Heidegger's involvement with Nazism, to wait until all the evidence is in
before judging him, especially the testimony of the lengthy correspondence between Heidegger and Hannah Arendt, which the executors of
Heidegger's estate have declared off limits for three generations.[96]

In the light of the resonantly unsaid I have retrieved, however, the
condemnation of Heidegger's "scandalously inadequate" synecdochical
equation by his critics takes on a different resonance; one that, if it does
not exonerate him of the charge of indifference to the difference or forgetfulness of the forgotten (as it is not at all intended to do), nevertheless
stirs the roots of the question of Heidegger's philosophical project. On
the one hand, it suggests that for Davidson and the American editors of
Critical Inquiry (as well as for all the other humanist critics who have been
afforded prosecutor credentials by the publication of Farías's "biography/
history") this judgment is self-serving, and for the poststructuralist contributors to the supplement it is self-defeating. On the other, it suggests
that, however morally ambiguous, Heidegger's "silence" about the
Nazi's "Final Solution" has its positive ontological, cultural, and sociopolitical implications in an age characterized by what Foucault has called
"the regime of truth." Could it even be that this "unpardonable" *faute*
was in some paradoxical sense an act of courage—a willingness to risk
the condemnation of the moralists' tribunals—in the face of the overwhelming pressure exerted by the dominant humanist discourse to publicly confess guilt?[97] Is it possible, in other words, to read Heidegger's
silence as an "I prefer not to": a brave refusal to capitulate to the "truth"
of the repressive hypothesis, to the "juridico-discursive" principle that

truth is incommensurable with the violence of power?[98] Whatever the viability of this possibility, which I am sure will strike Heidegger's humanist critics as outrageous, there *is*, despite the blinded compromises of Heidegger's discursive practices of the rectorate and the vestigial metaphysics of his thought at large, *the fact of* his influence on an essentially emancipatory contemporary (post-Vietnam) discourse that in turn has validated and energized the resistance of a multiplicity of historically specific constituencies of the human community, constituencies hitherto spoken for, marginalized, repressed, excluded, or, most insidiously of all, accommodated by the dominant Occidental (anthropological/technological/(neo-)imperial) sociopolitical order. As such a contradiction, it bears witness not simply against the humanist prosecutors' judgment of Heidegger's thought, but against the humanist "repressive hypothesis": the very idea of Truth that his humanist accusers have relied on to prosecute their "case" against Heidegger.

Notes

Foreword

1. See Emmanuel Lévinas, *Autrement qu'être ou aù-delà de l'essence* (The Hague: Nijhoff, 1978).
2. *Critical Inquiry* 15 (Winter 1989), pp. 407–88.
3. This special issue was significant in that it marked the first issue of *boundary 2* not under the official editorship of William V. Spanos, and was made up of essays by the editorial collective as well as an interview with Spanos conducted by Paul A. Bové, the new editor of *boundary 2*.
4. *boundary 2* 17 (Summer 1990), pp. 199–280.
5. *Critical Inquiry* 15, p. 423. Davidson's source is Wolfgang Schirmacher, *Technik und Gelassenheit* (Freiburg, 1984).
6. *Critical Inquiry*, p. 424.
7. *boundary 2* 17, p. 216.
8. *boundary 2* 17, p. 215.
9. *The Heidegger Controversy: A Critical Reader*, ed. Richard Wolin (New York: Columbia University Press, 1991), p. 163.
10. Victor Farías provides these facts with a lurid narrative frame in *Heidegger and Nazism*, trans. Paul Burrell and Gabriel Ricci (Philadelphia: Temple University Press, 1989). For a fine assessment of this work and the Heidegger controversy in general, see Richard Wolin, *The Heidegger Controversy*, pp. 1–23 and 282–310, as well as David Carroll's foreword to Lyotard's *Heidegger and "the jews,"* trans. Andreas Michel and Mark Roberts (Minneapolis: University of Minnesota Press, 1990), vii–xxix.
11. Philippe Lacoue-Labarthe, *La fiction du politique* (Strasbourg, 1987), p. 81, trans. Richard Wolin, *The Heidegger Controversy*, p. 296.

12. William V. Spanos, *Repetitions: The Postmodern Occasion in Literature and Culture* (Baton Rouge: Louisiana State University Press, 1987), p. 195.

1. On Heidegger's Destruction and the Metaphorics of Following: An Introduction

1. As Karsten Harries has observed, the question of Heidegger's affiliation with Nazism has been the topic of public controversy on at least three other occasions. The first occurred in the pages of Jean-Paul Sartre's *Les Temps Modernes* shortly after the end of World War II; the second, in 1953 after the publication of *Introduction to Metaphysics*, in which "Heidegger chose to let what he had said earlier [in the 1935 lecture course that constitutes the matter of this book] about the 'inner truth and greatness' of the National Socialist movement pass without comment. . . . "; the third, in 1976, after the publication of the now notorious *Spiegel* interview (given ten years before but not published until after Heidegger's death according to his wishes). "Introduction," *Martin Heidegger and National Socialism: Questions and Answers*, ed. Gunther Neske and Emil Kettering (New York: Paragon House, 1990), pp. xv–xix. First published in Germany in 1988.

2. Philippe Lacoue-Labarthe, "Annexe: sur le livre de Victor Farías's *Heidegger et le nazisme,*" *La fiction du politique: Heidegger, l'art et la politique* (Paris: Christian Bourgois, 1987), pp. 173–88. See also Heinrich Ott, "Paths and Wrong Paths: On Victor Farías's Critical Study of Heidegger," *Martin Heidegger and National Socialism*, pp. 133–39. I put "facts" in quotation marks not simply because the representation of events in general as facts are always ideologically informed, but because, as Lacoue-Labarthe, Ott, and others have shown, some of the facts that Farías invokes against Heidegger are simply mistaken or misrepresented by the process of interpretating them.

3. Arnold I. Davidson, "Question Concerning Heidegger: Opening the Debate," in "A Symposium on Heidegger and Nazism," ed. Arnold I. Davidson, *Critical Inquiry* 15: 2 (Winter 1989), p. 425. The quotation from Lévinas is taken from "As if Consenting to Horror," trans. Paula Wissing, *Critical Inquiry* 15, p. 487; that from Cavell, from "A Cover Letter to Molière's *Misanthrope*," *Themes out of School*, p. 103.

4. Jacques Derrida, "Comment Donner Raison? 'How to Concede, with Reasons,' " trans. John P. Leavey in a special issue, "Heidegger: Art and Politics," *Diacritics* 19: 3–4 (Fall–Winter 1989), p. 4.

5. Luc Ferry and Alain Renaut, *Heidegger et les modernes* (Paris: Bernard Grasset, 1988), p. 119, my translation. See also Ferry and Renaut, *La pensée 68: Essai sur l'anti-humanisme contemporain* (Paris: Gallimard, 1985). English translations: *Heidegger and Modernity*, trans. Franklin Philip (Chicago: University of Chicago Press, 1990); *French Philosophy of the Sixties: An Essay on Antihumanism*, trans. Mary Schnackenberg Cattani (Amherst: University of Massachusetts Press, 1990). The American humanist who most overtly—and reductively—utilizes Farías's *Heidegger et le nazisme* (and the recent disclosure of the collaborationist journalism of Paul de Man) for the purpose of delegitimating the antihumanist left discourses Heidegger's thought has enabled is David H. Hirsch in *The Deconstruction of Literature: Criticism after Auschwitz* (Hanover, N.H.: Brown University Press, 1991). Referring, for example, to Frank Lentricchia's invocation of "Foucault's Americaphobic ideology" in behalf of reclaiming the historicity and worldliness of the literary

text, Hirsch observes sardonically: "Lentricchia's own account of the philosophical forces that have brought us to the brink of this new 'historicism' reflects a characteristic blindness to recent history, thus creating a historical void in which Martin Heidegger, a crucial player in the development of contemporary theory, is severed from an unfortunate but crucial historical context. It is generally agreed that the conflux of postwar French theories that is now labeled postmodernism has been fueled by the philosophizing of Martin Heidegger. In the case of Derrida, the debt is openly acknowledged. In the case of Foucault, the Heideggerian influence is more elusive. Nevertheless, we can see it quite clearly in [Lentricchia's characterization of Foucault's 'effective history' not as 'a new historicism, but the old one disturbed, questioned, its duplicities and its techniques illuminated']. If Lentricchia is correct about Foucault, then there can be no doubt that this 'old [historicism] . . . is a Heideggerian historicism. And if there were any doubt of the Heideggerian roots here, they are removed by the peroration, which identifies itself not only in the notion of 'the deconstructive project,' but which reeks, in its diction, of the Heidegger Rektoratsrede of 1933, when Heidegger called on the German university students to follow their Führer bravely and energetically, and filled with self-assurance. In short, Lentricchia, through Foucault, presents Heidegger and his philosophy-aesthetics in a 'privileged' manner that sets Heidegger himself above criticism and outside history" (pp. 57–58). And again, in a concluding chapter titled "Deconstruction and Humanism after Auschwitz": "Thanks to Victor Farías's courage and tenacious detective work, we can no longer ignore the question of the connection between the thinking of Martin Heidegger and his long-term affiliation with, and lifetime refusal to repudiate, Nazi ideology. It is now clear that Heidegger's attraction to National Socialism and his extended membership in the Nazi Party were consistent with, rather than aberrant to, his thinking. By the same token, it is also becoming possible to contemplate connections between National Socialism and the post-Auschwitz perpetuation of Heidegger-inspired antihumanist theories in the guise of what has come to be called postmodernism" (pp. 255–56).

6. Martin Heidegger, *Being and Time*, trans. John Macquarrie and Edward Robinson (New York: Harper & Row, 1962), p. 363; hereafter cited in my text as BT.

7. As the translators suggest in the note to this climactic passage of *Being and Time*: "In resolute repetition one is having, as it were, a conversation with the past, in which the past proposes certain possibilities for adoption, but in which one makes a rejoinder to this proposal by 'reciprocating' with the proposal of other possibilities as a sort of rebuke to the past, which one now disavows. (The punning treatment of 'weider' and 'wider' is presumably intended.)" In Heidegger's later texts, this "*Erwiderung*," which might be better translated by the oxymoron "antagonistic dialogue," will become "*Auseinandersetzung*."

8. Davidson, "Questions Concerning Heidegger," pp. 416, 422. The quotation from Heidegger derives from "The Thing," *Poetry, Language, Thought*, trans. Albert Hofstadter (New York: Harper & Row, 1971), pp. 183–84. Davidson's reduction of the temporal/differential being of Heidegger's being to Being, of repetition to a self-confirming circularity, and, therefore, of *Auseinandersetzung* (dialogic confrontation) to a blind following of the Word of the Führer—the result of reading backwards, which is to say of not reading Heidegger's texts—informs the condemnatory discourse of virtually all the American humanists who have appropriated the European debate for the post-Vietnam American context. See especially, Richard Wolin, *The Politics of Being: The Political Thought of Martin Heidegger* (New York: Columbia University Press, 1990); Hirsch, *The Deconstruction of Literature:*

Criticism after Auschwitz; and Tom Rockmore, *On Heidegger's Nazism and Philosophy* (Berkeley: University of California Press, 1992).

9. This erased understanding of "loyalty" is not limited to *Being and Time* (the pre-National Socialist phase of Heidegger's thought). It is fundamental to his thought at large. We find it, for example, in the lectures of 1935 published later as *Einführung in die Metaphysik* (Tübingen: M. Niemeyer, 1953), the period immediately following his resignation of the rectorship, the period Heidegger's humanist critics invoke to challenge his later claim that he broke with historical Nazism at that time: "Introduction to metaphysics" means . . . an introduction to the asking of the fundamental question. . . . A leading into [*Einführung*] the asking of the fundamental questions is . . . not a going to something that lies and stands somewhere; no, this leading-to is itself a questioning advance, a preliminary questioning. It is a leading for which in the very nature of things there can be no following. When we hear of disciples, "followers," as in a school of philosophy for example, it means that the nature of questioning is misunderstood. Such schools can exist only in the domain of scientific and technical work." *Introduction to Metaphysics*, trans. Ralph Mannheim (New Haven: Yale University Press, 1959), p. 16.

We also find it in a text as late as "The Question Concerning Technology" (1953), this time in the context of the much maligned "destining": "Always the unconcealment of that which is goes upon a way of revealing. Always the destining of revealing holds complete sway over men. But that destining is never a fate that compels. For man becomes truly free only insofar as he belongs to the realm of destining and so becomes one who listens, though not one who simply obeys" *Basic Writings*, ed. David Farrell Krell (New York: Harper & Row, 1977), p. 306.

10. Jacques Derrida, "Structure, Sign, and Play in Discourse of the Human Sciences," *Writing and Difference*, trans. Alan Bass (Chicago: University of Chicago Press, 1978): "It has always been thought that the center, which is by definition unique, constituted that very thing within a structure which while governing structure, escapes structurality. This is why classical thought concerning structure could say that the center is, paradoxically, *within* the structure and *outside it*. The center is at the center of the totality, and yet, since the center does not belong to the totality (is not part of the totality), the totality *has its center elsewhere*. The center is not the center. The concept of centered structure—although it represents coherence itself, the condition of the *epistémé* as philosophy or science—is contradictorily coherent. And as always, coherence in contradiction expresses the force of a desire. The concept of centered structure is in fact the concept of a play based on a fundamental ground, a play constituted on the basis of a fundamental immobility and a reassuring certitude, which itself is beyond the reach of play" (p. 279).

11. Michel Foucault, "Revolutionary Action 'Until Now'," *Language, Counter-Memory, Practice: Selected Essays and Interviews*, ed. Donald F. Bouchard (Oxford: Blackwell, 1977), pp. 221–22.

12. One very significant indication of the viability of this hypothesis is the emergence after the end of the Cold War of a recuperative humanist discourse in which three related focuses are clearly discernable: (1) the revelations about Paul de Man's and Martin Heidegger's totalitarian affiliations, which are invoked to delegitimize posthumanist theory; (2) the representation of the emergence of "theory" (by which is usually meant deconstruction) in the academy as a usurpation by totalitarian radicals and the imposition of a reversed McCarthyism that evaluates performance and disposes privileges and rewards according to the "politically correct" tenets of "theory"; and (3) the events of 1989–90 in Eastern Europe, which are represented not simply as the triumph of Western democracy, but of American

culture in the context of and against the effort of posthumanists to "undermine" the American literary canon and, more generally, the core curriculum, which exist to safeguard and transmit this culture. This tripartite recuperative ideological strategy is epitomized, even if the first focus is invisible (no doubt because the names and the discourses would be meaningless to the American television public) in the following remarkably telling excerpt from an interview with Lynne Cheney, chairperson of the National Endowment for the Humanities, conducted by the panelists of the ABC News program "This Week with David Brinkley" (Sunday, January 6, 1991): "Well, I think that education, not just in our schools, but in our colleges and universities, is the shadow on what might otherwise be a sunny prediction for the next century and America's role in it. If you look at culture from a global perspective, there is every reason to be optimistic. The events of Eastern Europe and the Soviet Union of the past year or so have, in many ways, been affirmations of American culture, not just of our political system and our economic system, but people have read our books and they've seen our films and they've listened to our music and they've liked what they've read and seen and heard. . . . I think perhaps the most serious symptom [that casts its shadow across the sunny future of the world and America's role in it] is this idea of political correctness, that there are some thoughts that it is now proper to express and some thoughts that it is improper to express. Perhaps the most worrisome aspect of political correctness to me is one that you [the politically conservative syndicated columnist, George Will] hit on a little bit in the earlier conversation. Somehow, Western civilization, that whole long story of human failure and triumph and thought and achievement, has become politically incorrect in many places. It's become regarded as oppressive and indeed, it is the wellspring of those many, many attributes that we have as a country that people throughout the rest of the world envy. We saw students in Tienanmen Square, we saw students in Prague and in Budapest and Warsaw who know John Locke better than our students do because we don't teach John Locke as much as we used to, if we teach him at all." What Lynne Cheney says about the "triumph of American democracy" in the Cold War in this interview has, in fact, been theorized in terms of the "end of history" by Francis Fukuyama in a by now famous and influential essay, "The End of History?," *The National Interest* 16 (Summer 1989), 3–18, recently expanded to book length, *The End of History and the Last Man* (New York: The Free Press, 1992). In these politically conservative texts, Fukuyama essentializes the recent historical events in Eastern Europe that have borne witness to the collapse of Stalinist communism by turning orthodox Marxism on its head: by invoking Hegel's interpretation of history against the Marxist appropriation to demonstrate that the triumph of the *principles* of (American) democracy is the consequence of the historical dialectic.

13. Martin Heidegger, "Letter on Humanism," *Basic Writings*, p. 197.
14. Antonio Gramsci, *Selections from the Prison Notebooks*, ed. and trans. Quintin Hoare and Geoffrey Nowell Smith (New York: International Publishers, 1971), p. 12; Louis Althusser, "Ideology and Ideological State Apparatuses (Notes Toward an Investigation)," in *Lenin and Philosophy and Other Essays*, trans. Ben Brewster (New York: Monthly Review Press, 1971), pp. 127–86.
15. Walter Benjamin, "Theses on the Philosophy of History," *Illuminations*, ed. Hannah Arendt (New York: Schocken, 1969), pp. 256–57. Given the present context vis-à-vis Heidegger and Nazism, the affiliation I attribute to Heidegger and Benjamin will be dismissed as an act of hermeneutic violence. In response, I would cite Arendt's prefatory remarks: "This amazing revival, particularly of classical culture [precipitated by "the break in tradition"], which since the forties has been

especially noticeable in relatively traditionless America, began in Europe in the twenties. There it was initiated by those who were most aware of the irreparability of the break in tradition—thus in Germany, and not only there, first and foremost by Martin Heidegger, whose extraordinary, and extraordinarily early, success in the twenties was essentially due to a 'listening to the tradition that does not give itself up to the past but thinks of the present.' [*Kants These über das Sein* (Frankfurt, 1962), p. 8] Without realizing it, Benjamin actually had more in common with Heidegger's remarkable sense for living eyes and living bones that had sea-changed into pearls and coral, and as such could be saved and lifted into the present only by doing violence to their context in interpreting them with 'the deadly impact' of new thoughts, than he did with the dialectical subtleties of his Marxist friends" (p. 46).

16. Raymond Williams, *Marxism and Literature* (Oxford: Oxford University Press, 1977), p. 82. This phrasing is fundamental to Williams's neo-Marxist argument against the economism of classical Marxist theory, especially the base/superstructure model that determined its interpretation of cultural phenomena as well as history: "It is only when we realize that 'the base,' to which it is habitual to *refer* [dynamic historical] variations, is itself a dynamic and internally contradictory process—the specific activities and modes of activity, over a range from association to antagonism, of real men and classes of men—that we can begin to free ourselves from the notion of an 'area' or a 'category' with certain fixed properties for deduction to the variable processes of a 'superstructure.' The physical fixity of the terms exerts a constant pressure against just this realization.

  Thus, contrary to a development in Marxism, it is not 'the base' and 'the superstructure' that need to be studied, but specific and indissoluble real processes within which the decisive relationship, from a Marxist point of view, is that expressed by the complex idea of 'determination.' "

17. Michel Foucault, "What Is an Author?" *Language, Counter-Memory, Practice*, p. 131.

18. For my extended analysis of this failure, see chapter 5, "The University in the Vietnam Decade: The Refusal of Spontaneous Consent and the Crisis of Command," in *The End of Education: Toward Posthumanism* (Minneapolis: University of Minnesota Press, 1993).

19. Fredric Jameson, *The Political Unconscious: Narrative as a Socially Symbolic Act* (Ithaca, N.Y.: Cornell University Press, 1981), pp. 53–54.

2. Breaking the Circle: Hermeneutics as Dis-closure

1. Martin Heidegger, *The End of Philosophy*, trans. Joan Stambaugh (New York: Harper & Row, 1973). This translation was originally published as a part of volume 2 of *Nietzsche* (Pfullingen: Verlag Günther Neske, 1961).

2. I use the conventional capitalization only when I refer to the word "Being" as a substantive, i.e., as it is represented in the Western ontotheological tradition.

3. See Joseph Frank, "Spatial Form in Modern Literature," *Sewanee Review* 53 (Spring, Summer, and Autumn 1945), pp. 221–40, 433–45, 643–65; reprinted in *The Widening Gyre: Crisis and Mastery in Modern Literature* (New Brunswick, N.J.: Rutgers University Press, 1963, pp. 3–62). It is of considerable importance for the task of deconstructing the Western literary tradition to observe that Frank and those who follow him in his Kantian use of the term as a definition of the modernity of the symbolist/imagist imagination do so without reference either to Henri

Bergson's use of the same term in *Time and Free Will: An Essay on the Immediate Data of Consciousness*, trans. F. L. Pogson (New York: Macmillan, 1910) to define and criticize the reality perceived by the positivistic consciousness, or to T. E. Hulme's summary of Bergson's analysis and critique in "The Philosophy of Intensive Manifolds," *Speculations: Essays on Humanism and the Philosophy of Art*, ed. Herbert Read (New York: Harcourt, Brace, 1924), pp. 123–214. See especially, Jeffrey R. Smitten and Ann Daghistany, *Spatial Form in Narrative* (Ithaca, N.Y.: Cornell University Press, 1981). Proponents of "spatial form" thus inadvertently point to the ultimately logocentric ground of both the objective and subjective, positivistic and idealistic, realistic and symbolist standpoints and thereby undercut the allegedly radical modernity of Modernism. They thus also corroborate Heidegger's account of the continuity of the binary ontotheological tradition.

4. Martin Heidegger, *Being and Time*, trans. John Macquarrie and Edward Robinson (New York: Harper & Row, 1962), p. 265; SZ, p. 222. Further references to this text will be abbreviated to BT and incorporated in the text in parentheses. As in the above, the citation will also include abbreviated reference to the original German version, *Sein und Zeit*, 7th ed. (Tübingen: Neomarius Verlag, 1953).

5. Samuel Beckett, *Watt* (New York: Grove Press, 1959). On his arrival "in the midst at last, after so many tedious years spent clinging to the perimeter" (p. 41), Watt, like his predecessor Arsene, experiences "irrefragible" premonitions "of imminent harmony" (p. 40). He conceives of Knott's "establishment" as its *logos*, its unmoved mover, its Word. Then "something slips" (p. 42) and everything suddenly changes. A rupture in the referential surface of the plenary circle occurs, so to speak, and Watt finds himself in a *terra incognita* "grounded" in a mysterious and elusive absence. His ec-centric predicament is symbolized by the picture hanging in Erskine's room: "A circle, obviously described by a compass, and broken at its lowest point, occupied the middle foreground, of this picture. Was it receding? Watt had that impression. In the eastern background appeared a point, or dot. . . . Watt wondered how long it would be before the point and circle entered together upon the same plane. . . . Watt wondered if they had sighted each other, or were blindly flying thus, harried by some force of merely mechanical mutual attraction, or the playthings of chance. . . . And he wondered what the artist had intended to represent . . . a circle and its centre in search of each other, or a circle and its centre in search of a centre and a circle respectively, or a circle and its centre in search of its centre and a circle respectively, or a circle and its centre in search of a centre and its circle respectively, or a circle and a centre not its centre in search of its centre and its circle respectively. . . . " (pp. 128–29).

6. I refer the reader to W. B. Macomber, *The Anatomy of Disillusion: Martin Heidegger's Notion of Truth* (Evanston, Ill.: Northwestern University Press, 1967), for an excellent study of the subject.

7. Macquarrie and Robinson translate *Angst* as "anxiety." I have let this translation stand in the passage quoted below from *Being and Time*.

8. Thomas Langan, *The Meaning of Heidegger: A Critical Study of an Existential Phenomenology* (New York: Columbia University Press, 1961), p. 23. This condition is what I will later call *Dasein's* "occasion," because of the word's resonant etymology. See especially, chapter 4, "The Indifference of *Différance*: Retrieving Heidegger's Destruction." See also Heidegger's destruction of the word "causality" in "The Question Concerning Technology," *The Question Concerning Technology and Other Essays*, trans. William Lovitt (New York: Harper & Row, 1977), p. 7.

9. Søren Kierkegaard, *The Concept of Dread*, trans. Walter Lowrie (Princeton, N.J.: Princeton University Press, 1957), p. 38. The parallel with Heidegger is virtually

absolute, except that Kierkegaard puts the argument in theological rather than ontological terms. Here he uses the term "innocence" where Heidegger uses "everyday-being," though in "Letter on Humanism" the latter speaks of man in this state as *Homo animalis* (*Basic Writings*, ed. David Farrell Krell [New York: Harper & Row, 1977], pp. 189–242). "In this state [innocence] there is peace and repose [Heidegger's terms are 'tranquility and familiarity']; but at the same time there is something different which is not dissension and strife, for there is nothing to strive with. What is it then? Nothing. But what effect does nothing produce? It begets dread. This is the profound secret of innocence, that at the same time it is dread." In a footnote to his discussion of Section 40, "The Basic State-of-Mind of Anxiety as a Distinctive Way in which Dasein Is Disclosed," Heidegger writes, "The man who has gone farthest in analysing the phenomenon of anxiety . . . is Søren Kierkegaard. Cf. *Der Begriff der Angst* . . ." (BT, 492). For a fuller treatment of this relationship, see Chapter 3, "Heidegger, Kierkegaard, and the Hermeneutic Circle."

10. See also BT, 393 ff.; SZ, 342 ff.
11. Martin Heidegger, "What Is Metaphysics?" trans. R. F. C. Hull and Alan Crick, in *Existence and Being*, intro. Werner Brock (Chicago: Henry Regnery, 1949), p. 336, my emphasis.
12. Heidegger, "What Is Metaphysics?," p. 335. See also BT, 179–82; SZ, 140–42; and BT, 391–96; SZ, 341–45.
13. See especially, "Letter on Humanism" and *Discourse on Thinking* (originally entitled *Gelassenheit*), trans. John M. Anderson and E. Hans Freund (New York: Harper & Row, 1966). In opposition to the Western "will to power," Heidegger grounds the relationship between *Dasein* and being in *Gelassenheit*, in letting be, or letting being be.
14. Paul Tillich, *The Courage to Be* (New Haven: Yale University Press, 1952), p. 36. Though Tillich's analysis is existential-theological rather than existential-ontological, his way of putting *Dasein*'s impulse to transform dread into fear is illuminating—if "God" is read as "being": "This human mind is not only, as Calvin said, a permanent factory of fears—the first in order to escape a God, the second in order to escape anxiety: and there is a relationship between the two. For facing the God who is really God means facing also the absolute threat of nonbeing. The 'naked absolute' (to use a phrase of Luther's) produces 'naked anxiety'; for it is the extinction of every finite self-affirmation [read 'anthropomorphic metaphysics'], and not a possible object of fear and courage" (p. 39).
15. John Keats, *The Letters of John Keats*, vol. 1 (Cambridge, Mass.: Harvard University Press, 1958), pp. 192–94. See also Iris Murdoch, "The Sublime and the Beautiful Revisited," *Yale Review* 49 (1959–60), pp. 269–70; and Charles Olson, *The Special View of History*, ed. Ann Charters (Berkeley, Calif.: Oyez, 1970), pp. 14, 32–33, 41–46. References to Keats's letter pervade Olson's prose and poetry. The relationship between Heidegger's critique of the humanist will to power and early Modernist literature has been made by Nathan A. Scott in *Negative Capability: Studies in the New Literature and the Religious Situation* (New Haven: Yale University Press, 1969). See especially "The Literary Imagination in a Time of Dearth," pp. 59–88. Negative capability should not, as the oxymoron suggests, be understood as a license for passivity or, as in the case of American Modernists like Lionel Trilling, who invoked Keats's phrase against a progressive activist American criticism, to valorize a "Hegelian" dialectic (the *Aufhebung*) that internalized historical conflict in the public sphere and annuled the imperative to *praxis*. See, for example, Trilling, "The Meaning of a Literary Idea," *The Liberal Imagination: Essays on*

Society and Literature (New York: Harcourt Brace Jovanovich, 1978), pp. 280–81. See chapter 3, "Charles Olson and Negative Capability," in my *Repetitions: The Postmodern Occasion in Literature and Culture* (Baton Rouge: Louisiana State University Press, 1987), pp. 107–47.

16. See, for example, "Force and Signification," in *Writing and Difference*, trans. Alan Bass (Chicago: University of Chicago Press, 1978): In the process of interrogating the "structuralism" of Jean Rousset's representation of Corneille's oeuvre, Derrida writes: "for the sake of determining an essential 'Corneillean movement,' does one not lose what counts? Everything that defies a geometrical-mechanical framework—and not only the pieces which cannot be constrained by curves and helices, not only force and quality, which are meaning itself, but also *duration*, that which is pure qualitative heterogeneity within movement—is reduced to the appearance of the inessential for the sake of this essentialism or teleological structuralism. Rousset understands theatrical or novelistic movement as Aristotle understood movement in general: transition to the act, which itself is the repose of the desired form. Everything transpires as if everything within the dynamics of Corneillean meaning, and within each of Corneille's plays, came to life with the aim of final peace, the peace of the structural *energeia*: *Polyeucte*" (pp. 20–21).

17. Because Heidegger puts the antithesis of these three phases—*Gerede* (idle talk), *Zweideutigkeit* (ambiguity), and *Neugier* (curiosity)—in terms of inauthentic everyday-being-in-the-world, his analysis of these in *Being and Time* does not lend itself immediately to the discussion of literary hermeneutics. In order to clarify the applicability of this triadic opposition to this field of inquiry, the antitheses to the authentic phases should be understood in terms of the systematized or "metaphysical" version of everyday-being-in-the-world: objective distance, calculation, assertion. For Heidegger's account of idle talk, ambiguity, and curiosity, see BT, 211–24; SZ, 167–80.

18. Wallace Stevens, "An Ordinary Evening in New Haven," *The Collected Poems* (New York: Knopf, 1954), p. 473.

19. See also BT, 408–25; SZ, 356–64. In *An Introduction to Metaphysics*, trans. Ralph Mannheim (Garden City, N.Y.: Anchor Books, 1961), Heidegger puts the spatializing imperative of derived knowledge in terms of the historical transformation of *physis* (the "emerging power" of be-ing) into *eidos* (idea, i.e., "appearance or what is seen"): "From the standpoint of space, the difference between appearing [as *physis*] and appearing [as *eidos*] is this: appearing in the first and authentic sense as bringing-itself-to-stand in togetherness involves space, which it first conquers; as it stands there, it creates space for itself; it produces space and everything pertaining to it; it is not copied. Appearing in the second sense emerges from an already finished space; it is situated in the rigid measures of this space, and we see it by looking towards it. The vision makes the thing. Now this vision becomes decisive, instead of the thing itself. Appearing in the first sense opens up space. Appearing in the second sense merely circumscribes and measures the space that has already been opened" (p. 153).

See also Macomber, *The Anatomy of Disillusion*, p. 85. For a suggestive application of the phenomenologically derived map metaphor to post-Renaissance literary form and culture, I refer the reader to John Vernon, *The Garden and the Map: Schizophrenia in Twentieth-Century Literature and Culture* (Urbana: University of Illinois Press, 1973). Using Husserl and Erwin Strauss (*Phenomenological Psychology: Selected Essays* [New York: Basic Books, 1966]) rather than Heidegger as the source of his phenomenological analysis of the modern mind, Vernon inevitably restricts his critique to the "map consciousness" of the literature grounded in empirical science. He fails to perceive that the idealist/symbolist "garden consciousness" he prefers, in beginning prior to the "fall"—i.e., from a privileged origin—is also a spatial imagination and thus, like the map consciousness, inside the metaphysical tradition.

20. Heidegger, *An Introduction to Metaphysics*, p. 161.

21. Heidegger, "What Is Metaphysics?," *Existence and Being*, p. 344. See also Langan, *The Meaning of Heidegger*, pp. 11 and 72. I use the word "grounded" ironically to contrast the traditional metaphysicians' pursuit of transcendental heights with Heidegger's phenomenological insistence on returning to the things themselves— to worldly origins—implied, for example, in the paradoxical title "The Way Back into the Ground of Metaphysics."

22. Theodore Kisiel, "Translator's Introduction" to Werner Marx, *Heidegger and the Tradition* (Evanston, Ill.: Northwestern University Press, 1971), p. xxiv.

23. Heidegger, *An Introduction to Metaphysics*, p. 161. My emphasis, except for the earlier Greek and Latin words.

24. As W. B. Macomber observes in *The Anatomy of Disillusion*, "Heidegger rejects all conceptions of knowledge which are formed on the basis of an analogy with *vision*. In vision more than any other sense man dissociates himself from his world, and when knowledge [i.e., the knowledge of *logos* as reason or judgment] comes to be regarded as absolute or underived, its nature is invariably expressed in visual terms: Plato's *eidos* and *idea*, Descartes' 'clear and distinct ideas,' Hume's 'representations,' Kant's *Anschauung* and *Vorstellungen*, Husserl's *Wesensschau*" (pp. 60–61). See also pp. 128, 143, 144, 149 ff. In a footnote he also cites *Sein und Zeit*, *Platons Lehre von der Wahrheit mit Brief über den Humanismus*, *Vorträge und Aufsatz*, and *Holzwege*, and quotes Otto Pöggeler, *Der Denkweg Martin Heideggers* (Pfullingen: Neske, 1962): "Vision is divested of its priority which corresponds to the noetic priority of pure contemplation" (p. 4). See also *An Introduction to Metaphysics*, pp. 52, 151 ff.

25. Martin Heidegger, "The Age of the World Picture," *The Question Concerning Technology and Other Essays*, trans. William Lovitt (New York: Harper & Row, 1977), p. 128. Hereafter cited as AWP in my text.

26. See chapter 3, "Heidegger, Kierkegaard, and the Hermeneutic Circle." The Kierkegaardian-Heideggerian critique of re-presentation/re-collection applies equally to the objective hermeneutics of re-cognition of Emilio Betti and E. D. Hirsch, Jr.

27. I have modified William Lovitt's translation to focus a certain resonance vis-à-vis representation found in Marjorie Grene's translation of Heidegger's essay in *Measure* 2 (Summer 1951); reprinted in *boundary 2* 4 (Winter 1976), pp. 269–84.

28. See David Farrel Krell's valuable essay "Art and Truth in Raging Discord: Heidegger and Nietzsche on the Will to Power," *boundary 2* 4 (Winter 1976), pp. 379–92. I am concerned in this essay not so much with demonstrating the relationship between Heidegger's thematization of the will to power over temporality informing the metaphysical discourse of anthropology and the Occidental political tradition as with traditional (including New Critical and structuralist) interpretive practice. To establish a continuity between the ontological/aesthetic focus of this chapter and the next and the ontological/political focus of the last two chapters, however, I refer the reader to Heidegger's *Parmenides*, vol. 54 *Gesamtausgabe* (Frankfurt am Main: Vittorio Klosterman, 1982). English translation, *Parmenides*, trans. André Schuwer and Richard Rojcewicz (Bloomington: Indiana University Press, 1992). In these lectures, Heidegger's ontological analysis of the Cartesian *Umkehrung* in terms of the visual/spatial metaphorics of re-presentation is repeated at the site of politics. In these lectures, more specifically—and in a manner that I take to mark his disaffiliation with Nazism—Heidegger identifies representational thought with

(Roman) imperialism. For my discussion of Heidegger's *Parmenides*, see chapter 5, Heidegger and Foucault: The Politics of the Commanding Gaze."

29. Mircea Eliade, *Cosmos and History: The Myth of the Eternal Return*, trans. Willard R. Trask, (New York: Harper & Row, 1959), p. 123. See also Paul Tillich, "The Struggle Between Time and Space," *Theology and Culture*, ed. Robert C. Kimball (New York: Oxford University Press, 1974): "The ultimate symbol found by Greek philosophers for the immovable being is the sphere or circle, the most perfect representation of space," p. 34. The relationship between the Platonic concept of circular time and Greek tragedy is brilliantly developed in Tom F. Driver, *The Sense of History in Greek and Shakespearean Drama* (New York: Columbia University Press, 1960).

30. Significantly, Heidegger's phenomenological description of the " 'worldless' " *Dasein* as "free-floating" probably derives from Kierkegaard's analysis of the ironic aesthete, who, in a Hegelian *Aufhebung*, transcends the limits of actuality by achieving the infinitely negative possibilities of mind: the ability to "hover."

31. I. A. Richards, *Principles of Literary Criticism* (London: Routledge and Kegan Paul, 1924), pp. 245–50. See also my essay, "The Paradox of Anguish: Some Notes on Tragedy," *Journal of Aesthetics and Art Criticism* 24 (Summer 1966), pp. 525–32.

32. Virginia Woolf, *The Common Reader: First Series* (New York: Harcourt Brace, 1925), p. 15; T. S. Eliot, "Ulysses, Order, and Myth," reprinted from the *Dial* (1923), in *Forms of Modern Fiction*, ed. William Van O'Connor (Bloomington: Indiana University Press, 1959), p. 123.

33. Worringer's and Hulme's accounts of the arts of these non-Western cultures are, perhaps needless to say, *representations* determined by an Occidental perspective, i.e., "Orientalist," in Edward Said's term.

34. This quotation is from Archibald MacLeish's "Ars Poetica" (1926), which may have its source in I. A. Richards's statement that "it is never what a poem says that matters, but what it is." Quoted in Cleanth Brooks, *Modern Poetry and the Tradition* (New York: Oxford University Press, 1965), p. 48.

35. Frank, "Spatial Form in Modern Literature," pp. 229–30. See also William J. Handy, *Modern Fiction: A Formalist Approach* (Carbondale: Southern Illinois University Press, 1971), p. 15.

36. One should consider, in this context, the New Critical delegitimation of open-ended texts in the name of the "fallacy of imitative form."

37. See especially Jacques Derrida, *Speech and Phenomena: And Other Essays on Husserl's Theory of Signs*, trans. David Allison (Evanston, Ill.: Northwestern University Press, 1973).

38. Heidegger appropriately calls the hermeneutic stance *Gelassenheit* ("letting be" or "releasement") in his later thought. It is an open question, however, as to whether or not Heidegger assumes this hermeneutic stance in his exegeses of the texts of Hölderlin and Trakl during the period of his rectorate.

39. I am borrowing the metaphor of the petrifying gaze from Jean-Paul Sartre. See especially *Being and Nothingness: An Essay in Phenomenological Ontology*, trans. Hazel Barnes (New York: The Citadel Press, 1956), p. 406. I will make the crucial extension of my ontological/literary appropriation of Sartre's metaphorics of "the look" (*le regard*) to include the politics of Michel Foucault's "panoptic gaze" in chapter 5, "Heidegger and Foucault: The Politics of the Commanding Gaze."

40. W. B. Macomber, *The Anatomy of Disillusion*, p. 103.

41. See also BT, 384–88; SZ, 335–38; and *An Introduction to Metaphysics*, p. 17.

42. Heidegger epitomizes this paradoxical relation between futural orientation and re-membrance in the following way: "*Only an entity which, in its Being, is essentially*

futural *so that it is free for its death and can let itself be thrown back upon its factical 'there'
by shattering itself against death—that is to say, only an entity which, as futural, is equiprimordially in the process of* having-been, *can, by handing down to itself the possibility
it has inherited, take over its own thrownness and be* in the moment of vision *for* 'its
time.' *Only authentic temporality which is at the same time finite, makes possible something like fate—that is to say, authentic historicality*" (BT, 437; SZ, 385; Heidegger's
emphasis).

43. Heidegger, *An Introduction to Metaphysics*, p. 9.
44. Heidegger, *An Introduction to Metaphysics*, p. 10.
45. Charles Olson, *The Maximus Poems* (New York: Jargon/Corinth Books, 1960),
    dedication page; p. 77. Olson's source is the late Ezra Pound, for whom the *Cantos*
    are a "periplum / not as land looks on a map / but as sea bord seen by men sailing"
    ("Canto LIX"). See the chapter on "Charles Olson and Negative Capability" in
    my *Repetitions*, pp. 138–42.
46. Hans-Georg Gadamer, *Truth and Method* (New York: The Seabury Press, 1975), p.
    340. See also Richard Palmer, *Hermeneutics: Interpretation Theory in Schleiermacher,
    Dilthey, Heidegger, and Gadamer* (Evanston, Ill.: Northwestern University Press,
    1969), pp. 198–201.
47. Understood in the context of the Heideggerian destruction of the tradition, Harold
    Bloom's influential post-New Critical gesture, in *The Anxiety of Influence* and his
    other books, toward establishing a "new" literary history based on a genetic
    (patriarchal/dynastic) model turns out to constitute simply another, however more
    complex, manifestation of the mystified ontotheological literary tradition. See
    Paul Bové, *Destructive Poetics: Heidegger and Modern American Poetry* (New York:
    Columbia University Press, 1980), pp. 7–31.
48. Paul de Man, "The Rhetoric of Blindness: Jacques Derrida's Reading of Rousseau,"
    Blindness and Insight: Essays in the Rhetoric of Contemporary Criticism (New York:
    Oxford University Press, 1971), p. 116.
49. De Man, "The Rhetoric of Blindness," p. 107. See also, "Form and Intent in the
    American New Criticism," *Blindness and Insight*, p. 32.
50. De Man, "Criticism and Crisis," *Blindness and Insight*, p. 17. Further references to
    this essay will be abbreviated to CC and incorporated in the text.
51. See my essays "Modern Drama and the Aristotelian Tradition: The Formal Imper-
    atives of Absurd Time," in *Contemporary Literature* 12 (Summer 1971), pp. 345–72;
    and "The Detective and the Boundary: Some Notes on the Postmodern Literary
    Imagination," in *boundary 2* 1 (Fall 1972), pp. 147–68; reprinted in *Repetitions*, pp.
    13–49.
52. J. Hillis Miller, "The Antitheses of Criticism: Reflections on the Yale Collo-
    quium," *MLN* 81 (December 1966), reprinted in *Velocities of Change: Critical Essays
    from MLN*, ed. Richard Macksey (Baltimore: Johns Hopkins University Press,
    1974), p. 151.
53. Miller, "The Antitheses of Criticism," p. 152.
54. Søren Kierkegaard, *Repetition: An Essay in Experimental Psychology*, trans. Walter
    Lowrie (New York: Harper & Row, 1964), p. 33. See also Kierkegaard, *Johannes
    Climacus or, De Omnibus Dubitandum Est and A Sermon*, trans. T. H. Croxall (Stan-
    ford: Stanford University Press, 1958).
55. See also Kierkegaard, *Johannes Climacus*, pp. 151–55.
56. Kierkegaard, *Repetition*, pp. 52–53. Kierkegaard's emphasis. Kierkegaard, or rather
    Vigilius Haufniensis, the pseudonymous author, quotes this crucial passage from
    Repetition in *The Concept of Dread*, trans. Walter Lowrie (Princeton, N.J.: Princeton

University Press, 1957), pp. 16–17. For my analysis of this intertextual gesture see chapter 3, "Heidegger, Kierkegaard, and the Hermeneutic Circle."

57. It is this difference that makes a difference disclosed by the temporal structurality of the hermeneutic circle that radically distinguishes my retrieval of temporality out of the traditional (New Critical and structuralist) spatial model from that of the "reader response" criticism enabled by the hermeneutics of Wolfgang Iser. See especially *The Implied Reader: Patterns of Communication in Prose and Fiction from Bunyan to Beckett* (Baltimore: The Johns Hopkins University Press, 1974).

3. Heidegger, Kierkegaard, and the Hermeneutic Circle

1. Martin Heidegger, *Being and Time*, trans. John Macquarrie and Edward Robinson (New York: Harper & Row, 1962), Sect. 2, p. 25. Further references to *Being and Time* will be incorporated in the text in parentheses and will include the abbreviation BT, the section number, and the page number. Since the translation is often problematic, I will also include abbreviated references to the original German version, *Sein und Zeit*, 7th ed. (Tübingen: Neomarius Verlag, 1953). While "Being" is consistently capitalized in the translation, and therefore in all quotations from *Being and Time*, in my text I will use "being" or "be-ing," when I wish to refer to its verbal (and renewed) sense, and "Being" when I refer to its nominative (traditional) sense.

2. See W. B. Macomber, *The Anatomy of Disillusion: Martin Heidegger's Notion of Truth* (Evanston, Ill.: Northwestern University Press, 1967), pp. 44 ff. The phrase "referential surface" is important for my purposes because its reference to inauthentic reality in spatial terms (map/icon) points to the causal relationship between the *spatialization of time*—the reduction of the "hermeneutic as" to the "apophantic as"—and the covering up and forgetting of being.

3. See also BT, 32, 188–92; SZ, 149–51. Specifically, the forestructure of *Dasein* as interpreter consists of fore-having (*Vorhaben*); fore-sight or point of view (*Vorsicht*), which " 'takes the first cut' out of what has been taken into our fore-having, and . . . does so with a view to a definite way in which this can be interpreted"; and fore-conception (*Vorgriff*), the conceptualizability of that which "is held in our fore-having and toward which we set our sight 'foresightedly' " (BT, 32, 191; SZ, 150). The "fore-structure," that is, is another way of referring to the ek-static or temporal character of *Dasein*, to its always ontic/ontological status. The crucial point, as Michael Gelven points out, "is that the fore-structure comes from Dasein's involvement in the world as ready-to-hand; not as purely calculative function of the present-at-hand." *A Commentary on Heidegger's "Being and Time"* (New York: Harper Torchbooks, 1970), p. 95.

4. For another version of this crucial movement, see Heidegger's definition of the "leap" in *An Introduction to Metaphysics*, trans. Ralph Mannheim (Garden City, N.Y.: Anchor Books, 1961), p. 5.

5. The great importance that Heidegger attributes to the hermeneutic circle is suggested by the fact that he invokes it as a governing concept of his theory of interpretation, in an increasingly full way, at least three times in *Being and Time*: BT, 5, 27–28; SZ, 7–8; BT, 32, 192–95; SZ, 151–53; and BT, 63, 362–63; SZ, 314–15.

6. T. S. Eliot, *The Family Reunion, The Complete Poems and Plays, 1909–1950*, (New York: Harcourt Brace, 1952), p. 250.

7. A. R. Ammons, "Corsons Inlet," *Collected Poems, 1951–71*, (New York: Norton, 1972), p. 148.

8. In an important conversion of Heidegger's hermeneutics of understanding into literary interpretation Paul de Man puts this reversal of the Modernist representation of the relation between whole and part as follows: "Literary 'form' is the result of the dialectic interplay between the prefigurative structure of the foreknowledge and the intent at totality of the interpretative process. This dialectic is difficult to grasp. The idea of totality suggests closed forms that strive for ordered and consistent systems and have an almost irresistible tendency to transform themselves into objective structures. Yet, the temporal factor, so persistently forgotten, should remind us that the form is never anything but a process on the way to its completion. The completed form never exists as a concrete aspect of the work that could coincide with a sensorial or semantic dimension of the language. It is constituted in the mind of the interpreter as the work discloses itself in response to his questioning. But this dialogue between work and interpreter is endless. The hermeneutic understanding is always, by its very nature, lagging behind: to understand something is to realize that one had always known it, but, at the same time, to face the mystery of this hidden knowledge. Understanding can be called complete only when it becomes aware of its own temporal predicament and realizes that the horizon within which the totalization can take place is time itself. The act of understanding is a temporal act that has its own history, but this history forever eludes totalization." This is found in "Form and Intent in the American New Criticism," *Blindness and Insight: Essays in the Rhetoric of Contemporary Criticism* (New York: Oxford University Press, 1971), pp. 31–32. As I have noted, however, de Man's insistence on the ontological priority of temporality over form is belied by his practice. See also Stanley Romaine Hopper, "Introduction," *Interpretation: The Poetry of Meaning*, ed. Hopper and David L. Miller (New York: Harcourt, Brace & World, 1967), pp. xv–xvi. For another useful account of Heidegger's version of the hermeneutic circle, see Gelven's *A Commentary on Heidegger's "Being and Time,"* pp. 176–81. In justifying the conclusion that the hermeneutic circle is not a vicious circle, however, Gelven invokes the analogy of the cumulative enrichment of meaning that comes with repeated listening to a Beethoven sonata. In so doing, he fails to point to the kind of temporality that is prior to the temporality of incremental repetition: the temporal process of listening to the sonata itself.

9. The translators of *Being and Time*, Macquarrie and Robinson, translate *Wiederholung* as "repetition" (others, as "retrieval") and add in a footnote: "This English word is hardly adequate to express Heidegger's meaning. Etymologically, 'wiederholen' means 'to fetch again'; in modern German usage, however, this is expressed by the cognate separable verb 'wieder . . . holen,' while 'wiederholen' means simply 'to repeat' or 'do over again.' Heidegger departs from both these meanings, as he is careful to point out. For him, 'wiederholen' does not mean either a mere mechanical repetition or an attempt to reconstitute the physical past; it means rather an attempt to go back to the past and retrieve former *possibilities*, which are thus 'explicitly handed down' or 'transmitted' " (BT, 74, 437). Neither they nor, as far as I know, his commentators refer to Heidegger's source in Kierkegaard's texts. As a result a crucial dimension of the meaning of this important term is left out of play.

10. E. D. Hirsch, *Validity in Interpretation* (New Haven: Yale University Press, 1967).

11. See also Hans-Georg Gadamer, *Truth and Method*, (New York: Seabury Press, 1975), p. 274. Heidegger's definition of "repetition" as "reciprocal rejoinder to" and "disavowal of" that which has been handed down constitutes the source of

Gadamer's "fusion of [historical and present] horizons (*Horizontverschmelzung*)." This relationship is developed at greater length in my essay "Postmodern Literature and the Hermeneutic Crisis," *Union Seminary Quarterly Review* 34: 2 (Winter 1979), pp. 119–31.

12. See Richard E. Palmer, *Hermeneutics: Interpretation Theory in Schleiermacher, Dilthey, Heidegger, and Gadamer* (Evanston, Ill.: Northwestern University Press, 1969), pp. 86–88, 118–21, 130–32. For the importance of Kierkegaard's critique of the aesthetic consciousness for Hans-Georg Gadamer's dialogic hermeneutics, see Gadamer, *Truth and Method*, pp. 85 ff. and 112 ff.

13. Søren Kierkegaard, *The Concept of Irony, with Constant Reference to Socrates*, trans. with introduction by Lee M. Capel (London: Collins, 1966), pp. 154–55.

14. Søren Kierkegaard, *Repetition: An Essay in Experimental Psychology*, trans. with introduction and notes by Walter Lowrie (New York: Harper Torchbooks, 1964), p. 33. See also Søren Kierkegaard, *Johannes Climacus or De Omnibus Dubitandum Est and a Sermon*, trans. with an assessment by T. H. Croxall (Stanford: Stanford University Press, 1958). In distinguishing between the Cartesian/Hegelian methodology of systematic doubt and existential doubt (and extending this distinction to include that between disinterestedness and interest and between recollection and repetition), Kierkegaard in this seminal work (unpublished in his lifetime) remarkably prefigures Husserl's and especially Heidegger's interpretations of the phenomenological reduction, the principle of intentionality (care), and the hermeneutic circle. See especially pp. 151–55.

15. See especially Eliade's account of the development of the primitive cyclical perspective, and its return to the timeless time (*in illo tempore*), into Plato's essentialist philosophy of Forms. *Cosmos and History: The Myth of the Eternal Return*, trans. Willard Trask (New York: Harper Torchbooks, 1959), pp. 34–35, 120–22.

16. Kierkegaard, *Repetition*, pp. 52–53. The emphasis is mine except for Kierkegaard's telling italicizing of both instances of the word "interest."

17. Kierkegaard, *Johannes Climacus*, pp. 151–52. T. H. Croxall misses the connection with Heidegger's *Dasein* in his otherwise helpful introductory commentary on Kierkegaard's "interest": "Philosophy 'abstracts' life from factuality in order to think about it, and in doing so it pushes its way into the abstract sphere of 'possibility' (the opposite of actuality). True philosophy uses both the terms 'possible' and 'actual,' but the actuality it deals with is really false because its content has been removed or 'annulled.' It is merely treated as something to be thought about idealistically and in the abstract. Such thinking is a dispassionate, disinterested process, involving no more than the Latin *interesse* in its root meaning of 'being between,' or being there. The 'existing individual,' on the other hand, is interested in the other sense of the Latin word, i.e., 'being concerned' " (p. 88).

18. Kierkegaard, *Repetition*, p. 131.

19. Søren Kierkegaard, *Either/Or: A Fragment of Life*, trans. David F. Swenson and Lillian Marvin Swenson (Princeton, N.J.: Princeton University Press, 1946), vol. 1, p. 31.

20. Kierkegaard, *Repetition*, pp. 133–34. The transitive use of the verb "to think" should not be overlooked.

21. "Editor's Introduction," *Repetition*, p. 4. The central importance that Kierkegaard attaches to the term "interest" (as opposed to "disinterest") and thus to existential repetition is made eminently clear not only in the polemic against Professor Heiberg's misunderstanding, which "occupies . . . 55 pages in Kierkegaard's papers" (the crucial passage of which Walter Lowrie has translated and quoted at length in his introduction), but also in *The Concept of Dread* (Princeton, N.J.:

Princeton University Press, 1957). In the latter, Vigilius Haufniensis, the pseudonymous author, quotes the crucial passage from *Repetition* to lend authority to his thesis that "Sin [an existential category] belongs to ethics [in this case a universal category] only insofar as upon this concept it [ethics] founders . . . ": In the process, he thematizes the significance that Heiberg fails to understand: " 'Repetition is the *interest* of metaphysics and at the same time the interest upon which metaphysics founders. Repetition is the solution in every ethical view [in this case an existential category]; repetition is a *conditio sine qua non* of every dogmatic problem.' The first sentence [in *Repetition* all this is one sentence] contains an allusion to the thesis that metaphysics is disinterested, as Kant affirmed of aesthetics. As soon as interest emerges, metaphysics steps to one side. For this reason the word 'interest' is italicized. The whole interest of subjectivity [the existential self] emerges in real life, and then metaphysics founders. In case repetition is not posited, ethics [like metaphysics] remains a binding power [a principle that objectifies and determines existence]; presumably it is for this reason he [Constantius] says that 'it is the solution in every ethical view.' . . . In the sphere of spirit . . . the problem is to transform repetition into something inward, into the proper task of freedom, into freedom's highest interest, as to whether, while everything changes, it can actually realize repetition. . . . All this Professor Heiberg has failed to observe" (pp. 16–17).

22. See note 21.

23. Søren Kierkegaard, *Either/Or*, trans. David F. Swenson, Lillian M. Swenson, and Walter Lowrie, with revisions by Howard A. Johnson (Garden City, N.Y.: Anchor Books, 1959), vol. 1, pp. 31–32. The identity of metaphysics and aestheticism assumes even greater significance when one considers the relationship between A's definition of recollection and Hegel's term *aufgehoben*, which Kierkegaard interprets as one of the central concepts of the Hegelian system. The word means "raised" or "taken up" but, as Robert Bretall points out in a note on its use by William Afham, the aesthete of Kierkegaard's *Stages on Life's Way*, "to render precisely its philosophical significance, we should have to say 'cancelled as a separate entity while preserved as part of a larger whole.' " *A Kierkegaard Anthology* (Princeton, N.J.: Princeton University Press, 1951), p. 189. Kierkegaard's interrogation of the Hegelian *Aufhebung*, that is, enables the postmodern critique of dialectical thought usually represented as passing from Heidegger to Derrida and the poststructuralists.

24. Louis Mackey, *Kierkegaard: A Kind of Poet* (Philadelphia: Pennsylvania University Press, 1971), p. 17.

25. Søren Kierkegaard, *Stages on Life's Way*, trans. Walter Lowrie (New York: Schocken Books, 1967). The quotations have been drawn from "The Prefatory Note" to "In Vino Veritas: A Recollection," pp. 27–36.

26. Kierkegaard, *Stages on Life's Way*, p. 29.

27. According to Kierkegaard, whose interpretation of Greek culture derives from the German (Romantic) classicist representation, Greek (Aristotelian) tragedy is one of the purest forms of aesthetic recollection. This is why, in a number of places in his work, notably in *Fear and Trembling*, he conceives it as a literary form that, like metaphysics, must be surpassed. In this he is at one with the postmodern literary imagination, which rejects tragedy—at least the modern representation of its form and function—on the grounds that its evasive circularity (i.e., spatial form) is an especially virulent form of humanistic anthropomorphism that gains distance from death and finitude—the principle of nothingness itself—by imposing a human

order on, and thus justifying in the teleology of form, what is in fact meaningless. This is implicit in the drama of the absurd, but receives theoretical expression in Robbe-Grillet, "Nature, Humanism, Tragedy," *For a New Novel: Essays on Fiction*, trans. Richard Howard (New York: Grove Press, 1963), pp. 49–75. This essay itself is an amplification of the following Brechtian epigraph from Roland Barthes: "Tragedy is merely a means of 'recovering' human misery, of subsuming and thereby justifying it in the form of necessity, a wisdom or a purification: to refuse this recuperation and to investigate the techniques of not treacherously succumbing to it (nothing is more insidious than tragedy) is today a necessary enterprise" (p. 49).

28. See my essays "Modern Literary Criticism and the Spatialization of Time: An Existential Critique," *Journal of Aesthetics and Art Criticism* 29 (Fall 1970), pp. 87–104; " 'Wanna Go Home, Baby?': *Sweeney Agonistes* as Drama of the Absurd," *PMLA* 85 (January 1970), pp. 8–20; "Modern Drama and the Aristotelian Tradition: The Formal Imperatives of Absurd Time," *Contemporary Literature* 12 (Summer 1971), pp. 345–73; "The Detective and the Boundary: Some Notes on the Postmodern Literary Imagination," *boundary 2* 1 (Fall 1972), pp. 147–68; rpr. in *Repetitions: The Postmodern Occasion in Literature and Culture* (Baton Rouge: Louisiana State University Press, 1987), pp. 13–49.

29. Stephen Crites, "Pseudonymous Authorship as Art and as Act," in Josiah Thompson, ed., *Kierkegaard: A Collection of Critical Essays* (New York: Anchor Books, 1972), p. 210.

30. Kierkegaard, *The Concept of Dread*: "Irony is free . . . from all cares of actuality . . . when one is free in this way, only then does one live poetically, and it is well-known that irony's great demand was that one should live poetically" (pp. 296–97). To avoid misleading the reader, since Kierkegaard is himself a supreme ironist, I should add that Kierkegaard distinguishes between the centerless kind he privileges, which he calls "mastered irony," and that "romantic irony" in this quotation, which he also calls "unmastered irony."

31. Kierkegaard, *Either/Or* (Princeton edition), vol. 1, p. 29. Note the similarity between the state of mind of Kierkegaard's aesthete (who spatializes according to an idealistic model) and that of Dostoevsky's "underground man," whose condition is the consequence of the circular perceptual imperatives of the dominant discourse of the "straightforward gentlemen" who spatialize time according to a positivistic model: "Then–it is still you [the 'straightforward gentlemen'] speaking—new economic relations will be established, all ready-made and computed with mathematical exactitude, so that every possible question will vanish in a twinkling, simply because every possible answer to it will be provided. Then the crystal palace will be built. Then—well, in short, those will be halcyon days. Of course there is no guaranteeing (this is my comment now) that it will not be, for instance, terribly boring then (for what will one have to do when everything is calculated according to the table?) but on the other hand everything will be extraordinarily rational. Of course boredom may lead you to anything. After all boredom sets one to sticking golden pins into people [the allusion is to Cleopatra's fondness for "sticking gold pins into her slave-girls' breasts and deriving enjoyment from their screams and writhing], but all that would not matter. What is bad (this is my comment again) is that for all I know people will be thankful for the golden pins then." In Fyodor Dostoevsky, *Notes from Underground and The Legend of the Grand Inquisitor*, trans. Ralph E. Matlaw (New York: E. P. Dutton, 1960) pp. 22–23.

32. Kierkegaard, *The Concept of Irony*, p. 308.

33. Ibid.
34. Ibid., pp. 311–12.
35. W. B. Yeats, "The Phases of the Moon," *Collected Poems* (New York: Macmillan, 1956), p. 162.
36. W. B. Yeats, "Byzantium," *Collected Poems*, p. 244. I read the last three lines of this stanza to be parallel with the preceding clause, which has the expressive word "break" as its predicate. The smithies and the marbles (the aesthetic recollection) thus "break" not only "bitter furies of complexity" (the imbalance or incommensurability of body and soul: the condition which precipitates anxiety [*Angst*] and is the source of motion, i.e., the existential or ek-sistential "self") but also "begotten" images and "that dolphin-torn, that gong-tormented sea," i.e., generative life in time.
37. Samuel Beckett, *Waiting for Godot* (New York: Grove Press, 1954), p. 7. This phrase constitutes the first speech of the play and occurs repeatedly throughout at precisely and ironically the point where the circular process returns to its starting point, *in illo tempore*, as it were. The "zero zone" is also the locus of Thomas Pynchon's *V.* and *Gravity's Rainbow*, postmodern novels that, like Beckett's plays and fiction, pursue the logical economy of the Modernist plenary circle to its emptied-out and contradictory end.
38. Samuel Beckett, "Ding-Dong," *More Pricks than Kicks* (New York: Grove Press, 1972), p. 31. The previous quotation is from *Purgatorio*, Canto IV, trans. Dorothy Sayers (Baltimore: Penguin Books, 1955). Dante finds Belacqua on the second ledge of Anti-Purgatory sitting in a fetal position under the shade of a massive boulder:

> "Oh good my lord," said I, "pray look at this
> Bone-lazy lad, content to sit and settle
> Like sloth's own brother taking of his ease!"
>
> Then he gave heed, and turning just a little
> only his face upon his thigh, he grunted:
> "Go up then, thou, thou mighty man of mettle."

Dante recognizes "sloth's own brother" as Belacqua by "the grudging speech, and slow / Gestures," and asks him "why dost thou resignedly / Sit there?" Belacqua answers in words that betray his indolent nature:

> "Brother," said he, "what use to go up?
> He'd not admit me to the cleansing pain,
> That bird of God who perches at the gate.
>
> My lifetime long the heavens must wheel again
> Round me, that to my parting hour put off
> My healing sighs; and I meanwhile remain
>
> Outside, unless prayer hastens my remove—
> Prayer from a heart in grace; for who sets store
> By other kinds, which are not heard above?"

Though Belacqua is in Anti-Purgatory, the reference to Sloth suggests that Beckett also has in mind Virgil's discourse on love—the true agency of motion—in which Sloth is the fourth of the seven evil modes of love, exactly between the triad of hate (Pride, Envy, Wrath)—the active absence of love—and the triad of excessive love of that which is good (Avarice, Gluttony, Lust). Thus Sloth is definable as dedifferentiation of the difference that makes a difference and the neutralization of motion.

39. The "transitional" voice in this "moral" history of circularity in the modern period is the "existential" T. S. Eliot, the Eliot of "The Love Song of J. Alfred Prufrock," *Sweeney Agonistes*, and above all the figure of Tiresias in *The Waste Land*. See my essays, "Repetition in *The Waste Land*: A Phenomenological De-struction," *boundary 2*, 7 (Spring 1979), pp. 225–85, and " 'Wanna Go Home, Baby?': *Sweeney Agonistes* as Drama of the Absurd," *PMLA* 85 (1970), pp. 8–30.

40. See Josiah Thompson, "The Master of Irony," *Kierkegaard: A Collection of Critical Essays*: "The task of the ironist, Kierkegaard suggests, is to master irony, indeed to overcome it [just as the task of the destructive phenomenologist for Heidegger is to "overcome" metaphysics]. And this stage of mastered irony is described in the final section of the dissertation as a stage where actuality is again actualized. 'Actuality will therefore not be rejected,' Kierkegaard writes, 'and longing shall be a healthy love, not a kittenish ruse for sneaking out of the world' " (p. 120). The quotation from *The Concept of Irony* occurs on p. 341.

41. Søren Kierkegaard, *Concluding Unscientific Postscript*, trans. David F. Swenson and Walter Lowrie (Princeton, N.J.: Princeton University Press, 1941), p. 547. In this appropriately titled text, the pseudonymous Johannes Climacus, in an appendix ("For an Understanding with the Reader"), writes that "everything [in the book] is so to be understood that it is understood to be revoked, and this book has not only a Conclusion but a Revocation." See also p. 548.

42. Crites, "Pseudonymous Authorship as Act and as Art," pp. 217–18. The quotation from Kierkegaard occurs in *Repetition*, p. 133. Like Pirandello's Manager in *Six Characters in Search of an Author* (another work that prefigures postmodernism), Constantine Constantius, the psychologist-observer, and other Kierkegaardian aesthetes, especially Johannes, the author of "Diary of the Seducer," take great pains to "arrange," to "plot," the unique and contingent lives of others into their recollections, their fictions orchestrated from the end. Kierkegaard also notes, in *The Concept of Irony*, the "poetic" Lisette's habit (in Schlegel's *Lucinde*) of referring to herself in the third person (which is equivalent to her furnishing of her luxurious room with mirrors that reflect her image from every angle) to objectify her "unmanageable" life: "When referring to her own person she usually called herself 'Lisette,' and often said that were she able to write she would then treat her story as though it were another's, although preferring to speak of herself in third person. This, evidently, was not because her earthly exploits were as world historical as a Caesar's. . . . It was simply because the weight of this *vita ante acta* was too heavy for her to bear. To come to herself concerning it, to allow its menacing shapes to pass judgment upon her, this would indeed be too serious to be poetical" (p. 311). It is precisely this representational aesthetic impulse to objectify absurd existence that Beckett and Pynchon, for example, raise havoc with in their postmodern novels. This representation, which is a reification and "setting before" of that which is unrepresentable, is the aesthetic equivalent of Heidegger's analysis of the metaphysical *Vorstellung*. See especially "The Age of the World Picture," trans. William Lovitt in *The Question Concerning Technology and Other Essays* (New York: Harper & Row, 1977), pp. 127 ff.

43. Crites, "Pseudonymous Authorship as Art and as Act," p. 218. The most significant difference between Kierkegaard and Heidegger resides primarily in their understanding of the self. Whereas Kierkegaard's tendency is to assume the ultimate self-presence of the "exceptional self," Heidegger, as I have suggested in my discussion of the forestructure that always already guides inquiry, problematizes its "my-ownness." For Kierkegaard, the subject tends to be an ontological subject; for Heidegger, it is always already an ontic/ontological subject: "The authentic

existentiell understanding is so far from extricating itself from the way of interpreting Dasein which has come down to us [the ontic], that in each case it is in
terms of this interpretation, against it, and yet again for it, that any possibility one
has chosen is seized upon in one's resolution" (BT, 74, 435; SZ, 383).

44. Søren Kierkegaard, *Stages on Life's Way*, trans. Walter Lowrie (Princeton, N.J.:
Princeton University Press, 1945), p. 314.

45. Crites, "Pseudonymous Authorship as Art and as Act," pp. 223–24.

46. This fundamental characteristic of Kierkegaard's art is virtually missed by Edith
Kern in her study of his "existential fiction" in *Existential Thought and Fictional
Techniques: Kierkegaard, Sartre, Beckett* (New Haven: Yale University Press, 1970).
Despite her valuable discussion of Kierkegaard's elaborate use of personae to
achieve distance from his characters, she fails to perceive the full implications of
his disavowal of their views—especially the views of his artists, which, as Josiah
Thompson observes, "if anything . . . are the views he has outlived or out-
thought" ("The Master of Irony," p. 112). She fails, in other words, to attend to
Kierkegaard's avowal at the end of *The Concept of Irony* that irony must be mastered
in behalf of the recovery of "actuality." Thus she sees his work as imperfect versions of the *Künstlerroman* of the German Romantic tradition, in which the artist-
hero transcends the messiness of temporal existence through the discovery of aesthetic form, i.e., an inclusive irony. In so doing, she makes Kierkegaard, despite
the imperfection of his form, a precursor of the epiphanic Modernist novel, of
Proust's *A la recherche du temps perdu*, of André Gide's *The Counterfeiters*, of James
Joyce's *Portrait of the Artist as a Young Man*, and even of Jean-Paul Sartre's *Nausea*:
what I have called the novel of spatial form. One is compelled to conclude that
Kern has read Kierkegaard's existentialist novel (and Sartre's, for that matter) from
a Modernist (Symbolist) perspective. See my essay, "The Un-Naming of the
Beasts: The Postmodernity of Sartre's *La Nausée*, *Criticism* 20 (Summer 1978), pp.
223–80; repr. *Repetitions*, pp. 51–106.

47. Wallace Stevens, "Notes Toward a Supreme Fiction," *Collected Poems*, (New York:
Alfred Knopf, 1961), p. 383.

48. Heidegger, *An Introduction to Metaphysics*, p. 32. This quotation is problematized
by its textual/historical context: Heidegger's disillusionment with Nazi practice
without a renunciation of his adherence to "the inner truth and greatness of the
[National Socialist] movement" (*Introduction*, p. 166) and the world-historical destiny of the German language. For my intervention in the debate over this sensitive
question, see chapter 6, "Heidegger, Nazism, and the 'Repressive Hypothesis.' " For
Heidegger's version of "repetition" as an aspect of the existential analytic (and for
its dialogic implications for hermeneutics), see especially BT, 73, 432; SZ, 380–81.

49. Gotthold Lessing, *Laocoön: An Essay upon the Limits of Painting and Poetry*, trans.
Ellen Frothingham (New York: Noonday Press, 1957), p. 91.

50. Joseph Frank, "Spatial Form in Modern Literature," *Sewanee Review* 53 (Spring,
Summer, Autumn 1945), pp. 221–40, 433–45, 643–65; rpr. in *The Widening Gyre:
Crisis and Mastery in Modern Literature* (New Brunswick, N.J.: Rutgers University
Press, 1963), pp. 3–62. The quotation from Lessing occurs on p. 7 of the latter.

51. Charles Olson, "The Human Universe," *Selected Writings*, ed. with introd. by
Robert Creeley (New York: New Directions, 1966), p. 54. The passage is worth
quoting in full to suggest the remarkable parallel between the postmodernism of
Heidegger and that of the contemporary poet: "We have lived long in a generalizing time, at least since 450 B.C. And it has had its effects on the best of men, on
the best of things. Logos, or discourse [he means the derivative language of asser-
tion], for example, has, in that time, so worked its abstractions into our concept

and use of language that language's other function, speech, seems so in need of restoration that several of us go back to hieroglyphics or to ideograms to right the balance." The distinction here is between language as the act of the instant and language as the act of thought about the instant.

52. Here I am taking exception to Jacques Derrida's and Paul de Man's interpretation of the historical relationship between speech (*parole*) and writing (*écriture*). Where they *emphasize* the speech act as the abiding purveyor of the principle of (self-) presence and the model of Western literature, I *emphasize* writing (in the sense of the spatialization of time), at least since the invention of the printing press. Ultimately, I agree with Derrida and de Man that speech itself is a writing. It is their characteristic universalization of the historically specific contexts of the speech/ writing opposition that I am objecting to. Whereas they call for the "free play" of *écriture* as the agency of surpassing metaphysics and metaphysical literature, I am suggesting with Heidegger in *Being and Time* and postmodern poets like Charles Olson and Robert Creeley that the modern occasion, which has privileged the printed Book as the agency of reproducing the dominant culture, demands the "grounding" of literary production in speech understood as the "act of an instant" of a being-in-the-world, as that temporally differential mode of discourse that resists the spatialization of time. Unlike the orality of, say, tribal ritual poetry, this kind of speech act, it must be emphasized, has its source not in presence (a substantial and self-identical self), but, as Heidegger insists in *Being and Time*, in nothingness, a groundless ground. I have vastly oversimplified a very complex issue. I refer to this issue here simply to point out that Derrida's and de Man's Heidegger is not the Heidegger of *Being and Time* but a Heidegger interpreted (or deconstructed) through the eyes of poststructuralist linguistics.

53. Gadamer, *Truth and Method*, pp. 330 ff., 344 ff., 487 ff. Indeed, this is the fundamental thesis of Gadamer's ironically entitled book. See also Richard Palmer, *Hermeneutics*, p. 168. It is especially the existential theologians—Karl Barth, Rudolph Bultmann, Paul Tillich, Ernst Fuchs, etc.—who have developed Heidegger's concept of care into a dialogic hermeneutics. See, for example, James Robinson, "Hermeneutics Since Barth," *The New Hermeneutic: New Frontiers in Theology, II* (New York: Harper & Row, 1964): "With the development of hermeneutics from Karl Barth's *Romans* to Bultmann's 'demythologizing,' the flow of the traditional relation between subject and object, in which the subject interrogates the object, and, if he masters it, obtains from it his answer, has been significantly reversed. For it is now the object—which should henceforth be called the subject matter—that puts the subject in question. This is true not simply at the formal level, in inquiring as to whether he understands himself aright, i.e., is serious, but also at the material level, in inquiring as to whether the text's answers illumine him" (pp. 23–24). One of the most suggestive theological accounts of the phenomenology of dialogue is to be found in Heinrich Ott, "Hermeneutics and Personhood," in *Interpretation: The Poetry of Meaning*, pp. 14–33. Based on his reading of Dietrich Bonhoeffer, Ott's essay also presents the hermeneutic situation generated by the transformation of picture into voice as risk: "It is not that I simply 'consume' his thought. . . . In this case I simply would not yet have understood. Rather, my notions change and are forced open, my presuppositions are modified and my horizon widened; I gain new dimensions of understanding and expression. It is precisely by putting at stake what I bring with me into the encounter that I myself am changed and am lifted above what I bring as my own" (pp. 23–24). This existential theological hermeneutics of the voice is vestigially logocentric, and thus has been surpassed. But it should not be forgotten, as unfortunately it has been in the aftermath of the post-

structuralist linguistic turn, that the dialogics it was committed to was a profound activism, as the role it played in the civil rights / antiwar movement of the 1960s bears witness.

4. The Indifference of Différance: Retrieving Heidegger's Destruction

1. Barbara Johnson, "Nothing Fails Like Success," in *World of Difference* (Baltimore: Johns Hopkins University Press, 1987), pp. 11–16. This essay, written for a session of the 1980 MLA meetings on "The Future of Deconstruction" sponsored by the Society for Critical Exchange, was originally published in *Deconstructive Criticism: Directions*, *SCE* 8 (Fall 1980), ed. Vincent B. Leitch. Since the publication of this piece, Johnson has attempted to harness deconstruction to sociopolitical questions (as some of the later essays in *World of Difference* make clear). But it is still the justification of deconstruction articulated in this essay that determines her effort. This is borne out by the privileged place she gives it in the volume. As she observes in a note to the reprinted text, "While I would want to argue some of the points a bit differently now (and perhaps with different examples), the basic thrust of the essay seems to me to be, if anything, even more relevant today" (p. 213). The following essay also had its origins in that MLA session. But it constitutes a much revised and greatly expanded version of that talk (also published in *Deconstructive Criticism: Directions*).

2. I am referring especially, though not exclusively, to those American critics, mostly followers of Derrida, who have appropriated deconstruction for literary criticism: most notably Paul de Man, J. Hillis Miller, Jonathan Culler, Joseph Riddel, and the legion of students they have trained. Among American followers of Derrida who escape in some degree the charge of blindness to the radical sociopolitical imperatives of deconstruction are Christopher Fynsk, *Heidegger: Thought and Historicity* (Ithaca, N.Y.: Cornell University Press, 1986); Rodolphe Gasché, *The Tain of the Mirror* (Cambridge, Mass.: Harvard University Press, 1996); Samuel Weber, *Institution and Interpretation* (Minneapolis: University of Minnesota Press, 1987); and especially Gayatri Spivak, *In Other Worlds: Cultural Politics* (New York: Routledge, 1988).

My use of the phrase "blindness of oversight" should not be confused with Paul de Man's "blindness of insight," which is essentially descriptive: it posits that blindness is intrinsic to inquiry and thus always already unavoidable. Without denying the validity of de Man's descriptive insight, my use of "blindness of oversight" is intended as an act of criticism. It derives from Louis Althusser's remarkably Heideggerian critique of the metaphysical vision that "Marxism" reinscribes into its interpretive discourse after Marx (and his development of the "problematic" and of "symptomatic reading"):

"Science: it can only pose problems on the terrain and within the horizon of a definite theoretical structure, its problematic, which constitutes its absolute and definite condition of possibility, and hence the absolute determination of *the forms in which all problems must be posed*, at any given moment in the science.

"This opens the way to an understanding of the determination of the *visible* as visible, and conjointly, of the invisible as invisible, and of the organic link binding the invisible to the visible. Any object or problem situated on the terrain and within the horizon, i.e., in the definite structured field of the theoretical problematic of a given theoretical discipline, is visible. We must take these words literally.

The sighting is thus no longer the act of an individual subject, endowed with the faculty of 'vision' which he exercises either attentively or distractedly; the sighting is the act of its structural conditions, it is the relation of immanent reflection between the field of the problematic and *its* objects and *its* problems. Vision then loses the religious privileges of divine reading: it is no more than a reflection of the immanent necessity that ties an object or problem to its conditions of existence, which lie in the conditions of its production. It is literally no longer the eye (the mind's eye) of a subject which *sees* what exists in the field defined by a theoretical problematic: it is this field itself which *sees itself* in the objects or problems it defines—sighting being merely the necessary reflection of the field on its objects. . . .

"The same connexion that defines the visible also defines the invisible as its shadowy obverse. It is the field of the problematic that defines and structures the invisible as the defined excluded, *excluded* from the field of visibility and *defined* as excluded by the existence and peculiar structure of the field of the problematic; as what forbids and represses the reflection of the field on its object, i.e., the necessary and immanent inter-relationship of the problematic and one of its objects. . . . These new objects and problems are necessarily *invisible* in the field of the existing theory, because they are not objects of this theory, because they are *forbidden* by it. . . . They are invisible because they are rejected in principle, repressed from the field of the visible: and that is why their fleeting presence in the field when it does not occur (in very peculiar and symptomatic circumstances) *goes unperceived*, and becomes literally an undivulgeable absence—since the whole function of the field is not to see them, to forbid any sighting of them." ("From *Capital* to Marx's Philosophy," in Louis Althusser and Etienne Balibar, *Reading Capital* (London: Verso, 1970), pp. 25–26.

3. Barbara Johnson, "Nothing Fails Like Success," p. 11. See, for example, Meyer Abrams, "The Deconstructive Angel," *Critical Inquiry* 3, (Spring 1977), pp. 425–38 and "How To Do Things with Texts," *Partisan Review* 46: 4 (1979); Wayne Booth, *Critical Understanding: The Powers and Limits of Pluralism* (Chicago: University of Chicago Press, 1979); Gerald Graff, *Literature Against Itself* (Chicago: University of Chicago Press, 1979); Denis Donaghue, "Deconstructing Deconstruction," *The New York Review of Books* 27: 10 (June 12, 1980), pp. 37–41 and *Ferocious Alphabets* (New York: Columbia University Press, 1981); Eugene Goodheart, *The Skeptical Disposition in Contemporary Criticism* (Princeton, N.J.: Princeton University Press, 1984); Jürgen Habermas, "Modernity Versus Postmodernity," *New German Critique* 22 (1981), pp. 3–14, and *The Philosophical Discourse of Modernity: Twelve Lectures*, trans. Frederick Lawrence (Cambridge, Mass.: MIT Press, 1987), pp. 161–84; John Ellis, *Against Deconstruction*; Walter Jackson Bate, "The Crisis in English Studies," *Harvard Magazine* 85 (September–October 1982); Allan Bloom, *The Closing of the American Mind: How Higher Education Has Failed Democracy and Impoverished the Souls of Today's Students* (New York: Simon and Schuster, 1987); Roger Kimball, *Tenured Radicals: How Politics Has Corrupted Our Higher Education* (New York: Harper & Row, 1990); and David Lehman, *Signs of the Times: Deconstruction and the Fall of de Man* (New York: Poseidon Press, 1991).
4. Barbara Johnson, "Nothing Fails Like Success," p. 14. For examples of this type of criticism, see especially Edward Said, "The Problem of Textuality: Two Exemplary Positions," *Critical Inquiry* 4 (Summer 1978), pp. 673–714 and "Reflections on Recent American 'Left' Literary Criticism," *boundary 2* 8: 1 (Fall 1979), pp. 11–30 (rpr. in *The World, the Text, and the Critic* (Cambridge, Mass.: Harvard University Press, 1983), pp. 158–77; Fredric Jameson, "The Ideology of the

Text," *Salmagundi* 31–32 (1976), pp. 204–46 and *The Political Unconscious: Narrative as a Socially Symbolic Act* (Ithaca, N.Y.: Cornell University Press, 1981); John Brenkman, "Deconstruction and the Social Text," *Social Text* 1 (Winter 1979), pp. 186–88; Paul Bové, "Variations on Authority: Some Deconstructive Transformations of the New Criticism, in *The Yale Critics: Deconstruction in America*, ed. Jonathan Arac, Wlad Godzich, and Wallace Martin (Minneapolis: University of Minnesota Press, 1983), pp. 3–19; Jonathan Arac, "To Regress from the Rigor of Shelley: Figures in History in American Deconstructive Criticism," *boundary 2* 8: 3 (Spring 1980), pp. 241–58; Donald Pease, "J. Hillis Miller: The Other Victorian at Yale," *The Yale Critics*, pp. 66–89; Frank Lentricchia, *After the New Criticism* (Chicago: University of Chicago Press, 1980); and Michael Sprinker, "Textual Politics: Foucault and Derrida," *boundary 2* 8: 3 (Spring 1980), pp. 75–98. Prodded by this criticism from the left—and by Derrida's reorientation of his discourse toward political questions (since "The Principle of Reason: The University in the Eyes of Its Pupils," *Diacritics* 13 [Fall 1983], pp. 3–20)—Anglo-American deconstructive critics have recently begun to tease out the "radical" political implications of deconstruction. But the effort, when it has not been essentially defensive, has not developed a deconstructive/political discourse adequate to the critique of the left. See, for example, Christopher Norris, *The Conflict of Faculties* (London: Methuen, 1985), and, especially, Jonathan Culler, *Framing the Sign: Criticism and Its Institutions* (Norman: Oklahoma University Press, 1988), where, for example, the politically emancipatory possibilities of deconstruction are implicitly pitted against Michel Foucault's analysis of power relations in modernity: "If one were casting around for the theorist who did most to indicate that criticism could *not* structurally or systematically be an instrument of liberation, one might well pick the late Foucault, for whom apparently oppositional practices belong to the network of power: regulation masks itself by producing discourse which is apparently opposed to it but sustains the network of power. 'Power is tolerable,' he writes, 'only on condition that it mask a substantial part of itself. Power needs domains which seem outside power and which thereby serve it.' . . . This difficulty is not just an accident; it is tied to the most revolutionary contributions of his thinking about power" (p. 65). The assumption determining this critique is the characteristically deconstructionist reduction of historically specific power relations by raising power to transcendental status: power always already equals power. For Culler, as for the liberal humanists he ostensibly opposes, there is no distinction between those who have it and those who don't in any particular historical occasion. For Foucault, and for those critics of the left who follow him (the real target of Culler's criticism), power is indeed everywhere, but *in the world* it is also always unevenly distributed.

5. Martin Heidegger, "The Age of the World Picture," *The Question Concerning Technology and Other Essays*, trans. William Lovitt (New York: Harper & Row, 1977), pp. 115–54.

6. I am referring to the binary logic that informs Matthew Arnold's *Culture and Anarchy* (1869), the text, more than any other, that constitutes the enabling ground of modern humanistic criticism from Lionel Trilling through F. R. Leavis to those recent critics referred to above who have engaged deconstructive criticism in the name of interpretive decidability—and civilization. For an extended critique of Arnold's humanistic discourse undertaken from a destructive perspective, see the chapter entitled "The Apollonian Investment of Modern Humanist Education: The Examples of Matthew Arnold, Irving Babbitt, and I. A. Richards," in my *The End of Education: Toward Posthumanism* (Minneapolis: University of Minnesota Press, 1993).

7. Martin Heidegger, "Introduction II: The Twofold Task in Working Out the Question of Being: Method and Design of Our Investigation," *Being and Time*, trans. Joan Stambaugh, in *Basic Writings*, ed. Joseph Farrell Krell (New York: Harper & Row, 1977), pp. 67–68. The emphasis in the last paragraph is mine. I have used Stambaugh's translation in this instance rather than that of John Macquarrie and Edward Robinson, *Being and Time* (New York: Harper and Row, 1962), pp. 44–45, because of its more incisive foregrounding of the key terms of the definition of *Destruktion*. Henceforth I will refer to the latter except when recalling this passage.

8. Jacques Derrida, "Structure, Sign and Play in the Discourse of the Human Sciences," *Writing and Difference*, trans. Alan Bass (Chicago: University of Chicago Press, 1978), p. 279. See also "Plato's Pharmacy," *Disseminations*, trans. Barbara Johnson (Chicago: University of Chicago Press, 1981), pp. 63–172.

9. Derrida, "Structure, Sign and Play," p. 289.

10. See especially Derrida, "White Mythology: Metaphor in the Text of Philosophy," *Margins of Philosophy*, trans. Alan Bass (Chicago: University of Chicago Press, 1982), pp. 207–72; and "Force and Signification," *Writing and Difference*, trans. Alan Bass (Chicago: University of Chicago Press, 1978), pp. 3–30.

11. Derrida, "Structure, Sign and Play," p. 289.

12. Jacques Derrida, *Of Grammatology*, trans. Gayatri Spivak (Baltimore: Johns Hopkins University Press, 1976), p. 158. For Paul de Man, creative writing, unlike commentary about it, is self-consciously demystified from the start and exists to deconstruct the mystified expectations of the logocentric reader: "All literatures, including the literature of Greece, have always designated themselves as existing in the mode of fiction . . . when modern critics think they are demystifying literature, they are in fact being demystified by it." *Blindness and Insight: Essays in the Reading of Contemporary Criticism* (New York: Oxford University Press, 1971), pp. 102–4.

13. *Of Grammatology*, p. 158. Christopher Norris in *Derrida* (Cambridge, Mass.: Harvard University Press, 1987) insists on this moment in Derrida's text against those, especially literary deconstructors and the detractors of deconstruction who have taken Derrida's disclosure of indeterminacy as a license to say anything about a text: "As I have argued already—and will argue again—deconstruction is ill-served by those zealots of a limitless textual 'freeplay' who reject the very notions of rigorous thinking or conceptual critique. It is a premise of this book that the central issues of deconstruction can be set forth and defended in such a way as to engage the serious interest of philosophers in the 'other,' Anglo-American or analytic tradition" (p. 27). But, not accidentally, Norris's focus is not on the ideological specificity of "the conscious, voluntary, intentional relationship" between the writer and "the history to which he belongs," but on intellectually rigorous pursuit of the traditional logic, which alone can validate its aporetic essence.

14. Derrida, *Of Grammatology*, p. 158.

15. See especially Derrida, "The Principle of Reason: The University in the Eyes of Its Pupils," trans. Catherine Porter and Edward P. Morris, *Diacritics* 13: 3 (Fall 1983), pp. 3–20; "Racism's Last Word," trans. Peggy Kamuf, *Critical Inquiry* 12 (Autumn 1985), pp. 290–99; "But, beyond . . . An Open Letter to Anne McClintock and Rob Nixon," *Critical Inquiry* 13 (Autumn 1986), pp. 140–70; and "Force of Law: The Mystical Foundation of Authority," trans. Mary Quaintance, in a special issue on "Deconstruction and the Possibility of Justice," *Cardozo Law Review* 2 (July/August 1990), pp. 919–1045.

16. J. Hillis Miller, "Tradition and Difference," *Diacritics* 2: 4 (Winter 1972), p. 12.

17. Derrida, "Structure, Sign, and Play," p. 279. My emphasis. "Anxiety," it needs to

be recalled in the face of the persistent neglect of this crucial moment in Derrida's text by those whom J. Hillis Miller calls the "uncanny critics," is precisely the mood of being-in-the-world that, unlike fear, according to Heidegger, has no thing as its object: the nothing (*das Nichts*), which (as temporality in *Being and Time*) is the condition for the possibility of something. See chapter 3, "Heidegger, Kierkegaard, and the Hermeneutic Circle."

18. Derrida, *Of Grammatology*, p. 159. My emphasis.
19. Barbara Johnson, "Nothing Fails Like Success," p. 13.
20. Michael Sprinker, "Textual Politics: Foucault and Derrida," p. 92.
21. Jonathan Culler, *On Deconstruction: Theory and Criticism after Structuralism* (Ithaca, N.Y.: Cornell University Press, 1982), p. 109–110. My emphasis.
22. Edward Said, "Reflections on Recent American 'Left' Literary Criticism," p. 27. See also Pierre Macherey, *A Theory of Literary Production*, trans. Geoffrey Wall (London: Routledge and Kegan Paul, 1978): "the ideological background, which constitutes the real support of all forms of expression and all ideological manifestations, is fundamentally silent—one might say unconscious. But it must be emphasized that this unconscious is not a silent knowledge, but a total misrecognition of itself. If it is silent, it is silent on that about which it has nothing to say. We should therefore preserve the expression in all its ambiguity: it refers to that ideological horizon which conceals only because it is interminable, because there is always something more, but it refers also to that abyss over which ideology is built. Like a planet revolving round an absent sun, an ideology is made of what it does not mention: it exists because there are things which must not be spoken of. This is the sense in which Lenin can say that "Tolstoy's silences are eloquent" (pp. 131–32).

    In invoking Said's Gramscian notion of "affiliation," I do not want to suggest that such a politically left version of the critique of ideology supersedes Heidegger's destructive discourse. For, as I will show at length in the next chapter, "Heidegger, Foucault, and the Politics of the Gaze," the failure of these "worldly critics," as Edward Said calls them, to acknowledge the ontological question—specifically, to admit ontological determination as an ideological register—in their ontic critique of capitalism or the disciplinary or hegemonic society is, in the context of contemporary power relations, as limiting for critique as Heidegger's minimization of ontic (sociopolitical) determinations.

23. Jacques Derrida, "White Mythology," *Margins of Philosophy*, trans. Alan Bass (Chicago: University of Chicago Press, 1982), p. 268.
24. Ibid., p. 269. In identifying the metaphorics of the rising and setting sun with the East and the West respectively, Derrida is alluding to Hegel, "Introduction," *Lectures on the Philosophy of History*, trans. J. Sibree (New York: Colonial Press, 1900), pp. 109–110. The quotes, however, are from Rousseau, *Essay on the Origin of Language*, trans. John Moran (New York: Frederick Ungar, 1966), pp. 12 and 11.
25. Derrida, "La parole soufflée," *Writing and Difference*, p. 178.
26. Derrida, "White Mythology," p. 267.
27. See Edward Said, "The Problem of Textuality: Two Exemplary Positions," pp. 678 ff. See also Jacques Derrida, *Of Grammatology*: "The names of authors or of doctrines have here no substantial value. They indicate neither identities nor causes. It would be frivolous to think that 'Descartes,' 'Leibniz,' 'Rousseau,' 'Hegel,' etc., are names of authors, of the authors of movements or displacements that we thus designate. The indicative value that I attribute to them is first the name of a problem. If I provisionally authorize myself to treat this historical struc-

ture by fixing my attention on philosophical or literary texts, it is not for the sake of identifying in them the origin, cause, or equilibrium of the structure. But as I also do not think that these texts are the simple *effects* of structure, in any sense of the word; as I think that *all concepts hitherto proposed in order to think the articulation of a discourse and of an historical totality are caught within the metaphysical closure that I question here*, as we do not know of any other concepts and cannot produce any others, and indeed shall not produce so long as this closure limits our discourse; as the primordial and indispensable phase, in fact and in principle, of the development of this problematic, consists in questioning the internal structure of these texts as symptoms; as that is the only condition for determining these symptoms *themselves* in the totality of their metaphysical appurtenance; I draw my argument from them in order to isolate Rousseau and, in Rousseauism, the theory of writing" (p. 99). Derrida's emphasis.

28. This is Hegel's oblique (metaphorical) reference to the dialectics of the *Aufhebung*: "Here [in the East] rises the outward physical Sun, and in the West it sinks down: here consentaneously rises the Sun of self-consciousness, which diffuses a nobler brilliance. The History of the World is the discipline of the uncontrolled natural will, bringing it into obedience to a Universal principle and conferring subjective freedom," *Lectures on the Philosophy of History*, pp. 109–110; quoted in Derrida, "White Mythology," p. 269.

29. See chapters 5 and 6.

30. Barbara Johnson, "Nothing Fails Like Success," pp. 15–16. Johnson is clearly invoking and amplifying Derrida's reference to "*surprise*" in his excursus, the "Question of Method," in *Of Grammatology*: "This brings up the question of the usage of the word 'supplement': of Rousseau's situation within the language and the logic that assures to this word or this concept sufficiently *surprising* resources so that the presumed subject of the sentence might always say, through using the 'supplement,' more, less, or something other than what he *would mean [voudrait dire]*. This question is therefore not only of Rousseau's writing but also of our reading. We should begin by taking rigorous account of this *being held within [prise] or this surprise*: the writer writes *in* a language" (p. 158).

31. For a fully developed example of destructive criticism that historically situates the kind of ideological power inhering in a logocentric text and its institutional affiliations, see the chapter entitled "Percy Lubbock and the Craft of Supervision," in my *Repetitions: The Postmodern Occasion in Literature and Culture* (Baton Rouge: Louisiana State University Press, 1987), pp. 149–88.

32. Miguel de Cervantes, *Don Quixote*, trans. J. M. Cohen (Harmondsworth, England: Penguin, 1950), p. 531. For an amplification of this point, see "Postmodern Literature and Its Occasion: Retrieving the Preterite Middle," in my *Repetitions*, pp. 268–70.

33. Michel Foucault, "Mon corps, ce papier, ce feu," *Histoire de la folie à l'age classique* (Paris: Editions Gallimard, 1972), p. 602. My translation. See also Edward Said, "The Problem of Textuality," pp. 700–701.

34. Edward Said, "The Problem of Textuality," pp. 700–701. The first emphasis is mine.

35. Barbara Johnson, "Nothing Fails Like Success," p. 14.

36. In referring to the feminist/Marxist exception, I am not unmindful of a certain neo-Marxist sociopolitical criticism in which deconstruction plays an important part—for example, that of Ernesto Laclau and Chantal Mouffe in *Hegemony and Social Strategy* (London: Verso, 1987). There is, however, a crucial difference between the two. Whereas the former accommodates feminist criticism and

neo-Marxism to deconstruction, the latter accommodates deconstruction to neo-Marxism.

37. Christopher Norris, *Derrida* (Cambridge, Mass.: Harvard University Press, 1987), pp. 94–95.

38. Raymond Williams, *Marxism and Literature* (New York: Oxford University Press, 1977), pp. 77.

39. Michel Foucault, *Histoire de la folie*, p. 602. Quoted in Edward Said, "The Problem of Textuality," p. 702. My translation.

40. Barbara Johnson, "Nothing Fails Like Success," p. 14. For a powerful complementary analysis of the failure of deconstructive critics to examine the institutional conditions of possibility of their own "adversarial" discourses and thus their complicity with their "adversaries" (the New Critics) in a "self-preserving act which . . . fuels the institution with its own impotence" (p. 6), see Paul Bové, "Variations on Authority: Some Deconstructive Transformations of the New Criticism," *The Yale Critics: Deconstruction in America*, ed. Jonathan Arac, Wlad Godzich, Wallace Martin (Minneapolis: University of Minnesota Press, 1983), pp. 3–19; reprinted in *Mastering Discourse: The Politics of Intellectual Culture* (Durham, N.C.: Duke University Press, 1992) pp. 47–64.

41. Jacques Derrida, "Entre crochets: Entretien premiere partie," *Digraphe* 8 (April 1976), 113. My emphasis. I am indebted to Christopher Fynsk for bringing this interview to my attention, though I read its "politics" differently from the way he does in "A Deceleration of Philosophy," *Diacritics* 8 (Summer 1978), 80–90, which reviews GREPH'S *Qui a peur de la philosophie?* See also Derrida, *Positions*, trans. Alan Bass (Chicago: University of Chicago Press, 1981).

42. *The Oxford Dictionary of English Etymology*, ed. C. T. Onions (Oxford: Clarendon Press, 1966), p. 916. For a reading of the relation between the Greek *theoría* and *théa* that distinguishes the "look" to which these Greek words refer in terms of an earlier "encountering look" and a later "grasping look," see Martin Heidegger, *Parmenides*, trans. André Schuwer and Richard Rojcewicz (Bloomington: Indiana University Press, 1992), pp. 107–10, 144–51.

43. James Joyce, *A Portrait of the Artist as a Young Man*, ed. Chester F. Anderson (New York: Viking, 1965), p. 215. The phrase "spatial form of *rendered* drama" brings together Henry James's apotheosis of the novel as a "showing," Percy Lubbock's appropriation of James in behalf of a theory of the novel and of interpretation as "spectacle," and Joseph Frank's definition of Modernism, partially indebted to James and Lubbock, as "spatial form." As the latter puts it in his extraordinarily influential essay "Spatial Form in Modern Literature," *Sewanee Review* 53 (Spring, Summer, Autumn 1945): "Aesthetic form in modern poetry, then, is based on a space logic that demands a complete re-orientation in the reader's attitude towards language. Since the primary reference of any word-group is to something inside the poem itself, language, in modern poetry is really reflexive: the meaning-relationship is completed only by the simultaneous perception in space of word-groups which, when read consecutively in time, have no comprehensible relations to each other. Instead of the instinctive and immediate reference of word and word-groups to the objects or events they symbolize, and the construction of meaning from the sequence of their reference, modern poetry asks its readers to suspend the process of individual reference temporarily until the entire pattern of internal references can be apprehended in a unity" (pp. 229–30).

44. Martin Heidegger, "Introduction II," *Being and Time*, in *Basic Writings*, pp. 65–66.

45. Martin Heidegger, *Introduction to Metaphysics*, trans. Ralph Mannheim (Garden City, N.Y.: Anchor Books, 1961), pp. 12–14.

46. Martin Heidegger, "Introduction II," *Being and Time*, in *Basic Writings*, p. 66.

47. See especially Jean-François Lyotard, *Heidegger et "les juifs"* (Paris: Galilee, 1988) and Philippe Lacoue-Labarthe, *La fiction du politique: Heidegger, l'art et la politique* (Paris: Christian Bourgois, 1987). Lyotard's criticism of Heidegger's failure to think the forgetting is categorical. Unlike Lacoue-Labarthe, he refuses to allow its historically specific European context to intervene in his indictment of Heidegger's failure to think the forgetting adequately.

48. Martin Heidegger, *Letter on Humanism*, trans. Frank A. Capuzzi, in *Basic Writings*: "The widely and rapidly spreading devastation of language not only undermines aesthetic and moral responsibility in every use of language; it arises from a threat to the essence of humanity. . . . Much bemoaned of late, and much too lately, the downfall of language is, however, not the grounds for, but already a consequence of, the state of affairs in which language under the dominance of the modern metaphysics of subjectivity almost irremediably falls out of its element. Language still denies us its essence: that it is the house of the truth of being. Instead, language surrenders itself to our mere willing and trafficking as an instrument of domination over beings," pp. 198–99.

49. Martin Heidegger, "The Age of the World Picture," *The Question Concerning Technology and Other Essays*, pp. 115–54.

50. Martin Heidegger, "The End of Philosophy and the Task of Thinking," *On Time and Being*, trans. Joan Stambaugh (New York: Harper & Row, 1972), pp. 58–59. My emphasis. See also "The Question Concerning Technology" and "The Age of the World Picture," in *The Question Concerning Technology*, pp. 3–35; 115–54. As we shall see in the next chapter, Heidegger in "Letter on Humanism" and the *Parmenides* lectures, will develop the sociopolitical implications of the "Roman reference"—the literal imperialist imperative informing the West's appropriation of the Roman tradition, which, according to Heidegger, founds itself on the epochal reduction of Greek *aletheia* to *veritas* (*adequaetio intellectus et rei*).

51. Edward Said, *Orientalism* (New York: Pantheon, 1978), p. 3.

52. Hans-Georg Gadamer, *Truth and Method*, trans. and ed. by Garrett Barden and John Cumming from the second (1965) edition of *Wahrheit und Methode* (New York: The Seabury Press, 1975): "Every finite present has its limitations. We define the concept of 'situation' by saying that it represents a standpoint that limits the possibility of vision. Hence an essential part of the concept of situation is the concept of 'horizon.' The horizon is the range of vision that includes everything that can be seen from a particular vantage point. Applying this to the thinking mind, we speak of narrowness of horizon, of the possible expansion of horizon, of the opening up of new horizons, etc. The word has been used in philosophy since Nietzsche and Husserl to characterise the way in which thought is tied to its finite determination and the nature of the law of the expansion of the range of vision," p. 269. Gadamer's definition of "horizon" is, I think, a translation of Heidegger's existential analytic of the temporal ek-stasies of *Dasein* in *Being and Time*.

53. It could be said that Heidegger's limitation of inquiry *in practice* to the ontological (the question of being) is corrected by Foucault's and Said's ontic orientation. But it could also be said that Foucault's and Said's limitation of inquiry *in practice* to the ontic (the question of power relations in the sociopolitical sphere) is corrected by Heidegger's ontological orientation, insofar as the former is not ontologically justified. This effort to read Heidegger with Foucault and Foucault with Heidegger, i.e., to "reconcile" destruction and genealogy, will be undertaken in chapter 5.

54. Louis Althusser, "Ideology and Ideological State Apparatuses (Notes Toward an

Investigation)," *Lenin and Philosophy and Other Essays*, trans. Ben Brewster (New York: Monthly Review Press, 1971), pp. 162 ff.

55. Jacques Derrida, "The Ends of Man," *Margins*, pp. 109–36. This essay, not incidentally, begins with a political statement disavowing any tacit affiliation with the official foreign policy of the United States vis-à-vis Vietnam that might be implied by participation in such a congress. However, since it undertakes a critique of Jean-Paul Sartre's existential appropriation of Heidegger's thought and, centrally, of Heidegger's alleged recuperation of "the old metaphysical humanism" (p. 119), the essay ends paradoxically in an implicit delegitimation of the most influential theoretical source of the protest movement in this country. This is not to say that Derrida should have refrained from pursuing his critique of Heidegger's understanding of "authenticity" in *Being and Time* and the existentialist appropriation of Heidegger's thought at this congress. It is to say, rather, that his failure on this politically charged occasion to acknowledge the positive role that the existentialist appropriation of Heidegger's thought played in energizing the American protest movement is a measure of the ahistorical tendencies of his own appropriation of the Heideggerian destruction.

56. Jacques Derrida, "The Ends of Man," *Margins*, p. 124. See also "*Ousia* and *Grammé*: A Note on a Note from *Being and Time*," *Margins*, pp. 63–64; and *Positions*, pp. 129–64.

57. Derrida, "The Ends of Man," *Margins*, pp. 127–28. My emphasis.

58. Ibid., p. 130. My emphasis.

59. For an extended account of this reduction of Derrida's ("Heideggerian") understanding of textuality, see Rodolphe Gasché, "Deconstruction as Criticism," *Glyph 6* (Baltimore: Johns Hopkins University Press, 1981), pp. 177–215. See also Gasché, *The Tain of the Mirror: Derrida and the Philosophy of Reflection* (Cambridge, Mass.: Harvard University Press, 1988), pp. 255–70.

60. Martin Heidegger, "Introduction II," *Being and Time*, in *Basic Writings*, pp. 68–69.

61. Jacques Derrida, "*Ousia* and *Grammé*," in *Margins*, pp. 29–68.

62. Martin Heidegger, *Being and Time*, p. 310. See also "What Is Metaphysics?," trans. David Farrell Krell in *Basic Writings*, pp. 91–111, where Heidegger deconstructs the logic of "science"—its commitment to "something"—and discloses the (anxiety-provoking) nothing which is not simply the condition of its possibility but also that which science exists to domesticate: "But what is remarkable is that, precisely in the way scientific man secures to himself what is most properly his, he speaks of something different. What should be examined are beings only, and besides that—nothing; beings alone, and further—nothing; solely beings, and beyond that—nothing.

What about this nothing? The nothing is rejected precisely by science, given up as a nullity. But when we give up the nothing in such a way don't we just concede it? . . . If science is right, then only one thing is sure: science wishes to know nothing of the nothing. Ultimately this is the scientifically rigorous conception of the nothing. We know it, the nothing, in that we wish to know nothing about it.

Science wants to know nothing of the nothing. But even so it is certain that when science tries to express its proper essence it calls upon the nothing for help. It has recourse to what it rejects" (pp. 97–98).

63. Jacques Derrida, "*Ousia* and *Grammé*": "The concept of time, in all its aspects, belongs to metaphysics, and it names the domination of presence. Therefore we can only conclude that the entire system of metaphysical concepts, throughout its history, develops the so-called vulgarity of the concept of time (which Heidegger,

doubtless, would not contest) but also that an *other* concept of time cannot be opposed to it, since time in general belongs to metaphysical conceptuality. In attempting to produce this *other* concept, one rapidly would come to see that it is constructed out of other metaphysical or ontotheological predicates.

Was this not Heidegger's experience in *Being and Time*? The extraordinary trembling to which classical ontology is subjected in *Sein und Zeit* still remains within the grammar and lexicon of metaphysics. And all of the conceptual pairs of opposites which serve the destruction of ontology are ordered around one fundamental axis: that which separates the authentic from the inauthentic and, in the last analysis, primordial from fallen temporality" (p. 63). Here again, not incidentally, Derrida reads the metaphorics of proximity literally as spatial distance.

64. Martin Heidegger, "What Is Metaphysics?," *Basic Writings*, p. 103.

65. Again: "The authentic existentiell understanding is so far from extricating itself from this way of interpreting Dasein which has come down to us, that in each case it is in terms of this interpretation, against it, and yet again for it, that it seizes the chosen possibility in the resolution" (BT, 435; SZ, 383). See also Christopher Fynsk, *Heidegger: Thought and Historicity*, p. 112.

66. Jacques Derrida, "The Ends of Man," *Margins*, p. 126. One of the great ironies of Derrida's choice to emphasize Heidegger's vestigial metaphysics over his antimetaphysics, and its complicity with an "entire metaphorics of proximity, of simple and immediate presence" (which is also a system of values associated with the German *Volk*) is that it lends itself inadvertently to the recuperative anthropological project of those who, since the publication of Victor Farías's *Heidegger et le nazisme*, have gone all out to identify Heidegger's philosophical discourse at large with Nazism. To be more specific, Derrida's focus, in his reading of Heidegger's texts, on that aspect which justifies his substitution of *differance* for the ontological difference (textuality for being) is at one with, if far more nuanced than, that of humanists such as Arnold Davidson ("Questions Concerning Heidegger: Opening the Debate," *Critical Inquiry* 15 [Winter 1989], pp. 407–26), Richard Wolin (*The Politics of Being: The Political Thought of Martin Heidegger* [New York: Columbia University Press, 1990]), and Tom Rockmore (*On Heidegger's Nazism and Philosophy* [Berkeley: University of California Press, 1992]), who, in order to prove that Heidegger's Nazism was absolutely intrinsic to his concern with the *Seinsfrage* and thus abiding, have represented Heidegger's destructive interpretation of being precisely as the Being that it was Heidegger's insistent purpose to destroy: the Being that, whatever its particular representation in the ontotheological tradition, finally annuls human agency in favor of service to it.

67. See, for example, one of the passages Derrida quotes from "Letter on Humanism" (Krell, ed., *Basic Writings*, pp. 211–12): "Because man as the one who ek-sists comes to stand in this relation that Being destines (*schickt*) for itself, in that he ecstatically sustains it, that is, in care takes it upon himself, he at first fails to recognize the nearest (*das Nächste*) and attaches himself to the next nearest (*das Übernächste*). He even thinks that this is the nearest. But nearer than the nearest and at the same time for ordinary thinking farther than the farthest is *nearness* itself: the truth of Being." "The Ends of Man," *Margins*, p. 131.

68. The reading of Heidegger's metaphorics of nearness I have all too briefly sketched here is developed at length in chapter 6, this time in the context of the question of the relationship between the "metaphorics of proximity" and Heidegger's politics.

69. Martin Heidegger, "Words," *On the Way to Language* (New York: Harper & Row), p. 142.

70. Martin Heidegger, *Discourse on Thinking* (originally published under the title *Gelassenheit*), trans. John M. Anderson and E. Hans Freund (New York: Harper Torchbooks, 1966), p. 69.
71. Heidegger, *Discourse on Thinking*, p. 69. My emphasis.
72. Martin Heidegger, "The Question Concerning Technology," in *The Question Concerning Technology*: "It is in the sense of such a starting something on its way into arrival that being responsible is an occasioning or an inducing to go forward [*Ver-an-lassen*]. On the basis of a look at what the Greeks experienced in being responsible, in *aitia*, we now give this verb 'to occasion' a more inclusive meaning, so that it now is the name for the essence of causality thought as the Greeks thought it. The common and narrower meaning of 'occasion' in contrast is nothing more than striking against and releasing, and means a kind of secondary cause within the whole of causality" (pp. 9–10). As the translator observes, "*Ver-an-lassen* is Heidegger's writing of the verb *veranlassen* in noun form, now hyphenated to bring out its meaning. *Veranlassen* ordinarily means to occasion, to cause, to bring about, to call forth. Its use here relates back to the use of *anlassen* (to leave [something] on, to let loose, to set going), here translated 'to start something on its way.' *Anlassen* has just been similarly written as *an-lassen* so as to emphasize its composition from *lassen* (to let or leave) and *an* (to or towards). One of the functions of the German prefix *ver-* is to intensify the force of a verb. André Preau quotes Heidegger as saying: "*Ver-an-lassen* is more active than *an-lassen*. The *ver-*, as it were, pushes the latter towards a doing [*vers un faire*].' Cf. Martin Heidegger, *Essais et Conférences* (Paris: Gallimard, 1958), p. 16 n." If it is remembered that the distinction Heidegger makes between "occasioning" and "cause" is determined by *Dasein*'s *finite* being-in-the-world, we are justified, as I am doing here, in leaping across his terms to think Heidegger's distinction in terms of the Latin derivation of the English translation (from *cadere*: to fall, to perish). For the wider and deeper implications of this extension, see pp. 118–19.
73. Jacques Derrida, "*Ousia* and *Grammé*": "The displacement, a certain lateralization, if not a simple erasure of the theme of time and of everything that goes along with it in *Being and Time*, lead one to think that Heidegger, without putting back into question the necessity of a certain point of departure in metaphysics, and even less the efficacy of the "destruction" operated by the analytic of *Dasein*, for essential reasons had to go at it otherwise and, it may be said literally, to *change horizons*.

   "Henceforth, along with the theme of time, all the themes that are dependent upon it (and, par excellence, those of *Dasein*, of finitude, of historicity [in *Being and Time*]) will no longer constitute the transcendental horizon of the question of Being, but in transition will be reconstituted on the basis of the theme of the epochality of Being" (p. 64).
74. Martin Heidegger, "The Origin of the Work of Art," *Poetry, Language, Thought*, trans. Albert Hofstadter (New York: Harper & Row, 1971), p. 49. I have elsewhere invoked Fredric Jameson's appropriation of Heidegger's notion of the "rift" for his neo-Marxist discourse. See "Postmodern Literature and Its Occasion," *Repetitions*, pp. 274–75. Because Jameson interprets the metaphorics of "distance" in a "post-*Kehre*" text in a way that is radically different from Derrida's, it is worth repeating his reading for the light it throws on this occasion: "Heidegger . . . describes the effect and function of the 'authentic' work of art as the inauguration of a 'rift' between what he calls World and Earth—what we can rewrite in other language as the dimensions of History and the social project on the one hand, and Nature or matter on the other, ranging from geographical or ecological constraint all the way to the individual body. The force of Heidegger's description lies in the way in

which *the gap between these two dimensions is maintained*; the implication is that we all live in both dimensions at once, in some irreconcilable simultaneity. . . . We are at all moments in history and in matter; we are at one and the same time historical beings and 'natural' ones, living in the meaning-endowment of the historical project and the meaninglessness of organic life [read 'temporality'], *without any ultimate 'synthesis' between these two dimensions ever being possible or conceivable.* The Heideggerian formula thus *repudiates any such conception of a possible synthesis between History and Nature* (such syntheses are called 'metaphysics'), and at one and the same time repudiates a conception of the work of art which would aim at reuniting both symbolically, under some repression of History by Nature, or the reverse. The work of art can therefore *never heal this fundamental 'distance'*; but it can do something else, and better—it can stage the very tension between the two dimensions in such a way that we are made to live *within* that tension and to affirm its reality." "Interview," *Diacritics* 12 (Fall 1982), p. 136. My emphasis, except for "within."

In thus identifying Heidegger's understanding of the work of art as always instigating a rift between world and earth with Jameson's neo-Marxism, I am taking issue with Philippe Lacoue-Labarthe, who represents Heidegger's post-*Kehre* commitment to a "Greek" version of *Dichtung* as a continuous moment in a German "*national esthetisme*" deriving from the Greeks that culminates in the Nazis' identification of (Greek) art and the organic German *polis*. *La Fiction du politique: Heidegger, l'art et la politique* (Paris: Christian Bourgois, 1987), pp. 82 ff. It is true that Heidegger envisaged a German *polis* structured on the Greek model, in which the work of art and political community are continuous. As I will suggest in chapters 5 and 6, however, Heidegger explicitly disavows the German "classical Greek" tradition with which Lacoue-Labarthe identifies his discourse, because this tradition, which begins with Winckelmann, was mediated by the (imperial) Roman appropriation and reduction of Greek thinking, poetry, and education to the purposes of empire. It thus crucially misrepresents the political imperatives of Greek *poiesis*. Heidegger's projection of the work of art and the (nationalist) *polis* have therefore to be understood as uncentered—always already committed to instigating the rift—and thus anti-imperialist.

75. Martin Heidegger, "The Age of the World Picture," pp. 129–30. My emphasis. Indeed, in "The Question Concerning Technology," the triumph of "representation" (*Vorstellung*), the globalization of "enframement" (*Ge-stell*), which is to say, the totalized spatialization of time, in modernity "ends" in the reduction of its disseminations to "standing reserve" (*Bestand*) (pp. 17–21).

76. For an amplified reading of this tripartite "structure," see chapter 5, n. 9.

77. See my essay "Postmodern Literature and the Hermeneutic Crisis," *Union Seminary Quarterly Review* 34 (Winter 1979), pp. 119–31.

78. See Odo Marquand, *In Defense of the Accidental: Philosophical Studies*, trans. Robert M. Wallace (New York: Oxford University Press, 1991).

79. Like Foucault, who, after Nietzsche, identifies the will to power of Occidental metaphysics with "Egyptianism," I am invoking the traditional humanist binary opposition between Occident and Orient parodically: to suggest that its own discourse is inscribed by precisely what it attributes to the Orient: "Once the historical sense is mastered by a suprahistorical perspective, metaphysics can bend it to its own purposes and by aligning it to the demands of objective science, it can impose its own 'Egyptianism,' " "Nietzsche, Genealogy, History," *Language, Counter-Memory, Practice: Selected Essays and Interviews*, ed. Donald Bouchard and trans. Bouchard and Sherry Simon (Ithaca, N.Y.: Cornell University Press, 1977), p. 152.

80. Martin Heidegger, ". . . Poetically Man Dwells . . . ," *Poetry, Language, Thought*, pp. 221–22. See also "Building Dwelling Thinking," pp. 145–61.

81. Fredric Jameson, *Postmodernism, or the Logic of Late Capitalism* (Durham, N.C.: Duke University Press, 1990).

82. William Carlos Williams, *Paterson* (New York: New Directions, 1963), p. 50.

83. Charles Olson, "Letter 5," *The Maximus Poems* (New York: Jargon/Corinth Books, 1960), pp. 17–25. See also my essay, "Charles Olson and Negative Capability: A Phenomenological Interpretation," *Contemporary Literature* 21: 1 (Winter 1980), pp. 38–80; rpr. *Repetitions*, pp. 107–47.

84. Jacques Derrida, "Differance," *Speech and Phenomena: And Other Essays on Husserl's Theory of Signs*, trans. David B. Allison (Evanston, Ill.: Northwestern University Press, 1973), p. 139.

85. Ibid., p. 133.

86. Ibid., p. 139.

87. Ibid., p. 140.

88. Geoffrey Hartman, "Monsieur Texte: On Jacques Derrida, His *Glas*," *Georgia Review* 29 (Winter 1975), pp. 766–67.

89. Jacques Derrida, "Structure, Sign and Play," p. 292.

90. Michel Foucault, "Nietzsche, Genealogy, History," *Language, Counter-Memory, Practice*, p. 161.

91. J. Hillis Miller, "Stevens' Rock and Criticism as Cure, II," *Georgia Review* 30 (Summer 1975), pp. 335–38. For an extended critique of this essay, specifically the reduction of the affective resonances of the uncanny to an indifferent verbalism, see my "De-struction and the Critique of Ideology," in *Repetitions*, pp. 284–92.

92. J. Hillis Miller, "The Critic as Host," *Deconstruction and Criticism*, ed. Harold Bloom, Paul de Man, Jacques Derrida, Geoffrey Hartman, J. Hillis Miller (New York: Seabury Press, 1979), pp. 220–21.

93. Ibid., p. 237. My emphasis. See Jonathan Arac, "To Regress from the Rigor of Shelley: Figures of History in American Deconstructive Criticism," *boundary 2* 8 (Spring 1980), pp. 241–58. In fairness to Miller, it should be pointed out that in his most recent work, he has attempted to escape the kind of charge I am directing against his deconstructive practice by demonstrating its "ethical" imperatives. See *The Ethics of Reading: Kant, de Man, Eliot, Trollope, James, and Benjamin* (New York: Columbia University Press, 1987).

94. As Paul Bové says of deconstruction in general by way of his Foucauldian analysis of Paul de Man's assertion that not even such a "totally enlightened language, regardless of whether it conceives of itself as a consciousness or not, is unable to control the recurrence, in its readers as well as in itself, of the errors it exposes" (*Allegory Reading*, p. 219, n. 36): "One cannot say of these remarks [to the effect that "reading/writing produces allegory"] with Gerald Graff that they are referentially self-contradictory. Such a comment is unappreciative of de Man's ironic play with the levels of discourse in such a statement. Nor can one argue that this is *merely* pessimism or impotence. The difficulty consists in realizing how these seemingly despairing remarks *produce* texts and representations of writing/reading and criticism which have power. It is the quintessence of deconstruction that it responds to the decline of academic literary criticism [the reference is to the failed hegemony of the New Criticism] by inscribing within the academy a project for preservation. The repetitiveness of deconstruction is an institutional necessity fortunately fulfilled by the vigorous texts of subtle critics." "Variations on Authority," p. 17.

95. Barbara Johnson, "Nothing Fails Like Success," p. 16.

96. Geoffrey Hartman, "Monsieur Texte: On Jacques Derrida, His *Glas*": "We may not be able to use the instrument properly, though its best use is as a critical rather than positive or ideological philosophy" (p. 782). See also Christopher Fynsk, "A Decelebration of Philosophy," *Diacritics*.

97. Geoffrey Hartman, "Monsieur Texte," pp. 759, 768.

98. Søren Kierkegaard, *The Concept of Irony*, trans. Lee Capel (Bloomington: Indiana University Press, 1971), pp. 336–42. See also chapter 3, "Heidegger, Kierkegaard, and the Hermeneutic Circle."

99. I. A. Richards, *Principles of Literary Criticism*, 2nd ed. (London: Routledge and Kegan Paul, 1926), pp. 250–52. See also Cleanth Brooks, *Modern Poetry and the Tradition* (New York: Oxford University Press, 1965), p. 41. My emphasis, except on the words *"disinterested"* and *"detached."*

100. Recently, it is true, deconstructionists, under the pressure of the massive critique by politically left critics, and following the lead of Derrida, have begun to address the question of the ethics and/or politics of deconstruction. See, for example, J. Hillis Miller, *The Ethic of Reading*; and Christopher Norris, *The Conflict of Faculties*; Barbara Johnson, *A World of Difference* (Baltimore, Md.: Johns Hopkins University Press, 1987); Jonathan Culler, *Framing the Sign*; Tobin Sebers, *The Ethics of Criticism* (Ithaca, N.Y.: Cornell University Press, 1988); and Samuel Weber, *Institution and Interpretation* (Minneapolis: University of Minnesota Press, 1987). This is a welcome initiative. But insofar as it remains essentially defensive in practice it is inadequate to the challenge. It continues to be disciplinary in its commitment to *writing* as base and thus determinitive, not dialogic, vis-à-vis political and cultural critique.

101. Søren Kierkegaard, *Two Ages. The Age of Revolution and the Present Age: A Literary Review*, ed. and trans. Howard V. Hong and Edna Hong (Princeton: Princeton University Press, 1978), p. 77. I am grateful to Paul Bové for bringing this passage to my attention. See his "The Penitentiary of Reflection: Søren Kierkegaard and Critical Activity," *boundary 2* 9: 1 (Fall 1980), pp. 233–58; Kierkegaard's emphasis. See also Michel Foucault, "Intellectuals and Power: A Conversation with Gilles Deleuze," *Language, Counter-Memory, Practice*, pp. 205–17.

102. Edward Said, "Reflections on Recent 'Left' Criticism," p. 20.

103. See Paul Bové, "A Free, Varied, and Unwasteful Life: I. A. Richards' Speculative Instruments," *Intellectuals in Power: A Genealogy of Critical Humanism* (New York: Columbia University Press, 1986).

104. On deconstruction as a commodified discourse that takes its place within the logic of late capitalism, see Fredric Jameson, *Postmodernism, or the Cultural Logic of Late Capitalism*.

105. Friedrich Nietzsche, "On Truth and Falsity," *The Portable Nietzsche*, ed. and trans. Walter Kaufman (New York: Penguin, 1954), p. 46.

106. Jacques Derrida, "Force and Signification," *Writing and Difference*, pp. 26–27.

5. Heidegger and Foucault: The Politics of the Commanding Gaze

1. Jacques Derrida, "Structure, Sign and Play in the Discourse of the Human Sciences," *Writing and Difference*, trans. Alan Bass (Chicago: University of Chicago Press, 1978): "The entire history of the concept of structure, before the rupture of which we are speaking, must be thought of as a series of substitutions of center for center, a linked chain of determinations of the center. Successively, and in a regulated fashion, the center receives different forms or names. The history of

metaphysics, like the history of the West, is the history of these metaphors and metonymies" (p. 279).

2. This chapter enacts a retrieval, refocusing, and development of a significant amount of the materials constituting chapter 2 of my *The End of Education: Toward Posthumanism* (Minneapolis: University of Minnesota Press, 1993), which establishes the theoretical ground for an interrogation of the modern university. My retrieval and amplification of the argument of that text is intended to provide an adequate context for intervening in the debate over Heidegger's politics, or rather the politics of Heidegger's philosophical discourse precipitated by the publication of Victor Farías's *Heidegger et le nazisme* (Paris: Editions Verdier, 1987); English trans., *Heidegger and Nazism* (ed. Joseph Margolis and Tom Rockmore and trans. Paul Burrell (French materials) and Gabriel R. Ricci (German materials).

3. Michel Foucault, *The History of Sexuality, Vol. I: An Introduction*, trans. Robert Hurley (New York: Pantheon Books, 1978), p. 17.

4. Friedrich Engels, "Letter of September 1890 to Bloch," quoted in Raymond Williams, *Marxism and Literature* (Oxford: Oxford University Press, 1977), pp. 79–80.

5. See Barry Smart, "On the Limits and Limitations of Marxism," *Foucault, Marxism and Critique* (London: Routledge and Kegan Paul, 1983), pp. 4–31. Smart traces the origins of the European "crisis of Marxism" to "a series of events which took place in 1968," namely "the events of May '68 in France" and "the Prague Spring" in Czechoslovakia. These events precipitated a general awareness among Western Marxists that Marx's and Engels's adversarial discourse was essentially determined by the dominant bourgeois/capitalist discourse, i.e., the nineteenth century *epistémé*, and thus is subject to the same limitations as the latter.

6. See Louis Althusser, "Contradiction and Overdetermination," *For Marx*, trans. Ben Brewster (London: New Left Books, 1977), pp. 111–12.

7. Williams, *Marxism and Literature*, pp. 77–78. See also Ernesto Laclau and Chantal Mouffe, *Hegemony and Social Strategy* (London: Verso, 1988).

8. Williams, *Marxism and Literature*, pp. 80–81.

9. This is a fundamental motif, often referred to as "the Europeanization of the earth and man," in Heidegger's critique of modernity. See, for example, Martin Heidegger, "The End of Philosophy and the Task of Thinking," *Basic Writings*, ed. David Farrell Krell (New York: Harper & Row, 1977): "The end of philosophy proves to be the triumph of the manipulable arrangement of a scientific-technological world and of the social order proper to this world. The end of philosophy means the beginning of the world civilization base upon Western thinking" (p. 327).

10. Martin Heidegger, *Being and Time*, trans. John Macquarrie and Edward Robinson (New York: Harper & Row), pp. 170. *SZ*, 131. Heidegger analyzes these indissoluble structures of being-in-the-world in Sections 28–38, pp. 169–224. For a more fully articulated version of the point I am making about the equiprimordiality of these structures, see Alex Argyros, "The Warp of the World: Deconstruction and Hermeneutics," *Diacritics* 16: 3 (Fall 1986). In a significant qualification of Jacques Derrida's curiously literal reading of Heidegger's hermeneutics, Argyros reads this tripartite structure, the "collective name" of which is *Dasein* (p. 48), not as the agency of disclosing "meaning": the transcendental Truth of Being. It is, rather, the condition that renders *Dasein* always already historical (worldly) and the truth it articulates undecidable, that is, a necessary construction always open to and in need of destruction, the hermeneutic circle: "It is inaccurate . . . to think of meaning as lying 'before' or 'beneath' discourse. Indeed, it is precisely such a temporal or geological model that Heidegger would have us abandon. Meaning

does not point to a temporarily obscured sense lurking behind a sign or symbol. Nor is it simply a receptacle enclosing or supporting understanding. The meaning of Being is not a transcendental essence grounding Heidegger's hermeneutic. Meaning is simply that intimation of an answer necessary to any inquiry. As the possibility of investigation, *Dasein* is that entity which, uniquely touched by Being with the gift of curiosity, *is* the hermeneutic circle. And if Heidegger claims that the circle is the only legitimate mode of philosophic inquiry, his position should not be read as normative. To the contrary, meaning, the circularity of any gesture of interpretive investigation, is that prior articulation of *Dasein*'s environment that radically precludes the possibility of a simple, simply real, or punctual world. The meaning of Being is that meaning's other name, the world, must already have been read before it may be encountered. . . . As opposed to Husserl, for whom the presence of the present is the ultimate guarantor of truth, Heidegger 'grounds' experience in an interpretive bed of meaning which, dispersed as it is in a fore-structure preceding any possible present, is radically unphenomenal. Indeed, since meaning, the possibility of articulation, is always discursive, and insofar as discourse is less a system of constituted signs than the spacing which founds them (as well as other entities), Heidegger posits *Dasein* as that being which is defined by the precomprehension of a world which is itself nothing more than its own precomprehension or interpretation. The meaning of Being, then, would be the 'truth' of Being if by 'truth' is understood a concept that is as deeply historical, as profoundly unbounded, as Derrida's 'differance' " (pp. 53–54).

What is lacking in Argyros's brilliant reading of Heidegger's text, is specification of the concept "world." Like Heidegger, he fails to draw out the cultural and sociopolitical implications of his essentially ontological analysis of an understanding of interpretation grounded on the equiprimordiality of state of mind, understanding, and discourse. Thus in the end his reading remains trapped in the base/superstructure model. Nevertheless, it points toward the opening I am undertaking to achieve in this text.

11. Martin Heidegger, "The Rectorate 1933/34: Facts and Thoughts," trans. Karsten Harries, *Review of Metaphysics* 38: 3 (March 1985), p. 498.

12. Martin Heidegger, "On the Essence of Truth," trans. John Sallis, *Basic Writings*, ed. David Farrell Krell (New York: Harper & Row, 1977), p. 120. Heidegger's powerfully persuasive critique of truth as correctness in favor of truth as *aletheia* (unconcealment) is a constant of his thinking, and should be brought into play against a central motif of his recent humanist critics, most reductively and vocally represented by Tom Rockmore in *On Heidegger's Nazism and Philosophy* (Berkeley: University of California Press, 1992). Rockmore represents Heidegger as a "seer of Being" (p. 128), who arrogantly affirmed his truth as "correct" against the "erroneous" truth of the entire Western philosophical tradition. Thus for Rockmore, Heidegger's *Auseinandersetzung* (dialogic encounter) becomes "confrontation" understood in the context of the Nazi *Kampf* (battle) (pp. 106 ff).

13. Martin Heidegger, "The Origin of the Work of Art," trans. Albert Hofstadter, *Basic Writings*, pp. 153–54; Heidegger's emphasis.

14. Heidegger, *Being and Time*, p. 43.

15. Some suggestion of the crudeness of Victor Farías's anecdotal approach to the question of Heidegger's complicity with Nazism is suggested by his attribution of Heidegger's "massive reservations about the so-called 'Latin' or 'Roman' " to "a radical xenophobia" that is "typical of a [German] tradition for which Abraham à Sancta Clara [the seventeenth-century German monk whose virulent anti-

Semitism, according to Farías, was a decisive influence on Heidegger throughout his life] was exemplary." *Heidegger and Nazism*, trans. Paul Burrill and Gabriel R. Ricci (Philadelphia: Temple University Press, 1989), p. 223.

16. Heidegger, *Being and Time*, pp. 437–38; SZ, 385–86. Heidegger's emphasis. For an extended reading of this crucial passage, see chapter 1, "On Heidegger's Destruction and the Metaphorics of Following."

17. Martin Heidegger, "Letter on Humanism," trans. Frank A. Capuzzi, *Basic Writings*, pp. 200–201.

18. As I have shown more fully in *The End of Education*, the Roman rhetoric that represents the disciplinary violence of education and the sociopolitical violence of ethnocentric colonialism in terms of "culture" and the bringing of "universal peace" informs the discourse and practice of imperialist projects throughout the history of the Occident. I am referring not only to those sanctioned by the *theologos* mediated by the Roman imperial model: for example, the projects of the Holy Roman Emperors and, from a different (Calvinist) representation of the *theologos*, of the American Puritans. (See Sacvan Bercovitch, *The American Jeremiad* [Madison: Wisconsin University Press, 1978], and my essay "De-struction and the Critique of Ideology" in *Repetitions: The Postmodern Occasion in Literature and Culture* [Baton Rouge: Louisiana State University Press], pp. 282–84). I am also referring to those justified on anthropological grounds (the projects of Napoleonic France, Victorian England, and, less overtly, of the modern United States). This duplicitous discursive practice is evident, for example, in the rhetoric of "deliverance" (Matthew Arnold) informing the "classical" education inculcated by the British public-school system in the late nineteenth and early twentieth centuries, the humanist system that trained an elite to administer the British colonies, and in the related rhetoric of the *Pax Britannica*, which justified the conquest and exploitation of "peripheral" nations and their peoples. The recalcitrant protagonist of George Orwell's *Burmese Days* (1934) puts this succinctly. Against his mocking self-representation as "Civis Romanum," Flores's culturally inscribed and self-deprecating Indian friend invokes the "public school spirit" of "Clive, Warren Hastings, Dalhousie, Curzon" and "the unswerving British justice and the Pax Britannica." To this, Flores responds, "Pox Britannica, doctor, Pox Britannica is its proper name. And in any case, whom is it pax for?" *Burmese Days* (New York: Harvest Books, 1962), pp. 38–48.

19. According to the historian Arno J. Mayer in *Why Did the Heavens Not Darken?: The Final Solution in History* (New York: Pantheon, 1988), the anti-Semitism of the Nazis and the German elite, on whose approbation they initially relied, was integrally related to but subordinated to their "crusade" against the Bolshevists (whom they referred to as the "judeobolshevists"). It is Arno's central thesis that the decision to exterminate the Jews—the "judeocide" or "Final Solution"—was made only after the disastrous failure of "Operation Barbarossa" in the East.

20. Éliane Escoubas, "Heidegger, la question romaine, la question impériale: Autour du 'Tournant,' " in *Heidegger: Questions ouvertes*, ed. Éliane Escoubas (Paris: Éditions Osiris, 1988), pp. 173–88.

21. Martin Heidegger, *Parmenides*, vol. 54 of *Gesamtausgabe* (Frankfurt am Main: Vittorio Klostermann, 1982), pp. 63–67. My translation.

22. Heidegger, *Parmenides*, pp. 58–61. My translation. In the *Parmenides* lectures, Heidegger continues to affiliate the Romanization of Europe with the Romance languages and to characterize the German language as intrinsically similar to the ancient Greek. But this does not warrant the simplistic conclusion that Farías (and other humanists) draw about his politics in 1942: that these lectures make clear his continuing "link to National Socialism," or demonstrate his "open and public sup-

port for the war unleashed by the Hitler regime" (*Heidegger and Nazism*, p. 276). The *Parmenides* lectures, as Éliane Escoubas suggests as well, can be read as Heidegger's acknowledgement of the significant degree to which modern Germany ("*Wir denken*. . . .") had absorbed the Roman reference (and the "imperial" perspective) since the Romantic period, especially since the beginning of the Third Reich. And in the *Parmenides* lectures, where he introduces the notion of strife as fundamental to the relationship between unconcealedness and concealedness (*aletheia* and *lethe*) in Greek thought and Greek tragedy, he writes: "If hardship and suffering are mentioned here [in Hesiod's *Theogony* (v. 226 ff.] as descendents of Strife [the goddess Eris], then precisely this origin in strife should teach us to avoid the modern interpretation. . . . Our usual interpretation of them in terms of lived experience is the main reason Greek tragedy is still entirely sealed off to us. Aeschylus-Sophocles on the one side, and Shakespeare on the other, are incomparable worlds. German humanism has mixed them up and has made the Greek world completely inaccessible. Goethe is disastrous." *Parmenides*, trans. André Schuwer and Richard Rojcewicz (Bloomington: Indiana University Press, 1992), p. 73. In "Letter on Humanism" he identifies "Winckelmann, Goethe, and Schiller" with the humanism and the *studium humanitatis* of *Homo romanus* (p. 201). These Parmenides lectures can thus also be interpreted as a disavowal of historical National Socialism. Heidegger's thesis that the German language, as opposed to English and French (and the other Romance languages), is intrinsically capable of retrieving the originary thinking of the Greeks and thus of saving the world from devastation by the calculative/imperial Roman tradition may be debated. But it is an ideological sleight of hand to identify this essential motif of his thought with the historical Nazi project.

23. Heidegger's analysis of this developed form of the imperial project, especially of the role played by the operations of power he reiteratively invokes with the German word *heissen*, which not only means "to command, enjoin, bid, order, direct," but also "to name, call, denominate," bears a striking resemblance to Althusser's analysis of ideology as the "*interpellation*" (or "hailing") of individuals as (subjected) subjects. See "Ideology and Ideological State Apparatuses (Notes Toward an Investigation)," *Lenin and Philosophy and Other Essays*, trans. Ben Brewster (New York: Monthly Review Press, 1971): "We observe that the structure of all ideology, interpellating individuals as subjects in the name of a Unique and Absolute Subject, is *specular*, i.e., a mirror-structure, and *doubly* speculary: this mirror duplication is constitutive of ideology and ensures its functioning. Which means that all ideology is *centered*, that the Absolute Subject occupies the unique place of the Centre, and interpellates around it the infinity of individuals into subjects in a double mirror-connexion such that it *subjects* the subjects to the Subject, while giving them in the Subject in which each subject can contemplate its own image (present and future) the *guarantee* that this really concerns them and Him, and that since everything takes place in the Family . . . 'God will *recognize* his own in it', i.e. those who have recognized God, and have recognized themselves in Him, will be saved.

    Let me summarize what we have discovered about ideology in general.

    The duplicate mirror-structure of ideology ensures simultaneously: (1) the interpellation of 'individuals' as subjects; (2) their subjection to the Subject; (3) the mutual recognition of subjects and Subject, the subject's recognition of each other, and finally the subject's recognition of himself; (4) the absolute guarantee that everything really is so, and that on condition that the subjects recognize what they are and behave accordingly, everything will be all right: Amen—'*So be it*' " (pp.

180–81). Behind Althusser's formulation of the subject of capitalism is Lacan's formulation of the subject of post-Freudian psychoanalysis; ahead of Althusser is Foucault's formulation of the subject of the disciplinary society. Is it exorbitant to say that Heidegger's formulation of the subject of humanism stands as point of departure of this chain?

24. Philippe Lacoue-Labarthe, *La fiction du politique: Heidegger, l'art et politique* (Paris: Christian Bourgois, 1987), p. 138. My translation.

25. Ibid., p. 63.

26. Heidegger, "Letter on Humanism," p. 219–20. It is impossible to determine what Heidegger means by Marx's attainment of "an essential dimension of history." But it would seem from his differentiation between Marx's understanding of alienation and Hegel's and, more significantly, his dissociation of Marx's history from the History represented by metaphysics, that he interprets it in a way that cuts against the grain of the essentialism of "Marxism," which is to say, in the terms that have more recently become fundamental to the neo-Marxist critique of the "economism" of "vulgar" Marxism.

27. Edward Said, "Reflections on Recent American 'Left' Criticism," *boundary 2* 8 (Fall 1979), p. 27; rpr. in William Spanos, Paul Bové, and Daniel O'Hara (eds.), *The Question of Textuality: Strategies of Reading in Contemporary American Criticism* (Bloomington: Indiana University Press, 1982), pp. 1–30; and in Edward Said, *The World, the Text, and the Critic* (Cambridge, Mass.: Harvard University Press, 1983), pp. 158–77: "To study affiliation is to study and to recreate the bonds between text and world, bonds which specialization and the institutions of literature have all but effaced. Every text is an act of will to some extent, but what has not been very much studied is the degree to which—and the specific cultural space by which—texts are made permissible. To recreate the affiliative network is therefore to make visible, to give materiality back to, the strands holding the text to the society, the author and the culture that produced it."

28. Michel Foucault, "Final Interview," *Raritan*, 5: 1 (Summer 1985), pp. 8–9.

29. Michel Foucault, "Nietzsche, Genealogy, History," trans. Donald Bouchard and Sherry Simon, *Language, Counter-Memory, Practice: Selected Essays and Interviews*, ed. Donald Bouchard (Ithaca, N.Y.: Cornell University Press, 1977), p. 152.

30. Michel Foucault, *Surveiller et punir: Naissance de la prison.* (Paris: Gallimard, 1975). In the English translation by Alan Sheridan, *Discipline and Punish: The Birth of the Prison* (New York: Pantheon, 1977; hereafter cited DP), the title obscures the crucial relationship between visual perception and power and thus diverts the reader from making the connection between the metaphysical tradition (and the cultural apparatuses to which it has given rise) and sociopolitical power; i.e., the affiliative relationship between Foucault's and Heidegger's discourses and, for that matter, the role of Sartre (I am referring to the enormous importance of "the look"—*le regard*—in the latter's discourse). Foucault's brilliant genealogy of the modern disciplinary society is an extension and deepening of his "archeological" analysis of the cultural significance of insanity and disease in the eighteenth century in *Madness and Civilization: A History of Insanity in the Age of Reason*, trans. Richard Howard (New York: Vintage Books, 1973) and *The Birth of the Clinic: An Archeology of Medical Perception*, trans. A. M. Sheridan Smith (New York: Vintage Books, 1975). The genealogy of discipline is further developed in *The History of Sexuality, Vol. I: An Introduction*, trans. Robert Hurley (New York: Pantheon, 1978).

31. Michel Foucault, "Truth and Power," *Power/Knowledge: Selected Interviews and Other Writings, 1972–1977*, ed. Colin Gordon (New York: Pantheon, 1980), p. 112. My emphasis.

32. In "In the Empire of the Gaze: Foucault's Denigration of Vision in Twentieth-Century French Thought," *Foucault: A Critical Reader*, ed. David Couzens Hoy (Oxford: Basil Blackwell, 1986), Martin Jay contextualizes Foucault's analysis of modern panopticism by drawing attention to its affiliation with the interrogation of sight "carried out by a wide and otherwise disparate number of French intellectuals beginning with Bergson." Although it is not exactly true that this motif of Foucault's thought is a "hitherto unexamined one," it does contribute significantly to making "sense of his remarkable work, in particular the source of its puzzling critical impulse": "Beginning with Bergson's critique of the spatialization of time, the French interrogation of sight has tended increasingly to emphasize its more problematic implications. The link between privileging vision and the traditional humanistic subject, capable of rational enlightenment, has been opened to widespread attack. The illusions of imagistic representation and the allegedly disinterested scientific gaze have been subjected to hostile scrutiny. The mystification of the social imagery and the spectacle of late capitalist culture have been the target of fierce criticism. And the psychological dependence of the ideological 'I' on the totalizing gaze of the 'eye' has been ruthlessly exposed" (p. 178). Unfortunately, as the quoted passage itself suggests, Jay's delimitation of the context to the modern French interrogation of visualism—to its origins in Bergson's critique of science as the "spatialization of time (*durée réele*)"—tends to identify Foucault's with the critique of empirical science. It thus obscures the affinities of Foucault's "denigration of vision" with Heidegger's and the larger (historical) context it is the purpose of this chapter to thematize: that which understands the ideological continuity between the "objectivity" of empirical science and the "disinterestedness" of "lyrical" humanism. Further, in failing to indicate the degree to which French structuralism (Claude Lévi-Strauss and Gérard Genette, for example) enhanced the authority of visualism and the spatial model, it obscures Foucault's poststructuralist project.

33. See Martin Heidegger, "Plato's Doctrine of Truth," trans. John Barlow, *Philosophy in the Twentieth Century*, vol. 3, ed. William Barrett and Henry Aiken (New York: Random House, 1962), pp. 251–69.

34. William V. Spanos, "Postmodern Literature and Its Occasion: Retrieving the Preterite Middle," *Repetitions: The Postmodern Occasion in Literature and Culture* (Baton Rouge: Louisiana State University Press, 1987), pp. 200–05. Foucault refers to the circular fortresses Sebastien Le Preste de Vauban built for Louis XIV in *Surveiller and punir*, but dismisses them as an architectural geometry intended to facilitate the observation of "external space," (DP, 172). On the other hand, he invokes Claude-Nicholas Ledoux's (1736–1806) circular salt works at Arc-et-Senans as a precursor of Jeremy Bentham's Panopticon: "The perfect disciplinary apparatus would make it possible for a single gaze to see everything constantly. A central point would be both the source of light illuminating everything, and a locus of convergence for everything that must be known: a perfect eye that nothing could escape and a centre towards which all gazes would be turned. This is what Ledoux had imagined when he built Arc-et-Senans; all the buildings were to be arranged in a circle, opening on the inside, at the centre of which a high construction was to house the administrative functions of management, the policing functions of surveillance, the economic functions of control and checking, the religious functions of encouraging obedience and work; from here all orders would come, all activities would be recorded, all offenses perceived and judged; and this would be done immediately with no other aid than an exact geometry. Among all the reasons for the prestige that was accorded in the second half of the eighteenth century to circular

architecture, one must no doubt include the fact that it expressed a certain political utopia" (DP, 173–74. See also Foucault, "The Eye of Power," *Power/Knowledge,* pp. 147–48. What Foucault fails to recognize in emphasizing the "epistemic break" occurring in the age of the Enlightenment, is that his description and analysis of the function of Ledoux's Arc-et-Senans applies *mutatis mutandis* to, say, Campanella's circular utopian City of the Sun modelled on the orderly circular macrocosm and governed from the center by the Platonic "Metaphysician" (also called "Sun" on the analogy with its planetary counterpart in the Copernican astronomy). Tommaso Campanella, *La Citte del Sole: Dialogo Poetico/The City of the Sun,* bilingual ed. trans. Daniel J. Bonno (Berkeley: University of California Press, 1981), pp. 26 ff.

The point I am making about the circle as the perennial image of beauty and perfection *and* power is inadvertently made by at least two contemporary humanist art historians who have written on the history of the circular city: E. A. Gutkind, *Urban Development in Western Europe: France and Belgium* (New York: Free Press, 1970), vol. 5 of Gutkind, *International History of City Development,* 8 vols.; and Norman J. Johnston, *Cities in the Round* (Seattle: University of Washington Press, 1983). Both, but especially Johnston, interpret the military/disciplinary uses to which the circular/utopian model was increasingly put after the Renaissance as a tragic betrayal of the ideal envisaged by Plato, and by the Renaissance humanists, in which the circular city is represented as the worldly manifestation of eternal cosmic beauty, whereas all the evidence, including that of their own texts, points to them as the historically specific fulfillment of the latent power that theorists of the circular city, both utopian and practicing architects and engineers, recognized in this totalizing geometry of beauty from the beginning. See, for example, Johnston, *Cities in the Round,* p. 45. For an interesting study (influenced generally by Foucault) on the relationship between Vauban's fortresses and the literature of eighteenth-century France, see Joan DeJean, *Literary Fortifications: Rousseau, Laclos, Sade* (Princeton, N.J.: Princeton University Press, 1984).

35. Foucault cites this enabling text in the interview "Space, Knowledge, and Power," in *The Foucault Reader,* ed. Paul Rabinow (New York: Pantheon, 1984), but characteristically minimizes without denying any influence it might have had in the articulation of a relay between spatial and political economies: "In discussing Rome, one sees that the problem revolves around Vitruvius. Vitruvius was reinterpreted from the sixteenth century on, but one can find in the sixteenth century— and no doubt in the Middle Ages as well—many considerations of the same order as Vitruvius; if you consider them as *reflections upon.* The treatises on politics, on the art of government, on the manner of good government, did not generally include chapters or analyses devoted to the organization of cities or to architecture. The *Republic* of Jean Bodin does not contain extended discussion of the role of architecture, whereas the police treatises of the eighteenth century are full of them" (p. 240).

36. Campanella, *Citte del Sole,* p. 54, 55.

37. Although Foucault does not acknowledge it, the immediate source of his phrase is no doubt Jean-Paul Sartre's *le regard* ("the look"), which, one recalls, like Medusa's eye, transforms the threatening and unpredictable, because ultimately unknowable, "other" into stone. See *Being and Nothingness: An Essay in Phenomenological Ontology,* trans. Hazel Barnes (New York: Citadel Press, 1964), p. 406. Sartre's extended phenomenological account of "the look" can be found in *Being and Nothingness,* pp. 228–78. For one of Sartre's many fictional and dramatic instances of

"the look," see the Dr. Rogé / Achilles entry in *Nausea*, trans. Lloyd Alexander (New York: New Directions, 1964), pp. 92–96. Ultimately, of course, as Foucault also seems to be aware, the specific image goes back to the commonplace visual depiction of God's all-seeing eye looking down on the vainly concealed sinner in Renaissance emblem books, which is accompanied by the following verse:

"Behinde a fig tree great, him selfe did ADAM hide:
And thought from GOD hee there might lurke, & should not bee espide.
Oh foole, no corners seeke, though thou a sinner bee;
For none but GOD can thee forgive, who all thy waies doth see."

See, for example, Geoffrey Whitney, *A Choice of Emblems* (Leyden, 1586), p. 229.

38. From Foucault's demystified perspective, as from Heidegger's, the term "Enlightenment" assumes an ironic significance. The emphasis on the spatializing eye, which deliberately forgets or conceals temporal being for the sake of power over "it," becomes not simply a blindness, but a blinding oversight. For a similar critique of the Enlightenment, see Max Horkheimer and Theodor Adorno, *Dialectic of the Enlightenment*, trans. John Cumming (New York: Herder and Herder, 1972).

39. Of this "new knowledge of man," Marjorie Hope Nicolson, the celebrated humanist literary historian, says nothing in her celebratory account of the rise of the technology of optics in *Newton Demands the Muse: Newton's Optics and the Eighteenth-Century Poets* (Princeton, N.J.: Princeton University Press, 1946).

40. Max Weber, *The Protestant Ethic and the Spirit of Capitalism*, trans. Talcott Parsons (New York: Scribners, 1958), pp. 104–5.

41. Though Foucault is referring here specifically to Jean Baptiste de la Salle's "dream of the ideal classroom in *Conduite des écoles chrétiennes* (B.N. Ms. 11759), it is clear that the reference is intended to apply to other disciplinary institutions as well.

42. According to Foucault, "the power of the Norm appears" when the emergent disciplines combine with "other powers—Law, the Word (*Parole*), and the Text, Tradition"—and with surveillance—to become fundamental to the pedagogical economy of power in modern society: "The Normal is established as a principle of coercion in teaching with the introduction of a standardized education and the establishment of the *écoles normales* [teacher training colleges]. . . . Like surveillance and with it, normalization becomes one of the great instruments of power at the end of the classical age." DP 184. See also p. 192.

43. See, however, n. 33.

44. Michel Foucault, "The Eye of Power," p. 152. The affiliative relation between Rousseau and Bentham to which Foucault points is also suggested by the fact that Claude-Nicholas Ledoux, the eighteenth-century French architect whose circular manufactory, Arc-et-Senans, according to Foucault, prefigured Bentham's Panopticon, was an avowed Rousseauist. See my "Postmodern Literature and Its Occasion: Retrieving the Preterite Middle," in *Repetitions*, pp. 203–5. See also Jean de Jean, "*Julie* and *Emile*: 'Studia la Matematica,' " *Literary Fortifications*, pp. 112–90.

45. Michel Foucault, *The History of Sexuality, Volume I: An Introduction*, trans. Robert Hurley (New York: Pantheon Books, 1978), p. 10. For Foucault's generalization of the "repressive hypothesis" to include other sociopolitical sites besides the sexual—i.e., his recognition of its polyvalency—see also "Truth and Power," in *Power/Knowledge*, pp. 109–33.

46. Hubert L. Dreyfuss and Paul Rabinow, *Michel Foucault: Beyond Structuralism and Hermeneutics* (Chicago: University of Chicago Press, 1982), pp. 129–30. I emphasize "clarity" to suggest what is unthematized in Dreyfuss's and Rabinow's

otherwise perceptive representation of Foucault's interpretation of the "repressive hypothesis": the eye/light/center constellation—the Apollonian principle, as it were—inscribed in this view of power relations.

47. Michel Foucault, *The History of Sexuality*, pp. 88–89. Elsewhere Foucault observes: "The monarchy presented itself as a referee, a power capable of putting an end to war, violence, and pillage and saying no to these [feudal] struggles and private feuds. It made itself acceptable by allocating itself a juridical and negative function, albeit one whose limits it naturally began at once to overstep. Sovereign, law, and prohibition formed a system of representation of power which was extended during the subsequent era by the theories of right: political theory has never ceased to be obsessed with the person of the sovereign. Such theories still continue today to busy themselves with the problem of sovereignty. What we need, however, is a political philosophy that isn't erected around the problem of sovereignty, nor therefore around the problems of law and prohibition. We need to cut off the king's head: in political theory that has still to be done" ("Truth and Power," *Power/ Knowledge*, p. 121).

48. Martin Heidegger, "A Dialogue on Language (Between a Japanese and an Inquirer)", trans. Peter D. Hertz, in *On the Way to Language* (New York: Harper & Row, 1971), p. 15. See also Heidegger, "The End of Philosophy and the Task of Thinking," *Basic Writings*: "The end of philosophy proves to be the triumph of the manipulable arrangement of a scientific-technological world and of the social order proper to this world. The end of philosophy means the beginning of the world civilization based upon Western European thinking" (p. 377).

49. See also Lewis Munford, *The Myth of the Machine: The Pentagon of Power* (New York: Harcourt Brace Jovanovich, 1970), pp. 148 ff.

50. For an extended account of the complicity of humanist knowledge production with Napoleon's imperial project—one profoundly indebted to Foucault's genealogical discourse (and his thematization of the "panoptic gaze")—see Edward Said, *Orientalism* (New York: Vintage Books, 1979): "But dealings with the Muslims were only a part of Napoleon's project to dominate Egypt. The other part was to render it completely open, to make it totally accessible to European scrutiny. From being a land of obscurity and a part of the Orient hitherto known at second hand through the exploits of earlier travellers, scholars, and conquerors, Egypt was to become a department of French learning. Here too the textual and schematic attitudes are evident. The Institut, with its teams of chemists, historians, biologists, archeologists, surgeons, and antiquarians, was the learned division of the army. Its job was no less aggressive: to put Egypt into modern French; and unlike the Abbé Le Mascrier's 1735 *Description d'Égypte*, Napoleon's was to be a universal undertaking. Almost from the first moments of the occupation Napoleon saw to it that the Institut began its meetings, its experiments—its fact-finding mission, as we would call it today. Most important, everything said, seen, and studied was to be recorded, and indeed was recorded in that great collective appropriation of one country by another, the *Description de l'Égypt*, published in twenty-three enormous volumes between 1809 and 1829" (pp. 83–84).

51. Michel Foucault, "Revolutionary Action: 'Until Now,' " *Language, Counter-Memory, Practice*, pp. 221–22.

52. Martin Heidegger, "The Age of the World Picture," *The Question Concerning Technology and Other Essays*, trans. William Lovitt (New York: Harper & Row, 1977), pp. 133–34. In "Appendix 10" of this essay, Heidegger defines "anthropology" as "that interpretation of man that already knows fundamentally what man is and hence can never ask who he may be. For with this question it would have to confess

itself shaken and overcome. But how can this be expected of anthropology when the latter has expressly to achieve nothing less than the securing consequent upon the self-secureness of the *subjectum*?" (p.153). This momentous question, which the anthropological problematic is blind to, is precisely the question that Foucault asks in his discourse at large.

53. For succinct accounts of this genealogy, see Nietzsche, *On the Genealogy of Morals* in *On the Genealogy of Morals and Ecce Homo*, trans. Walter Kaufmann (New York: Vintage Books, 1967), pp. 146–47; and Martin Heidegger, "Letter on Humanism," *Basic Writings*, pp. 232–33.

54. A telling example of this representation of literary production in terms of empirical science can be found in Michel Foucault, "The Life of Infamous Men," *Power, Truth, Strategy*, ed. Meaghan Morris and Paul Patton and trans. Meaghan Morris and Paul Foss (Sydney, Australia 1979). Here he says that the birth of the novel "forms part of the great [panoptic] system of constraint by which the [post-Enlightenment] West compelled the everyday to bring itself into discourse." p. 91. Foucault is, of course, referring to the fiction of "Realism," epitomized by writers like Balzac and Zola, in which the fourth wall hiding the lives of the urban masses is stripped away for purposes of detailed observation—and domination—from a distance of that hitherto obscure, unknown—and threatening—world. This remark constitutes a brilliant insight into the origins of the nineteenth century realistic novel, but is it an accurate account of the origins of the novel as such? (One thinks, for example, of Mikhail Bakhtin's quite different genealogy.) Further, given the nineteenth century context, does it accurately represent novelistic production at large in that period?

55. See, for example, Richard Ohmann, *English in America: A Radical View of the Profession* (New York: Oxford University Press, 1976) and *Politics of Letters* (Middletown, Conn.: Wesleyan University Press, 1987). For an extended critique of Ohmann's vestigial and disabling use of the Marxist base/superstructure model, see chapter 5 ("The University in the Vietnam Decade: The Crisis of Command and the Refusal of Spontaneous Consent") in my *The End of Education*.

56. See, for example, Gerald Graff's inordinately influential *Professing Literature: An Institutional History* (Chicago: University of Chicago Press, 1987). Against what he refers to as the poststructuralist myth that the institution of literary studies (indeed, the university at large) in America is informed by a humanist consensus—a uniformative ideological center—Graff posits the view that it is essentially characterized by an inefficient fragmentation: "Although the turn of the century saw the imposition of a uniform canon of English literature, traditionalists complained that the curriculum had all but dissipated the civic potential of the canon by breaking up into such disconnected fragments that students could get no clear sense of its unity. Far from being organized on a centralized logocentric model, the American University is itself something of a deconstructionist, proliferating a variety of disciplinary vocabularies that nobody can reduce to the common measure of any metalanguage" (pp. 12–13). Graff's diagnosis, which is motivated by a liberal humanist impulse, is a telling instance of the persuasive accommodational power of the ruse of the repressive hypothesis.

57. For an extended, if provisional, theorization of the posthumanist project demanded by the self-destruction—the coming to its end, as it were—of the regime of truth in the decade of the Vietnam War, see my chapter entitled "The Intellectual and the Postmodern Occasion: Toward a Posthumanist Paideia" in *The End of Education*.

6. Heidegger, Nazism, and the "Repressive Hypothesis": the American Appropriation of the Question

1. Victor Farías, *Heidegger et le nazisme* (Paris: Lagrasse, 1987); the *Critical Inquiry* "Symposium on Heidegger and Nazism," 15 (Winter 1988) containing Hans-Georg Gadamer, "Back from Syracuse?," trans. John McCumber, pp. 427–30; Jürgen Habermas, "Work and Weltanschauung: The Heidegger Controversy from a German Perspective," trans. John McCumber, pp. 431–56; Jacques Derrida, "Of Spirit," trans. Geoff Bennington and Rachel Bowlby, pp. 457–74; Maurice Blanchot, "Thinking the Apocalypse: A Letter to Catherine David," trans. Paula Wissing, pp. 485–88; Philippe Lacoue-Labarthe, "Neither an Accident nor a Mistake," trans. Paula Wissing, pp. 481–84; Emmanuel Lévinas, "As if Consenting to Horror," trans. Paula Wissing, pp. 485–88. With the exception of Gadamer's contribution, which does not address the issue of Heidegger's culpability, all these selections chosen for publication are severely critical not only of Heidegger the man but, despite disclaimers (especially in the case of Habermas), of Heidegger's philosophical discourse, above all, that which follows his assumption of the rectorship of Freiburg University in 1933. In its selection of the materials of this "Symposium," that is, the editor fails to provide an adequate representation of the European debate. In excerpting from the larger texts of Derrida and Lacoue-Labarthe (both written before the publication of Farías's book), he also maximizes the negative elements of their texts, which are considerably more sympathetic to Heidegger's philosophical thought than these excerpts suggest.

2. Arnold Davidson, "Questions Concerning Heidegger: Opening the Debate," *Critical Inquiry* p. 408. Hereafter cited QCH in my text. Contrary to Davidson's representation, Heidegger's affiliation with German National Socialism has also been well known in American intellectual circles at least since the end of World War II, filtered as it was through the eyes of Jean-Paul Sartre, Maurice Merleau-Ponty, and the French existentialists in general, and of such Christian and Jewish existentialist theologians as the German expatriate Paul Tillich, Reinhold Niebuhr, Rudolph Bultmann, Gabriel Marcel, and Martin Buber, to name only the most prominent of those whose writing was widely and enthusiastically discussed in the postwar period and during the decade of the Vietnam War and the protest movement.

3. See Philippe Lacoue-Labarthe, "Sur le livre de Victor Farías *Heidegger et le nazisme*," in *La Fiction du politique* (Paris: Christian Bourgois, 1987), pp. 173–88. This review is a reprint with modifications originally published in *Le Journal litteraire*. The English version appeared under the title "Required Reading," trans. Stuart Barnett and Lynn Festa, *Diacritics* 19: 3–4 (Fall–Winter 1989), pp. 38–48.

4. Since the publication of the *Critical Inquiry* symposium, several books and collections of essays identifying Heidegger's thought with Nazism (and, in some degree or other, the antihumanist discourses Heidegger's thought enabled with forms of totalitarian politics) reflecting Davidson's explicitly humanist perspective on the question have been published in the United States; most notably, Richard Wolin, *The Politics of Being: The Political Thought of Martin Heidegger* (New York: Columbia University Press, 1990); Wolin, ed., *The Heidegger Controversy* (New York: Columbia University Press, 1992); David H. Hirsch, *The Deconstruction of Literature: Criticism After Auschwitz* (Hanover, N.H.: Brown University Press, 1991); Tom Rockmore, *On Heidegger's Nazism and Philosophy* (Berkeley: University of California Press, 1992).

5. See, however, Jacques Derrida, "Comment Donner Raison? 'How to Concede,

with Reasons,' " trans. John P. Leavey, Jr., a special issue titled "Heidegger: Art and Politics," *Diacritics* 19: 3–4 (Fall–Winter 1989), pp. 4–9: "The principal destination, the form, and the brevity of this note call for some precisions. Its context was very determining. It was autumn 1987. At the same time as the publication of my book *De l'esprit* . . . , Farías's *Heidegger et le nazisme* . . . had just appeared in France. Whatever the difference between the two books, the question of Nazism was central to them. In certain newspapers and through a kind of rumor, one perceived at that time the violence of a condemnation. This condemnation claimed to reach, well beyond Nazism and Heidegger, the very reading of Heidegger, the readers of Heidegger, those who had been able to refer to (even were it to pose on its subject deconstructive questions), still more those who promised to take an interest in (even were it to judge and to think, as rigorously as possible), Nazism and Heidegger's relationship to Nazism. The gravest and most obscurantist confusions were then maintained, sometimes naively, sometimes deliberately. It was not only, but it also was, rather evidently, a question of banning the reading of Heidegger and of exploiting what was believed to be a strategic advantage, in France, in France above all, against all thought that took Heidegger seriously, even if in a critical or deconstructive mode" (p. 4). This is an acutely perspicacious, important, and welcomed observation. Nevertheless, one is compelled with the force of irony, given Derrida's awareness of the violence of a condemnation in France that reached "well beyond Nazism and Heidegger" to include the deconstructive discourse in large part enabled by Heidegger, to ask this question: Why did Derrida accept the invitation of the editors of *Critical Inquiry* to contribute (especially the particular excerpt from *L'esprit* that appears in it) to its "Symposium on Heidegger and Nazism," which also, however more "mediately" than in the French press, reaches well beyond Nazism and Heidegger to include the posthumanist discourses that threaten the hegemony of the discourse of humanism and its institutional apparatuses? Is it that Derrida would discriminate between the "immediate presentations" of "the press," which he overdetermines in his effort to preserve Heidegger's text *for reading* from journals such as *Critical Inquiry*, which, in providing a forum for "critical inquiry" eschews "immediate presentation" and its "armed declarations and morality lessons," its "platforms [*tribunes*] and its tribunals [*tribuneaux*]"? It is Derrida, if anyone, who should know that such journals are, in their "pluralist" understanding of truth, no less ideological apparatuses of the dominant sociopolitical order than the media; indeed, that the difference between them is a difference of the visibility (and efficaciousness) of power. See also Joseph Kronick, "Dr. Heidegger's Experiment," *boundary 2* 17: 3 (Fall 1990), pp. 116–53. In this judicious review of the debate over the relationship between Heidegger's thought and politics, Kronick observes, "What distinguishes this debate from earlier ones, both in France and now in America, is not, in the final analysis, the new information that proves beyond question that Heidegger actively supported the Nazi regime, but the way in which the controversy has turned into an assault upon deconstruction and what we could call postmodern antihumanism" (p. 129).

6. As the editor of *boundary 2: a journal of postmodern literature and culture*, I must acknowledge my contribution to the process that has institutionalized the term "postmodernism." Nevertheless, I have come to realize that this word is misleading and in some ways disabling in its all-encompassing, which is to say dedifferentiating, generality. It obscures, if it does not annul, the fundamental point of departure of the oppositional discourses in question: that they exist to interrogate the anthropological subject; i.e., the discourse of Man. For an extended discussion

of this terminology, see my *End of Education: Toward Posthumanism* (Minneapolis: University of Minnesota Press, 1993).

7. Luc Ferry and Alain Renaut, *Heidegger and Modernity*, trans. Franklin Philip (Chicago: University of Chicago Press, 1990). Ferry and Renaut's book is an updating, afforded by the publication of Farías's *Heidegger et le nazisme*, of their earlier *La pensée 68: Essai sur l'anti-humanisme contemporain* (Paris: Gallimard, 1985), a virulent attack on the emergent "new left" in France, with chapters devoted to critiques (in terms of the "return of the Subject") of the "French Nietzscheanism" of Michel Foucault, the "French Heideggerianism" of Jacques Derrida, the French Marxism of Pierre Bourdieu, and the "French Freudianism" of Jacques Lacan. Published in English as *French Philosophy of the Sixties: An Essay on Antihumanism*, trans. Mary Schnackenberg Cattani (Amherst: University of Massachusetts Press, 1990). Ferry and Renaut's (mis)representation of Heidegger's and "Heideggerianism's" antihumanist discourses as discourses that fundamentally deny *agency* is the basis of the humanist critique. This representation will be addressed later in my text.

8. Jürgen Habermas, "Work and Weltanschauung," p. 448.

9. The quotation derives from Heidegger, "The Rectorate 1933/34: Facts and Thought," trans. Karsten Harries, *Review of Metaphysics* 38 (March 1985), p. 498. Hereafter cited R in my text.

10. The quotation derives from Heidegger, "The Thing," *Poetry, Language, Thought*, trans. Albert Hofstadter (New York: Harper & Row, 1971), pp. 193–94. The most extreme and sustained version of this familiar humanist representation of Heidegger's "later" understanding of being—one that practices the very violence of retrospective spatial reading it alleges against Heidegger's discourse—can be found in Tom Rockmore, *On Heidegger's Nazism and Philosophy*. Rockmore insistently represents Heidegger as a "seer of Being" (p. 128) and his "concept of truth as disclosure" as one depending on "the ability to see into history, to grasp the essence of what is with respect to the present and future" (p. 127). This representation of Heidegger's antivisionary hermeneutics as visionary culminates in an "explanation" of Heidegger's ethical irresponsibility: "There is a continuous line of argument leading from the Enlightenment commitment to reason to the insistence on responsibility as the condition of morality, which peaks in Kant's ethical theory. When Heidegger attributes ultimate causal authority to Being, he clearly reverses the Enlightenment view that through the exercise of reason human beings can attain dominion over the world and itself. In the final analysis, if Heidegger is correct, human actions depend on the gift of Being, hence on a suprahuman form of agency. Heidegger's insistence on Being as the final causal agent signals an abandonment of the idea of ethical responsibility. If responsibility presupposes autonomy, and autonomy presupposes freedom, then to embrace Being as the ultimate explanatory principle is tantamount to casting off the idea of ethical responsibility, the possibility of any moral accountability whatsoever.

"Heidegger's rejection of the idea of responsibility other than through the commitment to Being is incompatible with the assumption of personal moral accountability. This consequence, which follows rigorously from his position, calls for two comments. First, it in part explains his failure ever to take a public position on the well-known atrocities perpetrated by the Nazi movement to which he turned. If one's ontological analysis does not support the concept of personal responsibility, then one does not need to react on the personal level to what, from Heidegger's perspective, can be attributed to Being. Second, Heidegger's rejection of personal responsibility in his later thought denies a fundamental tenet of his own earlier position. In *Being and Time*, Heidegger had maintained that authenticity required a resolute choice of oneself. But if choice depends on Being, then in the final analysis, as Heidegger clearly saw, the only choice is the choice for or against Being" (p. 238).

11. The quotation derives from Kant, "What Is Enlightenment?," *Foundations of Metaphysics*, trans. Lewis White Beck (Indianapolis, 1959), p. 87.

12. The quotation derives from Emmanuel Lévinas, "As If Consenting to Horror": "But doesn't this silence, in time of peace, on the gas chambers and death camps lie beyond the realm of feeble excuses and reveal a soul completely cut off from any sensitivity, in which can be perceived a kind of consent to the horror?" (p. 487).

13. The quotation derives from Heidegger, "Letter on Humanism," *Basic Writings*, ed. David Farrell Krell (New York: Harper & Row, 1977), p. 213. See also the massive condemnation of Paul de Man's "dehumanized" and "dehumanizing" deconstructive discourse in the wake of the revelation of his early collaborationist journalist writing, most prominently, David Lehman, *Signs of the Times: Deconstruction and the Fall of de Man* (New York: Poseidon Press, 1991), and David Hirsch, *The Deconstruction of Literature: Criticism after Auschwitz*.

14. The by now notorious passage quoted by Davidson derives from an unpublished text made prominent by Philippe Lacoue-Labarthe in *La Fiction du politique*, p. 58. The latter's source is a citation in Wolfgang Schirmacher, *Technic und Gelassenheit* (Freiburg: Karl Alber, 1984). This passage has been invoked as a primary evidence not simply of Heidegger's moral callousness, but of the fundamental complicity of his philosophy with the historical Nazi project by virtually every humanist critic of Heidegger, continental and American, since the publication of Farías's *Heidegger et le nazisme*. See, for example, Richard Wolin, "The French Heidegger Debate," *New German Critique* 45 (Fall 1988), pp. 158–59; *The Politics of Being*, 168–69; and "Introduction," *The Heidegger Controversy*, p. 15; David H. Hirsch, *The Deconstruction of Literature*, pp. 18–19; and Tom Rockmore, *On Heidegger's Nazism and Philosophy*, pp. 241–42.

15. Quoted in Jürgen Habermas, "Work and Weltanschauung," p. 453.

16. Ibid. See also Thomas Sheehan, "Heidegger and the Nazis," *The New York Review of Books* (June 16, 1988), p. 42, and Richard Wolin, "The French Heidegger Debate," *New German Critique* 45 (Fall 1988), pp. 135–61. For Sheehan, this passage (as well as a passage from another lecture given the same day ["The Danger"] and Heidegger's response to Marcuse) is "characterized by a rhetoric, a cadence, a point of view that are damning *beyond commentary*" (my emphasis).

17. It will be objected that Heidegger's notion of the indissoluble continuum of being is precisely what identifies his thought, especially during and after the rectorate, with the totalitarian program of Nazism. Against this objection I would recall the testimony of Heidegger's recapitulation of the "Rectorate Address" in "The Rectorate 1933/34," where he opposes the "old" (disciplinary specialism) and the "new" (the official Nazi Party's insistence on reducing the different disciplines to an all-encompassing "political science" base) in favor of an alternative idea of the university that understands the various disciplines or fields of knowledge as a continuum or unity which, unlike the Nazi Party's, is "grounded" in the "essence of truth": "What let me hesitate until the very last day to assume the rectorate was the knowledge that with what I intended I would necessarily run into a twofold conflict with the "new" and the 'old.' The 'new' meanwhile had appeared in the form of 'political science' [*politische Wissenschaft*], the very idea of which rests on a falsification of the essence of truth [As Karsten Harries observes, ' "Political" here means "politicized." Truth was to be given a basis in the *Volk*. This led to the

attempt to create a "German mathematics," a "German physics," etc.'] The 'old' was an effort to remain responsible to one's "specialty," to help advance it and to utilize such advance in instruction, to reject all reflection on the foundations of science as abstract-philosophical speculations . . . but not to engage in reflection and, *thus engaged*, to think and to belong to the university" (R, pp. 482–83). If we recall Heidegger's representation of *Befindlichkeit* (the occasion of *Dasein*'s thrownness in temporality), *Verstehen* (understanding) and *Rede* (discourse) in *Being and Time* and his analysis of "the essence of truth" as *aletheia* (as opposed to *veritas* as *adequaetio intellectus et rei*) originary (temporal) thinking (as opposed to derivative, spatial thinking), it can be seen that Heidegger's understanding of the indissoluble relation between the sites of knowledge and between the university and the *polis* is substantially different from that of the Nazi Party precisely in the sense that the latter would totalize the various superstructural sites and the relationship between the university and the German socius in terms of "the idea of 'the political character of science,' " which is to say, in terms of a (racist) *technological* base or essence. It was, I submit, Heidegger's recognition of this *essentialist* essence in Nazism's historical cultural and political practice that precipitated not simply his resignation of the rectorship, but his eventual identification of Nazism with the nihilism of the two versions of "the universal rule of the will to power, now understood to embrace the planet. Today everything stands in this historical reality, no matter whether it is called communism, or fascism or world democracy." (R, p. 486).

18. However illiberal, indecorous, and improper it may seem to liberal humanist academics committed to the "autonomy of philosophy," I will contaminate my discourse by reference to my personal experience in World War II: I was a prisoner of war in Dresden at the time of the massive Allied fire bombing, and I bore witness to the horror not only of that dreadful night and day, but during the following days when those of us who were still alive in the *Arbeiten Kommandos* were assigned the task of searching the charred rubble of the totally devastated city for bodies of the incinerated dead, piling them or their members into horse-drawn wagons and hauling them away for mass burial. That, I can assure those who have been outraged by Heidegger's "pronouncement," was not a potential. It was, however easy it might be to discriminate between this and the gas chambers and death camps, immediate and actual—a "face-to-face . . . experience of horror."

19. Lacoue-Labarthe insistently equivocates on this crucial question. Immediately after his emphatic single-sentence paragraph judgment of Heidegger's 1949 statement as "scandaleusement insufficiente," he writes: "La raison [for Heidegger's inability or unwillingness to pronounce this difference] . . . est extrêmement *simple*: c'est que l'extermination des Juifs (et sa programmation dans le cadre d'une 'solution finale') est un phénomène *pour l'essentiel* ne relève d'aucune logique (politique, économique, sociale, militaire, etc.) autre que spirituelle, fût-elle dégradée, et par conséquence historiale. Dans l'apocalypse d'Auschwitz ce n'est ni plus ni moins que l'Occident, en son essence, qui s'est révélé—et qui ne cesse, depuis, de se révéler. Et c'est à la pensée de cet événement que Heidegger a manqué. [The reason is extremely *simple*: it's that the extermination of the Jews (and its programming in the framework of a 'final solution') is a phenomenon that follows *essentially* no logic (political, economic, social, military, etc.) other than a spiritual one, degraded as it may be, and therefore a historial one. In the Auschwitz apocalypse, it was nothing less than the Occident, in its essence, that revealed itself—and that continues, ever since, to reveal itself. And it is that event that Heidegger failed to think]" (*Fiction*, p. 59). Here as elsewhere in his text, Lacoue-Labarthe appears to

want it both ways: the extermination of the Jews was devoid of any "historial logic, whether political, economic, social, military, etc.," yet the "apocalypse of Auschwitz" was nothing more nor less than the exposure of the *essence* of the West. (The same kind of equivocation, if not contradiction, manifests itself in "Post-scriptum 2," pp. 73–81, where Lacoue-Labarthe answers his French critics' charge that he privileges the extermination of the Jews over other historical instances of mass murder.) For Heidegger, the *essence* of the West, i.e., that which *increasingly* determines its self-representation and historical practices (including the Nazis' manufacture of corpses in the gas chambers and death camps) is the logic of tech-nology. In his postwar retrieval of the period of the rectorate, moreover, Heideg-ger, we recall, identifies the planetary triumph of technology (*Technic*) in the mod-ern world as "the historical reality" in which "everything stands . . . no matter whether it is called communism or *fascism* or world democracy" (my emphasis). In what sense, then—if we understand these "-isms" as practices as well as systems of thought—beyond Heidegger's "failure" to speak publicly and at length (to apologize for) the "Final Solution," is Heidegger's statement lacking? Elsewhere, though not in terms addressing the question of Heidegger's "*faute*" as such, Lacoue-Labarthe betrays the qualification (contradiction?) I have thematized more specifically and starkly: "Le nazisme est un humanisme, en tant qu'il repose sur une détermination de l'*humanitas* à ses yeux plus puissante, c'est-à-dire plus effec-tive, que tout autre. Le sujet de l'auto-création absolue, même s'il transcende toute les déterminations du sujet moderne dans une position immédiatement naturelle (la particularité de la race), rassemble et concrétise ces mêmes déterminations . . . et s'institue comme *le* sujet, absolument parlant [Nazism is a humanism insofar as it rests on a determination of *humanitas* that, in its view, is more powerful, that is, more effective, than any other. The subject of absolute self-creation, even if it transcends all other determinations of the modern subject in occupying an imme-diately natural position (the particularity of race), brings together and concretizes these same determinations . . . and constitutes itself as *the* subject, absolutely speaking]" (*Fiction*, p. 138). Lacoue-Labarthe implicitly distinguishes the Nazis' from Heidegger's understanding of humanism as the fulfillment of the imperatives of *techne* by identifying the former with "le sujet de l'auto-fictionnement" (pp. 138–39). But he goes on to say, "On voit immédiatement les traits qui interdisent *ab-solument* qu'on rabatte ce schème [Rosenberg's biologism] sur le discours que tient à la même époque Jünger sur la *Gestalt* du Travailleur et *a fortiori* sur celui que tient Heidegger—lequel au reste n'a jamais caché son mépris à l'égard de Rosenberg—sur l'oeuvre d'art, la *Dichtung*, le peuple et l'histoire [One immediately sees the traits that make it *absolutely* impossible to confuse this schema with Jünger's ar-gument on the *Gestalt* of the Worker and, *a fortiori*, with the arguments of Heideg-ger—who, furthermore, never troubled to conceal his contempt for Rosenberg—concerning the work of art, *Dichtung*, the people and history]" (pp. 138–39).

20. I want to emphasize that this hierarchizing rhetorical maneuver is not unique to Davidson. It is repeated in virtually all the humanist critiques of Heidegger that invoke this passage. It is, alas, also Lacoue-Labarthe's: "Mais elle est scandaleuse, et donc piteusement insuffisante, parce qu'elle omet de signaler que *pour l'essentiel*, dans sa version allemande . . . l'extermination de masse fut celle des Juifs, et que cela fait une différence incommensurable avec la pratique économico-militaire des blocus ou même l'usage de l'armement nucléaire. *Sans parler de l'industrie agro-ali-mentaire*. . . . [But it is scandalous and therefore pitiably inadequate because it omits to mention that *essentially* . . . in its German version mass extermination was

an extermination of the Jews and that this is incommensurably different from the economic-military practice of blockades or even the use of nuclear arms. Not to speak of the agriculture industry. . . .]" (*Fiction*, p. 58).

21. Davidson cannot, however, refrain entirely from appealing to the authority of a prominent "autonomous" spokesman for "public reason": "I am indebted here," he writes in a footnote at this precise point, "to a conversation with Stanley Cavell that was essential in helping me formulate these issues" (QCH, 424).

22. This dialogue took place "in 1953/54, on the occasion of a visit by Professor Tezuka, of the Imperial University of Tokyo." It was published in 1959 in *Unterwegs zur Sprache* (Pfulligen: Verlag Günther Neske). My quotation is from Martin Heidegger, *On the Way to Language*, trans. Peter D. Hertz (San Francisco: Harper & Row, 1971), pp. 15–16. See also Martin Heidegger, "The End of Philosophy and the Task of Thinking," *Basic Writings*, ed. David Farrell Krell (New York: Harper & Row, 1977), originally published in *Zur Sache des Denkens* (Tübingen: Max Niemeyer Verlag, 1969): "The end of philosophy proves to be the triumph of the manipulable arrangement of a scientific-technological world *and the social order proper to this world*. The end of philosophy means the beginning of the world civilization based upon Western European thinking" (p. 327; my emphasis).

23. In keeping with this dual strategy, the Honolulu Conference included high-ranking military officers, the entire presidential cabinet, and a large contingency of technical advisors and, on the other hand, the triumvirate of generals (Nguyen Cao Ky, Nguyen Van Thieu, and Nguyen Huu Co), who, with the sanction of the United States, proclaimed themselves the government of the noncountry South Vietnam after the third military coup following the collapse of Diem's American-sponsored brutally dictatorial regime in August 1963.

24. Douglas Anderson, Corpsman, 3rd Battalion, 1st Marines, Nui Kim San, Feb. 1967-Feb. 1968, in Al Santoli, ed., *Everything We Had: An Oral History of the Vietnam War by Thirty-Three American Soldiers Who Fought It* (New York: Ballantine, 1981), p. 69.

25. Tim O'Brien, *Going After Cacciato* (New York: Dell, 1978), p. 300. See also Michael Herr, *Dispatches* (New York: Avon, 1978), pp. 1–2; and Philip Caputo, *A Rumor of War* (New York: Ballantine, 1977), *passim*.

26. Herman Rapaport, "Vietnam: The Thousand Plateaus," *The Sixties without Apologies*, ed. Sohnya Sayres, Anders Stephanson, Stanley Aronowitz, Fredric Jameson (Minneapolis: University of Minnesota Press, 1984), p. 138.

27. Andrew F. Krepinevich, Jr., *The Army and Vietnam* (Baltimore: The Johns Hopkins University Press, 1986): "The Army concept" that determined American military strategy throughout the Vietnam War, according to Krepinevich, was, despite token gestures to accommodate itself to the "low-intensity" conditions of guerrilla warfare, fundamentally that which determined military strategy in Europe in World War II: "The Army Concept of war is, basically, the Army's perception of how wars ought to be waged and is reflected in the way the Army organizes and trains its troops for battle. The characteristics of the Army Concept are two: a focus on mid-intensity, or conventional, war and a reliance on high volumes of firepower to minimize [American] casualties—in effect, the substitution of material cost at every available opportunity to avoid payment in [American] blood" (p. 5). What Krepinevich's rhetoric insistently obscures in his otherwise persuasive identification of the "Army Concept" with European warfare (in the term "conventional," for example) is precisely what the NLF and NVA intuitively exploited: its Eurocentric commitment to a narrative of closure (the promise/fulfillment structure that terminates in unconditional victory). See, in this respect, Michael

Herr's brilliant reading of the American military command's reading of the "Battle of Khe Sahn" in *Dispatches*: "It is impossible to fix the exact moment in time when it happened, or to know, really, why. All that was certain was that Khe Sahn had become a passion, the false love object in the heart of the Command. It cannot even be determined which way the passion travelled. Did it proceed from the filthiest ground-zero slit trench and proceed outward, across I Corps to Saigon and on (taking the true perimeter with it) to the most abstract reaches of the Pentagon? Or did it get born in those same Pentagon rooms where six years of failure had made the air bad, where optimism no longer sprang from anything viable but sprang and sprang, all the way to Saigon, where it was packaged and shipped north to give the grunts some kind of reason for what was about to happen to them? In its outline, the promise was delicious: Victory! A vision of as many as 40,000 of them out there in the open, fighting it out on our terms, fighting for once like men, fighting to no avail. There would be a battle, a set-piece battle where he could be killed by the numbers, killed wholesale, and if we killed enough of him, maybe he would go away. In the face of such a promise, the question of defeat could not even be considered, no more than the question of whether, after Tet, Khe Sahn might have become militarily unwise and even absurd. Once it was locked in place, Khe Sahn became like the planted jar in Wallace Stevens's poem. It took dominion everywhere" (pp. 113–14). For a brilliant analysis of the ideological relay Herr's identification of Stevens's poem with the command's (and America's) "mission" in Vietnam is pointing to, see Frank Lentriccia, "Anatomy of a Jar," in *Ariel and the Police: Michel Foucault, William James, Wallace Stevens* (Madison: University of Wisconsin Press, 1988), pp. 3–27.

This motif, which relates the "Army Concept" with the Eurocentric structure of consciousness, is pervasive in the political conscious or unconscious of the representations of the Vietnam War at large. See also Tim O'Brien, *Going After Cacciato*. "They did not know even the simple things. . . . No sense of order or momentum. No front, no trenches laid out in neat parallels. No Patton rushing for the Rhine, no beachheads to storm and win and hold for the duration. They did not have targets. They did not have a cause. . . . " (p. 320); and Philip Caputo, *A Rumor of War*: "It was not warfare. It was murder. We could not fight back against the Viet Cong mines or take cover from them or anticipate when they would go off. Walking down the trails, waiting for those things to explode, we had begun to feel more like victims than soldiers. So we were ready for a battle, a traditional, set-piece battle against regular soldiers like ourselves" (p. 273).

28. For provocative, if not finally adequate, accounts of this multi-situated effort of the culture industry to recuperate the continuity of the myth of America's world historical mission, see the special issue of *Cultural Critique* entitled "American Representations of Vietnam," 2 (Spring 1985) and John Hellman, *American Myth and the Legacy of Vietnam* (New York: Columbia University Press, 1986).

29. Herman Rapaport, "Vietnam: The Thousand Plateaus," p. 139. As Fredric Jameson has observed in passing, the Vietnam War was the first "postmodern war." "Postmodernism, or, The Cultural Logic of Late Capitalism," *New Left Review* 146 (July/August 1984), p. 14; reprinted with revisions in *Postmodernism; or, The Logic of Late Capitalism* (Durham, N.C.: Duke University Press, 1991). What Jameson neglects to add is that its postmodernity was determined by one of the relay of "others" struggling to e-merge from the domination of the imperial cultural and sociopolitical narrative of the collective Occidental Subject.

30. The name "Viet Cong" means "Vietnamese Communist" and was not acceptable to the NLF because it was invented by the Diem regime to associate the NLF with

the base-superstructure of Stalinist Marxism, a model of the revolution that Ho Chi Minh had specifically rejected. See Frances FitzGerald, *Fire in the Lake: The Vietnamese and the Americans in Vietnam* (New York: Vintage, 1973), p. 299.

31. Frances FitzGerald, *Fire in the Lake: The Vietnamese and the Americans in Vietnam*, pp. 498–500. See also Philip Caputo, *A Rumor of War*, for an example of the obverse side of this binarist representation: Commenting on the omission of reference to "any explanatory or extenuating circumstance" in the court-martial charge that he was guilty of the premeditated murder of two South Vietnamese civilians, Caputo writes: "Later, after I had time to think things over, I drew my own conclusions: the explanatory or extenuating circumstances was the war. The killings had occurred in war. They had occurred, moreover, in a war whose sole aim was to kill Viet Cong, a war in which those ordered to do the killing often could not distinguish the Viet Cong from the civilians, a war in which civilians in 'free-fire zones' were killed every day by weapons far more horrible than pistols or shotguns. The deaths of Le Dung and Le Du could not be divorced from the nature and conduct of the war. . . . But to raise those points in explanation would be to raise a host of ambiguous moral questions. It could even raise the question of the morality of American intervention in Vietnam. . . . Therefore, the five men in the patrol and I were to be tried as common criminals. . . . If we were found guilty, the Marine Corps's institutional conscience would be clear. Six criminals, who, of course, did not represent the majority of America's fine fighting sons, had been brought to justice. Case closed. If we were found innocent, the Marine Corps could say, 'Justice has taken its course, and in a court-martial conducted according to the facts and the rules of evidence, no crime was found to have been committed.' Case closed again. Either way the military won" (p. 306). See also Daniel Lang, *Casualties of War* (New York: Pocket, 1989); first published in *The New Yorker* (October 18, 1969).

32. See David Halberstam, *The Best and the Brightest* (New York: Random House, 1972), *passim*. This appallingly crude American phrase, according to Halberstam, epitomized the discourse of the civilian bureaucracy in Washington, D.C., planning and directing the war in Vietnam. In reducing the resistant complexities of this history—above all, the struggle of the Vietnamese people for self-determination—to a technical problem with a solution, it can be seen to be the discursive equivalent of the military/political technology that devastated Vietnam in pursuit of a decisive victory for the "free world." Compare the following extract from a book entitled *Die Tageszeitung als Mittel der Staatsführung* (1933) by one Theodor Lüddecke (director of the Press Institute at the University of Halle) quoted in Werner Hamacher, "Journals, Politics: Notes on Paul de Man's Wartime Journalism," *Responses: On Paul de Man's Wartime Journalism*, ed. Werner Hamacher, Neil Hertz, and Thomas Keenan (Lincoln: University of Nebraska Press, 1989): "The written word will once again return to its original purpose—that is, to trigger actions and to prepare them. The organized masses will constitute the new state; thus, this state will not stop where the official bureaucracy stops. Every citizen will be, in one form or another, an agent of the state. . . .

"In a technical respect, a dictatorship is, among other things, a rationalization of political work. *It reduces both the time needed for devising constructive plans and the channels through which they are carried out.* . . .

"The entire German national economy is a large business, and the entire nation is its work force. In business only one opinion may reign if its production goal is to be achieved" (p. 447).

33. FitzGerald, *Fire in the Lake*: "From 1969 on, Nixon expanded and intensified the

air war, doubling the total tonnage of bombs dropped so that after two years and a few months of his administration the United States had dropped more bombs on Indochina than it had in both the European and the Pacific theatres during World War II. The tactical strikes in South Vietnam continued while the B-52s expanded their operations in northern Laos, turning a large percentage of the Lao population and most of the montagnard tribes into refugees. U.S. air operations over Cambodia finished the job the troops had taken on, killing thousands of people and displacing millions" (p. 556).

34. See Jonathan Schell, "The Village of Ben Suc," in *The Real War* (New York: Pantheon, 1988), pp. 52–188; and, especially, John Duffet, ed., *Against the Crime of Silence: Proceedings of the International War Crimes Trial* (New York: Simon and Schuster, 1970).

35. Michael Herr, *Dispatches*, p. 2. As Herr suggests, by way of the parodic phonetic allusion to the voice of the John Wayne of the Hollywood Western, this is not endemic to the Vietnam occasion. It is a violent "know-how" that has its origins in the pioneer spirit and the westward expansion of the American frontier that culminated in the genocide of native Americans.

36. Tim O'Brien, *Going After Cacciato*, p. 107.

37. It was precisely this reified or technological "American" perspective which understood the Vietnamese earth as commodity that alienated the American soldier: not simply in the sense of his utter inability to understand the language and culture it informed, but of his desperate bewilderment in the face of an enemy who did not play by the Western rules of "enframement" by which he was inscribed. See especially, the chapter entitled "The Things They Didn't Understand," in Tim O'Brien, *Going After Cacciato*: "Not knowing the language, they [the soldiers in Paul Berlin's squad] did not know the people. They did not know what the people loved or respected or feared or hated. They did not recognize hostility unless it was patent, unless it came in a form other than language; the complexities of tone and tongue were beyond them. Dinkese, Stink Harris called it: monkey chatter, bird talk. Not knowing the language, the men did not know whom to trust. Trust was lethal. They did not know false smiles from true smiles, or if in Quang Ngai a smile has the same meaning it had in the States. 'Maybe the dinks got things mixed up,' Eddie once said, after the time a friendly-looking farmer bowed and smiled and pointed them into a minefield. 'Know what I mean? Maybe . . . well, maybe the gooks cry when they're happy and smile when they're sad. Who the hell knows? . . . I mean, hey, this here's a different culture.' Not knowing the people, they did not know friends from enemies. They did not know if it was a popular war, or, if popular, in what sense. . . . They did not know religions or philosophies or theories of justice. More than that, they did not know how emotions worked in Quang Ngai. . . . Emotions and beliefs and attitudes, motives and aims, hopes—these were unknown to the men in Alpha Company, and Quang Ngai told nothing. 'Fuckin' beasties,' Stink would croak, mimicking the frenzied village speech. 'No shit, I seen hamsters with more feelings' " (p. 309–10).

38. Frances FitzGerald, *Fire in the Lake*, p. 11. In her analysis of Vietnamese culture, FitzGerald draws heavily from the research of the noted French scholar of Asian religions Paul Mus. See especially, *Viet-Nam: Sociology d'une guerre* (Paris: Editions du Seuil, 1952); "Cultural Backgrounds of Present Problems," *Asia* 4 (Winter 1966) pp. 10–21; and "The Role of the Village in Vietnamese Politics," *Pacific Affairs* 23 (September 1949), pp. 265–72.

39. According to Frances FitzGerald, by 1972, at the time of the publication of her profoundly moving book, "Out of a population of seventeen million, there are

now five million refugees. Perhaps 40 or 50 percent of the population, as opposed to the 15 percent before the war, live in and around the cities and towns. The distribution is that of a highly industrialized country, but there is almost no industry in South Vietnam. And the word 'city' and even 'town' is misleading. What was even in 1965 [when the bombing began] a nation of villages and landed estates is now a nation of *bidonvilles*, refugee camps, and army bases. South Vietnam is shattered so no two pieces fit together" (*Fire in the Lake*, pp. 569–70). Since then, of course, we have had the painful spectacle of the "boat people" and mass exile to foreign countries where, by and large, these refugee Vietnam immigrants are not wanted.

40. Frances FitzGerald, *Fire in the Lake*, p. 572.

41. See my chapter entitled "The University in the Vietnam Decade: The Crisis of Command and the Refusal of Spontaneous Consent," *The End of Education: Toward Posthumanism* (Minneapolis: University of Minnesota Press, 1993).

42. Richard Ohmann, *English in America: A Radical View of the Profession* (New York: Oxford University Press, 1975): "To put the obvious label on the paradigm [that characterizes all the memoranda] it is a model for *problem solving*. . . . Any model reduces complexity—exchanges faithfulness to reality for finiteness. If you have to decide something tomorrow or next week, it is helpful, maybe necessary, to sort reality out on a familiar grid. A problem-solving model supplies a grid that connects reality to a desired future by one or more acts. To do that, it must pick out those elements from reality that have the most salient ties to the desired future. This is, of course, an abstraction of elements from the present in a way that reflects one's own needs and interests" (p. 196).

It is worth observing that this dedifferentiating model, which, according to Ohmann, is basic both to the memoranda that determined American foreign policy in Vietnam and the teaching of freshman composition in American educational institutions, is in general the circular model informing the metaphysical (Occidental) tradition at large, as understood by Heidegger, and in particular the panoptic model informing the disciplinary tradition of the Enlightenment, as understood by Foucault.

43. Richard Ohmann, *English in America*, pp. 199–202. In thus reducing "the suffering of the Vietnamese" into the frame of a problem-solving discursive economy, the "can do" memoranda of *The Pentagon Papers* betray a commitment to technique that, in its transformation of human beings into counters in a statistical system devoted to the efficient achievement of political ends, was not unlike that informing the discourse and practice of the Nazi planners (and their communication system) who understood their project as "a rationalization of political work" that "reduced both time needed for devising constructive plans and the channel through which they are carried out." See note 30.

44. Philip Jones Griffiths, *Vietnam, Inc.* (New York: Macmillan, 1971), p. 12. After the publication of this photographic documentary, Griffiths was refused re-entry to Vietnam by the American authorities.

45. Michael Herr, *Dispatches*, p. 2.

46. Philip Jones Griffiths, *Vietnam, Inc.* p. 15.

47. See especially, Edmund K. Oasa, "The Political Economy of International Agricultural Research: A Review of the CGIAR [Consultative Group on International Agricultural Research]: Response to Criticism of the 'Green Revolution,' " in *The Green Revolution Revisited: Critique and Alternatives*, ed. Bernhard Glaeser (London: Allen and Unwin, 1987), pp. 1–55.

48. Although Frances FitzGerald does not focus on the point I am making, her account

of American foreign policy in Vietnam following the Guam Conference in April 1967 bears witness to it: "At the Guam Conference President Johnson took the long-awaited step of putting all civilian operations under the command of General Westmoreland. His move signified that Washington no longer gave even symbolic importance to the notion of a 'political' war waged by the Vietnamese government. The reign of the U.S. military had begun, and with it the strategy of quantity in civilian as well as military affairs.

As assistant to Westmoreland, Robert Komer [civilian head of the Revolutionary Development Program] had something of the general's notion of scale. After all the history of failed aid programs, he believed that the only hope for success lay in saturation. . . . The U.S. government had no choice but to force its supplies upon the Vietnamese people: thousands of tons of bulgar wheat, thousands of gallons of cooking oil, tons of pharmaceuticals, enough seed to plant New Jersey with miracle rice, enough fertilizer for the same, light bulbs, garbage trucks, an atomic reactor. . . .

In part, of course, this aid was absolutely necessary, for the U.S. military was at the same time bombing, defoliating, and moving villages at such a rate that all the aid the United States could ship would not have been excessive as refugee relief. . . . Partly to solve this 'technical problem' of GVN efficiency, the United States sent in more American advisors. At the beginning of 1966 the mission had three or four civilians in every province capital; by the end of 1967 it had a small bureaucracy in each, comprising pig experts, rice experts, market and gardening experts, AID administrators, International Voluntary Service workers, English teachers, city planners. . . . " *Fire in the Lake*, pp. 461–62.

49. Michael Herr, *Dispatches*, pp. 44–45. In referring to Herr's rhetoric as Nietzschean carnival, I am invoking Michel Foucault's essay "Nietzsche, History, Genealogy," in *Language, Counter-Memory, Practice: Selected Essays and Interviews*, ed. Donald F. Bouchard (Ithaca, N.Y.: Cornell University Press, 1977): "The new historian, the genealogist, will know what to make of this masquerade [the historiography which, in monumentalizing history, bars 'access to the actual intensities and creations of life']. He will not be too serious to enjoy it; on the contrary, he will push the masquerade to its limit and prepare the great carnival of time where masks are constantly reappearing" (pp. 161–62).

The unsayability of the "face-to-face experience of horror" suffered by the Vietnamese peasantry as a consequence of the "suppression of the other, the human," by the technical advisors in general and the military directing the war in Vietnam, which compels Herr to Nietszchean parody, is attempted graphically (specifically in terms of the complicity between the agricultural advisors and the military) by Griffiths in the appalling "unofficial" sequence of photographs that constitute his resonantly entitled *Vietnam, Inc.* It begins with a juxtaposition of an image depicting MACV (Military Assistance Command Vietnam) military officers peering complacently (draped American flag in the center background) at a highlighted tactical map of Vietnam with images of a young Vietnamese woman harvesting a rice field, a venerable old peasant holding two stalks of rice, and several images depicting peasants in the rice paddies which are also recognizable as burial grounds. It ends with images of peasant refugees foraging in the garbage dumps (officially called "New Life Hamlets") to which they were relocated, and of peasants of all ages and both sexes mutilated by the American bombing of their villages. Like Herr's parody, Griffiths's sustained and relentless visual deconstruction of the official representation of the American intervention parallels my verbal analysis of what might justifiably be called the (American) technological sublime, but it evokes far more powerfully the enormity of the horror I have futilely tried to convey in words.

50. Louis Althusser and Etienne Balibar, *Reading Capital* (London: Verso, 1979), pp. 19 ff.

51. Noam Chomsky, "On War Crimes," *At War with Asia* (New York: Pantheon, 1970), pp. 298–99. In this representation of the Vietnamese enemy as "Asian horde," Hoopes's liberal discourse is no different from that of the American culture industry—particularly Hollywood. See, for example, John Wayne's *Green Berets* (1968), especially the depiction of the NVA's assault on the Marine base camp. Hoopes's discourse, it should be noted, also betrays an uneasy awareness that the strategy of the National Liberation Front and the North Vietnam Army was grounded in their penetration of the benign Christian humanist logic of the United States to its genocidal essence.

52. Jean-Paul Sartre, *On Genocide* (Boston: Beacon Press, 1968), pp. 81–82.

53. Herman Melville, *Moby-Dick*, ed. Harrison Hayford and Hershel Parker (New York: Norton Critical Editions, 1967), p. 161. My emphasis. See Sacvan Bercovitch, *The American Jeremiad* (Madison: University of Wisconsin Press, 1978), which traces modern America's global imperial project back to the Puritans' self-representation of their "Mission" as a divinely ordained "errand in the wilderness": "Insisting that the theocracy was the American chronometer, the ministers [in the late seventeenth century] drained it of its discrete theological and institutional content. Intent on preserving the past, they transformed it (as legend) into a malleable guide to the future. Seeking to defend the Good Old Way, they abstracted from its antiquated social forms the larger, vaguer, and more flexible forms of symbol and metaphor (*new chosen people, city on a hill, promised land, destined progress, New Eden, American Jerusalem*) and so facilitated the movement from visible saint to American patriot, sacred errand to manifest destiny, colony to republic to imperial power" (p. 92). Without subscribing to Bercovitch's interpretation of Melville's *Moby-Dick* and to his limited version of American ideology, I have appropriated his genealogy in my more radical account of the ideology informing the American intervention in Vietnam. See also John Hellman, *American Myth and the Legacy of Vietnam*, which broadly applies Bercovitch's analysis of seventeenth- and eighteenth-century American cultural production to the popular representations of American involvement in Vietnam.

54. Michel Foucault, "Nietzsche, Genealogy, History," pp. 160–61. The mask implicit in Herr's parodic portrait of the American major (as well as his equally Nietzschean portrait of the communications officer at Cu Chi in one of my epigraphs) is, perhaps needless to say, one step further removed from—in Jameson's and Baudrillard's term a "simulacrum" of—the "historical" figure with which the traditional historian identifies: it is, as it was for so many Americans involved in the Vietnam War, the hero of the John Wayne Western movie, including, of course, *The Green Berets*.

55. See Jacques Derrida, "L'enfer des philosophes," *Le Nouvel Observateur* (November 6–12, 1987), p. 172. Though Derrida demonstrates that Heidegger's philosophical discourse on "the people" (*die Volk*) was insistently opposed to the biologically determined racism of the official theorists of Nazism (Alfred Rosenberg, Ernst Krieck, Alfred Bäumler, etc.), he implicates it with Nietzsche's "metaphysical racism." But he also points out that "Nazism [and anti-Semitism] could have developed only with the differentiated but decisive complicity of other countries, of 'democratic' states, and of university and religious institutions" (p. 172).

56. Matthew Arnold, "The Modern Element in Modern Literature," in *On the Classical Tradition*, vol. 1 of *The Complete Prose Works*, ed. R. H. Super, 11 vols. (Ann Arbor: University of Michigan Press, 1960), p. 19. For an extended analysis of the repressive ideology (including its racism) informing Arnold's liberal humanist discourse, see "The Apollonian Investment of Modern Humanist Educational Theory: The Examples of Matthew Arnold, Irving Babbitt, and I. A. Richards," in my *The End of Education*.

57. For a telling example of the way American humanist intellectuals have exploited Victor Farías's renewed exposure of Heidegger's affiliation with Nazism and, above all, Heidegger's notorious "pronouncement" in behalf of recuperating the authority humanism has lost to poststructuralist thought since the 1960s, see David H. Hirsch, *The Deconstruction of Literature: Criticism after Auschwitz*. In a chapter titled "Derailing American Literary Criticism," which reaffirms the emancipatory accomplishments of liberal humanism (including the New Criticism) in the 1950s (the period bearing witness to the start of the Cold War)—without any reference to the virulent Gestapo-like tactics of McCarthyism and the tacit consent to them by most liberal humanists—Hirsch writes: "In the case of Heidegger, his unshakable faith in Nazism, his shameful unwillingness to speak out against Nazism after the war, and his obtuse paralleling of mechanized agriculture with the death camps made him a laughingstock to all but the most dedicated fanatics" (p. 18).

58. Martin Heidegger, *Parmenides*, vol. 54 of *Gesamtsausgabe* (Frankfurt am Main: Vittorio Klostermann, 1982), pp. 6–61. My translation. See also chapter 5, "Heidegger and Foucault: The Politics of the Commanding Gaze." It is worth observing here, for the sake of emphasizing the anti-Romanism of his Hellenism (that is, the anti-imperialism of his antihumanism), that what Heidegger discloses about the imperial Roman origins of humanist modernity by way of his critical genealogy of its "disinterested" discourse, is more or less overtly stated by T. S. Eliot in his repeated Christian humanist celebration of Virgil (as opposed to Homer) as the measure of the "universal classic"—his "centeredness," his "maturity," his "comprehensiveness," his "common style," his "historical sense," his sense of an "all-embracing destiny" (understood in terms of providential design)—during and after World War II (i.e., in the wars against German and later Soviet barbarism) as "the price of our freedom, the defense of freedom against chaos": "What then does this destiny, which no Homeric hero shares with Aeneas, mean? For Virgil's conscious mind, and for his contemporary readers, it means the *imperium romanum*. This in itself, as Virgil saw it, was a worthy justification of history. . . . I say that it was all the end of history that Virgil could be asked to find [the allusion is to the prefigurative typological role he plays in Christian providential history (in the biblical exegesis of the church fathers) and literature (Dante, for example)], and that it was a worthy end. And do you really think that Virgil was mistaken? You must remember that the Roman Empire was transformed into the Holy Roman Empire. What Virgil proposed to his contemporaries was the highest ideal even for an unholy Roman Empire, for any merely temporal empire. We are all, so far as we inherit the civilization of Europe, still citizens of the Roman Empire, and time has not yet proved Virgil wrong when he wrote *nec tempora pono: imperium sine fini dedi*" ("Virgil and the Christian World," *On Poetry and Poets* [London: Faber and Faber, 1957], pp. 129–30).

The quoted phrases in the introductory sentence are taken from "What Is a Classic?," *On Poetry and Poets*, pp. 52–71. For an extended analysis of the place and function of Eliot's Christian humanist prose writing in the cultural production of modernity, see "The Apollonian Investment of Modern Humanist Educational Theory: The Examples of Matthew Arnold, Irving Babbitt, and I. A. Richards," in my *The End of Education*.

59. What Foucault calls "the Roman reference" in his genealogy of the disciplinary society is pervasive and, despite its hitherto unnoticed prominence, determining in some fundamental ways. See chapter 5, "Heidegger and Foucault: The Politics of the Commanding Gaze."

60. Michel Foucault, "Truth and Power," *A Foucault Reader*, ed. Paul Rabinow (New York: Pantheon, 1984), pp. 72–73. See also Hubert L. Dreyfus and Paul Rabinow, *Michel Foucault: Beyond Structuralism and Hermeneutics* (Chicago: University of Chicago Press, 1982), pp. 128–33. Foucault's definition of humanism in "Revolutionary Action: 'Until Now,'" quoted in chapter 6, should also be considered in the light of his analysis of the "repressive hypothesis."

61. Antonio Gramsci, *Selections from the Prison Notebooks*, ed. and trans. Quintin Hoare and Geoffrey Nowell Smith (New York: International Publishers, 1971), p. 12. My emphasis.

62. See chapter 5, "The University in the Vietnam Decade," in my *The End of Education*.

63. Charles Frankel, *Education and the Barricades* (New York: W. W. Norton, 1968), pp. 72–73. My emphasis, except for "*specific*."

64. Michel Foucault, *The History of Sexuality, Vol. I*, trans. Robert Hurley (New York: Pantheon, 1978), p. 82. By the "juridico-discursive" view of power, Foucault means a relationship between the law and knowledge in which the former is secondary to the latter and is invoked only when spontaneous consent to the "truth" of knowledge is refused. As such, it is, as I am suggesting, related not only to Gramsci's analysis of the relationship between political and civil society and to Althusser's analysis of the relationship between ideological and (repressive) state apparatuses, but also to Heidegger's analysis of the relationship between the imperialism that takes the immediate form of *Niederwerfen* and that which takes the mediated form of *hintergehenden Umgehens*.

65. Against the inevitable objection that the relationship I am drawing between Heidegger's destruction and Foucault's more radical genealogy is an arbitrary one, I refer the reader to Michel Foucault, "Final Interview," *Raritan* 5: 1 (Summer 1985), pp. 8–9; originally published in *Les Nouvelles* (June 28, 1985). For a more extended account of this relationship, see chapter 5.

66. As the history of modernity, especially the example of the American intervention in Vietnam, suggests, the Occident = technology = ethnocentrism, if not racism. This equation, it should not be forgotten, is a fundamental one in Heidegger's postwar essays on technology.

67. Philippe Lacoue-Labarthe, *Fiction*, p. 71. For his discussion of the *césure* vis-à-vis Hölderlin, see pp. 64 ff.

68. In asserting that the event of Auschwitz was the revelation of the Occident's own essence, Lacoue-Labarthe adds: "Et c'est à la pensée de cet événement que Heidegger a manqué" (p. 59; "And it is that event that Heidegger failed to think"). I would certainly agree with Lacoue-Labarthe. But I would add a significant qualification. *Providing it is understood in the context of his reiteration of the motif of the "end of philosophy"* (a motif that traverses all his writing, from the first sentences of *Being and Time*, which refer to the forgetting of the question of being [*die Seinsfrage*] in modernity, through the proscribed lectures eventually published in *An Introduction to Metaphysics* [1953], to "The Rectorate 1933/34," published posthumously in 1983), Heidegger's "pronouncement" in 1949 can be seen to constitute the basis

for a more adequate analysis of this event, despite its brevity and abstraction. And this, precisely because Heidegger's discourse on the end of philosophy provides the basis of an interpretation of this event as an indissoluble relay that, however unevenly distributed the violence, encompasses the discourses and practices of the entire modern Occident, rather than as a pure event perpetrated by a singular agent at a singular site/time: the Nazis and the death camps and gas chambers between 1942–1945. This, I want to reiterate, is not to excuse Heidegger for his failure to discriminate between violences. It is, rather, to bring back into play the complicities of the "Occident" with the kind of violence perpetrated against the Jews by the Nazi regime, the complicities that humanists such as Davidson (with the inadvertent aid of Lacoue-Labarthe and other dissident French Heideggerians) all too easily efface in the name of the discourse of "truth," i.e., the repressive hypothesis.

69. See Arno J. Mayer, *Why Did the Heavens Not Darken? The "Final Solution" in History* (New York: Pantheon, 1991, p. 188. Like Habermas and others on the German left, Mayer, who refers to the Nazis' "Final Solution" in terms of its consequence to his own family, sees the "retrovisionist" historians in Germany as partaking in an effort "to rationalize the Nazi regime by characterizing it as intrinsically designed and essentially for the struggle against the 'greater evil' of Soviet communism." But he also rejects the disabling assumption that the Holocaust was without historical precedent and insists on the urgency of historicizing the Holocaust. Specifically, his research discloses that the anti-Semitism of the Nazis and the German elite was integrally related but practically subordinated to their anti-Bolshevism ("judeobolshevism") and that the "judeocide" as such—the "Final Solution"—was not independent of but contingent on the success of the Nazis' "crusade" in the East: that the decision to exterminate the Jews came only after "Operation Barbarossa" failed. Mayer's historicization of the Holocaust, that is, would undermine the essential ideological project of the conservative revisionist historians, who would separate German anti-Semitism from German anti-Bolshevism, reading the Holocaust as an aberration from the national character, in a strategy to bracket it in favor of focusing on the latter as representative of the continuity of German identity. Mayer's thesis about the dating of the decision to put the "Final Solution" into effect is, to be sure, the subject of heated debate.

70. Charles S. Maier, *The Unmasterable Past: History, Holocaust and German National Identity* (Cambridge, Mass.: Harvard University Press, 1988), p. 166. Maier (who, like Arno Mayer, prefaces his text with an account of the violence visited on his immediate forebears by the Nazis) broadly agrees with Jürgen Habermas's assessment of German revisionist accounts of the Holocaust—that the quest for national identity in the aftermath of the Third Reich constitutes an apologetics for Nazism aimed at recuperating the German right and the Cold War perspective toward the Soviet Union in the face of German democratization since the 1960s and the Gorbachev initiative. But he also points to and warns against making a "fetish of Auschwitz" in behalf of moral and political ends that make the victim a victimizer. See especially "Epilogue: Whose Holocaust? Whose History?," pp. 159–72. The degree to which even contemporary Israeli intellectuals of good will regarding the question of Palestinians are inscribed by and succumb to the dubious moral and political consequences of the prevailing discourse of the Holocaust is suggested in the response of Daniel Boyarin and Jonathan Boyarin to Edward W. Said's "Representing the Colonized: Anthropology's Interlocutors," *Critical Inquiry* 15 (Winter 1989), published in *Critical Inquiry* 15 (Spring 1989) and entitled "Towards a Dialogue with Edward Said." In their contribution to the exchange, these "Jewish nationalists" (as they refer to themselves) take Said especially to task for ("are most

critical of") "his occlusion of the fact that other options for Jewish self-renewal were obviated by genocide or Soviet repression" (p. 627). To this, Said answers: "I would have thought the Boyarins' reminder—monumental in its irrelevance to the suffering Palestinians—ought to be addressed to their fellow Jews, precisely those soldiers and politicians who are now engaged in visiting upon non-Jews many of the same evil practices anti-Semites waged against Holocaust victims who are ancestors and relatives of present-day Israelis. This deeply offensive attitude of the Boyarins dilutes the expressions of support for Palestinian self-determination that they occasionally allow themselves. What they cannot accept is that the Palestinian and Israeli positions are not symmetrical today, and that whatever the horror of Jewish suffering in the past it does not excuse, abrogate, or exonerate the practices of the Jewish state against the Palestinian people. There is, in short, a rank injustice against Palestinians by the Jewish state: this must be admitted, and not weakened by constantly calling on people to remember Jewish sufferings in the past, admittedly real and horrifying though they are" (pp. 636–37). Said's response to the Boyarins may appear to be unmannerly, a violation of propriety, to the gentlemanly—"liberal pluralist"—academic. But, I submit, his "unmannerly" discourse constitutes precisely a refusal of the critically disabling rules of discursive formation to which the Boyarins appeal in their call for a "dialogue" with Said that would desituate and rarefy the uneven historically specific occasion of the Palestinian people. In other words, Said's "impropriety" constitutes a refusal of the ruse of the "repressive hypothesis."

71. Jean-François Lyotard, *Heidegger and "the jews,"* trans. Andreas Michel and Mark Roberts, with a foreword by David Carroll (Minneapolis: University of Minnesota Press, 1990).

72. See especially chapter 2, "From Humanism to Nazism: Heideggerian Interpretations of Heidegger's Nazism," *Heidegger and Modernity,* pp. 31–54.

73. The editors of *Social Text* (Sohnya Sayre, Anders Stephanson, Stanley Aronowitz, Fredric Jameson), "Introduction," *The 60s Without Apology* (Minneapolis: University of Minnesota Press, 1984): "Trashing the 60s has become a strategic feature of the current struggle for hegemony" (p. 8).

74. Jean Beaufret, *Entrétien avec F. de Towarnicki* (Paris: PVF, 1984); François Fedier, "À propos de Heidegger: Une lecture denoncée," *Critique* 242 (July 1967), pp. 672–86, and *Heidegger, anatomie d'un scandale* (Paris: Laffont, 1988). See also the contributions of Fedier and Pierre Aubenque in *Le Debat* 48 (Paris: Gallimard, January-February 1988).

75. Martin Heidegger, *An Introduction to Metaphysics,* trans. Ralph Mannheim (New Haven: Yale University Press, 1959). This text, originally published in German by Max Niemeyer Verlag in 1953, "contains," as Heidegger notes, "the fully reworked text of the lectures bearing the same title that I delivered at the University of Freiburg in Breisgau in the summer semester of 1935," that is, shortly after his resignation as rector of the university.

76. What I have suggested about the enticingly reductive and derogating reading of Heidegger's thought enabled by the ruse of the repressive hypothesis applies as well, indeed, even more precisely, to the "Dossier" on "Martin Heidegger and Politics" compiled by Richard Wolin for *New German Critique* 45 (Fall 1988), pp. 91–161. Like the texts of the editor(s) of the *Critical Inquiry* "Symposium" and so many other humanist prosecutors in the trial of Martin Heidegger, though far more overtly and monolithically, this "leftist" prosecutor's "dossier" is predictably determined by the humanist truth/power opposition inscribed in his representation

of Heidegger's notorious "pronouncement" as a "simplistic ["antihumanist"; i.e., fascist] demonization of technology": "That 'the anti-humanist' philosophical framework of the later Heidegger can hardly be deemed the unqualified advance Lacoue-Labarthe and Derrida would have it, is indicated by a telling remark made by Heidegger in 1949 (well after his alleged *Kehre*): 'Agriculture today is a motorized food industry, in essence the same. . . . ' This cynical avowal—by the man who has staked a claim to being the leading philosopher of our time—is by no means an unrigorous aside, but pertains to the very crux of Heidegger's later philosophy as a critique of 'techne.' That the Freiburg sage can simply equate 'the manufacture of corpses in gas chambers and extermination camps' with 'mechanized agriculture' [note the predictable ellision of the other two more difficult terms] is not only a shockingly insensitive affront to the memory of the victims of the Nazi death camps—whose extermination in the remark just cited is treated as in essence no different from the productions of higher-yield crops. It is not only a gruesome equation of incomparables. It serves once more to deny the specifically German responsibility for these crimes by attributing them to the dominance of an abstract, supervening, world-historical process. It suggests, moreover, that other Western (as well as non-Western) nations who engage in mechanized food production, 'blockades,' and the manufacture of nuclear weapons, are in essence no different than the SS lieutenants who herded Jews into the gas chambers. It illustrates an extreme myopia concerning the various uses to which technology can be put in the modern world, an incapacity to distinguish between beneficial and destructive employment. It is in sum a simplistic demonization of technology. That the later Heidegger's philosophy is to such a great extent predicated on a demonization of 'technique' as exemplified by the 1949 observation just cited suggests a glaring flaw in his theoretical framework" ("The French Heidegger Debate," pp. 158–59; reprinted as "French Heidegger Wars," in *The Heidegger Controversy*, pp. 282–310).

Wolin's crude attack on Heidegger's "simplistic demonization of technology" also constitutes in large degree a move, like Davidson's, intended to preclude criticism of the discourse of "humanism" and the practices of "liberal democracies," which is to say, to exculpate them of their complicity by rendering their violences incommensurate to the violence instanced by the Nazi gas chambers and death camps. This is clearly suggested in the introduction of his "Dossier," where in a similar singularly monolithic attack on Heidegger's thought he writes, "It is the mentality of Heideggerian metaphysics itself which leads him to his fanatical condemnation of 'Americanism' (as well as 'liberalism,' 'publicity,' and 'technique')" (p. 94). See also Wolin, *The Politics of Being*, pp. 168–69; and "French Heidegger Wars," pp. 300–301.

77. Lacoue-Labarthe, *Fiction*, p. 43. The French word *"faute"* carries a much stronger meaning than *"erreur,"* something like a "crime" or "sin." Lyotard also subscribes to Lacoue-Labarthe's distinction, though he attributes it to Heidegger's forgetting of the forgotten (the "jews"). See *Heidegger and "the jews,"* pp. 79 ff.

78. Heidegger puts this "distress" in terms of the planetary hegemony of technology: "Was there not enough reason and essential distress to think in primordial reflection a surpassing of the metaphysics of the will to power ['now understood to embrace the planet'] and that is to say, to begin a confrontation (*Auseinandersetzung*) with Western thought by returning to its beginning? Was there not enough reason and essential distress, for the sake of such reflection on the spirit of the Western will, to awaken and to lead into battle that place which was considered the seat of the cultivation of knowledge and insight—the German university?" (R, p. 485).

But as the context makes quite clear, he is also alluding to the historically specific predicament of Germany and its people, the predicament he refers to in the 1935 lectures entitled *Introduction to Metaphysics*.

79. Alan Bullock, *Hitler: A Study in Tyranny*, revised ed. (New York: Bantam, 1961): "In Germany [unemployment] rose from 1,320,000 in September 1929, to 3,000,000 in September 1930, 4,350,000 in September 1931, and 5,102,000 in September 1932. The peak figures reached in the first two months of 1932, and again of 1933, were over six million. These, it should be added are the figures for only the registered unemployment in the country, nor do they take account of short-time working. Translate these figures into terms of men standing hopelessly on the street corners of every industrial town in Germany; of houses without food or warmth; of boys and girls leaving school without any chance of a job, and one may begin to guess something of the incalculable human anxiety and bitterness burned into the minds of millions of ordinary German working men and women. In the history of Great Britain it is no exaggeration to describe the mass unemployment of the early 1930s as the experience which had made the deepest impression on the working class of any in the present century. In Germany the effect was still more marked since it came on top of the defeat and the inflation, through which most of these people had already lived" (pp. 119–20).

80. See below, p. 249–50.

81. Heidegger, *An Introduction to Metaphysics*, p. 31.

82. Martin Heidegger, "Political Texts, 1933–1934," trans. William S. Lewis, in *New German Critique* 45, ed. Richard Wolin (Fall 1988), pp. 105–6. This address, somewhat misleadingly entitled "Declaration of Support for Adolph Hitler and the National Socialist State," as well as the other examples of Heidegger's "Political Texts," derives from the German original in Guido Schneeberger, *Nachlese zu Heidegger* (Bern: 1962). Lewis's translation of *Volksgemeinschaft* as "national community" should more accurately be rendered "community of the people."

83. Martin Heidegger, *An Introduction to Metaphysics*, pp. 31–32. As Jacques Derrida has observed, Heidegger's discourse of the rectorate period appropriates "spirit" (*Geist*) in behalf of articulating an understanding of the *self-affirmation* of the university that is free of the racism (biologism) of the Rosenbergs, Kriecks, and Bäumlers, but in so minimizing the ambiguity of his earlier use of the word in quotation marks, recuperated the fascist project of the self-identification of the Nazi subject and a "metaphysical" racism no less racist than the biological racism of official Nazism. There is, indeed, a thrust in this direction in Heidegger's discourse of the rectorate period that cannot and should not be gainsaid. However, it should not be overlooked in the passage quoted in my text—a passage that repeats Heidegger's definition of repetition (*Wiederholung*) articulated in *Being and Time* (II, 5, pp. 437–38) at the level of collectivity and determines the discourse of these lectures of 1935—that the adjective "spiritual" is qualified by the adjective "historical" ("historical-spiritual existence"), which, read in the context of *Being and Time*, would refer to *Dasein*'s radical *finitude/temporality* "grounded" in nothing (*das Nichts*). That is, even as early as 1935, immediately after Heidegger resigned from the rectorship, "spirit" is once again put under erasure, i.e., deprived of the denotation of self-presence in favor of an understanding of the word that is consonant with the always already deferral of presence—with the *ontic/ontological* hermeneutic circle—which precludes arrival, whether that of the individual or the *polis*. See especially the chapter entitled "Difference and Self-Affirmation" in Christopher Fynsk, *Heidegger: Thought and Historicity* (Ithaca, N.Y.: Cornell University Press, 1986), pp. 104–130. This chapter consists of a reading of "The Rectorate Address"

(in the context of *Introduction to Metaphysics*) that acknowledges Heidegger's "compromises" but warns against a reading of these "compromises" that, in assuming "a measure of philosophical purity or authenticity against which Heidegger's action might be judged," violates by overlooking the essence of Heidegger's thinking: "Philosophy, however, does not exist outside its sociopolitical context. Heidegger's own thought of finitude points to the necessity of thinking philosophy's inscription within the sphere of social institutions; it suggests that the practice of philosophy can never be disinterested. *But* the notion of finitude also suggests that philosophy's sociopolitical interests are exceeded, even disrupted, by its hyperbolical return to its own uncertain ["abyssal"] foundation in language—the foundation of any form of human production" (p. 112, my emphasis). In an important footnote to this passage Fynsk adds, "We should not lose sight of this dimension of the finitude of existence. As Heidegger explains in *Being and Time*, *Dasein* situates itself always within its factical situation and projects upon this situation: 'The authentic existentiell understanding is so far from extricating itself from the way of interpreting *Dasein* which has come down to us, that in each case it is in terms of this interpretation, against it, and yet again for it, that it seizes the chosen possibility in the resolution' (SZ, 383/435). Let us recall also the sentences quoted by Karsten Harries regarding the impossibility of divorcing philosophical inquiry from the concrete stance of the thinker within his or her ontic circumstances: 'Is there not, however, a definite ontical way of taking authentic existence, a factical ideal of *Dasein*, underlying our ontological interpretation of *Dasein*'s existence? That is so indeed. But not only is this fact one that must not be denied and that we are forced to grant; it must also be conceived in its *positive* necessity' (SZ, 310/358). As Harries observes, fundamental ontology cannot be pure" (p. 112).

These passages quoted by Fynsk are not isolated accidents. They are variations on Heidegger's revolutionary destructive/projective version of the hermeneutic circle.

84. Philippe Lacoue-Labarthe, *La Fiction*, p. 102.
85. Ibid., p. 130.
86. Ibid., p. 91.
87. Ibid., p. 130–31. Lacoue-Labarthe admits the crucial role that the "rift" (between world and earth) plays in Heidegger's discourse on art, particularly in "The Origin of the Work of Art." But it is Heidegger's seizure of the word *Gestell* and the constellation of terms radiating from it (*Herstellen* [produce], *Darstellen* [present], and *Feststellen* [institute, constitute] that he chooses to emphasize in his reading of the relationship between Heidegger's understanding of art and the polis: "La chaîne sémantique du *stellen* entre il est vrai en concurrence, dans ce passage parmi les plus risqués de Heidegger, avec la chaîne, d'une tout autre portée, du *reissen* (*Riss, Aufriss, Grundriss, Durchriss, Umriss*, etc.), où s'esquisse, une pensée de la *techne*, et par conséquent de la différence, a partir de l'incision, du trait ou du tracé 'ouvrant,' de l'entame ou de l'inscription—bref, de quelque chose qui n'est pas sans rapport avec l'archi-trace ou l'archi-écriture au sens de Derrida. Il n'empêche que l'oeuvre est *Gestalt*, c'est-à-dire *figura*, de la vérité, et que cette détermination—même si Heidegger ne pense surtout pas en terms de fiction, ni même d'imagination—consonne avec le motif onto-typologique du *Discours de Rectorat* [The semantic chain *Stellen*, it is true, enters into competition, in this passage, which is one of Heidegger's most audacious, with the chain, quite different in import, of *reissen* (*Riss, Aufriss, Grundriss, Durchriss, Umriss*, etc.), in which can be seen the outline of a thinking of *techne* and, as a consequence, of difference, on the basis of the incision, of the trait or 'inaugural' tracing, of the breaching or the inscrip-

tion—in short, of something which is not unrelated to the archi-trace or archi-writing in Derrida's sense. Nevertheless, the work is *Gestalt*, in other words, *figura*, of truth, and this determination—even if Heidegger certainly does not think in terms of fiction, not even of imagination—is consistent with the ontotypological motif of the *Rectorate Address*]" (p. 131). I would agree with Lacoue-Labarthe's representation of the relative weights of this aporia in Heidegger's text. My purpose for bringing the "rift" back into play is (1) to counter the humanist representation of Heidegger's discourse on art that renders it simply a later substitute for the *Führer* and (2) to posit a possibility, against Lacoue-Labarthe's reduction of the "unthought" rift motif to textuality, that renders the "Heideggerian" work of art an emancipatory praxis: neither a totalized art of closure nor an art of textual *différence*, but an art that always already destructures totalitarian structures: an art, in other words, that, in demystifying the Center/Metropolis, is anti-Roman (-humanist) and so anti-imperialist.

88. Lacoue-Labarthe is not unmindful of the Roman legacy informing Nazism: "L'Allemagne, ayant découvert le fond oriental (mystique, enthousiaste, nocturne, sauvage—*naturel*) de la Grèce, s'est régulièrement identifié à ce qu'on pourrait appeler, d'un point de vue historico-politique, l"ordre dorique' de las Grèce (le 'junonien' de Hölderlin, l"apollinien' de Nietzsche: rigoureux, délimité, solaire—*technique*). Et c'est évidemment là que Rome, qui n'a recueilli que cet héritage—à condition de la débarrasser des mièvreries hellénistiques et de la restituer à son austère grandeur militaire, paysanne et civique—, se superpose à l'image, qu'on en voulait indemne, de la Grèce. Le geste inaugural du national-socialisme n'est pas moins romaine, pour cette raison, ou moins spartiate-romain, que les gestes fondateurs de la Révolution, du Consulat ou de l'Empire. Il y avait du Pétrone dans Wagner, il y a eu du Néron dans Hitler [Having discovered the oriental (mystical, enthusiastic, nocturnal, savage—*natural*) depths of Greece, [Germany] regularly identified itself with what might be called, from a historical-political point of view, its "Doric order" (Hölderlin's "Junonian," Nietzsche's "Apollonian": rigorous, circumscribed, solar—*technical*). And it is obviously here that Rome, which received only that heritage—though rid of its Hellenistic mawkishness and restored to its austere military, peasant, and civic grandeur—becomes superimposed on the image, represented to be intact, of Greece. The inaugural gesture of National Socialism is no less Roman, for this reason, nor Spartan-Roman, than the founding gestures of the Revolution, the Consulate or the Empire. There was something of Petronius in Wagner, something of Nero in Hitler]" (pp. 107-8). But Lacoue-Labarthe subordinates this Roman reference to the Greek: "dans l'*agôn* mimétique qu'elle livre avec l'Ancien, l'Allemagne, dans la volonté qu'elle affiche depuis le *Sturm und Drang* de se démarquer de *l'imitation* de style 'latin' (a l'italienne et, surtout, à la française: l'enjeu politique est immense), cherche une autre Grèce que celle, tardive, qui s'est transmisse a l'Europe moderne à travers le filtrage romain. Au fond si l'Allemagne existe, on le voit bien avec la fracture de la Réforme luthérienne dont l'aire d'extension ne coïncide pas par hasard avec le tracé du *limes* impérial, c'est comme force de résistance à Rome et à tous ses tenant-lieu [In the mimetic *agon* it entered into with the ancient world, Germany sought, in the will it displayed from the *Sturm und Drang* onwards to dissociate itself from a "Latin" style *imitation* (in the Italian and, above all, French manner: the political stakes in this are immense), another Greece than that late one which had been transmitted to modern Europe through the Roman filter. At bottom, if Germany exists . . . it is as a force of resistance against Rome and all its substitutes" (p. 107). Whatever the

historical truth of this representation, the fact is that Heidegger identifies the German classical tradition inaugurated by Winckelmann with Roman humanism.

89. According to the cultural historian Frank M. Turner, in *The Greek Heritage in Victorian Britain* (New Haven: Yale University Press, 1981), Winckelmann's representation of Greek art of the fifth and fourth centuries in terms of a "classical restraint and harmony" which reflected " 'universal beauty and its ideal images,' " was mediated by late Greek or Hellenistic sculpture, since he was not familiar with earlier Greek statuary (p. 40). And his periodization of Greek art was determined by the "art history set forth by Quintilian and Cicero" (p. 43). Turner's book is devoted to demonstrating the influence of Greek art on British culture (and politics) from the Greek revival to the end of the nineteenth century; more specifically, on showing how Victorian Britain appropriated Greek antiquity in order to confirm its restrictive cultural and educational values, and to justify its imperial project. In this history, according to Turner, the German classical/humanist tradition initiated by Winckelmann plays a fundamental and enabling role. The British, *like* the Germans, distinguished between the Greeks and Romans, but only to recuperate a more sophisticated form of the latter's representation of the former. This becomes remarkably evident in Turner's account of Winckelmann's influence on Sir Joshua Reynolds: "Winckelmann's emphasis on the ideal character of Greek sculpture allowed British commentators to graft his criticism onto the existing aesthetics of British humanism. They were embodied in the *Discourses* of Sir Joshua Reynolds, delivered to the Royal Academy of Art between 1769 and 1790 . . . : 'The Art which we profess had beauty for its object; this is our business to discover and to express; the beauty of which we are in quest is general and intellectual; it is an idea that subsists only in the mind; the sight never beheld it, nor has the hand expressed it: it is an idea residing in the breast of the artist, which he is always laboring to impart, and which he dies at the last without imparting; but which he is yet so far able to communicate, as to raise the thoughts and extend the views of the spectator; and which, by a succession of art, may be so far diffused, that its effects may extend themselves imperceptibly into public benefits, and be among the means of bestowing on whole nations refinement of taste; which, if it does not lead directly to purity of manners, obviates at least their greatest deprivation, by disentangling the mind from appetite, and conducting the thoughts through successive stages of excellence, till that contemplation of universal rectitude and harmony which began by Taste, may, as it is exalted and refined, conclude in Virtue' " (pp. 43–44).

The resonant similarity between the Winckelmann appropriated by Sir Joshua Reynolds and the Winckelmann of Heidegger's "Letter on Humanism" is obvious: the function of their humanist version of "Greek" art is not to encourage originary thinking, but to produce a Roman "virtue": a nation of "manly" and dependable citizens. For an account of the influence of German Hellenism on Matthew Arnold's Roman Hellenism, see the chapter titled "The Apollonian Investment of Modern Humanist Educational Theory: The Examples of Matthew Arnold, Irving Babbitt, and I. A. Richards," in my *End of Education*.

90. Heidegger, "Letter on Humanism," *Basic Writings*, pp. 200–201. See also my discussion of Heidegger's *Parmenides* lectures (1942–43) in chapter 5, in which I suggest that Heidegger's insight into the "Romanness" of Nazism's "Greekness" precedes his postwar "Letter on Humanism." For Lacoue-Labarthe's discussion of German national aestheticism and its relation to ancient Greece, see *Fiction*, pp. 92–114.

91. Lacoue-Labarthe, *Fiction*, pp. 42–43. See also Fritz Stern, "National Socialism as

Temptation," *Dreams and Delusions: National Socialism in the Drama of the German Past* (New York: Vintage Books, 1989), pp. 147–92; and Michael E. Zimmerman, *Heidegger's Confrontation with Modernity: Technology, Politics, Art* (Bloomington: University of Indiana Press, 1990): "In evaluating Heidegger's enthusiastic endorsement of Hitler, we should recall that Roosevelt and many other Western politicians spoke well of Hitler's accomplishments for years after 1933. Moreover, the world came to Berlin in 1936 to take part in the Olympic Games. Heidegger was not alone in believing at first that Hitler could be persuaded to adopt a 'nobler' version of Germany's future than the one represented by racist ideologues and political hacks such as Rosenberg, Krieck, and Kolbenheyer" (p. 38).

92. Otto Wacker, State Minister for Instruction and Culture in Baden.

93. See chapter 4, "The Indifference of *Differance*: Retrieving Heidegger's Destruction." It is worth recalling at this important juncture in my argument that this essay undertakes, in part, an interrogation of Jacques Derrida's thematization of Heidegger's use of a constellation of metaphors radiating around the "proximity of Being"—"the values of neighboring, shelter, house, service, guard, voice, and listening"—to represent Heidegger's thought after the "turn" as "guided by the motif of Being as presence," where "everything transpires as if one had to reduce the ontological distance acknowledged in *Sein und Zeit* and to state the proximity of Being to the essence of man." ("The Ends of Man," *Margins of Philosophy*, trans. Alan Bass [Chicago: University of Chicago Press, 1982], pp. 128–30). Against this reading I suggest that the equally prominent spatial metaphorics Heidegger employs in his post-*Kehre* texts to characterize technological thought—"world picture," "commanding gaze," "enframing," "representation," etc.—compels us to read the claims of being from the perspective opened up by the de-struction of Being and the releasement of temporality from structure in *Being and Time* and the metaphorics of proximity in their "erased" sense. This is not by any means to suggest that Derrida's reading of Heidegger's late texts is wrong, but that they provide ample evidence for a reading that deconstructs Derrida's. I suggest, further, that what I say in that essay applies as well to Derrida's reading of Heidegger's appropriation of the word "spirit" in the "Rectorate Address," *Introduction to Metaphysics*, and other texts until 1939 in order to dissociate his project from the biologically informed racism of the official Nazi Party line: that, despite Heidegger's effort to free his discourse from Nazism, his invocation of "spirit" (without quotation marks) reinscribes the discourse of this period into the (geo)political project of the Nazis.

94. Fredric Jameson, "Interview," *Diacritics* 12 (Fall 1982), p. 136. In the context of the renewal of the debate over Heidegger's politics, Jameson would be considerably more meticulous in his account of Heidegger's extension of the dynamics of the rift and "the comparable philosophical act (the deconcealment of Being)" to "the act of political revolution (the inauguration of a new society, the production or invention of radically new social relations)." My point in invoking Jameson, however, is not to imply that his reading of Heidegger's text is objectively accurate. It is rather to show that certain fundamental nexuses in Heidegger's thought lend themselves to a productive dialogue with Marxist, or rather neo-Marxist, thought.

95. Heidegger, "Letter on Humanism," pp. 219–20.

96. I have this on the authority of the eminent translator of and commentator on Heidegger's text, David Farrell Krell. See also, Elizabeth Young Levy-Bruehl, *Hannah Arendt: For Love of the World* (New Haven: Yale University Press, 1982).

97. Though Jacques Derrida has not suggested this possibility as such, he has at least expressed his strong objection to the policing implicit in the anti-Heideggerians'

condemnation of Heidegger's silence about the Nazi death camps. In an interview with Jean-Luc Nancy in which he was asked to address Heidegger's silence, Derrida replied: "The excess of responsibility of which I was just speaking never authorizes silence. . . . I suppose, I hope that you are not expecting me only to say that 'I condemn Auschwitz' or that 'I condemn all silence on Auschwitz.' Concerning the latter phrase or its equivalents, I find the mechanism of the trials organized against all those who one believes can be accused of not having named or analyzed 'Auschwitz' a bit indecent, even obscene. . . . If we admit—and this concession seems to me evident everywhere—that the thing remains unthinkable, that we do not have discourse that can measure up to it, if we recognize that we have nothing to say about the real victims of Auschwitz, those same victims that we authorize ourselves to treat through metonymy or to name *via negativa*, then let people stop diagnosing the so-called silences and making the 'resistances' and 'nonthoughts' of just about everyone be confessed. Of course silence on Auschwitz will never be justified, but neither will the fact that people speak of it in such an instrumental way and to say nothing, to say nothing that is not self-evident, trivial, and that does not serve primarily to give themselves a good conscience, in order not to be the last to accuse, to give lessons, to take positions or to show off." " 'Il faut bien manger' ou le calcul du sujet: Entretien (avec J.-L. Nancy)," in *Cahiers Confrontation* 20 (Winter 1989), p. 113; quoted in David Carroll, "The Memory of Devastation and the Responsibilities of Thought: 'And let's not talk about that,' foreword to Jean-François Lyotard, *Heidegger and "the jews,"* pp. xxvii–viii.

98. See Karsten Harries, "Introduction," *Martin Heidegger and National Socialism,* ed. Günther Neske and Emil Kettering and trans. Lisa Harries (New York: Paragon House, 1990), p. xxxii. This possibility warrants a closer examination, given the uniformity and monolithic character of the humanist critics' condemnation of Heidegger's postwar "silence," but it cannot be undertaken here. Suffice it to invoke Heidegger's insistent reference to silence (*Schweigen*) from *Being and Time* to the *Beiträge zur Philosophie* and the *Parmenides* as a mode of discourse (*Rede*) that would counter not simply the "idle chatter" (*Gerede*) of *das Man,* that is, "the way things are publicly interpreted," but also and more fundamentally the discourse of the regime of truth (*adequaetio intellectus et rei*), the discourse that justifies its hegemony by always putting that which deviates from its way on trial. Could this be one aspect of what Heidegger is anticipating in the *Parmenides* lectures when, in a meditation on the Greek *lethe* as counter-essence of *aletheia,* he suggests the meaning "to be passed over in silence" and adds: "We reflect too rarely on the fact that the same Greeks to whom the word and speech were bestowed primordially could, for that very reason, keep silent in a unique way as well. For 'to keep silent' is not merely to say nothing. Without something essential to say, one cannot keep silent. Only within essential speech, and by means of it alone, can there prevail essential silence, having nothing in common with secrecy, concealment, or 'mental reservations' " (p. 108). See also *Being and Time,* pp. 203–10 and 341–48; and *Beiträge zur Philosophie,* pp. 78–79, 510. Tom Rockmore notes this possibility, but predictably—and with little effort to think Heidegger "doctrine"—dismisses it as a rationalization that only obscures Heidegger's arrogant and devious Nazi refusal to acknowledge his guilt before the tribunal of modern humanism: "Heidegger's idea of silence should be put in perspective. His point differs from Wittgenstein's view that one should be silent about what cannot be expressed in speech. Heidegger is not willing to take a skeptical stance, for instance by asserting that one should say nothing about what one cannot know. Rather, Heidegger's revised doctrine of silence [in the *Nietzsche* lectures and the *Beiträge*] . . . is intended to point to silence

as the highest level of speech. The modification is, however, significant, even 'convenient' in the present context, after the failure of the rectorate. For this revised view of silence provides Heidegger with a reason, rooted in his thought, to remain silent in an authentic manner, to refuse on philosophical grounds to say anything, anything at all, to decline in virtue of his theory to take a public position on the Holocaust, on Nazism, or on his view of Nazism. But one must wonder whether a form of thought can be authentic or even rigorous if this means to remain silent before the Holocaust whose central meaning it can neither express nor grasp." *On Heidegger's Nazism and Philosophy*, p. 203.

Index

Abrams, Meyer H., 82, 123, 129; "The Deconstructive Angel," 275, n. 3; "How to Do Things with Texts," 275 n. 3
Adorno, Theodor, 11, 19, 158; *Dialectic of the Enlightenment*, 295 n. 38
affiliation, 91–92
Althusser, Louis, 11, 12, 19, 128; antihumanism of, 189; and humanism, 188; on ideology, 108, 135; on ideological state apparatuses, 148, 187, 224; and interpellation, 291–92 n. 23; on the problematic, 183, 213, 274–75 n. 2
Ammons, A. R., 23; "Corsons Inlet," 60
Arac, Jonathan, 82; and critical genealogy, 177; "To Regress from the Rigors of Shelley," 276 n. 4, 286 n. 93
Arendt, Hannah, 250, 257 n. 15
Argyros, Alex: "The Warp of the World: Destructive Hermeneutics," 288–89 n. 10
Aristotle, 25, 27; and Modernism, 37–9; *Poetics*, 37, 112; on time, 112

Arnold, Matthew, 8, 20, 129, 290, 311 n. 56; and culture, 82; *Culture and Anarchy*, 276 n. 6; and the two cultures, 178. *See also* humanism
Augustine, St., 67; and the circular city, 157
Auschwitz, 149, 191, 195, 320–21 n. 98; as apocalyptic event, 230–34, 302–3 n. 19, 313 n. 69; and questionable political uses of, 234–35, 313–14 n. 70. *See also* Holocaust

Bakhtin, Mikhail, 297 n. 54
Balzac, Honoré de: and panopticism, 297 n. 54
Barthelme, Donald, 50; *The Dead Father*, 96, 179
Barthes, Roland: critique of tragedy, 269 n. 27
base/superstructure: limitations of, 134–38, 178–79, 258 n. 16
Bate, Walter Jackson, 129, 236; "The Crisis in English Studies," 275 n. 3
Bäumler, Alfred, 310 n. 55

William V. Spanos is professor of English and comparative literature at the State University of New York at Binghamton and was the founding editor of *boundary 2*. He is the author of *Repetitions: The Postmodern Occasion in Literature and Culture* (1987) and *The End of Education: Toward Posthumanism* (Minnesota, 1993), the editor of *Martin Heidegger and the Question of Literature* (1980) and the coeditor of *The Question of Textuality: Strategies of Reading in Contemporary American Criticism* (1982).